LIBRARY OF HEBREW BIBLE/
OLD TESTAMENT STUDIES

675

Formerly Journal for the Study of the Old Testament Supplement Series

Editors
Claudia V. Camp, Texas Christian University, USA
Andrew Mein, University of Durham, UK

Founding Editors
David J. A. Clines, Philip R. Davies and David M. Gunn

Editorial Board
Alan Cooper, Susan Gillingham, John Goldingay,
Norman K. Gottwald, James E. Harding, John Jarick, Carol Meyers,
Daniel L. Smith-Christopher, Francesca Stavrakopoulou,
James W. Watts

SEXUALITY AND LAW IN THE TORAH

Edited by

Hilary Lipka and Bruce Wells

LONDON • NEW YORK • OXFORD • NEW DELHI • SYDNEY

T&T CLARK
Bloomsbury Publishing Plc
50 Bedford Square, London, WC1B 3DP, UK
1385 Broadway, New York, NY 10018, USA
29 Earlsfort Terrace, Dublin 2, Ireland

BLOOMSBURY, T&T CLARK and the T&T Clark logo
are trademarks of Bloomsbury Publishing Plc

First published in Great Britain 2020
This paperback edition published in 2021

© Hilary Lipka, Bruce Wells, and contributors, 2020

Hilary Lipka and Bruce Wells have asserted their right under the Copyright, Designs and Patents Act, 1988, to be identified as the Authors of this work.

All rights reserved. No part of this publication may be reproduced or transmitted in any form or by any means, electronic or mechanical, including photocopying, recording, or any information storage or retrieval system, without prior permission in writing from the publishers.

Bloomsbury Publishing Plc does not have any control over, or responsibility for, any third-party websites referred to or in this book. All internet addresses given in this book were correct at the time of going to press. The author and publisher regret any inconvenience caused if addresses have changed or sites have ceased to exist, but can accept no responsibility for any such changes.

A catalogue record for this book is available from the British Library.

A catalog record for this book is available from the Library of Congress.

ISBN: HB: 978-0-5676-8159-1
PB: 978-0-5677-0382-8
ePDF: 978-0-5676-8160-7

Series: Library of New Testament Studies, ISSN 2513-8758, volume 675
Scriptural Traces, volume 23

Typeset by: Forthcoming Publications Ltd

To find out more about our authors and books visit www.bloomsbury.com and sign up for our newsletters.

Contents

Preface	vii
List of Abbreviations	ix
Notes on Contributors	xv

INTRODUCTION
    Hilary Lipka and Bruce Wells   1

1
CATEGORIES OF SEXUALITY INDIGENOUS
TO BIBLICAL LEGAL MATERIALS
    David Tabb Stewart   20

2
THE DAUGHTER SOLD INTO SLAVERY AND MARRIAGE
    Pamela Barmash   48

3
RACHEL'S BETROTHAL CONTRACT AND THE ORIGINS
OF CONTRACT LAW
    F. Rachel Magdalene   77

4
JUDAH, TAMAR, AND THE LAW OF LEVIRATE MARRIAGE
    Eryl W. Davies   111

5
ON THE BEDS OF A WOMAN:
THE LEVITICUS TEXTS ON SAME-SEX RELATIONS RECONSIDERED
    Bruce Wells   123

6
THE OFFENSE, ITS CONSEQUENCES,
AND THE MEANING OF זנה IN LEVITICUS 19:29
    Hilary Lipka   159

7
PRIESTLY MARRIAGE RESTRICTIONS
   Sarah Shectman   180

8
THE INHERITANCE INJUNCTION OF NUMBERS 36:
ZELOPHEHAD'S DAUGHTERS AND THE INTERSECTION
OF ANCESTRAL LAND AND SEX REGULATION
   M. L. Case   194

9
REPRODUCING TORAH:
HUMAN AND DIVINE SEXUALITY IN THE BOOK OF DEUTERONOMY
   Steffan Mathias   217

10
DIVORCE IN ARCHAIC CRETE:
COMPARATIVE PERSPECTIVES ON DEUTERONOMY 24:1-4
   Anselm C. Hagedorn   239

11
DIVORCE INSTRUCTION AND COVENANTAL UNFAITHFULNESS:
A NEW EXAMINATION OF THE REUSE OF DEUTERONOMY 24:1-4
AS METAPHOR IN JEREMIAH 3:1-10
   Kenneth Bergland   269

12
SEXUAL RELATIONS AND THE TRANSITION FROM HOLY PEOPLE
TO HUMAN SANCTUARY IN SECOND TEMPLE TIMES
   Hannah K. Harrington   286

Index of References   309
Index of Authors   320

PREFACE

This volume had its origins in a session of the Biblical Law program unit at the 2014 annual meeting of the Society of Biblical Literature in San Diego, California. Expanded versions of four of the five papers presented there are included in the volume; eight additional scholars have contributed papers as well. The topic of "sexuality and law" was timely in 2014, and the session was remarkably well attended. Much has changed within the legal and cultural landscape over the last several years, but the relevance of the topic remains. Debates—whether legal, religious, or cultural—over matters of sexuality are ongoing, and the work of scholars who study the Hebrew Bible can supply an important perspective to many of these discussions. It is hoped that readers will find the essays herein to be a valuable contribution to that endeavor.

Abbreviations

AASOR	Annual of the American Schools of Oriental Research
AB	Anchor Bible
ABD	*Anchor Bible Dictionary*. Edited by David Noel Freedman. 6 vols. New York: Doubleday, 1992
AfO	*Archiv für Orientforschung*
ÄgAbh	Ägyptologische Abhandlungen
AHw	*Akkadisches Handwörterbuch*. Wolfram von Soden. 3 vols. Wiesbaden: Harrassowitz, 1965–81
AJSR	*Association for Jewish Studies Review*
ALD	Aramaic Levi Document
AnBib	Analecta biblica
ANET	*Ancient Near Eastern Texts Relating to the Old Testament*. Edited by James B. Pritchard. 3d ed. Princeton: Princeton University Press, 1969
Ant.	*Jewish Antiquities*
AOAT	Alter Orient und Altes Testament
AOS	American Oriental Series
AsJT	*Asia Journal of Theology*
ASV	American Standard Version
AYBRL	Anchor Yale Bible Reference Library
b. Ber.	Babylonian Talmud, tractate *Berakhot*
b. Shab.	Babylonian Talmud, tractate *Shabbat*
BaAr	Babylonische Archive
BASOR	*Bulletin of the American Schools of Oriental Research*
BDB	Brown, Francis, S. R. Driver, and Charles A. Briggs. *A Hebrew and English Lexicon of the Old Testament*
BHS	*Biblia Hebraica Stuttgartensia*. Edited by Karl Elliger and Wilhelm Rudolph. Stuttgart: Deutsche Bibelgesellschaft, 1983
BibInt	*Biblical Interpretation: A Journal of Contemporary Approaches*
BibSem	The Bible Seminar
BJS	Brown Judaic Studies
BMes	Bibliotheca Mesopotamica
BR	*Bible Review*
BTB	*Biblical Theology Bulletin*
BZ	*Biblische Zeitschrift*

BZABR (= BZAR)	Beihefte zur Zeitschrift für altorientalische und biblische Rechtsgeschichte
BZAW	Beihefte zur Zeitschrift für die alttestamentliche Wissenschaft
CAD	*The Assyrian Dictionary of the Oriental Institute of the University of Chicago*. Chicago: The Oriental Institute of the University of Chicago, 1956–2006
CBC	Cambridge Bible Commentary
CBQ	*Catholic Biblical Quarterly*
CEB	Common English Bible
CHD	*The Hittite Dictionary of the Oriental Institute of the University of Chicago*. Edited by Hans G. Güterbock, Harry A. Hoffner Jr., and Theo P. J. van den Hout. Chicago: The Oriental Institute of the University of Chicago, 1980-
Cher.	*De cherubim*
CM	Cuneiform Monographs
ConBOT	Coniectanea Biblica: Old Testament Series
COS	*The Context of Scripture*. Edited by William W. Hallo and K. Lawson Younger Jr. 3 vols. Leiden: Brill, 2003
CSCO	Corpus Scriptorum Christianorum Orientalium. Edited by Jean Baptiste Chabot et al. Paris, 1903
CTH	*Catalogue des textes hittites*. Emmanuel Laroche. Paris: Klincksieck, 1971
CurBR	*Currents in Biblical Research*
DJD	Discoveries in the Judaean Desert
DMOA	Documenta et Monumenta Orientis Antiqui
DSD	*Dead Sea Discoveries*
EncJud	*Encyclopaedia Judaica*. Edited by Fred Skolnik and Michael Berenbaum. 2nd ed. 22 vols. Detroit: Macmillan Reference USA, 2007
ESV	English Standard Version
ExpTim	*Expository Times*
FAT	Forschungen zum Alten Testament
FCB	The Feminist Companion to the Bible
FOTL	Forms of the Old Testament Literature
FrGrH	*Die Fragmente der Griechischen Historiker*. Felix Jacoby. 5 vols. Leiden: Brill, 1923–
FRLANT	Forschungen zur Religion und Literatur des Alten und Neuen Testaments
GBS	Guides to Biblical Scholarship
GKC	*Gesenius' Hebrew Grammar*. Edited by Emil Kautzsch. Translated by Arthur E. Cowley. 2d. ed. Oxford: Clarendon, 1910
GMTR	Guides to the Mesopotamian Textual Record
HALOT	*The Hebrew and Aramaic Lexicon of the Old Testament*. Ludwig Koehler, Walter Baumgartner, and Johann J. Stamm. Translated and edited under the supervision of Mervyn E. J. Richardson. 4 vols. Leiden: Brill, 1994–99

HAR	*Hebrew Annual Review*
HBAI	*Hebrew Bible and Ancient Israel*
HCSB	Holman Christian Study Bible
HdO	Handbuch der Orientalistik
HL	Hittite Laws
HR	*History of Religions*
HSM	Harvard Semitic Monographs
HThKAT	Herders Theologischer Kommentar zum Alten Testament
HTR	*Harvard Theological Review*
HUCA	*Hebrew Union College Annual*
IBC	Interpretation: A Bible Commentary for Teaching and Preaching.
IC	*Inscriptiones Creticae*. Edited by Margherita Guarducci. 4 vols. Rome: La Libreria dello stato, 1935–50
ICC	International Critical Commentary
IEJ	*Israel Exploration Journal*
Il.	*Iliad*
IPArk	*Prozessrechtliche Inschriften der griechischen Poleis: Arkadien*. Edited by Gerhard Thür and Hans Taeuber. Vienna: Österreichische Akademie der Wissenschaften, 1994
JAOS	*Journal of the American Oriental Society*
JBL	*Journal of Biblical Literature*
JBQ	*Jewish Bible Quarterly*
JBS	Jerusalem Biblical Studies
JCS	*Journal of Cuneiform Studies*
JETS	*Journal of the Evangelical Theological Society*
JJP	*Journal of Juristic Papyrology*
JJS	*Journal of Jewish Studies*
JLA	*Jewish Law Annual*
JNES	*Journal of Near Eastern Studies*
JQR	*Jewish Quarterly Review*
JSJSup	Journal for the Study of Judaism in the Persian, Hellenistic, and Roman Periods Supplement Series
JSOT	*Journal for the Study of the Old Testament*
JSOTSup	Journal for the Study of the Old Testament Supplement Series
JSQ	*Jewish Studies Quarterly*
JSS	*Journal of Semitic Studies*
KBo	*Keilschrifttexte aus Boghazköi*
KJV	King James Version
KTU	*Die keilalphabetischen Texte aus Ugarit*. Edited by Manfried Dietrich, Oswald Loretz, and Juaquín Sanmartín. AOAT 24/1. Neukirchen-Vluyn: Neukirchener Verlag, 1976
KUB	*Keilschrifturkunden aus Boghazköi*
LAI	Library of Ancient Israel
LCL	Loeb Classical Library
LH	Laws of Hammurabi
LHBOTS	Library of Hebrew Bible/Old Testament Studies

LSCG	*Lois sacrées des cités grecques*. Franciszek Sokolowski. 2nd ed. Paris: de Boccard, 1969
LSTS	The Library of Second Temple Studies
LXX	Septuagint
m. Qidd.	Mishnah, tractate Qiddushin
MAL	Middle Assyrian Laws
MBPF	Münchener Beiträge zur Papyrusforschung und antiken Rechtsgeschichte
MT	Masoretic Text
NASB	New American Standard Bible
NEA	*Near Eastern Archaeology*
NET	New English Translation
NICOT	New International Commentary on the Old Testament
NIDB	*New Interpreter's Dictionary of the Bible*. Edited by Katherine Doob Sakenfeld. 5 vols. Nashville: Abingdon, 2006–2009
NIV	New International Version
NJB	New Jerusalem Bible
NJPS (=JPS)	*Tanakh: The Holy Scriptures: The New JPS Translation according to the Traditional Hebrew Text*
NLT	New Living Translation
NRSV	New Revised Standard Version
OBO	Orbis biblicus et orientalis
OBT	Overtures to Biblical Theology
Od.	*Odyssey*
OTL	Old Testament Library
OTS	Old Testament Studies
PBS	Publications of the Babylonian Section, University Museum, University of Pennsylvania
PRSt	*Perspectives in Religious Studies*
RB	*Revue biblique*
RevQ	*Revue de Qumran*
RHA	*Revue hittite et asianique*
RhM	Rheinisches Museum für Philologie
RSV	Revised Standard Version
SAA	State Archives of Assyria
SAAS	State Archives of Assyria Studies
SANE	Sources of the Ancient Near East
SAOC	Studies in Ancient Oriental Civilizations
SBLAIL	Society of Biblical Literature Ancient Israel and its Literature Series
SBLDS	Society of Biblical Literature Dissertation Series
SBLRBS	Society of Biblical Literature Resources for Biblical Study
SBLSymS	Society of Biblical Literature Symposium Series
SBLSP	Society of Biblical Literature Seminar Papers
SBLWAW	Society of Biblical Literature Writings from the Ancient World
ScrHier	Scripta hierosolymitana
SJLA	Studies in Judaism in Late Antiquity

Somn.	*De Somniis*
Spec. Laws	*On the Special Laws*
StBibLit	Studies in Biblical Literature (Lang)
STDJ	Studies on the Texts of the Desert of Judah
SVTP	Studia in Veteris Testamenti pseudepigraphica
T. Levi	Testament of Levi
TAD	*Textbook of Aramaic Documents from Ancient Egypt.* Edited by B. Porten and A. Yardeni. Winona Lake: Eisenbrauns, 1989
TBH	Transitional Biblical Hebrew
TDOT	*Theological Dictionary of the Old Testament.* Edited by G. Johannes Botterweck and Helmer Ringgren. Translated by John T. Willis et al. 8 vols. Grand Rapids: Eerdmans, 1974–2006
TGUOS	Transactions of the Glasgow University Oriental Society
ThTo	*Theology Today*
TOTC	Tyndale Old Testament Commentaries
TWAT	*Theologisches Wörterbuch zum Alten Testament.* Edited by G. Johannes Botterweck, Helmer Ringgren, and Heinz-Josef Fabry. 9 vols. Kolhammer, 1973–2000
UF	*Ugarit-Forschungen*
vac.	vacat (indicates the papyrus is blank at that point)
VT	*Vetus Testamentum*
VTSup	Supplements to Vetus Testamentum
WBC	Word Bible Commentary
WMANT	Wissenschaftliche Monographien zum Alten und Neuen Testament
ZA	*Zeitschrift für Assyriologie*
ZABR (= *ZAR*)	*Zeitschrift für altorientalische und biblische Rechtsgeschichte*
ZAH	*Zeitschrift für Althebräistik*
ZAW	*Zeitschrift für die alttestamentliche Wissenschaft*

CONTRIBUTORS

Pamela Barmash is Professor of Hebrew Bible at Washington University in St. Louis and has served as director of Jewish, Islamic and Near Eastern Studies there. She has been a fellow at the Hebrew University and at the Institute for Advanced Study, Princeton. She is the author of *Homicide in the Biblical World* (Cambridge University Press, 2005). She is the coeditor of *Exodus in the Jewish Experience: Echoes and Reverberations* (Lexington Books, 2015) and the editor of *The Oxford Handbook of Biblical Law* (Oxford University Press, 2019). She is currently working on a book on the Laws of Hammurabi.

Kenneth Bergland did his MA in the history of ideas at the University of Oslo, with special focus on philosophical ethics in the 20th century. His PhD dissertation, from Andrews University, was published as *Reading as a Disclosure of the Thoughts of the Heart* (Harrassowitz, 2019). It is a study on the reuse of instructions from the Torah in the prophets as a model for applied biblical ethics. He is presently working as a pastor in Vesterålen, in the north of Norway.

M. L. Case received her doctoral degree in Religious Studies from the University of Texas at Austin in May 2016. Her major concentration was Hebrew Bible, with minor concentrations in Women's and Gender Studies, Formative Judaism, and New Testament/Early Christianity. Her other research utilizes historical-critical, social-scientific, and feminist methodologies and theories to examine the social control of women and subordinate males in Judges 19-21 and the depiction of sexual activity in the Song of Songs. Case is currently the Postdoctoral Fellow in Judaic Studies at Virginia Polytechnic Institute and State University in Blacksburg, VA.

Eryl W. Davies is an Emeritus Professor at Bangor University, Wales, UK. He received his doctorate at the University of Cambridge for work on the ethics of the prophet Isaiah, which was subsequently published as

Prophecy and Ethics: Isaiah and the Ethical Traditions of Israel (JSOT Press, 1981). Subsequent publications include: *Numbers* (New Century Bible Commentary Series; Eerdmans, 1995); *The Dissenting Reader: Feminist Approaches to the Hebrew Bible* (Ashgate, 2003); and *The Immoral Bible: Approaches to Biblical Ethics* (T&T Clark, 2010). He was elected President of the Society for Old Testament Study in 2013, and Fellow of the Learned Society of Wales in 2015.

Anselm C. Hagedorn, DPhil habil., is Professor of Hebrew Bible and Ancient Judaism at the Universität Osnabrück in Germany. He read Theology at the universities of St Andrews, Göttingen, Notre Dame, and Heidelberg. His work focuses on various comparative aspects of Biblical and Archaic Greek Laws as well as on Biblical Prophecy and Mediterranean love lyrics. He is currently engaged in writing a commentary on the Song of Songs. Major publications include: *Between Moses and Plato: Individual and Society in Deuteronomy and Ancient Greek Law* (Vandenhoeck & Ruprecht, 2004); and *Die Anderen im Spiegel: Israels Auseinandersetzung mit den Völkern in den Büchern Nahum, Zefanja, Obadja und Joel* (de Gruyter, 2011).

Hannah K. Harrington, Professor of Old Testament at Patten University, Oakland, CA, for over thirty years, graduated from the University of California, Berkeley, in Near Eastern Studies (MA, 1985; PhD, 1992). She has written over seventy publications on Second Temple Judaism, including *Holiness: Rabbinic Judaism and the Graeco-Roman World* (Routledge Press, 2001); *The Purity Texts* (Sheffield Academic, 2004); "Leviticus," in *Women's Bible Commentary* (Westminster John Knox, 2012); *The Purity and Sanctuary of the Body in Second Temple Judaism* (Vandenhoeck & Ruprecht, 2019); and *Ezra and Nehemiah* (Eerdmans, forthcoming). Dr. Harrington has received four National Endowment for the Humanities Grants.

Hilary Lipka (PhD, Brandeis University) is an instructor in the Religious Studies Program at the University of New Mexico in Albuquerque, NM. She is the author of *Sexual Transgression in the Hebrew Bible* (Sheffield Phoenix, 2006). Her current research focuses on mapping the spectrum of biblical masculinities and femininities, examining the dynamic of holiness and desecration in Priestly literature, and exploring the intersection of sex, gender, and law in biblical texts.

F. Rachel Magdalene (J.D., University of Colorado School of Law; PhD, University of Denver and Iliff School of Theology Joint PhD Program) is a former lawyer and retired biblical scholar, having taught most recently at United Theological Seminary in Dayton, OH. Her scholarship includes numerous studies on biblical and ancient Near Eastern law and feminist hermeneutics. She is the author of *On the Scales of Righteousness: Neo-Babylonian Trial Law and the Book of Job* (Brown Judaic Studies, 2007) and first author (with Cornelia Wunsch and Bruce Wells) on *Fault, Responsibility, and Administrative Law in Late Babylonian Legal Texts* (Eisenbrauns, 2019).

Steffan Mathias is a scholar living in London. His PhD thesis, *Paternity, Progeny, and Perpetuation: Creating Lives after Death in the Hebrew Bible*, is forthcoming with Bloomsbury T&T Clark; it looks at biblical responses to male childlessness, particularly in texts relating to the institution of levirate marriage. His current research is focused on constructs of "ritual" and "moral" law in readings of Deuteronomy and applying literary theory to liturgical texts.

Sarah Shectman is a scholar and editor living in San Francisco, California. She is the author of *Women in the Pentateuch: A Feminist and Source-Critical Analysis* (Sheffield Phoenix, 2009) and coeditor, with Joel Baden, of *The Strata of the Priestly Writings: Contemporary Debate and Future Directions* (Theologischer Verlag, 2009). Her current research focuses on gender in the book of Leviticus, especially constructions of masculinity and femininity as reflected in language and regulations. She is the cofounder of SBAllies.

David Tabb Stewart (PhD, Near Eastern Studies, University of California, Berkeley) is professor of Ancient Near Eastern Religions and former chair of Religious Studies at California State University, Long Beach. Stewart's main research focus of "body and biblical law" takes account of dis/ability, gender, im/purity, sexuality, and LGBTQI interpretation. He is currently working on a book manuscript, *About Blank: A Biography of Leviticus*. Stewart is also a gamer, coauthoring with Adam Porter the academic game, *The Josianic Reform: Deuteronomy, Prophecy, and Israelite Religion*, and presenting workshops on academic game development in the US, China, and Mongolia.

Bruce Wells is Associate Professor of Middle Eastern Studies at the University of Texas at Austin where he specializes in the study of the Hebrew Bible and the ancient Near East. He is the author of *The Law of Testimony in the Pentateuchal Codes* (Harrassowitz, 2004), coauthor (with Raymond Westbrook) of *Everyday Law in Biblical Israel* (Westminster, John Knox 2009), and coauthor (with F. Rachel Magdalene and Cornelia Wunsch) of *Fault, Responsibility, and Administrative Law in Late Babylonian Legal Texts* (Eisenbrauns, 2019).

INTRODUCTION

Hilary Lipka and Bruce Wells

Every human society regulates sexual behavior, and every society for which we have any appreciable evidence appears to have implemented such regulation, in small or large measure, through the imposition of enforceable norms and expectations—that is, through law. The factors that motivate a given society to impose the norms that it does often remain unclear. It is easy to assume that the society held particular values about how life should be lived and order maintained and that it gave expression to those values through its laws, but the matter is not quite this simple. Law can take on a life of its own and exert a degree of influence on a society's values similar to or even greater than that which the latter are able to exert on it.[1] Moreover, the values embedded in the law may reflect those of previous generations[2] or of the individuals with substantial power and resources more than they do the values of the society at large.[3] Thus,

---

1. At the very least, law and social values have a mutually influential relationship. The literature on the matter is vast. For a relatively brief discussion with additional literature, see Robert D. Cooter, "Three Effects of Social Norms on Law: Expression, Deterrence, and Internalization," *Oregon Law Review* 79 (2000): 1–22. Among other questions, Cooter considers "how law can change behavior without deterring anyone" (ibid., 4); see also Cooter, "Do Good Laws Make Good Citizens? An Economic Analysis of Internalized Norms," *Virginia Law Review* 86 (2000): 1577–1601. For a discussion from the vantage point of biblical studies, see F. Rachel Magdalene, "Legal Science Then and Now: Theory and Method in the Work of Raymond Westbrook," *Maarav* 18 (2011): 17–53.

2. On the way in which law can speak to and influence future generations, see Austin Sarat and Thomas R. Kearns, "Writing History and Registering Memory in Legal Decisions and Legal Practices: An Introduction," in *History, Memory, and the Law*, ed. Austin Sarat and Thomas R. Kearns (Ann Arbor: University of Michigan Press, 1999), 1–24.

3. See the discussion of this point in Magdalene, "Legal Theory Then and Now," 26–8.

any analysis of the relationship between sexuality and law, especially within an ancient society, faces a complex set of challenges. Not only is the relationship between these two areas of human behavior and culture difficult to delineate, but each area also presents a variety of dimensions that deserve their own detailed exploration. Despite the hazards associated with this endeavor, however, we believe that a fresh analysis of how sexuality and law interface within the Hebrew Bible's most influential set of writings—namely, the Torah—will produce significant findings and insights. Recent advances in philological, historical, legal, and theoretical analysis have created opportunities to return to well-worn texts for new discoveries and interpretations. Here at the outset, then, we seek to introduce some of the key issues that will be examined in the book and to establish a modest theoretical basis for the ensuing discussions. We begin with remarks on the nature of sexuality and how it may be understood.

Sexuality/Sexualities

Sexuality encompasses both the ways in which we experience our bodies, pleasures, and desires, and how we interpret and make sense of those experiences. Yet our understanding of the erotic possibilities of the body is largely determined by time, place, and circumstances. What we see as being natural or unnatural, appropriate or inappropriate, and moral or immoral about particular sexual acts, behaviors, and choices in sexual partner—and even which feelings, acts, and behaviors we consider to be sexual—is shaped by the society and culture in which we live. It is instilled in us from birth by family, community, religious institutions, and other aspects of our culture. These societal and cultural sexual norms and mores[4] delineate the possibilities and the limits of our erotic lives.[5] Because sexual

---

4. Sexual norms in this context are the general behavioral standards of a community in regard to sexual conduct, while mores are a specific sub-set of behavioral norms in which determinations of right and wrong play a central role in regulating interpersonal relationships among members of society. See John DeLamater, "The Social Control of Sexuality," *Annual Review of Sociology* 7 (1981): 263–9; Kathleen McKinney, "The Sociological Approach to Human Sexuality," in *Alternative Approaches to the Study of Sexual Behavior*, ed. Donn Byrne and Kathryn Kelley (Hillsdale: Lawrence Erlbaum Associates, 1986), 106–7; and Margaret Mooney Marini, "Social Values and Norms," *Encyclopedia of Sociology*, ed. Edgar F. Borgatta and Rhonda J. V. Montgomery, 2nd ed., vol. 4 (New York: Macmillan Reference U.S.A, 2000), 2829.

5. A similar, somewhat longer version of this discussion on the nature of sexuality appears in Hilary Lipka, *Sexual Transgression in the Hebrew Bible*, Hebrew Bible Monographs 7 (Sheffield: Sheffield Phoenix, 2006), 1–8.

norms and mores can vary a great deal from society to society, and even from sub-group to sub-group within each society, there is little in the way of sexual behaviors or attitudes that may be considered universal.[6] What is sexually normative in one culture or sub-culture can have little in common with what is considered sexually normative in another. Dissimilarities can be found in what actions are viewed as sexual, which parts of the body are considered erogenous, and when, where, and with whom it is appropriate to engage in sexual activity, and the ways that different cultures and sub-cultures in different times and places make sense of erotic experiences can vary widely.[7] For that reason, every society at any given point

---

6. While many scholars accept this claim, it should be acknowledged that it is not without contest. There are those who take a more essentialist approach, maintaining that sexuality is a fixed essence that is almost entirely determined by biology; they see most aspects of sexuality and sexual behavior as universal. In contrast, social constructionists maintain that sexuality is largely a product of social conditioning. The essays in this collection reveal aspects of sexuality in biblical texts that provide evidence for the merits of taking the constructionist view, if the goal is to understand how sexuality was viewed in ancient Israel on its own terms. For a summary of the essentialist vs. constructionist debate over the nature of sexuality, see Jeffrey Weeks, *Sexuality*, 2nd ed., Key Ideas (London: Routledge, 2003), 6–8; Robert M. Buffington, "Introduction," in *A Global History of Sexuality: The Modern Era*, ed. Robert M. Buffington, Eithne Luibhéid, and Donna J. Guy (Malden: John Wiley & Sons, 2013), 1–6; and Marilyn B. Skinner, *Sexuality in Greek and Roman Culture*, 2nd ed., Ancient Cultures (Malden: Wiley-Blackwell, 2014), 9–13.

7. On the nature of sexuality and the diversity in how it is constructed in different societies, cultures, and sub-cultures, see William H. Davenport, "Sex in Cross-Cultural Perspective," in *Human Sexuality in Four Perspectives*, ed. Frank A. Beach (Baltimore: Johns Hopkins University Press, 1977), 117–21; Paul R. Abramson and Steven D. Pinkerton, "Introduction: Nature, Nurture, and In-Between," in *Sexual Nature, Sexual Culture,* ed. Paul R. Abramson and Steven D. Pinkerton (Chicago: University of Chicago Press, 1995), 5–6; Robert A. Padgug, "Sexual Matters: On Conceptualizing Sexuality in History," in *Culture, Society and Sexuality: A Reader*, ed. Richard Parker and Peter Aggleton (London and Philadelphia: UCL, 1999), 15–23; Weeks, *Sexuality*, 6–22; and Whitney Campbell and Nicholas E. Peterson, *Handbook on Sexuality: Perspectives, Issues and Role in Society* (New York: Nova Science Publishers, 2012), vii–xii. Sex is not as easy to define as one might think. Studies such as Stephanie A. Sanders and June Machover Reinisch, "Would You Say You 'Had Sex' If…?" *Journal of the American Medical Association* 281, no. 3 (1999): 275–77, and Stephanie A. Sanders, et al., "Misclassification Bias: Diversity in Conceptualisations about Having 'Had Sex,'" *Sexual Health* 7, no. 1 (2010): 31–4, have found that there is little consensus among the people they surveyed over what constitutes sex. Some people consider only penis-vagina intercourse with ejaculation to be sex, while others include a wider range of activities, including anal sex,

will actually have multiple sexualities in play, sometimes competing with one another. Additionally, what is considered normative and acceptable regarding sexual and gender roles within a particular society, culture, or sub-culture is not fixed but will shift as that society, culture, or sub-culture evolves.[8]

Given how diverse notions of sexuality can be among different societies, cultures, and sub-cultures, we cannot assume that those living in ancient Israel who created the biblical texts we have today had the same conception of sexuality that we do. In fact, they likely did not. Any study of sexuality within this culture so far removed temporally, geographically, and culturally from our own must consider the biblical construction of sexuality—that is, the ways in which sex was conceptualized and the cultural meanings that were attached to it—on its own terms. Moreover, it is important to keep in mind that the ideas of the biblical authors concerning what behaviors they considered sexual and how they viewed these behaviors not only differ from our own ideas about what is normative, but also, as will become evident from the essays in this book, exhibit differences among themselves. While some of these authors' views on sexuality may be representative of a large portion of the ancient Israelite population, at least in certain times and places, others likely present views that represent a minority opinion, limited to a small segment of the population. Thus, just as in our own time, it is more appropriate to talk about sexualities in the Hebrew Bible and in the culture that produced it, rather than one sexuality.[9]

---

oral-genital contact, and manual stimulation of genitalia by the hand and/or other body parts. If a randomly selected group of individuals from the present day U.S. have such different ideas about what is and is not considered sex, it is worth considering how different the understanding of sex might be for a culture much further removed from us temporally and geographically.

8. For a discussion of factors that influence how quickly or slowly societal norms and mores evolve, see Lipka, *Sexual Transgression in the Hebrew Bible*, 5, especially n. 15.

9. Some scholars, Michel Foucault foremost among them, observing how differently sex was constructed in the ancient world, have argued that it is inappropriate to use the term sexuality in reference to ancient cultures, since sexuality is a modern historical construct. See Michel Foucault, *The History of Sexuality, Volume 1: An Introduction*, trans. Robert Hurley (New York: Pantheon Books, 1978), 105–7; Arnold I. Davidson, "Sex and the Emergence of Sexuality," *Critical Inquiry* 14 (1987): 18–37; and Daniel Boyarin, "Are There Any Jews in 'The History of Sexuality'?" *Journal of the History of Sexuality* 5 (1995): 334–5. However, while it is true that our conception of sexuality in contemporary Western society as an identity primarily

This book provides a glimpse into the construction of sexuality—or multiple sexualities—in the Hebrew Bible and in ancient Israel through the lens of biblical law. Laws and legal customs provide insight into a society's standards, expectations, and ideals, both influencing and reflecting that society's norms and mores. In relation to sexuality, laws and legal customs dictate the nature of relations between various members of a family, household, and community regarding matters such as with whom one can have sexual relations, when and where sexual relations are appropriate, which forms of sexual expression are permissible, whom one can marry, and what options are available if one or both partners no longer want to be in the marriage. Since the focus of this book is on biblical law, it will be helpful to consider what biblical law is and what its relation may have been to the society and culture that produced it.

The Nature of Biblical Law

The concept of law can be difficult to define, even in a general sense, and legal scholars, anthropologists, and others continue to debate the issue. A functionalist definition would identify the roles or functions that what we call law typically fulfills, even if all of these do not have to be in operation before one can say that a legal system is in place. Such functions usually have to do with individual status (e.g., enslaved, married), the ownership and transfer of property (real or otherwise), agreements or contracts, settling disputes, norms for social behavior, and penalties for violators. What is of particular interest for this book is the effort to establish regulations (written or unwritten) for social behavior—regulations by which members of a given society are expected to conduct themselves and that can be enforced by that society's governmentally sanctioned judiciary

---

defined by one's choice of sexual partner is a modern construction and not applicable as such to the ancient world, that does not mean that there was no notion of sexuality in ancient cultures. As has been demonstrated by several scholars, it is appropriate to talk about sexuality (and sexualities) in the ancient world, so long as we do not confine our understanding of the term to our modern conceptions. The first chapter in this book goes into this issue in some depth. See, additionally, Amy Richlin, *The Garden of Priapus: Sexuality and Aggression in Roman Humor* (New York: Oxford University Press, 1992), xiv–xvii; Gwendolyn Leick, *Sex and Eroticism in Mesopotamian Literature* (London: Routledge, 1994), 5; Bernadette J. Brooten, *Love Between Women: Early Christian Responses to Female Homoeroticism* (Chicago: University of Chicago Press, 1996), 17–26; and Skinner, *Sexuality in Greek and Roman Culture*, 3–23.

system.¹⁰ Within the context of ancient Israel and what we can discern from biblical texts about possible legal practice within it, thinking of law in this way appears to work fairly well. One finds numerous regulations for behavior in the Torah, along with the implication that a body of rules existed even before YHWH communicated his laws to Moses at Sinai, and most of the regulations are presented as if they could be enforced by legal authorities. However, this raises the question of the relationship between biblical law and actual legal practice in ancient Israel. The biblical texts essentially constitute literature in the service of a religious agenda (or agendas), and we cannot assume that they provide a straightforward picture of ancient Israel's legal system.¹¹ It is necessary to ask, then, whether the contents of the biblical legal collections correlate with the law as it was practiced in ancient Israel and what the role of the collections might have been within ancient Israelite society and culture.¹²

Scholars vary a great deal as to how they view the relationship between biblical law and actual legal practice in ancient Israel and Judah, but current views on the issue can be divided into three general categories. First, a number of scholars hold that the biblical legal collections were meant to be authoritative in ancient Israel, although there are differences of opinion regarding the nature of that authority and the relationships between the collections. Some hold to the traditional notion that the legal material of the Pentateuch presents a comprehensive system of law that was supposed to be followed and enforced. They would see legal practice in ancient Israel as mostly conforming to Pentateuchal law¹³ or as looking to the biblical laws for authoritative precedents that judges should use to decide cases.¹⁴ Others understand the Pentateuchal legal texts as authori-

---

10. Bruce Wells, "What Is Biblical Law? A Look at Pentateuchal Rules and Near Eastern Practice," *CBQ* 70 (2008): 223 n. 2.

11. See Niels Peter Lemche, "Justice in Western Asia in Antiquity, or: Why No Laws Were Needed!," *Chicago-Kent Law Review* 70 (1995): 1695–1716.

12. Four extended legal collections are usually identified within the Pentateuch: the Covenant Collection or Book of the Covenant (Exodus 21–23; opinions on the textual boundaries of this collection vary); the Priestly Collection (found in parts of Exodus, Leviticus 1–16, and parts of Numbers), the Holiness Collection or Source (mainly in Leviticus 17–26), and the Deuteronomic Collection (Deuteronomy 12–26). For further discussion, see Bruce Wells, "Biblical Law," in *Encyclopedia of the Bible and Law*, ed. Brent Strawn, 2 vols. (New York: Oxford University Press, 2015), 1:39–50.

13. E.g., Gregory C. Chirichigno, *Debt-Slavery in Israel and the Ancient Near East*, JSOTSup 141 (Sheffield: Sheffield Academic, 1993), 354–7.

14. E.g., Ze'ev W. Falk, *Hebrew Law in Biblical Times: An Introduction*, 2nd ed. (Winona Lake: Eisenbrauns, 2001), 7–8, 11–13.

tative or attempting to be authoritative, but they do not view the legal collections as forming a coherent system of law. Rather, they observe that different legal collections at times seem to disagree with one another and, in some cases, try to revise one another.[15] Scholars who follow this line of thinking disagree as to how successful the authors of a given collection may have been in attempting to give their list of provisions the status of law, but they are generally agreed that the authors of each collection aspired to having their rules imposed on Israelite society and enforced. If the authors were successful, then one can assume substantial correlation between those authors' rules and Israelite legal practice, but, given the paucity of information regarding the latter, most scholars with this view remain agnostic about the degree of correlation that may have prevailed.

Second, another group of scholars understand the legal collections as academic treatises produced by scribal schools and based more or less on the practice of law in ancient Israel and Judah. Ample evidence demonstrates that scribes in multiple regions of the ancient Near East created such treatises (in the form of lists) as a way of cataloging knowledge about an array of topics such as omens or medical diagnoses and treatments. The legal collections found in the Hebrew Bible and in other ancient Near Eastern texts (e.g., the Laws of Hammurabi), according to this view, catalog legal knowledge and constitute a subcategory within the genre of academic treatises.[16] While those who take this approach do not see the legal collections as prescribing authoritative law, they believe that many of the provisions in the collections are accurate descriptions of the law and legal customs as they were practiced. These scholars also claim that the scribes composing the collections probably included hypothetical

---

15. Bernard M. Levinson, for example, who sees the legal collections mainly as literary works produced by scribes, views Deuteronomy and its laws as a radical attempt to revise and even overturn the Covenant Collection in Exodus (*Deuteronomy and the Hermeneutics of Legal Innovation* [Oxford: Oxford University Press, 1997], 3–22, 144–57). He also maintains that it is unclear how much of this agenda was enacted (*"The Right Chorale": Studies in Biblical Law and Interpretation* [Winona Lake: Eisenbrauns, 2011], 35–7, 68–86). Eckart Otto, on the other hand, believes that Deuteronomy borrowed from and added to existing scribal traditions in order to reform but not overturn previous laws and practices ("Kodifizierung und Kanonisierung von Rechtssätzen in keilschriftlichen und biblischen Rechtssammlungen," in *La Codification des lois dans l'antiquité*, ed. E. Levy [Paris: De Boccard, 2000], 120 and 123–4).

16. See the discussion in Marc Van De Mieroop, *Philosophy before the Greeks: The Pursuit of Truth in Ancient Babylonia* (Princeton: Princeton University Press, 2015), 157–70.

situations of their own making; some of these may have been unlikely actually to occur, and some functioned as so-called boundary scenarios—imagined events that tried to capture one extreme end or the other (or both) of a legal situation or problem.[17] The solutions that they provide to these scenarios were probably in keeping with how they believed their society would respond or, perhaps, ought to respond to these situations.

Third, there are those who view the legal collections as more theoretical or ideological in nature, in some cases created perhaps in the hope of influencing societal behavior or mores, but having little or no connection to actual legal practice at the time they were written. Some claim that the collections had their origins in wisdom traditions and came to function as repositories of advice that could guide individuals toward a righteous life.[18] Others identify a political origin for the collections and argue that they were composed in response to the projection of imperial power from Mesopotamia; the Covenant Collection, for example, was meant to "stand as a symbolic counterstatement to the Assyrian hegemony prevailing at the time of its composition."[19] In either case, this view distances the collections from a legal origin and function and is pessimistic regarding their usefulness when it comes to recovering the legal practice of ancient Israel. Any attempt to incorporate the collections into a study of law, according to this view, misunderstands the nature of the collections and is thus rendered problematic.

Out of all of these options, the least likely one is that the biblical legal collections functioned together as a comprehensive legal code; it also seems unlikely that they served as authoritative guidelines for judges. The legal collections are not comprehensive in scope and omit several important topics (e.g., sale and rental of property, dowry, adoption, the innocent buyer of stolen goods) that are treated in other ancient Near Eastern legal collections and that were probably of significance in ancient Israel as well.[20] Moreover, they do not provide a systematic description of

---

17. One of the foremost proponents of this overall view was Raymond Westbrook; see, in particular his "Cuneiform Law Codes and the Origins of Legislation," *ZA* 79 (1989): 201–22.

18. Anne Fitzpatrick-McKinley, *The Transformation of Torah from Scribal Advice to Law*, JSOTSup 287 (Sheffield: Sheffield Academic, 1999), 113–19.

19. David P. Wright, *Inventing God's Law: How the Covenant Code of the Bible Used and Revised the Laws of Hammurabi* (Oxford: Oxford University Press, 2009), 1–7, 346–59, quote on 346.

20. J. J. Finkelstein, *The Ox That Gored*, Transactions of the American Philosophical Society 71, part 2 (Philadelphia: The American Philosophical Society, 1981), 42–3, observes that even when everyday matters such as inheritance or marriage are

the rules for conducting legal proceedings, which one would expect if they were intended for use in a judicial context. We have little extra-biblical evidence to help determine the nature of the relationship between the biblical legal collections and the actual practice of law in ancient Israel,[21] and the biblical narrative evidence presents a rather ambiguous picture. One can find a few, often oblique, references to biblical law in narrative accounts,[22] but some behaviors prohibited in one or more of the biblical legal collections are not presented as problematic in some narrative texts.[23]

The relationship between biblical law and ancient Israel was most likely complex and multi-faceted. Some biblical laws may have played a role—and some were probably intended to play a role—in establishing certain legal practices in ancient Israel. Some laws may provide reasonably accurate reflections of ancient Israelite law and legal practice.[24] Some perhaps were the result of scribal musings, scholarly or theological reflection on ethical issues, and did not influence or reflect actual law and legal practice. Others were likely expressions of ideals that disclose how a certain segment of Israelite society viewed itself and believed that its community should behave. It is difficult to determine to what extent they represented mere ideals or were intended to influence social behavior

---

touched upon by the biblical laws, it is the unusual rather than the normative that is dealt with. See also Jan Joosten, *People and Land in the Holiness Code: An Exegetical Study of the Ideational Framework of the Law in Leviticus 17–26*, VTSup 67 (Leiden: Brill, 1996), 18–19.

21. On what little evidence there is, see Raymond Westbrook and Bruce Wells, *Everyday Law in Biblical Israel: An Introduction* (Louisville: Westminster John Knox, 2009), 15.

22. See, for example, what appears to be a citation of Deut. 24:16 in 2 Kgs 14:5-6. See also the story of Naboth's vineyard in 1 Kings 21, where two witnesses are made to testify against Naboth, perhaps to be in compliance with the laws in Num. 35:30; Deut. 17:6; and 19:15 (or laws similar to these). Some prophetic texts may also allude to provisions in the biblical legal collections. See, for example, the possible reference to Exod. 22:26 in Amos 2:8.

23. For example, see Athalya Brenner, *The Intercourse of Knowledge: On Gendering Desire and "Sexuality" in the Hebrew Bible*, Biblical Interpretation Series 26 (Leiden: Brill, 1997), 92–107, on the discrepancy between the notion of incest laid out in the legal collections and the presumably acceptable sexual unions found in the narrative texts. These discrepancies tend to occur more with the Holiness Source than the other collections.

24. Wells ("What Is Biblical Law?" 231–43) identifies points of congruence between certain laws in the Torah and legal practices in Mesopotamia and Syria; this supports, he suggests, the idea that some biblical laws do indeed accurately reflect the legal practice of ancient Israel and Judah.

and perhaps even influence legal practice. Thus, the Pentateuchal laws probably reflect ancient Israelite juridical practice to various degrees, some dictating, some influencing, some reflecting, and some having little relationship to actual law and legal practice.[25]

Nevertheless, all of these types of provisions can be considered legal discourse.[26] Even those provisions that may have had little relationship to Israelite legal practice were part of the broad array of legal discussions that undoubtedly took place throughout different quarters in ancient Israel. While some of these provisions exhibit affinities with other genres such as wisdom literature or general exhortation, the area of human intellectual and cultural endeavor that they are most closely aligned with is that of law. For this reason, we continue to employ the term "law" in referring to them. What we call biblical law, then, even if it did not provide a comprehensive law code that was put into practice in ancient Israel or authoritatively dictate what kings or judges must do, is valuable for helping us understand the societal norms and mores and legal practice in ancient Israel on two fundamental levels. First, in light of the reasoning above and the evidence from other ancient Near Eastern societies, there is sufficient warrant for claiming that a number of biblical provisions describe and reflect laws and legal customs as they were traditionally practiced, at least in certain times and places in ancient Israel.[27] Second,

---

25. In time, the Pentateuchal legal texts did become the basis of legislation, but that process of transforming the various legal collections into one authoritative body of law did not even begin until the time of Ezra. See Finkelstein, *The Ox That Gored*, 45–46; and Fitzpatrick-McKinley, *The Transformation of Torah from Scribal Advice to Law*, 146–77.

26. Eckart Otto, "Die Rechtshermeneutik des Pentateuch und die achämenidische Rechtsideologie in ihren altorientalischen Kontexten," in *Kodifizierung und Legitimierung des Rechts in der Antike und im Alten Orient*, ed. M. Witte und M. T. Fögen, BZABR 5 (Wiesbaden: Harrassowitz, 2005), 71–116.

27. Despite some biblical scholars' claims to the contrary, it is not a foregone conclusion that evidence from Mesopotamia demonstrates a clear lack of correlation between the legal collections and the documents of practice (e.g., contracts, trial records) from that region. In fact, ample work by Assyriologists shows a significant degree of correspondence between what is stated in the collections and what the documents of practice reveal to have been operative. See Herbert P. H. Petschow, "Die §§ 45 and 46 des Codex Ḥammurapi—Ein Beitrag zum altbabylonischen Bodenpachtrecht und zum Problem: Was ist der Codex Ḥammurapi?" *ZA* 74 (1984): 181–212; Gerhard Ries, "Ein Neubabylonischer Mitgiftprozess (559 v. Chr.): Gleichzeitig ein Eintrag zur Frage der Geltung keilschriftlicher Gesetze," in *Gedächtnisschrift für Wolfgang Kunkel*, ed. D. Nörr and D. Simon (Frankfurt: Klostermann, 1984), 345–63; Johannes Renger, "Noch einmal: Was war der 'Kodex Ḥammurapi':

other provisions provide insight into the sexual culture of ancient Israel, revealing which sexual behaviors were considered normative or even ideal, and which ones were considered problematic, among the various cultures and sub-cultures that produced these texts.

This Volume

The essays in this volume consider sexuality in the Hebrew Bible and in ancient Israel within the framework of the discourse of biblical law, with a focus on sexuality and law in the Torah. The book does not set out to provide a comprehensive overview of the treatment of sexuality in biblical law. Rather, it provides insight into the mindset of those who created the texts, the social and cultural milieu in which they lived, and the ideas they had regarding what was normative in relation to gender roles, sexual knowledge, sexual behavior, and those institutions (e.g., marriage) that influenced or were influenced by conceptions of sexuality. Of course, the Hebrew Bible does not present a mirror image of the cultures that produced it. Some sub-groups and their views are represented more than others, and their views and attitudes towards sexuality are presented as normative, though the reality of ancient Israel was surely more complex. Part of the challenge for an endeavor like this is accepting that, given the nature and limitations of the evidence available to us, there is much that we cannot know and will never know regarding sexual norms and mores in ancient Israel.

The chapters in the volume draw upon a wide array of strategies, methodologies, and approaches, including narrative criticism, philological analysis, feminist and gender theory, and comparative analysis. While the range of topics covered is diverse, several recurring subjects are interwoven throughout the book, especially the role and status of women within the household and within ancient Israelite society as a whole, as well as the degree of legal, religious, sexual, and economic agency and autonomy that women had available to them at various life (and particularly marital) stages. Other topics include the meaning of key terms and expressions in

Ein erlassenes Gesetz oder ein Rechtsbuch?" in *Rechtskodifizierung und soziale Normen im interkulturellen Vergleich*, ed. H.-J. Gehrke (Tübingen: Narr, 1994), 27–58; and Joachim Oelsner, "Erwägungen zu Aufbau, Charakter und Datierung des sog. 'Neubabylonischen Gesetzesfragments'," *AoF* 24 (1997): 219–25. In fact, some Assyriologists still maintain that the contents of the Laws of Hammurabi functioned as authoritative law for Old Babylonian society (e.g., Hans Neumann, "Recht im antiken Mesopotamien," in *Die Rechtskulturen der Antike: Vom Alten Orient bis zum Römischen Reich*, ed. U. Manthe [Munich: Beck, 2003], 55–122).

relevant texts, the role that concerns related to purity and impurity had on sexual and marital partner choice, and the responsibilities accorded to the *paterfamilias* in regulating the sexuality of members of his household. Among the more important questions addressed in the essays are: (1) What gender codes and expectations are embedded in these legal texts, and how are they reflected in their attempts to regulate certain aspects of sexuality, especially female sexuality? (2) What cultural conventions are implicit in the texts, and how much did they reflect the social realities of the time and place in which they were written? (3) What layers of interpretation and reinterpretation can be discerned in these texts, and what do these layers reveal about shifts in sexual norms and mores over time? and (4) What do these texts reveal about different types of sexualities that may have existed in ancient Israel?

In the opening essay, David Tabb Stewart posits that if we set aside contemporary notions of sexuality and examine what sexual behaviors are problematized and valorized in biblical texts, a sexual landscape quite different from our own emerges. Engaging in a comparative analysis of Hittite and biblical laws regulating sexuality, with a focus on the Holiness Collection, he contends that biblical law reflects a hierarchical system of divine, human, and bestial sexualities, along with a manifest concern with blurring the boundaries between these categories and with potential transgressions of sub-boundaries within the human category. Hittite laws reveal a sexual landscape that is in some ways quite different, but both sexual systems exhibit a concern with sexual behaviors that threaten to destabilize society. Stewart's essay provides a conceptual framework within which to consider the intersection of sexuality and law in the Torah on a holistic level, while the essays that follow highlight specific ways in which biblical authors navigate the regulation of sexuality within this larger conceptual matrix.

The next three essays consider ways in which the legal collections and descriptions of legal interactions in biblical narratives can reflect actual laws and legal procedures in ancient Israel, focusing on specific texts within the books of Genesis and Exodus. Pamela Barmash considers several questions raised by the law regarding the daughter sold into slavery in Exod. 21:7-11, including whether the law applied to all women sold into slavery or only daughters sold by their fathers for sexual purposes. She concludes that the former was likely the case, since the most common reason for a woman to be sold into slavery seems to have been for sexual purposes. She also explores what the status of the woman would have been in her master's household, and what the general intent of the law was, concluding that an important aspect of its intent was to protect the interests of the woman, who found herself in what was often a precarious situation. She also notes that due to loopholes in the law's wording, it may have been possible for an unscrupulous master to misuse this law for his own benefit.

The betrothal contract between Laban and Jacob for Rachel in Gen. 29:14-30 is the subject of the detailed study contributed by F. Rachel Magdalene. She maintains that at the center of the narrative lies an oral, informal contract for marriage in exchange for services rendered that was considered binding and enforceable, much in the same the way that modern informal contracts operate today. She contends that the presence of such an oral contract in this narrative reveals that the legal systems of the ancient world were far more developed and complex than previous scholarship has acknowledged and that, as a result, we must rethink outdated assumptions regarding the origins of contract law.

The question of how levirate marriage is depicted in Genesis 38, in light of the levirate law in Deut. 25:5-10 and its description in the book of Ruth, is addressed by Eryl W. Davies. Davies explores the legal background of the account of Judah and Tamar in Genesis 38 and addresses several questions about the nature of levirate marriage as it is depicted in this text. He asks whether the custom originally involved marriage between the brother-in-law and the widow (he believes it did), whether the levirate duty was optional or obligatory (he contends it was obligatory), and whether it extended, at one time, to the widow's father-in-law (he believes it did). He also considers the relationship between the three biblical texts that involve levirate marriage and identifies several stages throughout the evolution of the levirate law reflected in these texts.

The next three essays focus on the book of Leviticus, specifically the Holiness Collection, the biblical legal collection with the most material related to the regulation of sexuality, and each highlights a different aspect of its treatment of sexuality. Bruce Wells provides an innovative reading and interpretation of משכבי אשה in Lev. 18:22 and 20:13. Wells contends, arguing both on philological and contextual grounds, that rather than reading this phrase the way most scholars do, as an adverbial accusative of manner (e.g., "as one lies with a woman"), the phrase should be read as an adverbial accusative of location, translated as "on the beds of a woman." The connotation of "beds" in this context relates to the sexual and authoritative domain of a woman, and thus the law prohibits sexual relations with any Judean man married to a woman or with any males who are under the guardianship of a Judean woman. It was not meant to be a complete ban on male-with-male sex. Wells also considers these laws within the larger context of the sexual prohibitions in Leviticus 18 and 20, which he suggests may have reflected the authors' concern with preserving group identity and solidarity. They sought to distinguish their community not only from non-Judean groups around them but also from Judean groups who did not fully accept the same traditions and rules advocated by these authors regarding sexual boundaries.

The warning to fathers in Lev. 19:29 not to desecrate their daughters by letting them engage in זנה is the subject of the next essay. Hilary Lipka considers several questions raised by the verse, including how זנה should be translated in this context, the nature of the daughter's desecration and who is blamed for it, the impact of such behavior on the land, and how this admonition fits into the larger context of Leviticus 19 and its concern with achieving and maintaining holiness. She concludes that this verse warns fathers to keep control over their unmarried daughters' sexuality and not let them engage in sexually promiscuous behavior, because not only will it cause the daughters to profane themselves and thus lose holiness, but also such behavior poses a threat to the entire community. The authors view such behavior as contagious, with the ability to foster similar misbehavior in others, which in turn can lead to the land being filled with depravity (זמה) and then becoming defiled. The ultimate result becomes exile from the land.

Sarah Shectman's essay considers the priestly marriage restrictions in Lev. 21:7-8 and 13–15, which limit a priest's choice of wife to a virgin or a widow and the high priest's marriage prospects to a virgin of his own kin. She also discusses Ezek. 44:22, which extends the latter restriction to all priests, with the exception that a priest may marry the widow of another priest. Shectman provides an innovative thesis to explain the possible reasons for these regulations, in particular why a priest may marry a widow but not a divorced woman, focusing on what it is about the nature of marriage and its dissolution that renders divorced women, and at times widows, problematic as priestly spouses. She suggests that marriage creates a bond that moves beyond sexual relations and thus cannot simply be about sexual purity or stigma. That bond may be conceptualized in quasi-physical terms; it is not fully dissolved by divorce, and according to some biblical authors, it may not be fully dissolved by the death of the husband either.

Marital restrictions of a different kind are the subject of the next essay, in which M. L. Case considers the case of the daughters of Zelophehad. While in Num. 27:1-11, Zelophehad's daughters are allowed to inherit his ancestral land in the absence of sons, in Numbers 36 members of the tribe of Manasseh complain to Moses that if the daughters marry men outside their tribe, their land will go to their husbands. In response, Moses limits the daughters' marriage options to men within their own tribe. Case contends that the matter addressed in Numbers 36 is about more than simply keeping ancestral land in the family. The daughters, not under the control of a male head of household and in the possession of land which potentially gives them economic independence, threaten the social order of the Israelites, and thus there is a need to control them, and especially their sexuality. This is accomplished by placing restrictions on whom they can marry. Controlling the daughters' sexuality in this way not only mitigates the possibility of ancestral land leaving the tribe but also places the unattached daughters back under the control of male heads of households, namely, their new husbands.

The next two essays reflect on the intersection of sexuality and law in the book of Deuteronomy. Building upon the work of Michael Foucault, Steffan Mathias surveys the discourses of sexuality that pervade the book of Deuteronomy, and he explores how both the legal and narrative material in this book produce behavior that maintains relationships of sexual power, not just between men and women, but between the people and YHWH. Deuteronomy constructs sexuality as gendered, as powered, and as fundamentally reproductive, and it emphasizes the repeated teaching and passing down of Torah as that which enables and regulates fertility among the community. It is by the dutiful transmission of Torah that the people will remain fruitful and that proper social continuity will be ensured, while failure to follow the Torah will result in the converse: the loss of fertility and destruction of progeny. Thus, Mathias concludes, while male sexuality within Deuteronomy can be read as to an extent autonomous, it is always subservient to the procreative authority of YHWH.

One particular law in Deuteronomy that has continued to present challenges to scholars is Deut. 24:1-4. Anselm C. Hagedorn demonstrates how taking a comparative approach and considering this text's treatment of divorce within the larger ancient Mediterranean cultural milieu can provide illuminating results. His essay considers the treatment of divorce in ancient Crete, and in particular in the Gortyn Code, assessing how questions of status and property relate to each other in these laws and how their treatment of divorce relates to how divorce was practiced and regulated in other parts of the Greek world. Hagedorn then demonstrates how his analysis can provide new insight into divorce procedure in ancient Israel, generally, and Deut. 24:1-4, in particular.

The final two essays consider how certain Torah laws are utilized in later biblical texts in ways that both expand upon and transform the original laws, providing a glimpse into later perspectives on Pentateuchal texts addressing sexuality. Kenneth Bergland considers the implications of Jeremiah's reuse of the divorce and remarriage prohibition in Deut. 24:1-4 as a metaphor for the problematic relationship between God and Israel and Judah. Jeremiah, by changing the grounds for divorce from the relatively neutral כי־מצא בה ערות דבר of Deut. 24:1-4 to the wife's marital infidelity, alters and magnifies the nature of the pollution. While in Deut. 24:1-4, the husband is warned that it will pollute the land if he remarries a former wife who has since remarried, in Jer. 3:1-10, it is the wife (Israel) who has polluted the land through her promiscuities, and the husband YHWH bears no responsibility either for the dissolution of the marriage or for the defilement of the land. Lastly, while in Deut. 24:1-4, the husband cannot remarry the wife, the thrust of Jer. 2:1–4:4 is a call for Judah to repent and return to YHWH. It is an open invitation, demonstrating how YHWH is willing to defy any expectations based on the legal boundaries in Deut. 24:1-4 to welcome his people back again.

In the final essay, Hannah Harrington considers the shift in emphasis in the Second Temple period from conceiving of the temple and its cult as the divine sanctuary to the notion of the people of Israel as forming a human sanctuary which houses the presence of God. As a result of this development, the belief arose that this human sanctuary could be polluted by wrongful sexual relations—a belief that is reflected in concerns over sexual defilement, particularly through intermarriage, in both biblical and extra-biblical Second Temple literature. Harrington traces the evolution and development of this idea through several stages of the interpretation of Pentateuchal texts, including Exod. 19:6; 25:8; Lev. 20:3; and Deut. 23:3. Her study expands our understanding of the motivations underlying the heightened emphasis in Second Temple literature on preserving the sanctity and solidarity of the people by strict avoidance of intermarriage.

Taken together, these essays provide a foundation for those wishing to explore some of the different ways in which sexuality was understood and regulated in both the Hebrew Bible and the culture that produced it. From their own unique perspectives, the authors raise important questions at the intersection of sex, law, ideology, and religion. The essays' findings will, we hope, stimulate further discussion. They provide us with new options for understanding a broad range of critical issues: the landscape of Israelite and biblical sexualities; the ambiguous nature of marriage; the plight of those sold for sexual services; the significance of contract law and how it impinges on constructions of gender; the historical development of levirate marriage; the limitations in the prohibition on same-sex relations; the meaning and misunderstandings of זנה; the priestly view of suitable sex partners and its reasoning; the threat of independent and well-off women to the social order; the role of Torah in the rhetoric around divine reproduction; the comparative use of ancient Greek law; the role of marriage and divorce in prophetic metaphor; and the motives underlying the ban on intermarriage. As we have noted, the book is not a comprehensive exploration of sexuality and law, but the insights it provides will expand and advance our collective efforts to come to terms with the sexual culture of ancient Israel and the sexualities that existed within it.

Bibliography

Abramson, Paul R., and Steven D. Pinkerton. "Introduction: Nature, Nurture, and In-Between." In *Sexual Nature/Sexual Culture*, edited by Paul R. Abramson and Steven Pinkerton, 1–16. Chicago: University of Chicago Press, 1995.
Boyarin, Daniel. "Are There Any Jews in 'The History of Sexuality'?" *Journal of the History of Sexuality* 5 (1995): 333–55.
Brenner, Athalya. *The Intercourse of Knowledge: On Gendering Desire and 'Sexuality' in the Hebrew Bible*. Biblical Interpretation Series 26. Leiden: Brill, 1997.
Brooten, Bernadette J. *Love Between Women: Early Christian Responses to Female Homoeroticism*. Chicago: University of Chicago Press, 1996.
Buffington, Robert M. "Introduction." In *A Global History of Sexuality: The Modern Era*, edited by Robert M. Buffington, Eithne Luibhéid, and Donna J. Guy, 1–15. Malden: John Wiley & Sons, 2013.
Campbell, Whitney, and Nicholas E. Peterson. *Handbook on Sexuality: Perspectives, Issues and Role in Society*. New York: Nova Science Publishers, 2012.
Chirichigno, Gregory C. *Debt-Slavery in Israel and the Ancient Near East*. JSOTSup 141. Sheffield: Sheffield Academic, 1993.
Cooter, Robert D. "Do Good Laws Make Good Citizens? An Economic Analysis of Internalized Norms." *Virginia Law Review* 86 (2000): 1577–1601.
Cooter, Robert D. "Three Effects of Social Norms on Law: Expression, Deterrence, and Internalization." *Oregon Law Review* 79 (2000): 1–22.
Davenport, William H. "Sex in Cross-Cultural Perspective." In *Human Sexuality in Four Perspectives*, edited by Frank A. Beach, 115–63. Baltimore: Johns Hopkins University Press, 1977.
Davidson, Arnold I. "Sex and the Emergence of Sexuality." *Critical Inquiry* 14 (1987): 16–48.
DeLamater, John. "The Social Control of Sexuality." *Annual Review of Sociology* 7 (1981): 263–90.
Falk, Ze'ev W. *Hebrew Law in Biblical Times: An Introduction*. 2nd ed. Winona Lake: Eisenbrauns, 2001.
Finkelstein, J. J. *The Ox That Gored*. Transactions of the American Philosophical Society 71, part 2. Philadelphia: The American Philosophical Society, 1981.
Fitzpatrick-McKinley, Anne. *The Transformation of Torah from Scribal Advice to Law*. JSOTSup 287. Sheffield: Sheffield Academic, 1999.
Foucault, Michel. *The History of Sexuality, Volume 1: An Introduction*. Translated by Robert Hurley. New York: Pantheon Books, 1978.
Joosten, Jan. *People and Land in the Holiness Code: An Exegetical Study of the Ideational Framework of the Law in Leviticus 17–26*. VTSup 67. Leiden: Brill, 1996.

Leick, Gwendolyn. *Sex and Eroticism in Mesopotamian Literature*. London: Routledge, 1994.
Lemche, Niels Peter. "Justice in Western Asia in Antiquity, or: Why No Laws Were Needed!" *Chicago-Kent Law Review* 70 (1995): 1695–1716.
Levinson, Bernard M. *Deuteronomy and the Hermeneutics of Legal Innovation*. New York: Oxford University Press, 1997.
Levinson, Bernard M. *"The Right Chorale": Studies in Biblical Law and Interpretation*. Winona Lake: Eisenbrauns, 2011.
Lipka, Hilary. *Sexual Transgression in the Hebrew Bible*. Hebrew Bible Monographs 7. Sheffield: Sheffield Phoenix, 2006.
Magdalene, F. Rachel. "Legal Science Then and Now: Theory and Method in the Work of Raymond Westbrook." *Maarav* 18 (2011): 17–53.
Marini, Margaret Mooney. "Social Values and Norms." In *Encyclopedia of Sociology, Volume 4*, edited by Edgar F. Borgatta and Rhonda J. V. Montgomery, 2828–40. 2nd ed. New York: Macmillan Reference U.S.A, 2000.
McKinney, Kathleen. "The Sociological Approach to Human Sexuality." In *Alternative Approaches to the Study of Sexual Behavior*, edited by Donn Byrne and Kathryn Kelley, 103–29. Hillsdale: Lawrence Erlbaum Associates, 1986.
Neumann, Hans. "Recht im antiken Mesopotamien." In *Die Rechtskulturen der Antike: Vom Alten Orient bis zum Römischen Reich*, edited by U. Manthe, 55–122. Munich: Beck, 2003.
Oelsner, Joachim. "Erwägungen zu Aufbau, Charakter und Datierung des sog. 'Neubabylonischen Gesetzesfragments.'" *AoF* 24 (1997): 219–25.
Otto, Eckart. "Kodifizierung und Kanonisierung von Rechtssätzen in keilschriftlichen und biblischen Rechtssammlungen." In *La Codification des lois dans l'antiquité*, edited by Lévy, 77–124. Paris: De Boccard, 2000.
Otto, Eckart. "Die Rechtshermeneutik des Pentateuch und die achämenidische Rechtsideologie in ihren altorientalischen Kontexten." In *Kodifizierung und Legitimierung des Rechts in der Antike und im Alten Orient*, edited by M. Witte and M. T. Fögen, 71–116. BZABR 5. Wiesbaden: Harrassowitz, 2005.
Padgug, Robert A. "Sexual Matters: On Conceptualizing Sexuality in History." In *Culture, Society and Sexuality: A Reader*, edited by Richard Parker and Peter Aggleton, 15–28. London: UCL, 1999.
Petschow, Herbert P. H. "Die §§ 45 and 46 des Codex Ḫammurapi—Ein Beitrag zum altbabylonischen Bodenpachtrecht und zum Problem: Was ist der Codex Ḫammurapi?" *ZA* 74 (1984): 181–212.
Renger, Johannes. "Noch einmal: Was war der 'Kodex Hammurapi': Ein erlassenes Gesetz oder ein Rechtsbuch?" In *Rechtskodifizierung und soziale Normen im interkulturellen Vergleich*, edited by H. J. Gehrke, 27–58. Tübingen: Narr, 1994.
Richlin, Amy. *The Garden of Priapus: Sexuality and Aggression in Roman Humor*. New York: Oxford University Press, 1992.
Ries, Gerhard. "Ein Neubabylonischer Mitgiftprozess (559 v. Chr.): Gleichzeitig ein Eintrag zur Frage der Geltung keilschriftlicher Gesetze." In *Gedächtnisschrift für Wolfgang Kunkel*, edited by D. Nörr and D. Simon, 345–63. Frankfurt: Klostermann, 1984.
Sanders, Stephanie A., Brandon J. Hill, William L. Yarber, Cynthia A. Graham, Richard A. Crosby, and Robin R. Milhausen. "Misclassification Bias: Diversity in Conceptualisations about Having 'Had Sex.'" *Sexual Health* 7, no. 1 (2010): 31–4.

Sanders, Stephanie A., and June Machover Reinisch. "Would You Say You 'Had Sex' If...?" *Journal of the American Medical Association* 281, no. 3 (1999): 275–7.

Sarat, Austin, and Thomas R. Kearns. "Writing History and Registering Memory in Legal Decisions and Legal Practices: An Introduction." In *History, Memory, and the Law*, edited by Austin Sarat and Thomas R. Kearns, 1–24. Ann Arbor: University of Michigan Press, 1999.

Skinner, Marilyn B. *Sexuality in Greek and Roman Culture*. 2nd ed. Ancient Cultures. Malden: Wiley-Blackwell, 2014.

Van De Mieroop, Marc. *Philosophy before the Greeks. The Pursuit of Truth in Ancient Babylonia*. Princeton: Princeton University Press, 2015.

Weeks, Jeffrey. *Sexuality*. 2nd ed. Key Ideas. London: Routledge, 2003.

Wells, Bruce. "Biblical Law." In *Encyclopedia of the Bible and Law*, edited by Brent Strawn, 1:39–50. 2 vols. New York: Oxford University Press, 2015.

Wells, Bruce. "What Is Biblical Law? A Look at Pentateuchal Rules and Near Eastern Practice." *CBQ* 70 (2008): 223–43.

Westbrook, Raymond. "Cuneiform Law Codes and the Origins of Legislation." *ZA* 79 (1989): 201–22.

Westbrook, Raymond, and Bruce Wells. *Everyday Law in Biblical Israel: An Introduction*. Louisville: Westminster John Knox, 2009.

Wright, David P. *Inventing God's Law: How the Covenant Code of the Bible Used and Revised the Laws of Hammurabi*. Oxford: Oxford University Press, 2009.

1

CATEGORIES OF SEXUALITY INDIGENOUS
TO BIBLICAL LEGAL MATERIALS

David Tabb Stewart

The Problem of "Sexuality"

If "sexuality" is "the broad term that refers to categories of sexual desire,"[1] Daniel Boyarin argues that there is no *a priori* reason to assume that the Hebrew Bible has a system of sexuality—such as the binary opposition of homo- and heterosexuality. That is, he hypothesizes, "the Jewish culture of the biblical and talmudic periods was not organized around a system of sexual orientations defined by object choice."[2] He concludes instead that the Hebrew Bible confirms Foucault's thesis about the "history of sexuality": the ancient world does not "divide off sexual practices" as identities separate "from the general categories of forbidden and permitted."[3] Teresa Hornsby says categorically: "There

---

1. Teresa J. Hornsby, "Sexuality," in *The Oxford Encyclopedia of the Bible and Gender Studies*, vol. 2, ed. Julia M. O'Brien (Oxford: Oxford University Press, 2014), 290.
2. Daniel Boyarin, "Against Rabbinic Sexuality: Textual Reasoning and the Jewish Theology of Sex," in *Queer Theology: Rethinking the Western Body*, ed. Gerard Loughlin (Malden: Blackwell, 2007), 131.
3. Ibid., 141. See Michel Foucault, *The History of Sexuality, vol. 1: An Introduction*, trans. Robert Hurley (New York: Vintage, 1990), 37–8, 106; Foucault, *The History of Sexuality, vol. 2: The Use of Pleasure*, trans. Robert Hurley (New York: Vintage, 1990), 30–2. Foucault's regime of the permitted and forbidden is more complex than indicated in Boyarin's references. For example, the individual who

is no concept of sexuality to be discovered in the Bible; we can only know how the Bible has been used in the production and maintenance of modern sexualities."[4] But, while Julia Asher-Greve reminds us of the confusion of terminology about sexuality in ancient studies, she observes that "generalizing on the similarity *or difference* between contemporary and ancient cultures' gender/sexuality system(s) requires caution as ideas and concepts vary considerably."[5] Jeffrey Weeks argued in 1981 that categories of sexuality are created, and so the history of the concept is "a history of our discourses about sexuality."[6] And more recently in 2010 he offers that "'sexuality' is a historical construction, which brings together a lot of different biological and mental possibilities, and cultural forms."[7] This leaves open the possibility that an ancient culture might develop notions of "sexuality" different from our own. Therefore, what follows addresses Boyarin's skepticism about a sexuality system and Foucault's alleged reduction of ancient sexuality to the forbidden/permitted binary, while attempting to reconstruct the sexual/ity system of ancient Israel primarily by investigating the Holiness Code and contrasting it with the Hittite Laws.

Foucault's three-volume sketch of *The History of Sexuality* shows several twists and turns for the categories of sexuality deployed. He understands Greco-Roman culture as focusing on "practices of the self" and *askēsis*,[8] rather than codifying conduct or developing strict definitions

---

takes the notion of permitted and forbidden things into account makes use of not only behavioral or legal codes but also (b) cultural contexts that might allow loopholes (ibid., 2:25), *and* (c) different ways in which an individual "recognizes himself as obliged to put it in practice" (e.g., fidelity to a group, making oneself an example, etc.; ibid., 2:27). Consequently, one must turn to ancient texts beyond codes to visualize the surrounding corona of culture and self.

4. Hornsby, "Sexuality," 297.

5. Julia M. Asher-Greve, "From *La Femme* to Multiple Sex/Gender," in *Studying Gender in the Ancient Near East*, ed. Saana Svärd and Agnès Garcia-Ventura (University Park: Eisenbrauns, 2018), 17–18 (emphasis mine). She adds: "A survey of the terms *gender*, *sex*, and *sexuality* in Assyriology, Egyptology, and Classics shows authors often avoid precision" (ibid., 20).

6. Jeffrey Weeks, *Sex, Politics, and Society: The Regulation of Sexuality since 1800* (London: Longman, 1981), 7, and see also 5, 11, 285–7.

7. Jeffrey Weeks, *Sexuality*, rev. ed. (London: Routledge, 2010), 7–8.

8. Foucault, *History of Sexuality*, 2:73, 77, where he indicates that "training" body and soul in the care of the self was key for an individual to form themselves as a "moral subject." Foucault understands *askēsis* as distinct from the moral code itself (2:31).

of what is forbidden.⁹ In the second century CE, Artemidorus, in his *Oneirocritica*,¹⁰ becomes agitated about dreams of "unnatural" sexual behaviors.¹¹ Foucault discusses how Artemidorus envisioned "ways to deviate from nature in sexual relations by the very nature of one's partners."¹² This notion of behaviors "against nature" also occurs in Philonic and Pauline literature of the previous century. What is interesting here are Artemidorus's five possibilities: "relations with gods, with animals, with corpses"— which occur in what follows below—and "relations with oneself and relations between women."¹³ The issue for the last two is unnatural penetration.¹⁴

If the "unnatural" can emerge in dreams, Foucault also observes the emergence of the "illicit *and* unnatural" in the West's reaction to intersex people. "For a long time hermaphrodites [*sic*] were criminals, or crime's offspring, since their anatomical disposition, their very being confounds the law."¹⁵ With whom can an intersex person "naturally" have sex?

Thus, on the one hand, felt "problems" like this bring the two binary paradigms of "licit and illicit" and "natural and unnatural" to an intersection. Their offspring are the zero-marked "illicit" category ("natural" does not need to be marked) and the "unnaturally illicit." In Foucault's schema, adultery and rape were left in the unmarked category. But before the nineteenth century the category of "illicit and unnatural'" expanded to include behaviors "essentially different" from adultery and rape: marrying close relatives, practicing sodomy (primarily bestiality), seducing nuns, engaging in sadism, violating cadavers, and deceiving one's wife.¹⁶

---

9. Ibid., 2:30.

10. Artemidorus, *The Interpretation of Dreams* [*Oneirocritica*], trans. Richard J. White (Park Ridge: Noyes, 1975).

11. Michel Foucault, *The History of Sexuality, vol. 3: The Care of the Self*, trans. Robert Hurley (New York: Pantheon, 1986), 23.

12. Ibid., 3:24.

13. Ibid.

14. With an object or by self. However, male–male penetration is "not a transgression of nature" because it conforms to the penetrative "manly" role (ibid., 3:24).

15. Ibid., 1:38.

16. Ibid., 1:39. "The area covered by the Sixth Commandment began to fragment." Some forms of adultery and rape were condemned less, but other forms were thought unnatural and thus "essentially different." "Deceiving one's wife," although Foucault doesn't discuss it, appears to be distinguished from what might be called an "open relationship."

On the other hand, "licit sex" shifts focus away from the ancient Greek "care of self" to the "deployment of sanguinity." "Sanguinity" understood that the family's role was "to anchor sexuality in the interchange of sexuality and alliance."[17] Thus the foci of concern were marital alliances with new extended families and fecundity. Foucault argues that the nineteenth century put into operation—in contrast to these three categories of sanguinity, illicit sex, and unnatural and illicit sex—a way to speak about "and formulate the *universal* truth of sex."[18]

The "deployment of sexuality" as a notion, then, "engender[ed] a continual extension of areas and forms of control."[19] That is, the details of what was to be controlled, both the licit and the illicit, became more and more fine-grained.[20] This development meant that "to speak of *sexuality as a historically singular experience*…presupposed the availability of tools [to analyze] three axes": (1) "sciences (*savoirs*)" to make the fine-grained distinctions; (2) "systems of powers that regulate its practice"; and (3) "forms within which *individuals…recognize themselves as sexual subjects*" (emphases mine).[21] Foucault acknowledges that what he originally planned "was a history of the experience of sexuality, where experience is understood as the correlation between [a] fields of knowledge, [b] types of normativity, and [c] *forms of subjectivity in a particular culture*. To speak of sexuality in this way, *I had to break with the conception that…sexuality was conceived of as a constant*."[22] Foucault's "Aha!" moment was that sexuality was *not* a singular experience and *not* a constant.

Thus, turning to the modern North American and European set of sexualities—those that have crystallized around subjectivity and emerge from the work of late nineteenth-century sexologists, and then Freud, Lacan, and others—these too have been unraveling for some time. Kinsey's spectrum of seven positions of homo-/heterosexual self-identification (numbered from 0-6), ranging from complete heterosexual identification (0) to complete homosexual identification (6), moved away from the assumed binary seventy years ago.[23] Positions one to five might be read

17. Ibid., 1:108.
18. Ibid., 1:69 (emphasis mine). 19.
19. Ibid., 1:106.
20. Ibid., 1:107.
21. Ibid., 2:4.
22. Ibid. (emphasis mine).
23. The seven-point continuum ranges from "zero," exclusively heterosexual, to "six," exclusively homosexual. Thus "one" is predominantly heterosexual with incidental homosexual experience; "two" is predominantly heterosexual with more

as gradations of bisexuality. If one then moves from a one-dimensional line to a plane, a simple matrix operation reveals a fourth position, non-desire or "asexuality"—something Kinsey almost recognized with his position "X" for non-reported behavior. Judith Butler's shift away from a focus on sexuality to "the production and maintenance of gender and sex itself"[24] has opened space for a cissexual and trans* reshuffling of the deck. While cissexuality, with its focus on mental gender and bio-sex alignment, enfolds hetero-, homo-, and to some degree bisexuality, mental and physical non-alignment encompasses trans*, intersex, and maybe asexuality.[25] That is to say, cissexuality and trans* categories themselves are not neat but have somewhat fuzzy boundaries when overlaid by the homo-/hetero-/bi-/asexuality matrix. Both the matrix and the cis-/trans* binary push one to think in terms of multiple dimensions. A 3D universe of gender, biological phenomena (such as intersex bodies), and sexuality gives one a star map of galactic clusters, single stars, and traveling bodies in between. An intellectual move toward acknowledging the uniqueness of anyone's sexual positionality would include all genderqueer, gender-fluid, or gender non-binary persons.

---

than incidental homosexual experience; "three" is equally hetero- and homosexual and so forth. "X" is an eighth category for someone with no reported sexual activity (which we might be tempted to think of as "asexual" except that the modern term refers to attraction, not lack of reporting). Kinsey also resisted calling positions "one" to "five" on his scale "bisexual." He reserved "bisexual" for what we now call "intersex." See Alfred C. Kinsey, Wardell B. Pomeroy, and Clyde E. Martin, *Sexual Behavior in the Human Male* (Philadelphia: W. B. Saunders, 1948), 638, 647, 651; Alfred C. Kinsey et al., *Sexual Behavior in the Human Female* (Philadelphia: W. B. Saunders, 1953), 472, 494, 499.

24. Hornsby, "Sexuality," 295.

25. David Tabb Stewart, "LGBT/Queer Hermeneutics and the Hebrew Bible," *CurBR* 15, no. 3 (2017): 289–314. With reference to "trans*": "The asterisk (*) stands for all the possible combinations with 'trans'—transgender, transsexual, trans-man, transwoman, and people transgressing gender categories such as crossdressers, eunuchs, those who are gender ambiguous or gender fluid, etc." (ibid., 314). "Intersex," once labelled "pseudo-hermaphroditism," refers to a "whole series of bodily positions between male and female, a set containing a host of syndromes [sixteen mentioned by the Intersex Society of North America, 'Intersex conditions,' http://www.isna.org/faq/conditions, accessed 25 April 2019]. Estimates of incidence range from 1.7 percent to as high as 2.7 percent, depending upon how many of the syndromes are counted as intersex conditions" (ibid., 309). See also David Tabb Stewart, "Sexual Disabilities in the Hebrew Bible," in *Disability Studies and Biblical Literature*, ed. Jeremy Schipper and Candida Moss (New York: Palgrave Macmillan, 2011), 78–81.

This brings us to the central problem of categorization when discussing "sexuality"—we are not dealing with monothetic categories that share at least one characteristic and where species might be distinguished by only one difference.[26] Rather, "family resemblances," using Wittgenstein's famous term,[27] are less neat. Species within a polythetic category draw from a collection of attributes but may not share any in particular. Likewise, sexualities are not Linnaean taxa, dividing biological species into clear genera, phyla, etc. As Gericke suggests, the problem of category in the Hebrew Bible is a problem of Israelite ethnophilosophy. That is, one cannot expect to develop a systematic unified philosophy from Israelite folk categories, but one could speak of a "synthesis of knowledge."[28] Moreover, "the Hebrew Bible's authors [do] not spell out [their] assumptions…. The texts' fundamental presuppositions about the world were assumed to be common knowledge."[29] Thus, if sexualities can be sorted in different ways, like gender, and are a socially produced invention, created and culturally constructed, one might well ask again whether Israelite society, analogously to late- and postmodernity, did indeed invent its own sex and gender system, including indigenous notions of sexuality. And if so, what is it? To answer this, one must attempt to identify the folk categories associated with sexual behaviors and the "common knowledge" assumptions that undergird them.

What follows brackets both the "constancy" of the notion of "sexuality" and the idea that "sexuality is a historical singular experience." That is, "sexuality" can vary in different places and climes just like other abstractions such as "law" or "disability."[30] Instead, a close reading of Israelite and Hittite legal texts, with some comparands from other genres and from elsewhere in the ancient Near East, suggests that fine-grained regulation of sexual behaviors did not arise only in the nineteenth century, and that different ways to organize "sexuality" already existed.

26. The problem of "murkiness" referred to by Asher-Greve, "From *La Femme*," 22.
27. Ludwig Wittgenstein, *Philosophical Investigations* (Malden: Blackwell, 2001), sections 66–7.
28. Jaco Gericke, *The Hebrew Bible and Philosophy of Religion*, SBLRBS 7 (Atlanta: SBL, 2012), 174.
29. Ibid., 449.
30. Stewart, "Sexual Disabilities," 69–71.

A Biblical Sexual Landscape

If we set aside contemporary notions of homo-, hetero-, bi-, a-, trans*, and cissexuality and examine what sexual behaviors are problematized and valorized in ancient Israel, a different sexual landscape emerges (see Figure 1). That is, some things are strictly forbidden—adultery, incest, sex with animals and heavenly beings, and menstrual sex; some things are commanded—reproductive sex; some things fall in-between—not strictly outlawed but viewed negatively, or valued but not commanded; and some things are neutral, neither rejected nor recommended. There is a spectrum of prohibition and permission that can be graded by degrees of penalty or affirmation. This arrangement of biblical sexual behaviors undermines any simplistic binary regime of the forbidden and permitted.

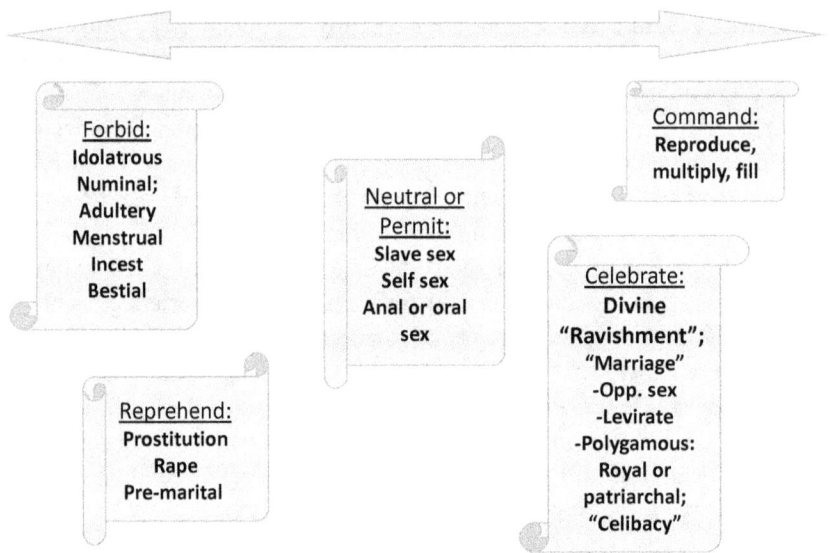

Figure 1. Spectrum of Sexual Relations

Two objects of sexual desire are different from those commonly thought of in contemporary Western society: divine or numinal beings and animals. As to the former, the relations of the בני האלהים with human daughters (Gen. 6:1-4), the attempted rape of the angelic visitors (Gen. 19:1-5), the Molekh practices (Lev. 18:21; 20:1-5), the "whoring after" (לזנות אחרי) ghosts and familiar spirits (Lev. 20:6, 27), and even the worship of other gods as a kind of "whoring" or promiscuity (זנות; Deut. 31:16) violate the hierarchical chain of being—the divine, the human, and the beastly as in Ps. 8:5-9 (see Figure 2). A human (בן אדם) made "a little less than divine" (מעט מאלהים) stands above domestic animals (צנה ואלפים) and wild (בהמות שדי), as well as air (צפור שמים) and marine (דגי הים) creatures, which are all placed underfoot (תחת רגליו). From an Israelite's perspective, "desire" could flow in either direction—from divine to human or human to divine. For example, the בני האלהים desire human women; the men of Sodom desire the divine visitors (מלאכים).

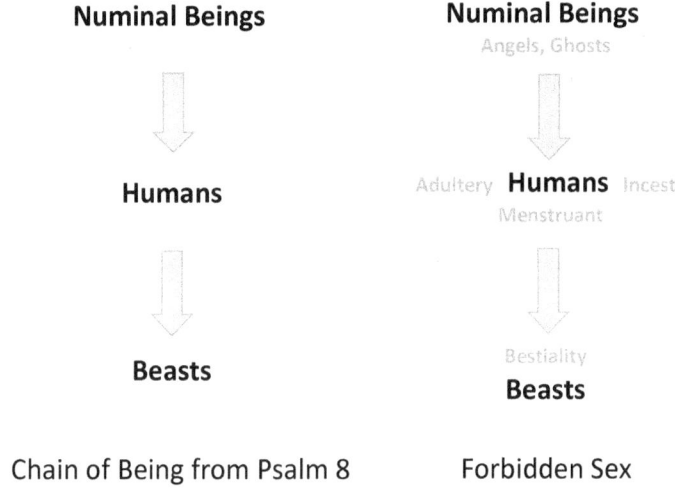

Figure 2. Biblical Sexual Landscapes

The divine ravishment of Jeremiah—with the Divine Being as the dominant and Jeremiah as the submissive (Jer. 20:7-18)—is treated differently. Though Jeremiah had been commanded to be celibate (Jer. 16:1-2), he may not be asexual. His desire must run in some direction—a divine direction? The apparent Israelite prohibition of divine/human sexual relations is not categorical even if one were to take all the texts concerning such as mythical or metaphorical. In Figure 1 "divine ravishment" would come under the category of celebrated behaviors. In Mesopotamian myth, the goddess Ishtar/Inanna takes many human lovers including Tammuz, a shepherd, and Ishullanu. For that matter, she attempts to seduce Gilgamesh who refuses her and the erotic desire of the divine.[31]

---

31. Neal Walls, *Desire, Discord and Death: Approaches to Ancient Near Eastern Myth*, ASOR Books 8 (Boston: American Schools of Oriental Research, 2001), 47.

Something like "promiscuity" with spirits of the dead might also exist in Hittite sexual law. HL §190α imagines sex, or a dream about sex, between a living person and a deceased (*akkantit*)— a ghost or possibly a corpse—in a context of incest laws. This behavior is *natta ḫaratar*, "not an offense," but still *waštul*, here meaning a "(polluting) sexual offense" (see Figure 3a).[32]

As for animals (see Figure 3b), האדם finds no mate among them in the Garden of Eden (Gen. 2:18-24, esp. v. 20), and yet the phallic snake approaches Eve (Gen. 3:1-7). These stories may function as warnings to a cattle-tending culture to avoid sex with animals—a behavior that Kinsey found in about 14% of his 1940s male sample,[33] but rarely practiced by women (only two of his female sample reported actual coitus).[34] The commands against penetrating, approaching, and allowing the sexual approach of animals (Exod. 22:18; Lev. 18:23; 20:15-16) are evidence that interspecies relations existed in ancient Israel on the principle that laws are not made for nothing. The language of the laws also shows that desire flows in two directions. Leviticus 18:23 and 20:15-16 acknowledge that humans are approached by, as well as sexually approach, animals.[35]

Biblical Law
Death penalty:
- Idolatry as *zĕnût* (Deut. 31:16)
- Pass "seed" to Molekh (Lev. 20:1-5 + 18:21)
- *Zĕnût* with ghosts or familiar spirits (Lev. 20:6, 27)

Not an offence:
- Divine ravishment (Jer. 20:7-18)

Hittite Law
Not an offense:
- "Dream" or "real" sex with dead person or ghost (HL §190α)— *natta ḫaratar*

Figures 3a: Biblical vs. Hittite Law: Numinality

---

32. Figures 3a, 3b, 5a, 5b, and 5c below offer an extended comparison between ancient Israelite and Hittite legal materials.

33. Kinsey, Pomeroy, and Martin, *Sexual Behavior in the Human Male*, 670–1, 674.

34. Kinsey et al., *Sexual Behavior in the Human Female*, 505, 509. Of the women sampled, 3.6% acknowledged having fantasies, but only two reported coitus. Note the apparent rarity of this behavior.

35. E.g., Lev. 18:23b (תעמד לפני...לרבעה, "present herself before…to lie down") suggests the behavior is active and voluntary. That is, the woman entices the animal. See David Tabb Stewart, "Ancient Sexual Laws" (PhD diss., University of California, Berkeley, 2000), 99.

Biblical Law
Death penalty for man or woman and animal:
- All bestiality—*all three receive*
- *death penalty whether human or*
- *animal initiates* (Lev. 20:15-16)

Diagnosed as "confusion":
- Woman's initiating bestial realtions diagnosed as tebel

Hittite Law
Death penalty to both:
- Man with cow or sheep (HL §§187-188)—*ḫaratar, ḫurkel, waštul*; king's gate judgment—if spared still polluted
- Man with pig or sheep (HL §199α)—*ḫaratar, katta, waštai*; king's gate judgment—if spared still polluted

Death penalty to both only for animal; sheep substituted for human killed:
- Ox springs at man (HL §199β)—*ḫaratar*

Unpunished but human polluted:
- Pig springs at man (HL §200aγ)
- Man with horse or mule (HL §200aα)—*kata waštai*

Figure 3b: Biblical vs. Hittite Law: Bestiality

Likewise, Ishtar/Inanna takes animal consorts: the *allalu*-bird, the wild lion, and the domesticated horse.[36] Perhaps this gives us one reason for the apparent categorical biblical rejection of this option. Leviticus 18:23b calls it "confusion," תבל. But by way of comparison, Hittite legal rules do not fully reject the behavior. They show three "degrees" of severity for bestiality, along with one animal-initiated instance that apparently bears no penalty other than possible continuing pollution. The first degree can be seen in the laws that deal with situations when a man has sex with a cow or sheep. This behavior is described as "an offense," "an unpermitted sexual pairing" causing severe pollution,[37] and "a sin or sexual offense" that is "impure/anomalous"[38] (*ḫaratar, ḫurkel, waštul*).[39] It is a crime that incurs the death penalty if the perpetrator is not spared by the king. When anyone "sins sexually with" (*katta waštai*) a pig or dog, this also incurs impurity and death for human and animal alike unless spared by

36. Walls, *Desire*, 47.
37. HL §§187-188. Alice Mouton, "The Sacred in Hittite Anatolia: A Tentative Definition," *HR* 55 (2015): 55. She inverts the degrees, calling the second degree the most dangerous, and the first degree "insignificant and…neutralized by ablutions."
38. As according to ibid.
39. See HL §§187-188, and Harry A. Hoffner, Jr., *The Laws of the Hittites: A Critical Edition*, DMOA 23 (Leiden: Brill, 1997), 147–9, 224–7, 276, 278, and 306.

the king (HL §199α). That these crimes are serious is signaled not just by the penalty but also by their judgment at the highest court—the king's or palace's gate, i.e., the royal court.[40] Even if perpetrators are pardoned, they still retain pollution such that they cannot appear in person before the king.

When an ox springs at a man, the ox must die, but the human does not die. This is a second-degree crime, and a sheep is killed in place of the human (HL §199β). However, a pig springing at a man in sexual excitement (HL §199γ) is not an offense (*natta ḫaratar*) at all; it falls into the third-degree category.[41] If a man has sex with a horse or mule, it is also *natta ḫaratar*, not punishable, even though it still defiles (HL §200a) like the dreamy ghost-sex above. Due to the defilement, "he shall not approach the king, nor shall he become a priest." Perhaps also here, but at least in the case of sheep and goats, the New Hittite ritual recorded in CTH 456.05 (KUB 41:11) provides a way to expiate the pollution of bestiality by the use of a scape-animal.[42]

Thus, one can say, ancient law and narrative *did* think about sexual behaviors that seem unlikely to us. They stem from an imagined hierarchy of relations among creatures. And, as a first approximation, they suggest regimes of desire that could be called "sexualities": "numinality," or perhaps better, "idolatry," and bestiality.

An Archaeology of Questions

But how did ancient peoples begin to think about this? Foucault in his later work offered some notes on what he calls "the archaeology of thought" (as opposed to an "archaeology of knowledge"). The archaeology of thought works somewhat like the linguistic projection of proto-languages from attested languages. Working backwards from grammars and lexica, applying known rules of language change to these data, the grammar and lexica of a proto-language can be triangulated. Likewise, working backwards from known solutions to a problem found in various literary genres such as law and narrative (and cross-linguistically with cultures in contact), one might triangulate the question asked, for which textual accounts constitute answers. Behind the question is the "problem" that

---

40. Ibid., 4–5.
41. Stewart, "Ancient Sexual Laws," 358–62.
42. See Emmanuel Laroche, "Catalogue des Textes Hittites: Premier supplément," *RHA* 30 (1972): 109. The text was published in Liane Jakob-Rost, *Hethitische Rituale und Festbeschreibungen*, KUB 41 (Berlin: Akademie-Verlag, 1970), no. 11 (labeled as a "Reinigungsritual gegen Sodomie" in the table of contents on p. iv).

first arose from the anxiety that individuals felt about something amiss or out-of-place. Thus, the "archaeology of thought" is an "archaeology of questions" arising from "problematizations."[43]

Steven Greenberg suggests that the question here might be: "What is human?" That is, sexual relations between humans and domestic animals blur the categories of human and animal and so raise the problem of human identity (as may numinality, but see below).[44] One might also say that "human-ness," or self-identification as a human being in human sexual relations, contrasts with this. In Hatti-land, bestial relations were polluting even when apparently accepted for caravaneers and cavalry—a pollution that could affect the royal throne as well as the perpetrator. Perhaps it raises the question of which sexual behaviors destabilize human society. Already this concern about destabilization can be seen in situations involving theft marriage vendettas (HL §37; cf. Judg. 21:20-23). Alternatively, the questions in Israelite society might have to do with the problem of fertility—raised continuously in Genesis. One can imagine people asking themselves, "How will we then reproduce?" or, with respect to numinality, "What constitutes idolatry in the face of a jealous God?" As we know, illicit sex became a metaphor for idolatry itself.

The Five Forbidden Sexual Behaviors in Leviticus

The discussion above follows what might be called the ladder of being—a structure presented in Psalm 8—to reposition several laws differently from their order of presentation in Leviticus 18–20. This approach offers a literary contextualization within the broader biblical corpus.[45] A second hermeneutical move labels sexual relations between beings on different steps of the ladder as ancient Israelite "sexualities"—numinality, human-focused, and bestiality. Leviticus also positions these laws within its own literary structures that place idolatry/numinality and bestiality among five forbidden behaviors.

---

43. Michel Foucault, "Polemics, Politics, and Problematizations: An Interview with Michel Foucault," in *Ethics: Subjectivity and Truth*, vol. 1 of *The Essential Works of Foucault 1954–1984*, ed. Paul Rabinow (New York: New Press, 1997), 111–19.

44. Steven Greenberg, "The Rationale of Category Confusion," in *Wrestling with God and Men: Homosexuality in the Jewish Tradition* (Madison: University of Wisconsin Press, 2004), 183.

45. An earlier version of this idea may be found in David Tabb Stewart, "Leviticus," in *The Queer Bible Commentary*, ed. Robert Goss et al. (London: SCM, 2006), 81.

These forbidden sexual behaviors—numinality, bestiality, adultery, incest, and menstrual sex[46]—in Foucault's regime would be forbidden because they implicate desire.[47] Adultery, the "great sin" of ancient Egypt and Ugarit,[48] incest of various stripes, and sex during menstruation or similar discharges are forbidden behaviors among humans—on the middle step of the ladder of being. Imagined, dreamed, or "real" sex acts with numina, along with sex with animals, are intercalated in the discussions of forbidden human/human sex at Leviticus 18 and 20. Indeed, they are given central positions in two of the four legal inserts: Lev. 18:19-23 (v. 21, Molekh) and 20:10-21 (vv. 15-16, beasts). This positioning stresses their importance.[49]

Leviticus chapters 18 through 20 form a sort of ancient triptych.[50] The two side panels (chs. 18 and 20) focus on sexual behaviors. Chapter 18 organizes the laws in two inset pieces: vv. 7-16 present ten commandments concerning incest, headed by a general rule in v. 6 and framed by a bridging section in vv. 17-18. The bridging section adds two rules that extend the incest prohibition to any mother–daughter or sister pairing. The second inset panel, vv. 19-23, contains a poem of seven commands. The poem arranges the seven laws in this order: no menstrual sex, no adultery, no Molekh sex, no profaning the divine name, no male–male incest,[51] no

---

46. Note that four of these intersect with the later rabbinic category, *gilluy arayot*, ("uncovering nakedness") mentioned in discussions of Noachide law, which can refer to sexual impropriety in general but traditionally refer to incest, adultery, pederasty, and bestiality in particular (*Gen. Rab.* 16:6; *Deut. Rab.* 2:25). The biblical phrase גלה ערוה ("uncover nakedness") is used in Lev. 18:6-16 and 20:18 for incest and menstrual sex.

47. He speaks of "the principle of 'desiring man'" (Foucault, *History of Sexuality*, 2:4). He pays very little attention to numinality and bestiality and no attention to menstrual sex.

48. See William L. Moran, "The Scandal of the 'Great Sin' at Ugarit," *JNES* 12 (1959): 280–1; and J. J. Rabinowitz, "The 'Great Sin' in Ancient Egyptian Marriage Contracts," *JNES* 18 (1959): 73.

49. Centrality in a focusing structure signals importance. See David Tabb Stewart, "Leviticus 19 as Mini-Torah," in *Current Issues in Priestly and Related Literature: The Legacy of Jacob Milgrom and Beyond*, ed. Roy E. Gane and Ada Taggar-Cohen (Atlanta: SBL, 2015), 316–22; Stewart, "Ancient Sexual Laws," 105.

50. For a fuller discussion of the structure of these chapters, see ibid., 299–323.

51.

51. Arguments for this understanding can be found elsewhere in Stewart, "LGBT/Queer Hermeneutics and the Hebrew Bible," 297–8. Most scholars do not interpret Lev. 18:22 and 20:13 as referring to male incest. For a critique of the dominant view

male-initiated bestiality, and no female-initiated bestiality. The centerpiece is a staircase structure featuring three divine names in v. 21, which condemns passing "seed to Molekh"—where "seed" can be understood as either "semen" or "offspring."

Leviticus 20 entertains sexual behaviors in two insets. Verses 2–5 pick up and elaborate on the Molekh prohibition, adding the cut-off penalty to this and the זנות ("promiscuity") of using אבת and ידענים, here referring to the tools of conjuration as a metonymy for "ghosts and familiar spirits" (v. 6). The second inset covers six groups of sex crimes: adultery (v. 10), acts of incest with the death penalty (vv. 11-14),[52] bestiality (vv. 15-16), acts of incest without the death penalty (v. 17), menstrual sex (v. 18), and more acts of incest without the death penalty, the last verse outlawing actual brother-in-law levirate marriage (vv. 19-21). The entire chapter is bookended with a second prohibition (v. 27) against relations with ghosts and familiars (see Figure 4). Chapter 19 mentions two special cases of adultery: one involving a "promised" slave girl (Lev. 19:20-22), and one that involves causing one's daughter to become promiscuous (להזנותה; v. 29), which results in the land becoming זמה ("infamous; depraved, lewd"; cf. Lev. 20:14).[53]

For narrative context, four of these five sexual behaviors are addressed directly or indirectly in Genesis as "cases"—adultery,[54] sex with angels,[55] incest,[56] and bestiality.[57] The book also briefly refers to the menstrual taboo.[58] Two of the five behaviors are addressed in other biblical laws. Exodus 22:18 explicitly forbids bestiality; Exodus, Deuteronomy, and Leviticus explicitly condemn adultery.[59] But Num. 5:11-31 and Deut. 22:13–23:1 extend the law of adultery to cover new cases: the suspected woman, the betrothed woman who proves not to be a virgin, and cases of rape distinguished from adultery by the location of the crime.

---

and a perspective that overlaps with but also diverges from mine, see Bruce Wells, "On the Beds of a Woman: The Leviticus Texts on Same-Sex Relations Reconsidered," Chapter 5 in this volume.

52. On Lev. 20:13 as referring to incest, see n. 51 above.

53. For a fuller discussion of the sense and significance of Lev. 19:29, see Hilary Lipka, "The Offense, Its Consequences, and the Meaning of זנה in Leviticus 19:29," Chapter 6 in this volume.

54. Genesis 12, 20, 26, and arguably also chs. 16, 34, 38–39.

55. Gen. 6:1-4; 19:1-11.

56. Indirectly in Gen. 9:20-24, but directly in Gen. 19:30-38; 35:22; 49:4, 57.

57. Indirectly in Gen. 2:18-20.

58. Gen. 31:33-35.

59. Exod. 20:13; Deut. 5:17; Lev. 20:10.

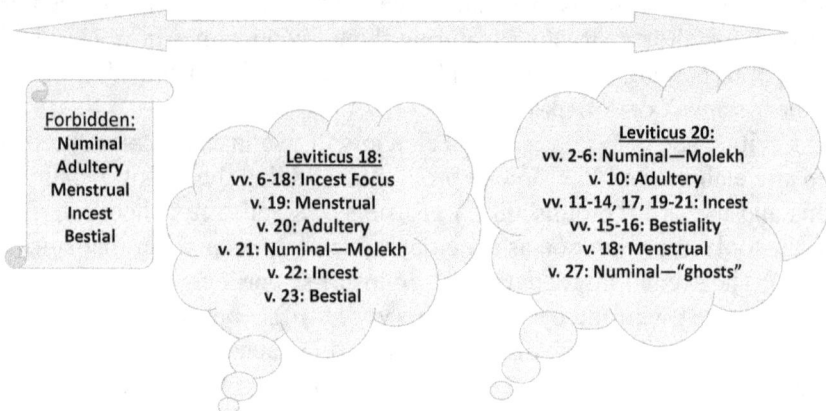

Figure 4. Forbidden Sexual Relations

Genesis exhibits the most anxiety about adultery—the "great sin" of Egypt and Ugarit. Using Foucault's "archaeology of thought," one can observe how texts move from anxiety to problematization and then crystallize the problem in a question—here, what is adultery anyway? In a series of six narrative cases it explores the boundaries: Sarah in Pharaoh's harem (Genesis 12); Abraham with his slave Hagar (Gen. 16:1-6); Sarah in Abimelech's harem (Genesis 20); Isaac's lie about Rebekah that could have led to her sexual endangerment (Genesis 26); Joseph's imprisonment after he was framed by Potiphar's wife (Genesis 39); and Judah mistaking Tamar for a prostitute (Genesis 38). The boundary conditions of adultery emerge as one considers slave status, lack of consent, ignorance concerning marital status, levirate marriage, and lack of consummation. When any of these conditions obtain, the behavior falls outside of adultery. But free status, consent, knowledge of marital status, and consummation of relations—or the husband consenting to place his non-slave wife in a royal harem—apparently are conditions that define adultery.

Moreover, the notion of adultery is not fully stable but sees further development in Leviticus and Deuteronomy, swapping out terminology[60] and adding in the resident alien's wife[61] and the betrothed woman as

---

60. Lev. 18:20 states: "Don't give your sperm flow (לא תתן שכבתך לזרע) to a fellow citizen's wife (אשת עמית)." The more graphic language here comports with the wordplays on זרע in v. 21 and שכבת in v. 23a. The term נאף becomes the word of choice in Lev. 20:10 and Deut. 5:18 (= Exod. 20:14). Deut. 22:22 focuses on the violation of a בעלת בעל, "husband's wife," making it the most general command.

61. Lev. 18:26 implicitly adds the resident alien's wife to the Israelite citizen's wife in 18:20.

adulterous subject/objects, respectively (see Deut. 22:23-24).[62] Leviticus 19:20-22 subtracts the "assigned" slave girl as a subject of adultery because she lacks agency. And "P" (Num. 5:11-31) adds an abortion ritual to satisfy the jealous husband of a suspect wife. The prohibition of adultery is asymmetrical in all cases since the husband remains free to have dalliances as long as they are not with another man's wife, while a woman is not so free. However, the special conditions associated with slave consent, i.e., the lack of agency, show that hierarchal social status cuts a different way: it excuses the slave and, to a lesser degree, the perpetrator.[63] In contrast, lack of agency, or at least the absence of equivalent status, in hierarchical relations between humans and non-humans intensifies punishments.

In Hatti-land, as in Deuteronomy, rape is also determined by location. If the act takes place in the mountains, the man is executed (HL §197α); if in the woman's house, she is executed as an adulterer (HL §197β). If a husband finds the pair in the act of adultery, he may kill them without penalty (HL §197γ). However, if the husband brings the case for royal judgment and asks for leniency for the wife, the king must also grant mercy to the paramour (HL §198). Figure 5a juxtaposes the punishments for adultery/rape in the Hittite Laws with those in biblical texts.

Biblical Law
- **Death by fire:** Any *zĕnût* by priests daughter (Lev. 21:9)
- **Death for both:** Ego takes married woman, wife of fellow citizen, or resident alien (Lev. 20:10)
- **Death for both:** adultery/rape with engaged free woman in town (Deut. 22:23-24)
- **Death of male alone:** rape of free woman in countryside (Deut. 22:25-27)
- **Cut-off penalty:** Levirate marriage with sister-in-law or daughter-in-law outlawed (Lev. 18:17-18 + 18:29; 20:21)
- *Ašām* **sacrifice of ram for male only:** adultery/rape of "promised" salve woman (Lev. 19:20-22)

Hittite Law
- **Death to both if not pardoned:** Ego with another man's wife (HL §197γ); husband may execute if found *inflagrante delicto*
- **Death to woman unless pardoned:** adultery/rape with free woman in woman's house (HL §198)
- **Death to male alone unless pardoned:** rape of free woman in mountains (HL §§197α, 198)
- **Levirate marriage not an offense:** HL §§192 and 193
- **Slave sex unpunished but can be polluting:** Sheep sacrificed as substitute if unpermitted pairing (HL §196)

Figure 5a. Biblical vs. Hittite Law: Adultery/Rape

62. Note that rape is subsumed, and not differentiated, in this and the following example. In Deut. 22:25-27 rape is distinguished by the location of the crime.

63. The slave woman receives no punishment; the offending third-party male must offer a relatively expensive ram as an אשם-sacrifice.

With respect to incest, it is not immediately apparent why Ham's look at Noah's body would bring a curse on the grandson Canaan in Genesis 9. But one possibility is that more than a look took place. "The nakedness of his father" (ערות אביו, Gen. 9:22) is eerily reminiscent of the incest language of uncovering "the nakedness of your father" in Lev. 18:7 (where the language functions as a marker of allusion). Indeed, when Jacob/Israel sings his song of tribal inheritance in Gen. 49:4, Reuben, the firstborn, is called out for sleeping with one of Jacob's wives—Bilhah—using the language of Lev. 18:22 (משכבי אביך, "lyings of your father"). The possibility of father–son and son–stepmother incest is implicitly forbidden in the general command against sexual relations with near-kin (Lev. 18:6) and explicitly forbidden in the commands against a male having sex with his father/mother (v. 7) and stepmother (v. 8). This last point is reinforced in the Deuteronomic cursing liturgy (Deut. 27:20) that echoes Genesis 9. While both Leviticus and Deuteronomy supplement the set of possible incestuous relations, the parade examples remain: son with father and son with (step-) mother (understood as an extension of the father). Likewise, in Hatti-land, incest with one's father or between son and mother is forbidden (HL §189). Incest with the stepmother is provisionally forbidden if her husband is still alive (HL §190γ). The parade examples of incest in both cultures are also inversions of family hierarchy, and as will be seen below, punished more severely (see Figure 5b).

Biblical Law
- **Death by fire:** Ego with two related women (e.g. mother + daughter, includes mother- in-law) (Lev. 20:14ab)
- **Death for both:** Ego with father's wife (mother or stepmother) or daughter-in-law (v. 12); male relatives (v. 13)
- **Cut-off penalty:** with brother's wife (Lev. 20:21)
- **Bear guilt:** paternal (half-)sister; maternal or paternal aunt (Lev. 20:17), or paternal by marriage (v. 18)

Hittite Law
- **Death for both if not pardoned:** Incest with father, mother, daughter, son (HL §189)—ḥurkel unpermitted sexual pairing')
- **Death if not pardoned:** Incest with stepmother, husband alive (HL §190γ)—ḥaratar, ḥurkel ('a punishable unpermitted sexual pairing')
- **Unpunished but polluting:** Incest with stepmother, husband dead (HL §190β)—natta ḥaratar, katta wastai ('unpunished but polluting sexual offence')

Figure 5b. Biblical vs. Hittite Law: Incest[64]

64. The Hittite Laws refer to additional incestuous acts. HL §195 forbids sexual contact with a brother's wife while the brother is alive, with a free man's stepdaughter

But what of menstrual sex?[65] Is this a plunge into abjection? Rachel shoos away her father Laban by pleading her period (Gen. 31:35). In Lev. 15:19-30, one is to wash, launder, and wait until sundown to resolve ritual impurity.[66] But in Lev. 18:19, menstrual sex is categorically forbidden. Leviticus 20:18 prescribes the divinely enforced "cut-off" penalty, a cutting off or failing of one's progeny.[67] The cut-off penalty was assigned in Lev. 18:29 as a general divine punishment for all named behaviors of the chapter (menstrual sex, adultery, incest, bestiality, and giving seed to Molekh) along with a punishment administered by the land: the people are "vomited out" (v. 28). Also of interest is Lev. 20:21's metaphorical use of נדה as a diagnostic term for sister-in-law incest, also forbidden in Lev. 18:16, but permitted elsewhere as the very definition of levirate marriage. Here it is analogized with menstrual sex. Why, the modern reader may ask, is menstrual sex such a big deal? In Lev. 20:18 a rationale is given: "he has laid bare her flow" or wellspring. So there is some hint here of woman's creative capacity—something shared with divinity—hence put off limits. The disciplining of menstrual sex thus evolves from taboo

---

while married to the free mother, and, if married to the free daughter, the mother-in-law and sister-in-law. Incest within these four affinal relationships is *ḫurkel*. The laws also mention relations that look like incest but are not. HL §194 permits a version of the two-woman incest that is forbidden in Lev. 18:18: a free man plus two slave sisters. HL §194 also permits the inverse: two brothers with the same free woman, and father and son with the same slave woman or prostitute. These three behaviors are *natta ḫaratar*. HL §193 permits levirate marriage by a brother-in-law, a father-in-law, and the brother of the father-in-law with a widow. Likewise, if a man's wife dies, he himself may marry her sister, i.e., his sister-in-law (HL §192).

65. Here I am writing as someone limited by not having felt any of what follows in my own body.

66. Lev. 15:24, 27. In the case of the זבה, the woman with dysmenorrhea, she waits and on the eighth day, after her discharge stops, offers two pigeons or turtledoves, one each for a purification offering and a burnt offering (Lev. 15:28-30). This recalls the parturient who offers two turtledoves after her period of "blood purification," if she is poor, or a lamb otherwise for a burnt offering and a turtledove for a purification offering (Lev. 12:6-8). Notice that this natural condition and its dysfunction call for intermediate steps—making sacrifices. For further discussion, see Tarja S. Philip, *Menstruation and Childbirth in the Bible: Fertility and Childbirth*, StBibLit 88 (New York: Lang, 2006), 43–60.

67. The "cut-off" may also or alternatively be a cut-off from joining ancestors in Sheol—a sort of afterlife death. See Jacob Milgrom, *Leviticus 1–16: A New Translation with Introduction and Commentary*, AB 3 (New York: Doubleday, 1991), 457–60; and Milgrom, *Leviticus 17–22: A New Translation with Introduction and Commentary*, AB 3A (New York: Doubleday, 2000), 1736.

and minor pollution control to something divinely punished as both an individual and national behavior. By contrast, in Hatti-land with its broad concern for pollution, menstrual and lochial discharges do cause pollution, but there does not seem to be a specific sexual prohibition for these.[68] That any sex with a woman ritually pollutes temple food workers may suggest a broader issue—but it is resolvable by washing. Only if the temple worker skips washing and serves the god's meal does he incur the death penalty.[69] For a comparison of the menstrual laws, see Figure 5c.

Biblical Law
- **Cut-off penalty for both:** "Uncover nakedness" of a woman during her flow (*dāwā*, Lev. 20:18). This also covers locial flows (Lev. 12:2-5)
- **Remain childless:** with brother's wife (Lev. 20:21)—diagnosed as *niddâ* (menstrual pollution)

Hittite Law
- **Death:** Any male–female sex before feeding the gods in a Temple without proper wash-up
- **Menstrual and lochial flows are polluting:** Ritual evidence for pollution and in some cases this requires sacrifice. No law against menstrual sex *per se*

Figure 5c. Biblical vs. Hittite Law:

If we return to Psalm 8's ladder of being (see Figure 2) and assign these last three forbidden behaviors to the central level, we have complicated the map of human desire. Some sexual practices (certain "homosexualities," if we contrast sexual relations on the horizontal axis between humans with those on the vertical axis) are forbidden—adultery, incest, and menstrual sex. Other "homosexualities" are permitted or overlooked. In contrast, the

---

68. Menstruation, along with lochial discharges, is seen as causing impurity in Hittite culture necessitating ritual responses, but there is no extant prohibition against menstrual sex. See Philip's discussion of Hittite childbirth in *Menstruation and Childbirth*, 118–19. See also Gary Beckman, *Hittite Birth Rituals: An Introduction*, SANE 1/4 (Malibu: Undena, 1974), 18, who indicates that "*maršaya* offerings" that "bestow purity" are offered for the parturient in KBo 17.65 rev. 5–9; *CHD* L–N 195b, which points out that KBo 5.2 i 4–5 speaks of drinking blood from a woman's body as *marša-* "unholy"; Mouton, "The Sacred in Hittite Anatolia," 50, for whom the menstrual blood in KBo 5.2 appears as "bewitched food"; and Jaan Puhvel, "Eshar, ishar," in *Hittite Etymological Dictionary*, 2:309, who refers to KUB 41.8 iii 24 + 17.27 iii 12–13 (= CTH 446), where the use of *eshariya-* "to bloody" is in a parallel structure ("let the ass bloody them, let the ox defecate on them") and may possibly suggest menstrual blood pollution. As Puhvel points out, **eshariya-* parallels *sehuriya-* ("urinate") in form.

69. Mouton, "The Sacred in Hittite Anatolia," 54–5, citing KUB 13.4 iii 68–83.

Hittites of the mid- to late thirteenth century BCE reject certain behaviors categorically (those that are *ḫurkel*) and grade others by degrees of impurity and social class. The Hittite schema reflects neither the Israelite ladder of being nor modern concerns with homo-/heterosexuality.

However, if "the forbidden" and "the permitted" are taken as categories of "sexuality," their subject matter cannot be easily divided by object of desire. The five principal, regulated sexual behaviors forbidden in Israelite law, and the three principal, regulated sexual behaviors covered by Hittite law, represent continua of permission, neutrality, reprehension, and condemnation. In Israelite law the forbidden/permitted binary is also not fully stable, as the laws undergo development over time by addition, emergence of case exceptions, and complete revision.[70] Even as a heuristic device, the notion of "the forbidden" and "the permitted" as categories of "sexuality" proves unsatisfactory.

Intersections of Graded Behaviors and Control Regimes

The possible hierarchalization of ancient Israelite sexual behaviors into "sexualities" partially erodes when one takes a harder look at graded behaviors or other regimes of sexual control (see Figure 6). Other categories intersect—i.e., the regime of purity associated with exchange of sexual fluids, social class heightening impurity and broadening or narrowing permission, and geographical location which determines whether a sexual law applies or not.

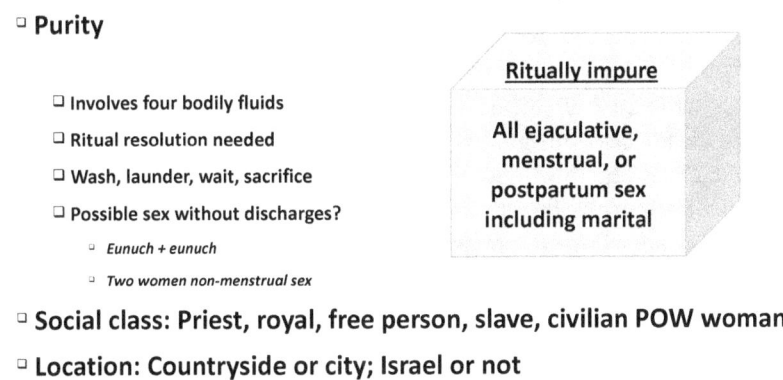

Figure 6. Other Israelite Regulatory Regimes

---

70. This is not to say that the Hittite Laws do not show development over time, but it is beyond the scope of this chapter. See Hoffner, *The Laws of the Hittites*, 5–11.

Graded Penalties; Graded Behaviors

If one of the principal behaviors that Leviticus regulates has an exception (ravishment by the God of Israel), three more are distinguished by degrees of penalty (Figures 5a-5c). Bestiality alone is consistently and categorically condemned in Israelite law. If we turn to the graded crimes starting with incest, death by fire is prescribed for a man having sex with a woman and her daughter, a kind of incest that would cover sex with the mother-in-law as well as with two women who were not affines (Lev. 20:14). All three are burned, suggesting this is a first-degree crime with an "enhancement." Likewise the priest's daughter who commits זנות (which would include adultery or incest among other things; Lev. 21:9) is also burned, though the enhancement seems to have something to do with impingement on the *cultus* through the father.[71] Death (by stoning) for first-degree crimes for both parties is prescribed for adultery (Lev. 20:10; Figure 5a); incest with father's wife (mother or stepmother); incest with a daughter-in-law (Lev. 20:12); incest with male relatives (Lev. 20:13);[72] and sex between a man or woman and an animal (Lev. 20:15-16), with the beast also being executed (Figure 3b). The person who gives seed to Molekh also dies (Lev. 20:2; Figure 3a), and the person who has concourse with ghosts or familiar spirits is specifically stoned (Lev. 20:27; Figure 3a). Thus nine sexual crimes are of the first degree, three with enhancements (burning; animal participant killed).

An "assigned" slave (Lev. 19:20-22) raped or seduced by someone other than her owner or promised husband is exempt from a penalty for "adultery." However, the perpetrator sacrifices a ram—apparently a second-degree penalty for the slave rapist. Both the man having sex with the נדה and the menstruant herself have their progeny "cut-off" (Lev. 20:18). In the case of incest with a brother's wife (when the brother is alive or dead, also designated as נדה), both partners are also "cut-off" (Lev. 20:21).[73] The third-degree penalty, "bearing one's guilt," falls to the incestor of a half- or full-sister who is the daughter of one's father (Lev. 20:17); the incestor of the maternal or paternal aunt (Lev. 20:19); and the

---

71. This is perhaps analogous to the deaths by fire of Nadab and Abihu, sons of Aaron, who brought in alien fire to the Tent of Meeting (Lev. 10:1-2), or Judah's sentence of Tamar for her alleged promiscuity (Gen. 38:24). For a fuller discussion of Lev. 21:9 and its rationale, see Sarah Shectman, "Priestly Marriage Restrictions," Chapter 7 in this volume.

72. See n. 51 above.

73. This represents a restriction on levirate marriage, permitting it only for degrees of relation beyond those mentioned in the Holiness Code, such as cousins-by-marriage (but not with a father-in-law, brothers-in-law, sons-in-law, or uncles-by-marriage).

incestor of the uncle's wife, or paternal aunt by marriage (Lev. 20:20). Thus, four of the five sexual "forbiddens" in the Holiness Code have the death penalty in first-degree versions of the violative behaviors. The exception is נדה-sex which has a second-degree penalty.

With respect to bestiality, Hittite law (HL §§187, 188, 199, 200aα) gives the death penalty to both the male perpetrator and animal (women are not mentioned) for a cow, sheep, pig, and dog. If an ox is the perpetrator, the animal is killed, and the man can sacrifice a sheep for himself. The ox here may stand for the class of both ox and sheep (Figure 3b). With respect to adultery, Hittite law prescribes death for both partners, who are executed either by vendetta (if *in flagrante delicto*) or by the court if the act occurred inside the woman's house (Figure 5a). Death is prescribed for the male alone if the woman is taken in the mountains. Death is also the penalty for incestuous acts in the nuclear family (father, mother, daughter, and son), notably including male–male incest and the stepmother if the father is still alive (Figure 5b). All three of the principal Hittite sexual crimes have death as a first- degree penalty, but only two make use of the first-degree diagnostic, the term *ḫurkel*, which designates the particular acts within the nuclear family, along with relations with a cow or sheep. Second-degree penalties all involve continuing pollution that must be resolved lest taint remain. Hittite law also contains several loopholes, including the possibility of royal pardon. One Hittite ritual suggests that incest might be resolved by sending off a decorated scape-animal which carries the pollution to the unlucky person who claims it. Finally, no behavior is condemned categorically since exceptions, pardons, and ritual interventions mitigate any penalties.

Diagnostic Terms

As noted above, Israelite sexual behaviors are often characterized by "diagnostic" terms like נדה (Lev. 18:19; 20:21). The woman with the beast (Lev. 18:23b) and daughter-in-law incest (Lev. 20:12) are both described as תבל, "confusion." Two-woman quasi-incest (Lev. 18:17; 20:14) and the father prostituting his daughter (Lev. 19:29) are זמה, "infamy; depravity; lewdness." Outside of biblical law, one finds that the rape of the פלגש, "secondary wife" in Judges 19, raping the נדה during her time of impurity, committing incest with father, mother, and daughter-in-law (Ezek. 22:9-10), along with raping one's own sister or half-sister, are all designated as זמה (Ezek. 22:11). However, committing incest with (or raping) one's sister or half-sister in Lev. 20:17 is diagnosed as חסד, "lovingkindness," inverted to mean "hated." Male–male incest is also specifically designated תועבה, "abhorrence" (Lev. 18:22; 20:13), along with adultery with another man's wife (Ezek. 22:11). Actually, all the sexual behaviors of Leviticus 18—that is all the principal forbiddens—are designated as תועבה in the peroration, including menstrual sex (Lev. 18:24-30). Thus the death penalty and the diagnostic terms זמה, תבל, and תועבה together mark first-degree sexual behaviors. The diagnostic term נדה marks one of the five forbiddens as a second-degree behavior, but תועבה marks menstrual sex with the same degree of abhorrence as the other principal behaviors in the Holiness Code. The rape of the menstruant linked to זמה in the Holiness Code's tradent, Ezekiel, marks the ultimate degree of horror.

Likewise, Hittite laws make use of diagnostic terms to describe degrees of sexual crimes as noted above—*ḫaratar*, *ḫurkel*, and *waštul*. These are used in various lexical "pileups" with questionable sexual behaviors. Thus, relations with cattle, sheep, and goats, incest with mother, son, or daughter, and incest with the stepmother while the father is living take all three terms, suggesting they are severe crimes. Some behaviors are described as *ḫaratar* and *ḫurkel* but not *waštul*. Thus, incest with daughter- or mother-in-law and incest with wife's sister when the wife is alive, or brother's wife when the brother is alive, or with "free" co-uterine sisters living in the same locale are diagnosed as second-degree crimes. Things that are only *ḫaratar* and *waštul* but not *ḫurkel*—bestiality with a pig or dog, an ox springing at a man with sexual excitement, rape in the mountains—are third-degree crimes by this rule of diagnostics. Things that are only *waštul*—bestiality with a horse or mule, a man at whom a pig springs in sexual excitement, sex with stepmother after the father has died—are diagnosed as "only" impure and *not* punished, and so represent a marginal status.[74]

Ritual Purity, Social Class, and Location as Control Regimes

Any Israelite sexual behaviors that involve discharges—seminal, gonorrheal, menstrual, or lochial flows—make a person impure or טמא (see Figure 6). This includes heterosexual sex in marriage. Seminal and menstrual discharges are resolvable by washing, laundering, and waiting, while sacrifices follow a waiting period after lochial, dysmenorrheal, or gonorrheal flows. However, any sexual relations that do not involve discharges including sex between two women or between eunuchs and others logically would not. When discharges cause impurity, it is only for ritual purposes—impairing the priest's ability to serve, preventing the eating of sacred donations, or delaying the resolving sacrifice until

---

74. Stewart, "Ancient Sexual Laws," 286.

sufficient time has passed. In Hatti-land, as noted above, lochial discharges pollute, as does any sex with a woman before serving food to the gods in a temple, when not followed by washing. This last one suggests that the Hittite priestly class might have special purity risks from sexual behavior. Moreover, *ḫurkel* represents a diagnosis of severe pollution and *waštul* a lesser degree of impurity. Thus, some of the sex crimes of the Hittites involve pollution.

The several social classes contemplated in biblical laws—high priest, priest, priestly family member, royals, Israelite free person, slave, civilian female POWs—have modified rules. Priests are restricted, for reasons of ritual impurity, in choosing marriage partners and in performing service in the temple; royals may get away with multiplying wives; slaves are sexually subject to their masters, except for the promised slave woman; and civilian POW women can be married against their will after thirty days of cleansing.

One might argue that different social statuses complicate the position of human beings on the ladder of being—royals climbing somewhat above human-ness as proto-gods; slaves falling somewhat below those who are free. For Hittites, those sexual behaviors that are neither *ḫurkel* nor *waštul*, and so are unpunished, also exhibit differences due to the role of social class as a factor. Sexual relations with two related women who are slaves or half-free (*arnuwalaš*) are allowed, as are relations involving a father and son who sleep with the same slave woman or prostitute.[75] However, just as two free brothers can have relations with the same free woman (not otherwise forbidden; HL §194), so a pair of male and female slaves who commit *ḫurkel* are not executed. When sexual partners are on the same social *niveau*, some latitude is granted. For *ḫurkel* crimes, free persons face execution, but slaves are resettled in different cities and have sheep killed in their place (HL §196). As in HL §199β, when an ox springs at a man and thereby causes pollution, the pollution is resolved by sacrificed sheep (and possible resettlement). This solution, rather than raising the question of slave agency, as with the promised slave girl in Leviticus 19, appears to be a response to their property-value. The ancient question here might be: who is human?

Finally, location is determinative for rape not only in Deuteronomy, but also in Hittite Law, and the Cretan Code of Gortyn. Further, all the laws of Leviticus 18, technically, only apply if one lives in the land (Lev. 18:24-30). So, while resident aliens were held to them, the people of other

---

75. The first two fall under HL §194. The situation where a father and son sleep with the same woman is explicitly rejected in Amos 2:7. See also Stewart, "Ancient Sexual Laws," 286.

nations were not. Likewise, Hittite law also complicates sexual behaviors in this way. Beyond substituting location for *mens rea* in cases of rape, the role of location is also important when permitting sexual relations by a free man with free, co-uterine sisters who live in different places (HL §191).

Thus, both Israelite and Hittite cultures exhibit multiple systems related to sexual behaviors. These additional categories mean that within both the biblical and Hittite sexual "systems" there are multiple intersections between these sets—things prohibited and not, gradations of behavior, pollution, the implications of diagnostic terms, and locations—not to speak of conflicts between laws or the literary presentation of laws that can influence the perceptions of their importance. The intersections of regimes of control complicate the analysis of sexual behaviors as a "system" and, therefore, the understanding of "sexuality."

Some Conclusions

This account of the biblical and Hittite sexual system(s) has offered two sketches of how sexuality could be accounted for if one examines the indigenous organization of the texts. First, forbidden sexual objects of desire ordered in a hierarchy suggests one way to avoid the imposition of modern categories other than the using the word "sexuality" itself. The texts attest that desire does exist as myth or as fantasy or in reality. But the hierarchical nature of the relations also shows that they stem from power and so would be forms of rape from a twenty-first-century perspective. To the degree they represent desire, one might then speak of numinality and bestiality and the collective sex of humans as "sexualities" in the biblical world. This thought experiment has shifted the axis of analysis from the horizontal to the vertical, from the forbidden and permitted relations among humans on the same level, to humans or species on different levels.

The insertion of the term "sexuality" into the discussion, for which there is no classical Hebrew or Hittite equivalent, leads to the question of how new abstractions might emerge in language. Langer argues that, emerging from dream and myth, "every new…idea about things evokes first of all some metaphorical expression."[76] "Really new ideas," she continues, "have their own modes of expression in the unpredictable creative mind."[77] So it is that the metaphorical ladder of being, read with

---

76. Susanne K. Langer, *Philosophy in a New Key: A Study in the Symbolism of Reason, Rite, and Art*, 3rd ed. (Cambridge: Harvard University Press, 1942), 114, 120, 163.

77. Ibid., 164.

the mythic or fantastical notion of זנות with divine beings in mind, allows for a hierarchy of beings that suggests categories of "sexuality" not yet named in the language. Calling the hierarchical relations "sexualities" becomes an act of translation.

Hittite law, while showing many similarities with biblical law (in the crimes presented, penalties, recognition of animal agency, use of diagnostic terminology, and concern for pollution), has several significant differences. The range of behaviors controlled is more limited in Hittite laws. Legal and ritual loopholes allow for royal pardon and for the ritual transfer of sexual pollutions to scape-animals. In a matrix formed by overlaying forbidden and permitted behaviors with polluting and non-polluting, sex engaged in by free men may be (1) forbidden and polluting (some bestiality and acts of incest), (2) forbidden and non-polluting (adultery and rape), (3) permitted and polluting (temple workers with women before serving divine meals), or (4) permitted and non-polluting (when some animals try to initiate sex; sex between a free man and certain affines; levirate marriage). The Hittites were concerned about animal–human sex and relations with the deceased, but the prohibition and punishment for these, along with adultery and incest, varied by social class. The Hittites were anxious about the sexual behaviors of free men with the free, the sex of free men with classes below their *niveau* (e.g., with half-free, slaves, and animals), and the sex of the unfree with each other and animals. A similar matrix for free and slave relations in ancient Israel would find no sexual acts that were forbidden but not polluting (#2), and only hypothetical but unattested behaviors not forbidden and not polluting (#4; see Figure 6). All sex in the Priestly literature is ritually polluting, but apparently most sex for the Hittites was not. Thus, the hierarchical sexuality of the Hittite free, dominant, and unfree contrasts with the hierarchical sexuality of Israelites with numina, humans, and beasts.

With respect to the questions suggested by retrojecting from practices observed in the two sets of texts, it seems that Israel and Hatti-land shared an answer to at least one. What sexual behaviors destabilize society? Adultery, rape, unregulated sex between some degrees of familial relation, and sex with someone with contagious pollution. For the Hittites, identifying things as "not an offense" was a way of forestalling social strife, just as labelling the avenger of theft marriage—"You are a wolf" (HL §37)— was a way of giving advance warning of trouble. However, whatever anxieties Hittites may have had about successful reproduction— how will we then reproduce?—are not sharply mirrored in the patchwork of rules about animal–human sex, but rather in birth rituals and not in any attested controls over menstrual sex. Neither did they seem much worried about sexual relations with the divine. Even if the Hittite *akkantit* was a ghost, HL §190α still makes sex with it "not an offense." Finally, it seems that the question, "Is sex with a divine being idolatry?" is, *ipso facto*, a question just for monotheists.

What is human? Who is human? What or whose kind of sex is fully human? The sexual laws of the Holiness Code and the Hittites ask different questions about humanity. For the Holiness Code, sex with humans, though restricted, is still human; sex up and down the ladder of being is not. For Hittite Law, free men are dominant humans and, with few restrictions, have wide latitude for sex down the ladder of social class. Half-free, slaves, and some domesticated animals are permitted or tolerated as objects of desire. Nevertheless, these different answers from Israelite and Hittite culture seem to be in the same musical key, the key of hierarchy.

Bibliography

Artemidorus. *The Interpretation of Dreams [Oneirocritica]*. Translation and commentary by Richard J. White. Park Ridge: Noyes, 1975.

Asher-Greve, Julia M. "From *La Femme* to Multiple Sex/Gender." In *Studying Gender in the Ancient Near East*, edited by Saana Svärd and Agnès Garcia-Ventura, 15–50. University Park: Eisenbrauns, 2018.

Beckman, Gary M. *Hittite Birth Rituals: An Introduction*. SANE 1/4. Malibu: Undena, 1974.

Boyarin, Daniel. "Against Rabbinic Sexuality: Textual Reasoning and the Jewish Theology of Sex." In *Queer Theology: Rethinking the Western Body*, edited by Gerard Loughlin, 131–46. Malden: Blackwell, 2007.

Foucault, Michel. *The History of Sexuality, Volume 1: An Introduction*. Translated by Robert Hurley. New York: Vintage, 1990.

Foucault, Michel. *The History of Sexuality, Volume 2: The Use of Pleasure*. Translated by Robert Hurley. New York: Vintage, 1990.

Foucault, Michel. *The History of Sexuality, Volume 3: The Care of the Self*. Translated by Robert Hurley. New York: Pantheon, 1986.

Foucault, Michel. "Polemics, Politics, and Problematizations: An Interview with Michel Foucault." Pages 111–19 in *Ethics: Subjectivity and Truth*. Volume 1 of *The Essential Works of Foucault 1954–1984*. Edited by Paul Rabinow. New York: New Press, 1997.

Gericke, Jaco. *The Hebrew Bible and Philosophy of Religion*. SBLRBS 70. Atlanta: SBL, 2012.

Greenberg, Steven. "The Rationale of Category Confusion." In *Wrestling with God and Men: Homosexuality in the Jewish Tradition*, 175–91. Madison: University of Wisconsin Press, 2004.

Hoffner, Harry A., Jr. *The Laws of the Hittites: A Critical Edition*. DMOA 23. Leiden: Brill, 1997.

Hornsby, Teresa J. "Sexuality." In *The Oxford Encyclopedia of the Bible and Gender Studies*, edited by Julia M. O'Brien, 2:290–7. Oxford: Oxford University Press, 2014.

Intersex Society of North America. "Intersex Conditions." http://www.isna.org/faq/conditions. Accessed 25 April 2019.

Jakob-Rost, Liane. *Hetitische Rituale und Festbeschreibungen*. KUB 41. Berlin: Akademie-Verlag, 1970.

Kinsey, Alfred. C., Wardell B. Pomeroy, and Clyde E. Martin. *Sexual Behavior in the Human Male*. Philadelphia: W. B. Saunders, 1948.

Kinsey, Alfred C., Wardell B. Pomeroy, Clyde E. Martin, and Paul H. Gebhard. *Sexual Behavior in the Human Female*. Philadelphia: W. B. Saunders, 1953.

Langer, Susanne K. *Philosophy in a New Key: A Study in the Symbolism of Reason, Rite, and Art*. 3rd ed. Cambridge: Harvard University Press, 1942.

Laroche, Emmanuel. "Catalogue des Textes Hittites: Premier supplément." *RHA* 30 (1972): 94–133.

Milgrom, Jacob. *Leviticus 1–16: A New Translation with Introduction and Commentary*. AB 3. New York: Doubleday, 1991.

Milgrom, Jacob. *Leviticus 17–22: A New Translation with Introduction and Commentary*. AB 3A. New York: Doubleday, 2000.

Moran, William L. "The Scandal of the 'Great Sin' at Ugarit." *JNES* 12 (1959): 280–1.

Mouton, Alice. "The Sacred in Hittite Anatolia: A Tentative Definition." *HR* 55 (2015): 41–62.

Philip, Tarja S. *Menstruation and Childbirth in the Bible: Fertility and Impurity*. StBibLit 88. New York: Lang, 2006.

Puhvel, Jaan. "Eshar, ishar." *Hittite Etymological Dictionary* 2:305–13.

Rabinowitz, J. J. "The 'Great Sin' in Ancient Egyptian Marriage Contracts." *JNES* 18 (1959): 73.

Stewart, David Tabb. "Ancient Sexual Laws." PhD diss., University of California, Berkeley, 2000.

Stewart, David Tabb. "Leviticus." In *The Queer Bible Commentary*, edited by Robert Goss, Deryn Guest, Mona West, and Thomas Bohache, 77–104. London: SCM, 2006.

Stewart, David Tabb. "Leviticus 19 as Mini-Torah." In *Current Issues in Priestly and Related Literature: The Legacy of Jacob Milgrom and Beyond*, edited by Roy E. Gane and Ada Taggar-Cohen, 299–323. Atlanta: SBL, 2015.

Stewart, David Tabb. "LGBT/Queer Hermeneutics and the Hebrew Bible." *CurBR* 15, no. 3 (2017): 289–314.

Stewart, David Tabb. "Sexual Disabilities in the Hebrew Bible." In *Disability Studies and Biblical Literature*, edited by Jeremy Schipper and Candida Moss, 67–97. New York: Palgrave Macmillan, 2011.

Walls, Neal. *Desire, Discord and Death: Approaches to Ancient Near Eastern Myth*. ASOR Books 8. Boston: American Schools of Oriental Research, 2001.

Weeks, Jeffrey. *Sex, Politics, and Society: The Regulation of Sexuality since 1800*. London: Longman, 1981.

Weeks, Jeffrey. *Sexuality*. Rev. ed. London: Routledge, 2010.

Wittgenstein, Ludwig. *Philosophical Investigations*. Malden: Blackwell, 2001.

2

The Daughter Sold into Slavery and Marriage

Pamela Barmash

The Book of the Covenant holds that a male slave is to be freed after six years of servitude while the female slave is not to be released (Exod. 21:2-11). This inequity has been an enigma for millennia, and perhaps it was so even in biblical times, since Deut. 15:12-18 pointedly revises the passage so that both male and female slaves are to be released in the seventh year. The passage in the Book of the Covenant appears to be aimed at providing the female slave with the protection of a marital relationship, but the proviso that she is to be released if her purchaser withholds her maintenance could be manipulated by a malicious purchaser. He could free himself of her if he intentionally denies what she is due, and then the protections afforded her by the statute would be undermined and negated. A further enigma is that although the daughter is forced into servitude, her status could be reversed: she would remain a slave if her purchaser was her sexual partner, but she would enjoy a return to free status if she were intended for his son. To understand how these conundrums developed, we must take into account how the sale of a daughter epitomizes the status of men and women and the nature of marriage and divorce in the Hebrew Bible.

The Daughter Sold into Slavery for Marriage

The passage on the daughter sold into slavery addresses the case of a family in dire economic straits, one that cannot provide a dowry for a daughter,[1] and in so doing, it opens a window on the life of an average Israelite.[2] Otherwise, the women portrayed in the Bible are exceptional: they are spouses or descendants of celebrated men, they are women who rose to prominence, or they are the subject of a tragedy.[3] The case of a daughter sold into slavery appears to be an unexceptional event: it occurs

1. It must be noted that the family's basic problem may have been its general debts, rather than lack of funds at the specific point in time that a daughter would require a dowry. The family's problem was that its poverty, whatever the cause, forced sons and daughters to be subjected to slavery, as in the situation recounted in Neh. 5:1-5. However, a daughter's value resided in her use in sexual intimacy and the bearing of progeny more than her labor, and it may be for this reason the people appealing to Nehemiah stated that their daughters have already been enslaved (rather than their sons). See Phyllis A. Bird, "Poor Man or Poor Woman? Gendering the Poor in Prophetic Texts," in *Missing Persons and Mistaken Identities: Women and Gender in Ancient Israel*, OBT (Minneapolis: Fortress, 1997), 74–5.

2. It is not clear what relationship the legal texts of the Bible had to law as practiced in ancient Israel. Were the legal texts a mirror of what actually occurred? Were they meant as amendments to the law that was put into practice? Or were they purely theoretical? Whose viewpoint do they manifest, whether in terms of geography (the entirety of ancient Israel, the southern or northern kingdoms, or a limited locality), or in terms of socio-economic class or religious circle? In the absence of inscriptions recording legal activity from ancient Israel, answering these questions may be hopeless. There are only two inscriptions that appear to deal with legal matters. A letter written on a potsherd, the Yavneh Yam or Meṣad Ḥashavyahu letter, records a laborer appealing to an administrator over the confiscation of his garment (Shmuel Ahituv, *Echoes from the Past: Hebrew and Cognate Inscriptions from the Biblical Period* [Jerusalem: Carta, 2008], 156–63), and a text expressing concern for those marginalized in society has been excavated from Khirbet Qeiyafa (Bob Becking and Paul Sanders, "Plead for the Poor and the Widow: The Ostracon from Khirbet Qeiyafa as an Expression of Social Consciousness," *ZABR* 17 [2011]: 133–48).

The literary elite who may have written the Book of the Covenant had a social position far different from the enslaved men and women who are the subject of the passage. They may have even been the ones who were their masters. This may have consequences: on the one hand, the members of a literary elite may have a rosier view of slavery, but on the other, their familiarity may have prompted a sharp critique of the institution of slavery. The audience for the Book of the Covenant may also have been an elite one; while there is evidence for increasing literacy in ancient Israel, it is not clear who had access to specific texts and what their characteristics were, whether in terms of literacy, gender, socio-economic class, religious status, or location (see I. Mendelsohn, "The Conditional Sale into Slavery of Free-Born Daughters in Nuzi and the Law of Ex. 21: 7-11," *JAOS* 55 [1935]: 190–5).

3. Phyllis A. Bird, "Images of Women in the Old Testament," in *Missing Persons and Mistaken Identities*, 13; and Carol Meyers, *Rediscovering Eve: Ancient Israelite Women in Context* (Oxford: Oxford University Press, 2012), 3.

to a family that cannot take care of a daughter's marriage through the normal process of marriage. The daughter is in a less favorable position and is more vulnerable to mistreatment. It is a sad calamity of daily life, not an exemplary case.[4]

The rules on slavery are articulated primarily as rules on manumission, but they also address the sexual use of slaves. Exodus 21:1-11 reads:

ואלה המשפטים אשר תשים לפניהם:
כי תקנה עבד עברי שש שנים יעבד ובשבעת יצא לחפשי חנם:
אם־בגפו יבא בגפו יצא אם־בעל אשה הוא ויצאה אשתו עמו:
אם־אדניו יתן־לו אשה וילדה־לו בנים או בנות האשה וילדיה תהיה לאדניה והוא יצא בגפו:
ואם־אמר יאמר העבד אהבתי את־אדני את־אשתי ואת־בני לא אצא חפשי:
והגישו אדניו אל־האלהים והגישו אל־הדלת או אל־המזוזה ורצע אדניו את־אזנו במרצע ועבדו לעלם:

וכי־ימכר איש את־בתו לאמה לא תצא כצאת העבדים:
אם־רעה בעיני אדניה אשר־לא/לו יעדה והפדה לעם נכרי לא־ימשל למכרה בבגדו־בה:
ואם־לבנו ייעדנה כמשפט הבנות יעשה־לה:
אם־אחרת יקח־לו שארה כסותה וענתה לא יגרע:
ואם־שלש־אלה לא יעשה לה ויצאה חנם אין כסף:

(2) When you purchase a Hebrew slave, he shall serve six years, and in the seventh year, he shall go free without payment.

(3) If he came in by himself, he shall go out by himself.
(4) If he was married, his wife shall go out with him.

(5) If his master gave him a woman and she bore him sons or daughters, the woman and her children shall be her master's, and he shall go out by himself.

6) If he says "I love my master, my woman, and my children, I shall not go free," his master shall lead him before God[5] and (then) shall lead him to the lintel and the doorposts. He will pierce his ear with an awl, and he will serve him forever.

---

4. For more on the precariousness of the subsistence agrarian economy of ancient Israel, see Roland Boer, *The Sacred Economy of Ancient Israel*, LAI (Louisville: Westminster John Knox, 2015), 53–109.

5. The reference to God in this verse and in 22:7–8 has been traditionally taken to refer to judges, as the Septuagint, the Peshitta, and the Targumim render the verse. However, it is more likely that this refers to an oath taken at either a local sanctuary or a home shrine to prevent or resolve a dispute. It is completely omitted in the law's reshaping in Deut. 15:12-18 because cult centralization, a central mission of the Deuteronomic reform, negates the legitimacy of a local shrine, whether freestanding

(7) If a man sells his daughter as a maidservant, she shall not go free as the slaves do.

(8) If she is displeasing in the eyes of her master, who designated her for himself,[6] he will allow her to be redeemed. He does not have the authority to sell her to a foreign nation because he has betrayed her.
(9) If he designated her for his son, he shall treat her according to the legal status of (free) daughters.[7]

or in-home. (And if the term does refer to judges, then there would be no reason for Deuteronomy to have omitted the mention of judges.)

6. This verse has a significant textual issue. The *Ketiv* reads יעדה לא אשר, and the verses should then be rendered "If she displeases her master who has not designated her, he shall let her be redeemed." This rendering implies that since she entered his household for sexual use, if he does not intend to use her in that way, he may not use her as a slave, and he must allow her to be redeemed. Her family obtained funds in her sale and would have to pay for her release. The *Qere* reads יעדה לו אשר, "If she displeases her master who designated her for himself, he shall let her be redeemed." The latter reading makes more sense in light of the contrast with the corresponding rule for his son in the next verse. Exodus 21:8 deals with the situation in which she is designated for the purchaser, while Exod. 21:9 addresses the situation in which she is designated for the purchaser's son. In either case, her purchaser's jurisdiction over her as her master is restricted. The suggestion that the verse should read ידעה לא אשר (i.e., "if she displeases her master who did not know her [in sexual intimacy])" also should be rejected in light of the matching cases of the purchaser and his son.

7. The term הבנות כמשפט means that she is to be treated as a daughter, a free-born woman, as opposed to the slave status to which she was relegated upon being purchased, with the consequence that she could not be used as a slave, if there was a delay in sexual union with the son; see Shalom M. Paul, *Studies in the Book of the Covenant in Light of Cuneiform and Biblical Law*, VTSup 18 (Leiden: Brill, 1970), 55. The similar term in Deut. 21:17, הבכורה משפט, refers to the legal rights of the firstborn; see Carolyn Pressler, "Wives and Daughters, Bond and Free: Views of Women in the Slave Laws of Exodus 21.2-11," in *Gender and Law in the Hebrew Bible and the Ancient Near East*, ed. Victor H. Matthews, Bernard M. Levinson, and Tikva Frymer-Kensky, JSOTSup 262 (Sheffield: Sheffield Academic, 1998), 159.

Michael Fishbane argues that Exod 21:9 is an interpolation because the referent in the following verse is to the original master, the father, not to the son and that the presence of the interpolated verse is made more jarring by the cross-reference signaled by the term כמשפט (*Biblical Interpretation in Ancient Israel* [Oxford: Clarendon, 1985], 209–11). In ritual texts, כמשפט refers to rules mentioned elsewhere in the text, rules omitted perhaps for the sake of brevity or laziness. The reference to the rules is used as a way of applying those rules to the matter under discussion. There is no need then, according to Fishbane, to repeat them. It is just a form of shorthand. By contrast, with respect to non-ritual legal texts, Fishbane argues that the cross-reference sheds new light on a situation that might arise and in essence transforms

(10) If he takes another woman, he shall not withhold her food, clothing, or conjugal rights.⁸

(11) If he does not supply her with those three, she shall go free without payment.

The statutes cohere as a carefully crafted passage composed of two units, both beginning with כי, and employing אם and ואם for the sub-units. The sub-units incorporate secondary cases introduced by אם, and cases complementary to the secondary cases are introduced with (ו)אם. A corresponding order may be discerned in the way the units are introduced. The clause "when you purchase a Hebrew slave...he will go free (יצא)" stands in contrast to the specification in the unit that begins with "when a man sells his daughter as a maidservant...she will not go free as the male slaves (לֹא תֵצֵא כְּצֵאת הָעֲבָדִים)." The repetition of key phrases cements the structural unity of the literary unit and emphasizes the correlation between the case and the remedy. The parallel language in Exod. 21:2 and 7 highlights the social context of the two units of the passage: both the male and female were compelled into servitude,⁹ and the distinguishing mark between them is their gender.¹⁰

the law. A woman may be sold to a particular man by her father, and the master is obligated to fulfill his pledge to marry her. If he does not wish to marry her, she goes free because the master has breached the contract, and if he takes an additional wife, she is guaranteed maintenance. However, v. 9 is not an interpolation because this stipulation deals with her being designated to marry the master's son in contrast to what happens to her in the case where she is designated for the father: she is to be treated according to the rules pertaining to free-born women.

8. Traditionally, the word ענה has been understood as conjugal rights, but Shalom M. Paul suggests that this refers to oil. See Paul, "Exod. 21:10: A Threefold Maintenance Clause," *JNES* 28 (1969): 48–51; and Paul, *Studies in the Book of the Covenant*, 56–61. This maintenance item appears in Mesopotamian law collections as the right of a child's wet-nurse (Laws of Lipit-Ishtar §32) or a prostitute who has given a man children (Laws of Lipit-Ishtar §27), not necessarily the rights of a wife, and the question is whether the intent of taking up with another woman means that she is marginalized. For a review of possible renderings, see Etan Levine, "On Exodus 21,10: *'Onah* and Biblical Marriage," *ZABR* 5 (1999): 133–64.

9. A number of circumstances could result in enslavement. Another statute in the Book of the Covenant prescribes that a thief who could not pay the penalty for his offense would be sold into slavery for the payment (Exod. 22:2). Presumably, in general, an Israelite could sell himself into slavery to pay off a debt. An Israelite who was owed a debt could apprehend the debtor or the debtor's dependents and enslave them (2 Kgs 4:1; Amos 2:6; 8:6; Isa. 50:1-2; Neh. 5:5).

10. Many factors could affect the economic situation of a family so as to prevent the family from possessing the wherewithal to provide the funds for the marriage

However, the relationship between the two cases in Exod. 21:2-11 is the subject of debate. Was the release in the seventh year meant to cover every Israelite, both male and female, forced into slavery and the case of the daughter sold by her father was then a special case of servitude?[11] Or did the release in the seventh year apply only to male Israelites, and was the daughter sold into slavery the only case of female servitude addressed in the passage? A number of scholars have argued that manumission applied only to men, either because Israelite women were not full members of the covenant and therefore did not need to be restored to their original free status,[12] or because they could not own property and therefore could not accrue debt.[13] Other scholars have argued that release was voided only for daughters sold as wives and that the passage did not deal at all with female slaves who were used for household or non-sexual labor.[14] It may also be that emancipation after six years was intended for all slaves and that the case of the daughter sold into slavery was the exceptional case.

Analyzing how Exod. 21:2-11 is a tightly knit literary unit with two interconnected concerns provides a solution. The passage is a set of laws providing safeguards for Israelite slaves as well as regulating the sexual use of slaves. A male slave can be used for procreation, and it would seem that the children he has with a slave-woman provided to him by his master would remain slaves since otherwise it makes no sense for the owner to have him procreate.[15] His sexual use does not change his status. However, a woman sold for sexual use becomes a permanent member of

---

of a daughter. The case of a son lacking the economic means needed for marriage may have been less common because a son had a primary right to patrimonial land, allowing him to have recourse to financial resources that a daughter might not have. The case of the daughters of Zelophehad demonstrates that only in unusual circumstances did daughters obtain rights to family land (Numbers 27).

11. The Septuagint follows this interpretation, reading in Exod. 21:7 that οὐκ ἀπελεύσεται ὥσπερ ἀποτρέχουσιν αἱ δοῦλαι, "the daughter sold into slavery will not be released as the other female slaves."

12. Anthony Phillips, "The Laws of Slavery: Exodus 21.2-11," *JSOT* 30 (1984): 61.

13. Gerhard von Rad, *Deuteronomy*, trans. Dorothea Barton, OTL (Philadelphia: Westminster, 1966), 107.

14. Gregory C. Chirichigno, *Debt Slavery in Israel and the Ancient Near East*, JSOTSup 141 (Sheffield: JSOT Press, 1993), 244-55.

15. It is safe to assume that the woman he is given is a slave herself (but it can be speculated that this slave woman is Canaanite, not Israelite). Bernard S. Jackson points out that it seems unlikely that an owner would give a slave a wife, a woman with whom he has a permanent formal relationship, and that the term אשה cannot

the household of the owner or his son and, therefore, she must receive certain protections of her own in place of manumission. It also must be noted that elsewhere in the Book of the Covenant, a slave is specifically denoted as both genders, with the male termed עבד and the female as אמה. The statutes on a slave killed or injured apply to both עבד and אמה, males and females (Exod. 21:20-21, 26-27). If there is conceptual and literary coherence to the Book of the Covenant, the case of the daughter sold into slavery was the only case meant to apply to females.[16] It does not envision any other option for Israelite female slaves.

The economic value of a daughter sold off for marriage is her value for sexual intimacy and procreation more than her labor,[17] and the amelioration of slavery finds special expression in the case of the daughter sold into slavery. She was either to have a permanent relationship with her master or master's son or be redeemed,[18] in contrast to the male slave who was to be emancipated after six years of servitude. This discrepancy may seem to be an inequity, but she entered slavery because her family could not provide the funds she would normally need for marriage. If she were to be freed after six years during which her sexuality could be used by her purchaser, releasing her would leave her vulnerable once again and probably worse off.

The daughter's vulnerability is protected in other ways. If the purchaser sours on her and refuses to take her in a permanent bond, the daughter sold into slavery is thereby protected by the requirement that the owner must let

---

always refer to a wife because the woman is termed אשה ("The 'Institutions' of Marriage and Divorce in the Hebrew Bible," *JSS* 56 [2011]: 234; and *Wisdom-Laws: A Study of the Mishpatim of Exodus 21:1–22:16* [Oxford: Oxford University Press, 2006], 91). Why would the master provide him with a sexual partner? The likelihood is that the master is using him to produce children, that is, more slaves (rather than benevolently providing him with a sexual outlet). Perhaps the master's purpose is to entice him to stay in servitude through an attachment to his partner and children. The option to remain in servitude assumes that the woman and/or her children do not ever obtain manumission and that in order to be with them, he must remain a slave.

16. Pressler, "Wives and Daughters, Bond and Free," 166–7.

17. Among the factors that would prompt a man to purchase the daughter may be that (1) purchasing her might be less expensive than the normal process undertaken for marriage; (2) his wife might be barren, and she could provide children; (3) she could provide additional children to a household that already had children; (4) the purchaser or his son might have personal characteristics that might make the usual process of marriage difficult, among other factors.

18. Since the passage does not mention whether the master could give her to a slave or to another free man, it can be argued that this cannot happen to her.

her be redeemed.¹⁹ She cannot be sold off to a foreign country. (This attests to the existence of an international sex trade even in antiquity.) But she is not released for free: her natal family must pay for her release because she has not had sexual relations with the purchaser. After sexual intimacy (and the loss of her virginity), she needs more protection. If her purchaser takes another woman, the statute prescribes that the maintenance rights of the daughter sold into slavery are not to be diminished. If her maintenance is withheld, she goes free without payment for her emancipation.²⁰ Because the purchaser has had sexual relations with her, he does not receive a payment. It would seem, then, that this is to her benefit.

There is, however, a serious defect in this proviso: a purchaser who wants to be with another woman could manipulate the situation and intentionally neglect to provide her with her maintenance. She is thereby deprived of the protection that she is supposed to be guaranteed. Even though she does not have to be redeemed and goes free without payment, she has been betrayed. The protection is flawed: the corrective can hurt her. It can be surmised that the intention of this proviso is that having to emancipate her for free might prompt her master to continue her maintenance, but he might be willing to lose her if he is sufficiently malicious.

This flaw arises because of the basic problematics arising from her status. When a daughter is sold into slavery, she occupies the status of slave. If she is designated for her purchaser, she remains a slave: she is called אמה,²¹ not אשה, who is sold (מכר), and her purchaser is called אדון, not בעל, husband. If the purchaser is not pleased with her, he must let her be redeemed, and if he deprives her of her maintenance, she is to go free without payment. But her status is altered if she is designated for his son.

She is deemed to have the same status as his daughters (and daughters-in-law) because she has a different sexual partner than her purchaser. The male slave has the option of choosing whether to stay with his master, but in the case of the female slave, the master is the one with the option of

---

19. It is not clear who redeems her. Presumably her natal family or her father in particular is to redeem her.

20. She does not receive a marriage settlement like a wife because she started out the relationship as a daughter sold into slavery. The stipulation that she can go free without payment, means that she does not have to pay him for being released, and that he does not need to give her anything.

21. אמה is the general term for female slave in the Book of the Covenant (Exod. 21:20-21, 26-27, 32; 23:12) and other Pentateuchal laws, except for Lev. 19:20. This last statute assumes that she cannot be in a marital relationship unless she is redeemed or released and may follow the principle of H, as exemplified in Leviticus 25, that Israelites cannot be permanent slaves.

choice—he can dislike her and allow her to be redeemed, he can decide to maintain her, or be freed of her by withholding her maintenance. She does not possess an option to choose.

Her patrimonial family's actions are also restricted.[22] In general, the members of a lineage could redeem a family member sold into slavery, but this general right was lost when she was sold for the purpose of sexual relations. It would come back into effect if the purchaser had designated her for himself but has broken faith with her. If he allocated her for his son, she gains the same status as a free wife and is treated as a free daughter-in-law would be. She does not return to the status of a slave, and it does not seem that according to this passage she can be designated for anyone other than the purchaser himself or his son.

Further, the language of designation in Exod. 21:8 rather than marriage indicates that she does not enjoy the status of a wife when the purchaser designates her for himself, but at which subordinate level of a sexual relationship was she? The term אשה is not limited to "wife," as evident in Exod. 21:4, and the only "marital" status for which there is a technical term in Biblical Hebrew is פילגש, whether the word is translated as concubine or secondary wife. Since the daughter was originally free, her rights are superior to an ordinary אמה, who can be sold abroad and for whom the master does not have to provide much maintenance, and it seems that if the daughter sold into slavery is designated for the purchaser's son, she has a higher status than otherwise. It is likely that there were different ranks of legitimate sexual relationships, but in order to determine what they were, we must delve into the status of men and women and the nature of marriage.

The Status of Men and Women in the Hebrew Bible

Israelite society as depicted in the Bible privileged males, especially those who act as the head of their בית אב, patrimonial joint family or lineage. Women as a general class were subordinated: gender inequity meant that real estate belonging to a lineage passed along male lines, and only to females in the absence of male heirs.[23] But status was nuanced, and rank could be fluid. There were hierarchies that restricted men as well as women. The priesthood, for example, was restricted to a certain circle of males. Male privilege could convey rights that were greatly restricted.

---

22. See M. L. Case, "The Inheritance Injunction of Numbers 36: Zelophehad's Daughters and the Intersection of Ancestral Land and Sex Regulation," Chapter 8 in this volume.

23. See ibid.

While patrilineal property was handed down along agnate lines, patrimonial land could not be sold outside the lineage even with this privilege. Owners were not able to convey title of their property outside of their lineage, as is possible in general with real estate in contemporary society. The preservation of patrilineal property within a lineage was crucial because land was the primary resource in ancient Israel. Male privilege existed and prevailed, but men could be greatly restricted in their rights.

Moreover, despite the general proclivity toward male privilege, ancient Israelite society was not a hierarchical society in which males dominated pervasively, at every level of society in every institution, social, economic, and political. Rather, ancient Israelite society was composed of individuals and social units that related to each other in a variety of vertical and horizontal relationships.[24] Within households, women exercised significant power and authority. Female professionals, such as healers, textile-makers, wet-nurses, and mourners, operated in their vocation with varying degrees of independence. Subordinates, whether male or female, found themselves in a dependent status because of class, age, economic means, and ethnicity. Carol Meyers observes:

> Power in pre-modern communities is hardly unitary. There were multiple loci of power in Israelite society, with women as well as men shaping household and community life. The gendered spheres of life within the household, except for sexuality, can be considered complementary rather than hierarchical; men controlled certain activities and subsistence tasks, women had sole expertise and responsibility in others, and some were shared. Furthermore, the existence of female professionals means that there were women's groups with their own hierarchies and that women functioned in public roles, some of which, including mourning, midwifery, certain types of musical performances, perhaps sorcery, were largely or exclusively female. Anthropologists studying pre-modern societies who are dissatisfied with the shortcomings of existing models of sociocultural complexity have suggested that *heterarchy* rather than *hierarchy* is a better way to understand complex traditional societies. The term *heterarchy* refers to an organizational pattern in which "each element possesses the potential of being unranked (relative to other elements) or ranked in different ways, depending on systemic requirements." Social systems can be related to each other laterally as well as vertically. In this conceptualization, the activities of Israelite women can be considered subsystems, each with its own rankings and statuses. Especially in professional groups but also in informal networks, women exercised leadership and dominance vis-a-vis other women in the

---

24. Bird, "Images of Women in the Old Testament," 44; and Meyers, *Rediscovering Eve*, 193–202.

system. Looking at women's systems, along with those of men, as constituents of the heterarchical complexity of Israelite society rescues women from the notion of oppression, as implied by the term patriarchy, and allows a more nuanced reading of their lives.[25]

Individuals could possess different rankings depending on the activity and social situation they were engaging in. They might have functioned in a subordinate role in one set of circumstances yet have enjoyed superior status in another context. It was also likely that the personal characteristics of individuals had consequences for their standing: certain character traits and actions enabled an individual to gain or lose status. Life was not rigidly structured in fixed hierarchical patterns but shifted in different situations over time.

The nature of status explains the circumstances of the daughter sold into slavery. The daughter's status and that of her children were imperiled because she was sold into slavery. The right of the father to sell his daughter is due to his authority over her as a parent, and both fathers and mothers had the right to sell their children (2 Kgs 4:1; Neh. 5:5). Generational rank meant that parents had authority over children: both fathers and mothers had jurisdiction over sons and daughters.[26] Parents possessed a vertical relationship over children, and the purchaser of a daughter sold into slavery also held a vertical relationship with her. She remained his אמה, his slave. But if she were designated for his son, their relationship was horizontal, and she was to be treated as a free-born daughter. In this case, her status as the slave of her intended husband's father was to be nullified. The obligation to marry her cannot be transferred from father to son, and so she must be treated by her former master according to the rules pertaining to daughters(-in-law). Her status was to be transformed.

Even without an abrupt change in fortune, individuals did not necessarily remain in the same rank. Women were able to maneuver for greater power within a household. A paternal house might witness a battle between maternal houses if the household were polygynous.[27] The first sons of each mother were rivals to succeed the father, and if the mothers were of different ranks, the son of a mother of higher rank had a natural

---

25. Carol Meyers, "Women: Biblical Period," *EncJud* (2nd ed.), 161.
26. Tikva Frymer-Kensky, "Virginity in the Bible," in Matthews, Levinson, and Frymer-Kensky, eds, *Gender and Law*, 96.
27. Cynthia R. Chapman, *The House of the Mother: The Social Roles of Maternal Kin in Biblical Hebrew Narrative and Poetry*, AYBRL (New Haven: Yale University Press, 2016), 38–50.

advantage. Narrative accounts depict the struggles of the sons of a low-status wife to succeed their fathers, and the resistance they encountered. In dialogue embedded in narratives, emphasizing an individual's status as אמה, "maidservant," or בן־האמה, "son of a maidservant," serves to denigrate that person: Sarah stresses Hagar's rank in trying to dispossess Ishmael (Gen. 21:10), and Jotham is portrayed as rebuking the citizens of Shechem for killing his father's sons and raising the son of his maidservant (בן־אמתו) to be king.[28]

The daughter sold into slavery could try to enhance her status. A woman could retain ties to the members of her father's household: just as a free woman could use her relationship with them to advance her position, a daughter sold for marriage could depend on them to maintain her status in her husband's house. The relationship to her natal family is the basis on which the statute provided her with protections. She could depend upon her enduring bond with her father's house to affirm her status in her purchaser's household because, if mistreated, she could seek the protection of her natal family: she could enjoy being redeemed from slavery, or she could be emancipated with her family's debt remitted, depending on the type of mistreatment.

A daughter sold into slavery found herself vulnerable: she had subordinate status, similar to an enslaved male, but the reason for her enslavement, her family's economic situation, made her situation precarious. The shifting fortunes in rank for men and women in Israelite society meant that her status could fluctuate for the better or the worse. Her vertical relationship vis-à-vis her purchaser could become a horizontal relationship with his son. The nature of marriage according to the Hebrew Bible could further aid or hinder her shifting fortunes.

Marriage and Divorce in the Hebrew Bible

While biblical texts do not manifest a complete set of procedures and laws for marriage and divorce, certain features are clear.[29] Marriage appears to be comprehended in two seemingly contradictory ways in the Hebrew

---

28. Terminology mirrors the low rank of a female slave: in direct address, the phrase עבדך/בן עבדך, "your servant/the son of your servant," is used to express humility, and the related phrase בן אמתך, "the son of your maidservant," intensifies the sense of humbleness (ibid., 196). The magnitude of the plague of the death of the firstborn is expressed as occurring from the firstborn of Pharaoh who sits on the throne to the son of the maidservant (שפחה) who is behind the hand-mill (Exod. 11:5).

29. See Sarah Shectman, "Priestly Marriage Restrictions," Chapter 7 in this volume.

Bible. That the man served as the active party in constituting a marriage is based on a number of pieces of evidence: the verbs, for example, employed in different genres of biblical texts, such as לקח אשה or נשא אשה, convey the assumption that the man initiated the marriage process and that marriage was the acquisition of the bride by the groom. But the words should not be taken at face value: despite the terminology of acquisition, the husband gained the right to marriage, not ownership of his wife. Furthermore, marriage is termed ברית, "a covenant," a term implying free consent to the agreement and a significant amount of mutuality (although not complete equality) in Mal. 2:14; Ezek. 16:8; and Prov. 2:17.[30]

Similarly, the only biblical legal text on divorce, Deut. 24:1-4, leaves the impression that only men could initiate divorce. If this was the case, a man was restricted in his right to divorce a wife only in unusual circumstances, and the right to a divorce was available to a woman only under unusual circumstances (Exod. 21:10-11; Deut. 22:13-29; 24:1-4).[31] It is possible, though, that this impression, that only men could initiate divorce, is due to the circumstances of the specific situation addressed in this text, the case of a man seeking to remarry a woman to whom he had once been married: since the husband was the active party in this case, in the absence of other biblical texts that might offer other information, the description leaves the impression that in all situations of divorce, the husband was the one to take the initiative.[32] The narrative of a Levite's concubine leaving him (Judg. 19:2) offers possible evidence that a woman could take the initiative in a divorce, but there are many interpretive difficulties with this passage.[33] Sources from outside the Bible offer evidence that the woman

---

30. Paul Kalluveettil, *Declaration and Covenant: A Comprehensive Review of Covenant Formulary from the Old Testament and the Ancient Near East*, AnBib 88 (Rome: Biblical Institute, 1982), 79. Dan. 11:6, 17 refers to a diplomatic marriage between the Seleucid and Ptolemaic dynasties, and the word מישרים or ישרים stands as a replacement for the word ברית, "covenant." But how much significance this had for the marriage of common people is hard to extrapolate.

31. A. Toeg, "Does Deuteronomy XXIV, 1-4 Incorporate a General Law on Divorce?" *Dine-Israel* 2 (1970): v–xxiv. See also Shectman, "Priestly Marriage Restrictions."

32. Meyers, "Women: Biblical Period," 158; Yair Zakovitch, "The Woman's Rights in the Biblical Law of Divorce," *JLA* 4 (1981): 28–46.

33. Among these difficulties is that the woman is termed a פילגש, "a concubine," and it is not clear whether the procedures of divorce would apply the same way to a wife and to a concubine. The text employs the term זנה to refer to her return to her father's house, and while it does not seem likely that this means that she engaged in sexual intimacy as a prostitute but more likely that her act was to reject the Levite,

did have the right to divorce. Mesopotamian texts indicate that women could initiate divorce,[34] and the Elephantine papyri, from an Israelite mercenary colony in Egypt in the fifth century BCE, attest to a woman's right to do so as well.[35]

whether her return constituted divorce is debatable. See Phyllis A. Bird, "'To Play the Harlot': An Inquiry into an Old Testament Metaphor," in *Missing Persons and Mistaken Identities*, 219–36.

34. In the Old Babylonian period, Mesopotamian marriage contracts assume that the wife could initiate divorce and put limits on her right to do so. A number of them restrict her right to do so in the same way that the husband's right was restricted: if either initiated divorce, they were subject to the same fine. However, the majority of extant marriage contracts from the same time period and same geographic territory restrict her right so much that her right to do so was voided: the husband was subject to a financial penalty, but she was subject to a severe penalty, such as being tied up and thrown in the river or sold into slavery. It may be speculated that women and their families of origin who agreed to such severe restrictions may have been in an inferior financial position vis-à-vis the husband. See Samuel Greengus, "The Old Babylonian Marriage Contract," *JAOS* 89 (1969): 505–32; Raymond Westbrook, *Old Babylonian Marriage Law*, AfO Beiheft 23 (Horn, Austria: Berger & Söhne), 112–38. Mesopotamian material chronologically overlapping with the biblical period shows a general decrease in a woman's right to initiate a divorce. Yet the wife's right to divorce reappeared from time to time. An unusual contract from Neo-Assyria allows the woman to divorce without penalty, but the man would have to pay twice the amount of the dowry. This was the marriage of the daughter of a high-ranking woman of the royal court to the chief court tailor. See Nicholas Postgate, *Fifty Neo-Assyrian Legal Documents* (Warminster: Aris & Phillips, 1976), no. 14; Karen Radner, *Die neuassyrischen Privatrechtsurkunden als Quell für Mensch und Umwelt*, SAAS 6 (Helsinki: The Neo-Assyrian Text Corpus Project, 1997), 159, 164–6; Martin Stol, *Women in the Ancient Near East*, trans. Helen Richardson and Mervyn Richardson (Berlin: de Gruyter, 2016), 202–3. Extant Neo-Babylonian contracts do not exhibit parity of any kind, and only the husbands enjoyed the right to divorce. See Stol, *Women in the Ancient Near East*, 209–33; Martha T. Roth, *Babylonian Marriage Agreements: 7th–3rd centuries B.C.*, AOAT 222 (Kevelaer: Butzon & Bercker; Neukirchen-Vluyn: Neukirchener Verlag, 1989), 14, 108–13, nos. 34–5; Cornelia Wunsch, *Urkunden zum Ehe-, Vermögens- und Erbrecht aus verschiedenen neubabylonischen Archiven*, Babylonische Archive 2 (Dresden: ISLET, 2003), 36 n. 3.

35. See texts B28, B36, and B41 in Bezalel Porten, *The Elephantine Papyri in English: Three Millennia of Cross-Cultural Continuity and Change*, 2nd ed. (Atlanta: SBL, 2011); and the discussion in Mordechai Akiva Freedman, *Jewish Marriage in Palestine: A Cairo Geniza Study* (Tel Aviv and New York: The Jewish Theological Seminary of America, 1980), 312–19. In regard to Babatha's *ketubbah* (Papyrus Yadin 10), a celebrated text from a later period (the Bar-Kochba revolt of 132–135 CE), it may be somewhat far-fetched to claim that the phrase in question means that the wife could implement a divorce at will: [ובכל זמן ד[י ת]מר לי [אחלף] ל]ך שטרא דנה כדי חזא]

The contradictory nature of marriage is manifested in other aspects of the marriage. The husband did have the right to an exclusive relationship with his wife in a way that a married woman did not have vis-a-vis her husband. The husband was also able to marry multiple wives. However, the assumption of a number of non-legal biblical texts, such as Gen. 2:24 and the Song of Songs, is of a monogamous relationship.

In the same vein, the husband could annul a wife's vow but did not have absolute power over his wife in biblical law.[36] Women had rights in a marriage, and it is striking that a wife was at least partly enfranchised. A husband could not sell his wife into debt-slavery.[37] In contrast, LH §117 allows a debtor to sell his wife, son, or daughter into bondage to pay off a debt with a limit of three years of servitude.[38] The Laws of Eshnunna §24 allows a creditor to distrain a debtor or a debtor's wife, children, or slaves to force payment of the debt.

Marriage was bilateral, and Millar Burrows locates the roots of marriage in barter, in an exchange between families.[39] What is helpful in his conceptualization is the focus on the reciprocity inherent in the

"And whenever you tell me, I will exchange for you this document, as is fitting." It most likely means that she is entitled to a replacement document. See Yigael Yadin et al., *The Documents from the Bar Kokhba Period in the Cave of Letters: Hebrew, Aramaic and Nabatean Papyri* (Jerusalem: Israel Exploration Society, 2002), 118–41, esp. 139–40; Yigael Yadin, Jonas C. Greenfield, and Ada Yardeni, "Babatha's Ketubba," *IEJ* 44 (1994): 75–99. See also Philip F. Esler, *Babatha's Orchard: The Yadin Papyri and an Ancient Jewish Family Tale Retold* (Oxford: Oxford University Press, 2017).

36. The limits of a husband's authority are manifested in the description of Eve as עזר כנגדו in Gen. 2:23; while it has been a crux interpretum for ages, the sense of the phrase is that even if the woman possesses a lesser status, as an עזר to the man, she is the man's counterpart, as implied from כנגדו. He is first among equals, and she was not in complete subordination to him. The following verse, Gen. 2:24, describes male and female pairing as a man leaving his mother and father and bonding with his wife. The man is active, and the woman is ostensibly less so. It is an image of near, but not quite, equals. At the same time, Gen. 3:16 presents an image of greater male dominance, especially in the realm of sexuality and procreation. Meyers offers an extensive analysis of the phrase in *Rediscovering Eve*, 70–6.

37. Biblical texts offer evidence for the sale of children but not for wives.

38. See Pamela Barmash, *The Laws of Hammurabi* (forthcoming), on whether this paragraph of the Laws of Hammurabi was law actually practiced.

39. Millar Burrows, *The Basis of Israelite Marriage*, AOS 15 (New Haven: American Oriental Society, 1940), 9–15. Paul Koschaker argued that marriage in Mesopotamia was effected through purchase, a viewpoint much debated by scholars. See Paul Koschaker, *Rechtsvergleichende Studien zur Gesetzgebung Hammurapis Königs von Babylon* (Leipzig: Veit, 1917), 137.

interchange. Where marriage transcended barter was the formation of a permanent relationship, perhaps adumbrated by the expectation that a successful barter would likely lead to further exchanges between the parties. It was not about an exchange of equal value, a "bride-price" for a bride, but about the establishment of mutual ties. The objects of value that were presented to the other side expressed and confirmed the social bond. It strengthened the alliance between families. The process of marriage created a network of relationships, rights, and duties between the parties and their natal families, and what the bride's and groom's families received from one another, the *mohar* and the dowry, was presumably used by the families to set up the couple's household[40] and perhaps also utilized to find a spouse for the bride's and groom's siblings and other relatives, creating further ties to other kinship groups.

The process of establishing a marital relationship was a way of creating a bond between two בית אב lineages. It established a new household with ties to both the husband's and wife's natal households. The wife retained the relationship she had with her natal family after she married, and she continued to have a relationship with her husband's family after he died. Two parties came to a mutual agreement and concurred on an exchange that created a new household that retained ties to the two prior households.

In the process of creating a marital bond, the groom took the lead because men were privileged in the legal sphere and, therefore, he was the one to initiate the formal process with the *mohar*, the betrothal gift,[41] the formal emblem of his commitment to the marriage.[42] He offered the *mohar* to the bride's father rather than to the bride for two reasons: (1) the higher status of males meant that her father served as head of the family; and (2) the bride was generally younger, and social rank depended not just on gender but on age as well. Only in unusual circumstances did a woman act for herself.[43]

40. See the complaint by Rachel and Leah that their father had used their money for himself (Gen. 31:15).

41. Often translated as "bride-price." Burrows suggested "compensation-gift," reflecting its origins as barter and its use in establishing a bond between families (*The Basis of Israelite Marriage*, 10–15).

42. The extent to which the initiative was the groom's can be seen in the book of Ruth, where Naomi and Ruth are depicted as expending great effort to prompt Boaz to undertake legal action. His declaration in Ruth 4:10 that he has acquired a wife is deeply ironic in light of the machinations that Naomi and Ruth are portrayed as undertaking in order to prompt him to act.

43. The narratives on Samson display ironic humor in that the hero's parents need to make the marriage arrangements, since Samson apparently has only seen the Philistine woman and has not spoken to her (Judg. 14:1-5).

The *mohar* was an emblem more than a payment: it signaled the creation of social, legal, and emotional bonds between the parties to the marriage. It was not temporary but effected a permanent relationship. And the groom was not the only one to provide a prestation. The bride's family gave her a dowry. The offering of a *mohar* for a woman started the process, and the interchange of offerings between parties finalized the marital bond.

But the case of the daughter sold into slavery did not fit the regular pattern of establishing a marital relationship: the sale of a person to another was distant and distinct from an interchange creating a permanent relationship. It was uneven and unequal. Reciprocity was compromised. It is a fair assumption that no one, male or female, would enter or place someone into servitude without dire need, and without the exchange of *mohar* and dowry, the daughter has entered into a different form of marital relationship, one with unresolved and unsettled aspects in comparison to the typical form of marriage. The daughter became the object of value.

She remained an אמה to her purchaser if she was designated for him, but she secured the status of a free daughter(-in-law) if she was designated for his son. Even in the case in which she remained an אמה, her owner's right to sell her was restricted. At the same time her ability to rely on her natal family was greatly limited compared to a primary wife.

The ambivalent, even somewhat amorphous, nature of the daughter's marital relationship may reflect that marriage was not yet an institution all that well defined beyond (primary) wifehood: the relationships between a man and other women with whom he had a legitimate bond had a range of characteristics, both formal and informal. This amplifies the fluidity in the vertical and horizontal relationships that determine status. Bernard S. Jackson is correct in noting that there may not have been a single conception of marriage that clearly distinguished its options from all other relationships.[44] Unlike contemporary marriage, which is under the administrative rule of a state with legislated formal procedures, a fully worked-out concept of marriage was still in formation.[45]

---

44. Jackson, "The 'Institutions' of Marriage and Divorce in the Hebrew Bible," 230–2.

45. As a consequence of this ambiguity, it may be that marriage contracts delineating detailed financial terms and property rights were negotiated only between families that possessed sufficient resources. But whether those contracts were normally in written form is not clear, and perhaps they were recorded textually only under a limited range of circumstances. This was the case as well elsewhere in the ancient Near East. How much this applies as well to divorce is unknown; a bill of divorce seems to be part of the process of divorce (Deut. 24:1-4; Isa. 50:1).

Narratives on a Maidservant's Quasi-marital Relationship

The ill-defined nature of the marital relationship of the daughter sold into slavery is illustrated vividly in narratives depicting the fluctuating fortunes of an אמה, a maidservant, and her children in what appear to be quasi-marital relationships, and situating the case of the daughter sold into slavery amidst those narratives sheds light on the nuances of her marital situation.

In shifting from legal texts to narratives, it must be noted that the genre in which law is depicted has an effect on its presentation.[46] A narrative is not a transcript of legal procedure: it may distort law for the sake of plot or character development. It can show how a legal system was perceived to operate and whether an action in the legal realm was deemed to be just or unjust. A narrative may convey what justice ought to be in the opinion of the author: it may aspire to moral justice, a model of justice in which victims are vindicated, hurts are acknowledged, and relationships are restored. In so doing, legal procedures and institutions may be reshaped (or perhaps distorted) in order to reach a more just conclusion.

The narratives illustrate negotiations over financial arrangements, the establishment of the household, and the celebratory feast. The laws treat financial arrangements such as the *mohar* explicitly and the dowry implicitly: the case of the daughter sold into slavery for marriage presumes that the father cannot provide a dowry and is forced to sell her rather than make the arrangements usual for a marriage. The narratives depict the *mohar* being paid in unusual ways, in labor, either prior to the marriage or as a promise after the marriage (Gen. 29:19-20), or, in the case of a warrior son-in-law of a king, in enemy foreskins (1 Sam. 18:25). The narratives also show the bride's family providing her with a dowry (Gen. 2:24; 29:24, 29; Josh. 15:18-19; Judg. 1:14-15; 1 Kgs 9:16).

Furthermore, although marriage in the Bible was an established practice that had social and legal aspects, it did not have religious aspects. Celebrations were held to mark the social change, but it remains unclear whether the procedure of joining a couple in matrimony in ancient Israel carried any religious overtones or meaning. It may be that prayers were invoked on behalf of the couple to have children, but more than that is unknown (Meyers, *Rediscovering Eve*, 159).

46. In contrast, law organizes human actions into a fixed set of patterns. Law aims for the predictable, and it has to curtail the complexity of a given case in order to accommodate categories and remedies. For more on narrative in comparison to law, see Pamela Barmash, "The Narrative Quandary: Cases of Law in Literature," *VT* 54 (2004): 1–16; "Law and Narrative in Genesis," *ZABR* 16 (2010): 211–23; and "Achieving Justice Through Narrative in the Hebrew Bible: The Limitations of Law and the Legal Potential of Literature," *ZABR* 20 (2014): 181–99.

In so doing, a narrative shapes marital law for the sake of the storyline. Jacob's deception of his brother is recompensed by Laban's deception of him when Jacob is tricked into marriage with Leah. Jacob's own mother instructs him to deceive his father, and it is her own brother who deceives Jacob.[47] The parallel double-dealing enriches the narrative. The bride's family appears to have taken advantage of the groom in the cases of Jacob and David: the standing of the bride's family is so superior to the groom's situation that the groom has no choice but to agree to the unfavorable request. The maidservants of Rachel and Leah provide for more children in a contest between sisters about who can bear (the most) children, and the unusual dowry of towns from a magnate to a daughter prompts its being mentioned.

Including female slaves in the rivalry of bearing children prompts the portrayal in Genesis of women of different marital status as providing legitimate offspring, offspring who are entitled to an inheritance.[48] Sarah, Rebecca, Rachel, and Leah give birth to heirs, and their status as wife is not contested. However, the status of other women is more ambiguous and less well-defined. Hagar, a שפחה, is given to Abraham as a surrogate by Sarah (Gen. 16:1-3), and she is termed an אמה to Abraham in Gen. 21:12.[49] Abraham considers Ishmael as his heir and the fulfillment of the divine promise (Gen. 17:18). Zilpah is a שפחה given by Laban to Leah on her marriage, and Bilhah is a שפחה given by Laban to Rachel on her marriage (Gen. 29:24). After Leah can no longer bear children, she gives Zilpah, again termed a שפחה, with the proviso that she is לאשה to Jacob (Gen. 30:9). Clearly, אשה does not necessarily mean a primary wife or perhaps

---

47. The narrative portrays how Laban manipulates the legal system to his advantage because of his greater power in his relationship with Jacob, and how he can distort the terms of a contract. Laban and Jacob have made a contract for Jacob to work seven years for Laban's daughter Rachel, but on the marriage night, Jacob discovers that Laban has brought in his other daughter. If Jacob walked away from further dealings with Laban, he would lose what he has already invested. He wants to wed Rachel too much (even if it appears that he has not looked upon her since falling in love with her and does not realize that he is in bed with Leah). For a detailed discussion of this narrative, see F. Rachel Magdalene, "Rachel's Betrothal Contract and the Origins of Contract Law," Chapter 3 in this volume.

48. It cannot be assumed that the stories in Genesis accurately preserve archaic law of the epoch in which they are set. See my "Law and Narrative in Genesis," 212–13.

49. An added complication may be whether the hypothesized Pentateuchal documents use different terms for female slave. See S. R. Driver, *The Book of Genesis* (London: Methuen, 1904), xiii.

any marital status. Rachel gives Bilhah, termed an אמה, as a surrogate to Jacob (Gen 30:3). Zilpah's children seem to be considered Leah's children, and while the tribes whose eponyms are children of Bilhah and Zilpah possess a lower status than the children of Leah and Rachel, they are still included among the tribes.

Narrative texts depict different family members engaged in negotiations over marriage, mirroring the shifting rankings. Brothers are involved, even when the father is alive. In the betrothal of Rebecca, it is her brother Laban who takes the lead (Gen. 24:53-60).[50] In the marriage negotiations between Dinah and Shechem, Hamor first approaches Jacob, but then it is Jacob's sons with whom he must deal (Gen. 34:14). The Song of Songs views marriage from the vantage point of a marriage-age daughter, and her brothers by her mother are the ones who are concerned with protecting her chastity (Song 1:6; 8:8-9).

Other narratives depict the father as the only one negotiating his daughter's marriage. Laban takes the lead in marrying his daughters Leah and Rachel off to Jacob (Genesis 29). Jethro/Reuel negotiates the marriage of his daughter Zipporah to Moses (Exod. 2:15-22). Saul dictates the terms of David's marriage to his daughters Merab and Michal (1 Sam. 18:17-30). In all of these narratives, the fathers have multiple daughters, and either no male heir is mentioned or there is no dispute as to who the male heir is. The groom is a fugitive in two of the cases, and in the third, the status of the father (King Saul) is much higher than that of the groom (David). The status of the groom as the younger son of his father may factor into the nature of the negotiations (although Moses' status is less clear).[51]

In contrast to the narratives, the statute about the daughter sold into slavery depicts the father as taking the lead because he is the only male who can sell her into slavery. Her brothers cannot sell their sister, even though she may have to be redeemed by the בית אב, the patrilineal family, whose leadership a brother would succeed.

The status of the children of the daughter sold into slavery is left unmentioned in Exod. 21:2-11. The narrative texts of Genesis indicate that the slave-woman's children are free,[52] and at least in the case of Leah,

---

50. For a detailed discussion of the betrothal contract between Laban and Jacob, and the consequences of Laban's breach of that contract, see Magdalene, "Rachel's Betrothal Contract and the Origins of Contract Law."

51. Chapman, *The House of the Mother*, 70. The father becomes involved when the household would be absorbing the groom for a period of time.

52. Although, according to LH §§170–171, a man's children by a slave woman are not able to inherit unless he formally adopts them, they appear to be deemed free, at least in the narratives of Genesis.

she names her maidservant's children, perhaps indicating that they are considered her children.⁵³ Although the children are free, they do have secondary status.⁵⁴ The slave-women Hagar, Bilhah, and Zilpah remain the slaves of Sarah, Rachel, and Leah respectively, and while they appear to have a marital bond with their husbands, it is not equal to that which Sarah, Rachel, and Leah enjoy; the slaves are still denoted as the אמה or שפחה of the husbands (Gen. 21:12; 32:23) despite the fact that the term לאשה, usually understood to mean "as a wife," is used to describe how the patriarchs relate to them (Gen. 16:3; 30:4, 9).⁵⁵ Their sons inherit their share of their father's property, and even Ishmael must be intentionally disinherited (Gen. 21:10-13). Whether the bond between concubine (פילגש) or slave woman (אמה or שפחה) and the man should be termed a secondary marriage or not a marriage at all is more of a red herring: the son of a mother of that status does have a right to inherit, but the narratives about Abraham show that their sons can be maneuvered out of an inheritance by being given a gift and sent away from the son deemed as the major heir (Gen. 25:5-6).

53. For more on the maternal prerogative of naming, see Ilana Pardes, *Countertraditions in the Bible: A Feminist Approach* (Cambridge: Harvard University Press, 1992), 40–3.

54. The Royal Steward inscription records the burial of a man with his אמה, signaling her great significance to him, despite her status as a slave. See N. Avigad, "The Epitaph of a Royal Steward from Siloam Village," *IEJ* 3 (1953): 137–52.

55. Abraham is described as taking Keturah לאשה, "as a wife," in Gen. 25:1, and yet she is called a פילגש in Gen. 25:6. Further, while Westbrook ("The Female Slave," in Matthews, Levinson, and Frymer-Kensky, eds, *Gender and Law*, 229–30) argues that a woman could not be both a wife (even a secondary one) and a slave, he notes that this was legally peculiar and observed that it would be bizarre that children would inherit their own mother as a slave. Westbrook's argument is based on a more rigid line of demarcation between law of personal status and law of property than actually was the case. A man inheriting his mother as a slave could be a possible consequence of legal slavery. Old Babylonian marriage contracts stipulate that the woman slave becomes the second wife of the man and the slave of the primary wife, and the Laws of Lipit-Ishtar §25 and LH §§170–171 distinguish between children of the primary and secondary wives. At Elephantine, the slave Tamet is freed by her master twenty-two years after another (free) man has married her. She is the sole wife to her husband. See Rainer Kessler, "Die Sklavin als Ehefrau: Zur Stellen der 'ĀMĀH," *VT* 52 (2002): 501–12; Bezalel Porten and Ada Yardeni, *Textbook of Aramaic Documents from Ancient Egypt* (Jerusalem: Magnes, 1989), B3.6; Stol, *Women in the Ancient Near East*, 205; and Jan A. Wagenaar, "The Annulment of a 'Purchase' Marriage in Exod 21, 7-11," *ZABR* 10 (2004): 221–3.

The daughter sold into slavery had a double liability against her. As a woman, her general status was lower than a man, and her sale into slavery put her at further disadvantage. The social system made her dependent. But the nature of her status and the inchoate nature of marriage for those who were not primary wives allowed leeway for factors that could both alleviate and exacerbate her situation. Her fortunes and the fortunes of her children could fluctuate. Her children might be free, and her sons might have the right to inherit from their father. But they could be finagled out of their inheritance. The pliable nature of status according to gender and the amorphous nature of marriage could protect a daughter sold into slavery. Nonetheless, her vulnerability lingered.

The Reshaping of the Slave Laws of the Book of the Covenant in Deuteronomy

The Deuteronomic counterpart to the Book of the Covenant (Deut. 15:12-18) reshapes the Exodus passage to deliberately propose a different set of protections for slaves, an outcome of the Deuteronomic program of social reform.[56] It incorporates the אמה in a direct and unambiguous way, appearing to indicate criticism of the Exodus passage.[57]

---

56. The reshaping is evidence for relative dating: the Deuteronomic passage is later than the Exodus passage. But this is not proof that all of Deuteronomy is later than the Book of the Covenant. The laws on slavery are placed at the beginning of the Book of the Covenant, and the second person form used in Exod. 21:2 is in stark contrast to 21:12–22:16. This prompts the question of whether this passage was originally part of the collection of statutes that make up the Book of the Covenant and whether its date of composition was at a different time from the other statutes (or at the same time as 22:17–23:19, a text that employs the second person). A number of methods have been employed to determine the date of biblical texts besides the dependence of one text on another. Using the level of social complexity as chronological evidence has failed to produce a fixed time period because an institution like debt-slavery could occur in a wide range of social conditions. Linguistic evidence seems the most secure, but even then, determining that the Book of the Covenant manifests Early (or Classical) Biblical Hebrew (or any other stratum of Biblical Hebrew) yields a wide time period. In the case of Early (or Classical) Biblical Hebrew, its time range is from some time in the First Temple period to the Exilic period. Another means of dating, the relationship of D to Josiah's reform narrated in 2 Kings 22–23, has complications. See Pamela Barmash, "Determining the Date of Biblical Legal Texts," in *Oxford Handbook of Biblical Law*, ed. Pamela Barmash (Oxford: Oxford University Press, 2019), 233–53.

57. Whether the laws on the release of slaves, either as evidenced in Exod. 21:2-11 or Deut. 15:12-18, were ever put into practice is debatable. Jer. 34:14 demonstrates that it was put into practice at best inconsistently or at worst not at all.

Deuteronomy 15:12-18 appears to be based on Exod. 21:2-11 because of the large number of parallel elements: the usage of words such as חפשי,[58] עברי,[59] and רצע;[60] the six-year term of service; manumission in the seventh year; the attention paid to the financial component of manumission; the option for the slave to decide whether to remain in bondage forever; and the ritual of assuming lifetime bondage.[61] The clustering of these parallel elements demonstrates that Deut. 15:12-18 has reshaped Exod. 21:2-11.

The Deuteronomy passage reshapes the Exodus passage both in content and literary form. While the Exodus statute begins by addressing the master, "When you purchase a Hebrew slave..." and then assumes the usual third person form of cuneiform casuistic legal formulation, the Deuteronomic law is entirely in the second person addressed to the master in order to motivate him to release his slave.[62] Even more strikingly, the Deuteronomic passage transforms the legal rulings of the Exodus statute. The requirement to manumit a slave is applied to both male and female slaves.[63] Exodus 21:2-7 provides for a male slave to go free in the

---

58. Other than these two passages, the word חפשי is not found elsewhere in the Pentateuch. It is employed a number of times in Jer. 34:9, 10, 11, 14, and 16, which address the manumission of slaves (most likely alluding to Deut. 15:1, 12-18).

59. These are the only statutes in which the word עברי appears. Elsewhere, the word occurs in passages where Israelites found themselves in a foreign context (e.g., narratives about Joseph, Gen. 39:17 and 41:12; about Egyptian bondage, Exod. 2:11 and 13; and about Jonah, Jon. 1:9).

60. This root is found only in these statutes.

61. The extent to which the Deuteronomic law is dependent on Exodus can be seen most clearly in comparing both sets of laws to Lev. 25:25-28, a formulation of laws on slavery that does not have a single echo of the Exodus passage. Leviticus 25:25-28 is a set of statutes that is independent of Exodus and Deuteronomy. For more on this issue, see Sara Japhet, "The Relationship Between the Legal Corpora in the Pentateuch in Light of the Manumission Laws," in *Studies in Bible 1986*, ScrHier 31 (Jerusalem: Magnes, 1986), 63–89; Bernard M. Levinson, "The Manumission of Hermeneutics: The Slave Laws of the Pentateuch as a Challenge to Contemporary Pentateuchal Theory," in *Congress Volume Leiden 2004*, ed. André Lemaire, VTSup 109 (Leiden: Brill, 2006), 281–324; John Van Seters, *A Law Book for the Diaspora: Revision in the Study of the Covenant Code* (New York: Oxford University Press, 2003), 82–95.

62. The statutes in Deuteronomy are replete with motive clauses in order to inspire the master to release his slave.

63. The awkward formulation אחיך העברי או העבריה, "your brother, the male or female Hebrew," is due to the splicing of the reference to both male and female in a passage dependent on earlier wording that did not include women. Even in contemporary English, the use of a pronoun to refer to both men and women is awkward

seventh year without his paying the master for his release. Deuteronomy 15:12-14 goes beyond the payment-free release and prescribes that the master provide compensation to the manumitted slave in the form of sheep and/ or goats, grain, and oil.⁶⁴ When a slave refuses manumission and asks to remain in the master's house, no mention is made in the Deuteronomic passage that his wife and children are the reason he wishes to remain because manumission would apply to them as well. The slave wishes to remain because he enjoys the positive situation he has with his master. Deuteronomy clarifies the Exodus process for the slave who refuses manumission: in Exodus, the procedure (והגישו אל־הדלת או אל־המזוזה ורצע אדניו את־אזנו במרצע) mandates that the master take the awl and pierce the slave's ear, but it is not so clear how the door or doorpost figures in this procedure. Presumably it is to serve as a rigid backdrop against which to pierce the slave's ear. The statute in Deuteronomy makes it clear: ולקחת את המרצע ונתתה באזנו ובדלת, "You shall take the awl and put it through his ear into the door." There is no mention of the clause, והגישו אל־האלהים, "he shall bring him to God," because local shrines are not legitimate after cult centralization.

The program of secularization and humanitarianism in Deuteronomy accounts for the transformation.⁶⁵ The provision of the newly freed slave with gifts is apparently to facilitate his/her ability to survive on his/her own. The extension of the manumission to female slaves reflects the legislator's humanistic concern,⁶⁶ as does the omission of any reference

and gives rise to infelicitous expressions as "he/she" or "s/he" or worse. Moreover, the statute in Deuteronomy is formulated so generally that it appears to encompass all women without exception. Lastly, Deut. 15:17 reads ואף לאמתך תעשה כן, a redundancy with an emphatic particle that stresses the modification of an earlier law that did not decree emancipation for female slaves.

64. It is clarified that a slave does not have to pay for manumission. In this way, going free חנם is quite the opposite of the way the master experiences the manumission of his slave in Exod. 21:2.

65. Moshe Weinfeld, *Deuteronomy and the Deuteronomic School* (Oxford: Clarendon, 1972; repr., Winona Lake: Eisenbrauns, 1992), 232, 272, 282–3. This also accounts for the rule against returning fugitive slaves to their master in Deut. 23:16. One wonders if 1 Sam. 22:2 could serve as evidence that debtors were not returned to be sold by their creditors. However, according to 1 Kgs 2:39-40, an Israelite master is depicted as going out to reclaim his slaves. Does this prove that Deuteronomy is legislating against the norm in ancient Israel or that fugitive slaves were returned to their masters in areas under non-Israelite control?

66. Deuteronomic laws mandate that men and women participate in ceremonies (Deut. 29:10, 17; 31:12). The festival celebrations refer to sons as well as daughters, male servants as well as female servants (Deut. 12:12, 18; 16:11, 14). Weinfeld argues

to the master giving a wife to the slave or the slave wishing to remain in his master's service in order to be with his wife. The master does not control the private life of his slave, or as Deuteronomy puts it, אחיך העברי או העבריה, "your fellow Israelite citizen." The master buys the slave's service, not his person. The slave's family life is independent of his master. The master is never referred to as אדון, "master," and the slave is referred to as "your fellow citizen." The master is commanded to set the slave free, whereas the rule in Exodus states impersonally that the slave will go free. The Deuteronomy law is formulated in the second person and addressed to the master in order to motivate him to release what he might think is a piece of property too valuable to manumit. Three reasons are offered to motivate the master to release his slaves: (1) the Israelites were slaves in Egypt, God freed them, and therefore they are commanded presumably to free their slaves (or obey God's command); (2) the slave has worked twice as hard as a hired worker; and (3) God will bless the Israelites who free their slaves.

The passage on the daughter sold into slavery in the Book of the Covenant and its Deuteronomic reshaping aim at ameliorating the circumstances of slavery. The Exodus passage protects the daughter by restricting her emancipation, keeping her in slavery but preventing her from being sold abroad in the sex trade and allowing her to be redeemed if the purchaser sours on her. It protects her by ordaining that she be provided with maintenance if he takes on another woman, and emancipates her if he withholds her maintenance. The Deuteronomic revamping of the Exodus passage provides for her emancipation, just as for a male slave, and furnishes her with the wherewithal in animals, grain, and oil to resume life as a free person.

Conclusion

The case of the daughter sold into slavery is an unexceptional tragedy befalling an average Israelite family that has fallen into dire financial straits. Her family's economic vulnerability prevents her from entering into marriage in the usual manner, and the statute in the Book of the Covenant aims at safeguarding her. She is not released after six years during which she could be used sexually by her purchaser because that

---

that the reason why the wife is not mentioned is not that she is to sit alone at home while all the other members of the household make the pilgrimage but rather that she, too, is addressed in the word "you," the recipient of the command, which applies equally to the husband and the wife (ibid., 291).

would leave her vulnerable. If he grows to dislike her, the statute denies him the ability to sell her abroad and provides for her to be redeemed, leaving her in the position she had before the sale. If he takes on another woman, she is to be provided with maintenance; otherwise, if she is denied maintenance, she is freed without payment, a disincentive to her master. This proviso could be manipulated by a malicious master who, willing to let her go for free, intentionally withholds her maintenance, and it may be surmised that the intention of this proviso is that having to emancipate her for free might prompt her master to continue her maintenance.

The somewhat mutable nature of status in Israelite society has a curious effect on the status of the daughter sold into slavery. An individual might possess a subordinate role in one circumstance but enjoy an enhanced status into another. The daughter sold into slavery remains an אמה, maidservant, to her purchaser. But if his son is to be her sexual partner, the relationship is no longer vertical—slave to master—but horizontal, and she is to be treated like a daughter(-in-law).

This fluidity is enabled by an ambivalent conception of marriage as both privileged for the male in certain aspects yet mutual in other aspects. Further enhancing the fluidity was that the parameters for marital relationships between the status of primary wife and concubine (פילגש) were not fully defined. These factors allowed the daughter sold into slavery to regain her free status when the purchaser's son became her intended sexual partner.

The statute in the Book of the Covenant aims at protecting the daughter with a number of provisos, but the Deuteronomic revamping of the slave laws pursues another path in the amelioration of slavery. All slaves are to be freed after six years of servitude, and they are to be provided with the financial means to resume free living.

Bibliography

Ahituv, Shmuel. *Echoes from the Past: Hebrew and Cognate Inscriptions from the Biblical Period*. Jerusalem: Carta, 2008.

Avigad, N. "The Epitaph of a Royal Steward from Siloam Village." *IEJ* 3 (1953): 137–52.

Barmash, Pamela. "Achieving Justice through Narrative in the Hebrew Bible: The Limitations of Law and the Legal Potential of Literature." *ZABR* 20 (2014): 181–99.

Barmash, Pamela. "Determining the Date of Biblical Legal Texts." In *Oxford Handbook of Biblical Law*, edited by Pamela Barmash, 233–53. Oxford: Oxford University Press, 2019.

Barmash, Pamela. "Law and Narrative in Genesis." *ZABR* 16 (2010): 211–23.

Barmash, Pamela. *The Laws of Hammurabi*. Forthcoming.

Barmash, Pamela. "The Narrative Quandary: Cases of Law in Literature." *VT* 54 (2004): 1–16.

Becking, Bob, and Paul Sanders. "Plead for the Poor and the Widow: The Ostracon from Khirbet Qeiyafa as an Expression of Social Consciousness." *ZABR* 17 (2011): 133–48.
Bird, Phyllis A. "Images of Women in the Old Testament." In *Missing Persons and Mistaken Identities: Women and Gender in Ancient Israel*, 13–51. OBT. Minneapolis: Fortress, 1997.
Bird, Phyllis A. "Poor Man or Poor Woman? Gendering the Poor in Prophetic Texts." In *Missing Persons and Mistaken Identities: Women and Gender in Ancient Israel*, 67–78. OBT. Minneapolis: Fortress, 1997.
Bird, Phyllis A. "'To Play the Harlot': An Inquiry into an Old Testament Metaphor." In *Missing Persons and Mistaken Identities: Women and Gender in Ancient Israel*, 219–36. OBT. Minneapolis: Fortress, 1997.
Boer, Roland. *The Sacred Economy of Ancient Israel*. Library of Ancient Israel. Louisville: Westminster John Knox, 2015.
Burrows, Millar. *The Basis of Israelite Marriage*. AOS 15. New Haven: American Oriental Society, 1940.
Chapman, Cynthia R. *The House of the Mother: The Social Roles of Maternal Kin in Biblical Hebrew Narrative and Poetry*. AYBRL. New Haven: Yale University Press, 2016.
Chirichigno, Gregory C. *Debt Slavery in Israel and the Ancient Near East*. JSOTSup 141. Sheffield: JSOT Press, 1993.
Driver, S. R. *The Book of Genesis*. London: Methuen, 1904.
Edenburg, Cynthia. "Ideology and Social Context of the Deuteronomic Women's Sex Laws." *JBL* 128 (2009): 43–60.
Esler, Philip F. *Babatha's Orchard: The Yadin Papyri and an Ancient Jewish Family Tale Retold*. Oxford: Oxford University Press, 2017.
Fishbane, Michael. *Biblical Interpretation in Ancient Israel*. Oxford: Clarendon, 1985.
Freedman, Mordechai Akiva. *Jewish Marriage in Palestine: A Cairo Geniza Study*. TelAviv and New York: The Jewish Theological Seminary of America, 1980.
Frymer-Kensky, Tikva. "Virginity in the Bible." In *Gender and Law in the Hebrew Bible and the Ancient Near East*, edited by Victor H. Matthews, Bernard M. Levinson, and Tikva Frymer-Kensky, 79–96. JSOTSup 262. Sheffield: Sheffield Academic, 1999.
Greengus, Samuel. "The Old Babylonian Marriage Contract." *JAOS* 89 (1969): 505–32.
Jackson, Bernard M. "The 'Institutions' of Marriage and Divorce in the Hebrew Bible." *JSS* 56 (2011): 221–51.
Jackson, Bernard M. *Wisdom-Laws: A Study of the Mishpatim of Exodus 21:1–22:16*. Oxford: Oxford University Press, 2006.
Japhet, Sara. "The Relationship between the Legal Corpora in the Pentateuch in Light of the Manumission Laws." In *Studies in Bible 1986*, 63–89. ScrHier 31. Jerusalem: Magnes, 1986.
Kalluveettil, Paul. *Declaration and Covenant: A Comprehensive Review of Covenant Formulary from the Old Testament and the Ancient Near East*. AnBib 88. Rome: Biblical Institute, 1982.
Kessler, Rainer. "Die Sklavin als Ehefrau: Zur Stellen der 'ĀMĀH." *VT* 52 (2002): 501–12.
Koschaker, Paul. *Rechtsvergleichende Studien zur Gesetzgebung Hammurapis Königs von Babylon*. Leipzig: Veit, 1917.
Levine, Etan. "On Exodus 21,10 '*Onah* and Biblical Marriage." *ZABR* 5 (1999): 133–64.

Levinson, Bernard M. "The Manumission of Hermeneutics: The Slave Laws of the Pentateuch as a Challenge to Contemporary Pentateuchal Theory." In *Congress Volume Leiden 2004*, edited by André Lemaire, 281–324. VTSup 109. Leiden: Brill, 2006.

Mendelsohn, I. "The Conditional Sale into Slavery of Free-Born Daughters in Nuzi and the Law of Ex. 21: 7-11." *JAOS* 55 (1935): 190–5.

Meyers, Carol. *Rediscovering Eve: Ancient Israelite Women in Context*. Oxford: Oxford University Press, 2012.

Meyers, Carol. "Women: Biblical Period." *EncJud* 21: 156–61.

Pardes, Ilana. *Countertraditions in the Bible: A Feminist Approach*. Cambridge: Harvard University Press, 1992.

Paul, Shalom M. "Exod. 21:10: A Threefold Maintenance Clause." *JNES* 28 (1969): 48–51.

Paul, Shalom M. *Studies in the Book of the Covenant in Light of Cuneiform and Biblical Law*. VTSup 18. Leiden: Brill, 1970.

Phillips, Anthony. "The Laws of Slavery: Exodus 21.2-11." *JSOT* 30 (1984): 51–66.

Porten, Bezalel. *The Elephantine Papyri in English: Three Millennia of Cross-Cultural Continuity and Change*. 2nd ed. Atlanta: SBL Press, 2011.

Porten, Bezalel, and Ada Yardeni, *Textbook of Aramaic Documents from Ancient Egypt*. Jerusalem: Magnes, 1989.

Postgate, Nicholas. *Fifty Neo-Assyrian Legal Documents*. Warminster: Aris & Phillips, 1976.

Pressler, Carolyn. "Wives and Daughters, Bond and Free: Views of Women in the Slave Laws of Exodus 21.2-11." In *Gender and Law in the Hebrew Bible and the Ancient Near East*, edited by Victor H. Matthews, Bernard M. Levinson, and Tikva Frymer-Kensky, 147–72. JSOTSup 262. Sheffield: Sheffield Academic, 1999.

Rad, Gerhard von. *Deuteronomy*. OTL. Philadelphia: Westminster, 1966.

Radner, Karen. *Die neuassyrischen Privatrechtsurkunden als Quell für Mensch und Umwelt*. SAAS 6. Helsinki: The Neo-Assyrian Text Corpus Project, 1997.

Roth, Martha T. *Babylonian Marriage Agreements: 7th–3rd centuries B.C.* AOAT 222. Kevelaer: Butzon & Bercker; Neukirchen-Vluyn: Neukirchener Verlag, 1989.

Stol, Martin. *Women in the Ancient Near East*. Translated by Helen Richardson and Mervyn Richardson. Berlin: de Gruyter, 2016.

Toeg, A. "Does Deuteronomy XXIV, 1-4 Incorporate a General Law on Divorce?" *Dine-Israel* 2 (1970): v–xxiv.

Van Seters, John. *A Law Book for the Diaspora: Revision in the Study of the Covenant Code*. New York: Oxford University Press, 2003.

Wagenaar, Jan A. "The Annulment of a 'Purchase' Marriage in Exod 21, 7-11." *ZABR* 10 (2004): 219–31.

Weinfeld, Moshe. *Deuteronomy and the Deuteronomic School*. Winona Lake: Eisenbrauns, 1992.

Westbrook, Raymond. "The Female Slave." In *Gender and Law in the Hebrew Bible and the Ancient Near East*, edited by Victor H. Matthews, Bernard M. Levinson, and Tikva Frymer-Kensky, 214–38. JSOTSup 262. Sheffield: Sheffield Academic, 1999.

Westbrook, Raymond. *Old Babylonian Marriage Law*. AfO Beiheft 23. Horn, Austria: Berger & Söhne, 1988.

Wunsch, Cornelia. *Urkunden zum Ehe-, Vermögens- und Erbrecht aus verschiedenen neubabylonischen Archiven*. Babylonische Archive 2. Dresden: ISLET, 2003.

Yadin, Yigael, Jonas C. Greenfield, and Ada Yardeni. "Babatha's Ketubba." *IEJ* 44 (1994): 75–99.
Yadin, Yigael, Jonas C. Greenfield, Ada Yardeni, and Baruch A. Levine. *The Documents from the Bar Kokhba Period in the Cave of Letters: Hebrew, Aramaic and Nabatean Papyri*. Jerusalem: Israel Exploration Society, 2002.
Zakovitch, Yair. "The Woman's Rights in the Biblical Law of Divorce." *JLA* 4 (1981): 28–46.

3

Rachel's Betrothal Contract and the Origins of Contract Law[*]

F. Rachel Magdalene

The great majority of legal historians have argued that the origins of modern British and American contract law can be found in Rome when its law of contracts became more fully established, possibly during the time of the early republic or even significantly later. Such historians, joined by scholars in the world of biblical studies, have maintained that there existed no oral, informal contracts that could be legally enforced in the ancient world before the Roman period.[1] According to this view, contracts

---

[*] This essay found its genesis in an Introduction to Hebrew Bible class many years ago now. Thus, many able hands were required to bring it to its current state. Foremost among them were Dr. Kent Harold Richards, Mr. Robert G. Buller, and Dr. Raymond Westbrook. I also owe a debt of gratitude to Dr. Tamara Eskenazi, Dr. Gregory A. Robbins, Dr. Samuel Greengus, Dr. Bernard M. Levinson, Dr. Judith Romney Wegner, Dr. David L. Peterson, Ms. Judith R. Heller, and Dr. Judith Streit for their careful reading of and valuable suggestions for this essay, and to the participants over the years of the Biblical Law Section of the Society of Biblical Literature, to whom I presented an earlier draft of this work. All errors of both commission and omission are, of course, mine. Some of the scholarly literature addressed in this study is older, but it is necessary to treat it carefully because it set the interpretive tone for how the issues I am dealing with have come to be understood in subsequent scholarship.

1. For those uninitiated into the vocabulary and principles of modern contract law, I would suggest Arthur L. Corbin, *Corbin on Contracts* (St. Paul: West, 1952); John D. Calamari and Joseph M. Perillo, *The Law of Contracts*, 3rd ed. (St. Paul: West, 1987); and Samuel Williston, *A Treatise on the Law of Contracts*, 2nd ed., 9 vols. (New York: Baker, Voorhis, 1936–38). On the formality or informality of a contract, Corbin explains: "A formal contract is one, the legal operation of which is dependent upon the form in which it is made, the mode of expression, and not upon

as we know them—contracts that are enforceable due to a bargained-for exchange of valuable consideration and that also involve the exchange of promises—did not exist in previous periods of antiquity.[2] This essay argues, however, that oral, binding, enforceable, informal contracts can indeed be found in the ancient world before the rise of Rome.

The present chapter offers an examination of the betrothal contract[3] between Laban and Jacob for Rachel recorded in the biblical text, at

the sufficiency of the consideration that is given in return for it. In such a case the formalities of writing or the execution determine the validity of the contract rather than the elements of assent and consideration [which are the determining factors of an informal contract]" (*Corbin on Contracts*, §5; cf. Williston, *A Treatise on the Law of Contracts*, §§12, 17–21, 205–21). Formal contracts usually include, in the modern world, contracts under seal, the recognizance, and the negotiable instruments and letters of credit (Calamari and Perillo, *The Law of Contracts*, §§1.9).

2. Consideration is that which creates a mutuality of obligation sufficient to find a contract (for example, I promise to sell you my car for $2000 / I promise to buy your car for $2000). See Corbin, *Corbin on Contracts*, §§109–70; Calamari and Perillo, *The Law of Contracts*, §§4.1–5.20; and Williston, *A Treatise on the Law of Contracts*, §§99–137A.

3. Raymond Westbrook points out that in examining the contracts surrounding the acts of betrothal and marriage, it is important to distinguish between marriage, marriage contracts, and betrothal contracts (*Old Babylonian Marriage Law*, AfO Beiheft 23 [Horn, Austria: Berger & Söhne, 1988], 31–2). With regard to distinguishing marriage and betrothal contracts, Westbrook states: "If, however, there is a lapse of time between conclusion of the marriage contract and the act of marriage (or inchoate marriage), this will constitute a period of betrothal, and the contract therefore may be more properly called a betrothal contract" (ibid., 32). The term marriage contract ought to be reserved for executed marriage contracts, rather than for executory contracts based on a promise to give the bride in marriage at some future date. Technically, then, the primary contract under examination here is a betrothal contract. For some of the more traditional views on the law and custom of marriage in ancient Israel, see Millar Burrows, *The Basis of Israelite Marriage*, AOS 15 (New Haven: American Oriental Society, 1940); and Ephraim Neufeld, *Ancient Hebrew Marriage Laws* (London: Longmans, Green, 1944). See also Leo G. Perdue et al., *Families in Ancient Israel*, The Family, Religion, and Culture (Louisville: Westminster John Knox, 1997); Etan Levine, *Marital Relations in Ancient Judaism*, BZABR 10 (Wiesbaden: Harrassowitz, 2009); and T. M. Lemos, *Marriage Gifts and Social Change in Ancient Palestine 1200 BCE to 200 CE* (Cambridge: Cambridge University Press, 2010). For discussion regarding possible background information provided by other ancient Near Eastern marriage laws and customs, see John Van Seters, "Jacob's Marriages and Ancient Near East Customs: A Reexamination," *HTR* 62 (1969): 377–95; Cyrus H. Gordon, "The Story of Jacob and Laban in Light of the Nuzi Tablets," *BASOR* 66 (1936–37): 25–7; and Bruce Wells, "First Wives Club: Divorce, Demotion, and the Fate of Leah in Genesis 29," *Maarav* 18 (2011): 101–29.

Gen. 29:14-30.⁴ I maintain that within this literary unit of the Hebrew Bible stands a contract narrative that reflects an extensive process of contract development and maturation. It discloses a request for bid, an offer, an acceptance, and a partial exchange of consideration, and then it continues on to deal with matters of potential breach, suit for enforcement, and settlement. At the center of this narrative lies an oral, informal contract that relies for its legal effect, not upon formal execution language or rites, but instead upon the exchange of legally valid consideration, much in the way that such modern contracts operate. Other texts have similar characteristics. Thus, there is to be found within the book of Genesis a genre that should be distinguished from other types of known contract chronicles.

I will argue in the course of this essay that we must rethink outdated assumptions regarding the origins of contract law that have colored our thinking about the subject for over 130 years. Legal systems do not necessarily evolve in the way that we have accepted. I maintain, instead, that the legal systems of the ancient world were far more developed than we have previously thought and that we owe a far greater debt to them than we have ever acknowledged. A corollary of this argument is that contract narratives such as the one in Genesis 29 can also reveal important aspects

---

4. A survey of just a few scholars shows the range of opinion on how to identify the boundaries of the relevant textual unit. The possibilities include: 29:14b-30 (Ephraim A. Speiser, *Genesis: A New Translation with Introduction and Commentary*, AB 1 [New York: Doubleday, 1964], 224–7); 29:15-30 (Gerhard von Rad, *Genesis: A Commentary*, 2nd ed. [Philadelphia: Westminster, 1972], 289–92; Stephen K. Sherwood, *"Had God Not Been on My Side": An Examination of the Narrative Technique of the Story of Jacob and Laban, Genesis 29,1–32,2* [Frankfurt am Main: Peter Lang, 1990], 75–9); 29:13-30 (Sharon P. Jeansonne, *The Women of Genesis: From Sarah to Potiphar's Wife* [Minneapolis: Fortress, 1990], 71–4); 29:15-28a (Robert Davidson, *Genesis 12–50*, CBC [Cambridge: Cambridge University Press, 1979], 152–5); 29:1-30 (Michael Fishbane, "Composition and Structure in the Jacob Cycle," *JJS* 26 [1975]: 30–1; Nahum M. Sarna, *Genesis: The Traditional Hebrew Text with the New JPS Translation* [Philadelphia: Jewish Publication Society, 1989], 201–6; and Claus Westermann, *Genesis 12–36: A Commentary* [Minneapolis: Augsburg, 1981], 461–8). For a more complex source-critical assessment, cf. Reinhard G. Kratz, *The Composition of the Narrative Books of the Old Testament*, trans. J. Bowden (New York: T&T Clark, 2005), 266, 296 n. 26, and 323 n. 21. Sherwood offers an excellent summary of the major issues in the dispute (*Examination of the Narrative Technique*, 75–9). My own view is that the unit begins at v. 14. From the point of view of the legal analysis, however, the unit might begin either at v. 14 or v. 15 because there is an imminent significant shift in the legal status of Jacob within Laban's household at both of those points. While there is a time shift at 14b, the legal transactions in vv. 14a and 15 seem tied and, therefore, appropriately held together.

of the relationship between law and marriage, sexual relations, and gender. It is the latter issues that occupy the focus of the negotiations and the consideration that is at stake in a narrative like this. Thus, a detailed look at contract procedure and a willingness to forgo assumptions about the primitive nature of law at this time and in this place should allow us to see how certain aspects of sexuality were handled by the legal system underlying the narrative.

In furtherance of my overall argument, I will examine first the history of the scholarship on the question of ancient contract law, elucidating many of the principles of the traditional evolutionary theory of contract development. I will then do a form-critical analysis of the relevant biblical text. In my efforts to draw out its legal significance, I will be using research methods taken from two very different worlds, that of law and legal history and that of biblical criticism. This might put some readers at a disadvantage because they are not familiar with both areas of scholarship. I will, therefore, attempt, through my notes, to assist those who are unversed in one field or the other. With this, I turn to a further word about method.

Mixing Methodologies

For those who spend their lives in the world of biblical and ancient Near Eastern studies, it can seem a strange undertaking to utilize the techniques, vocabularies, and principles of modern law and legal history in the exploration of biblical texts. It is not often done. Moreover, the Bible is not a well-studied document among contemporary legal historians. Consequently, a project such as this one can seem a bit foreign to both camps, and red flags can fly in great number. Yet, I maintain that it is a valuable exercise in furtherance of both legal and biblical scholarship.

While I will be utilizing some more modern legal concepts in the exploration of an ancient society, I do not want to suggest that ancient Israelites thought in modern contract categories. They did not. Hans J. Boecker warns against identifying modern ideas with ancient facts in an uncritical manner.[5] He further advises that the correspondence between modern and ancient legal terms, practices, and categories must always be demonstrated, not presumed. Yet, while the ancients did not think in modern terms, we do; thus, modern categories are, at a minimum, a useful way for us to enter into a more refined discourse concerning the

---

5. Hans J. Boecker, *Law and the Administration of Justice in the Old Testament and Ancient East*, trans. Jeremy Moiser (Minneapolis: Augsburg, 1980), 16–18.

problem of contract development in the ancient Near East. Just as we have brought the modern scholarly vocabularies, techniques, and principles of history, literature, comparative studies, sociology, and anthropology to bear on biblical texts, and, in so doing, have discovered more of the profound complexity and beauty of ancient life, it is equally important to bring modern legal concepts to bear on our discussions of biblical law. If our prior experience with new methodologies has any meaning, then to avoid this conversation for fear of misunderstanding our forebears is to assure that we will only partially understand them. While we must remain cognizant of the difficulties that can arise when we irresponsibly or overbroadly apply the methods, data, and theories of modern social scientific approaches, including a legal approach, to refuse to explore what a legal method might reveal in an investigation of biblical law would be a scholarly tragedy. The field has begun to recognize this and bring modern legal concepts to bear on the conversation. For example, we can see such usage in the work of the late Raymond Westbrook and that of Geoffrey P. Miller.[6] Consequently, this paper will follow suit and utilize the vocabulary of modern legal analysis in order to better explicate some basic principles of biblical contract law.

Finally, in following this path, I make another assumption that I should state clearly. I am most interested in understanding something of the realities of the legal system of ancient Israel and in other parts of the ancient Near East. In my analysis, I accept the form-critical and sociological premise that the literary genres of the Hebrew Bible are intimately connected to the social realities of the ancient world from which they came.[7] I believe that the social world of the text reflects something of

---

6. See, e.g., Raymond Westbrook, *Property and the Family in Biblical Law*, JSOTSup 113 (Sheffield: Sheffield Academic, 1991), 24–35; Westbrook, "The Character of Ancient Near Eastern Law," in *A History of Ancient Near Eastern Law*, ed. Raymond Westbrook, 2 vols., HdO 72 (Leiden: Brill, 2003), 1:1–90; and Geoffrey P. Miller, "Contracts of Genesis," *Journal of Legal Studies* 22 (1993): 15–45. See also the work of German legal historians concerning the doctrine, "Prinzip der notwendigen Entgeltlichkeit (principle of the need for consideration)," which describes the ancient legal rule whereby the ownership of a thing does not pass entirely to a new owner until the counter-consideration has been received by the original owner (discussed by Westbrook, *Property and Family in Biblical Law*, 26–8, esp. 27 n. 1).

7. With respect to form criticism, Erhard Gerstenberger put it best: there is an "intimate connection between the formal structures [of the text] and life settings" ("Psalms," in *Old Testament Form Criticism*, ed. John H. Hayes [San Antonio: Trinity University Press, 1974], 223). For a more general discussion of the method, see Gene M. Tucker, *Form Criticism of the Old Testament*, Guides to Biblical Scholarship (Philadelphia: Fortress, 1971). With respect to the application of social-scientific

the social world behind the text. A detailed discussion of this point is, however, beyond the scope of this study. Let us, then, investigate the history and state of scholarship on ancient contract law.

The Scholarship on Ancient Contract Law

In exploring the question of ancient contract law, the primary question before us must be the fundamental one: What is a contract? According to William L. Burdick:

> An obligation arises from contract when two or more persons enter into an agreement that is enforceable at law. The word contract (*contractus*) means, literally, a drawing together, and its juridical significance is a mutual agreement of the parties concerned.... However, even though there is an agreement there is not, necessarily, a contract. The fact that the parties agreed to do or not to do a certain thing did not always give rise to an obligation, even though they intended to create an obligation. There must be some legal cause or reason whereby the agreement becomes a contract, something that makes the agreement a legal bond or tie (*vinculum juris*).[8]

methods to biblical literature and the dialogue between the newer forms of literary criticism and social-scientific methods, see Norman K. Gottwald, *The Hebrew Bible: A Socio-Literary Introduction* (Philadelphia: Fortress, 1985), 20–34. Miller states concerning the social setting of the contractual material embedded in the stories of Genesis that many of the stories "served the important social function of embodying and culturally transmitting rules of customary law" ("Contracts of Genesis," 17, although I disagree with many of his particular findings).

8. William L. Burdick, *The Principles of Roman Law and Their Relation to Modern Law* (Holmes Beach: Gaunt & Sons, 1989), 431; see also Corbin, *Corbin on Contracts*, §2. For a discussion of the difficulty of finding a precise definition of a contract, see ibid., §3; and Calamari and Perillo, *The Law of Contracts*, §1.1. Corbin, in particular, notes additional confusion concerning the term because of its multiple usage: "A study of its common usage will show that the term 'contract' has been named to denote three different kinds of things in various combinations: (1) a series of operative acts of the parties expressing their assent...; (2) a physical document executed by the parties as an operative fact in itself and as lasting evidence of their having performed other necessary acts expressing their intentions; [and] (3) the legal relation of right in one party and duty in the other" (*Corbin on Contracts*, §3). Samuel Greengus indicates that the term for contract could have a multiplicity of referents even in antiquity. In discussing an Old Babylonian contract (PBS 7 90), he states: "The tablet is again referred to as *kanik riksāti* šināti 'the document of (i.e. recording) that agreement'; here, the term *riksātum* cannot refer to the document but only to the agreement or contract recorded therein" ("The Old Babylonian Marriage Contract," *JAOS* 89 [1969]: 509).

Some notion of contract exists in every culture whose polity organizes around a unit other than the clan, and even exists in some clan structures as well. As Henry Sumner Maine observed: "Neither Ancient Law nor any other source of evidence discloses to us a society entirely destitute of the conception of Contract."[9] For almost a thousand years, legal philosophers have been pondering why it is that legal systems recognize and enforce private agreements.[10] Though many questions remain unanswered, we do know that contracts are essential if a culture is to move into a polity that is not clan-based. Maine asserted:

> The movement of the progressive [sic][11] societies has been uniform in one respect. Through all its course it has been distinguished by the gradual dissolution of family dependency, and the growth of individual obligations in its place. The Individual is steadily substituted for the Family, as the unit of which civil laws take account. The advance has been accomplished at varying rates of celerity, and there are societies not absolutely stationary in which the collages of the ancient organisation can only be perceived by careful study of the phenomena they present. But, whatever its pace, the change has not been subject to reaction or recoil, and apparent retardations will be found to have been occasioned through the absorption of archaic ideas and customs from some entirely foreign source. Nor is it difficult to see what is the tie between man and man [sic][12] which replaces by degrees those forms of reciprocity in rights and duties which have their origin in the Family. It is Contract.[13]

---

9. Henry Sumner Maine, *Ancient Law* (London: John Murray, 1920 [1861]), 326.

10. See, e.g., Hugo Grotius, *Grotius on the Rights of War and Peace: An Abridged Translation*, ed. and trans. William Whewell (Cambridge: Cambridge University Press, 1953), II.11–12; and Immanuel Kant, *The Philosophy of Law: An Exposition of the Fundamental Principles of Jurisprudence as the Science of Right*, trans. W. Hastie (Clifton: A. M. Kelly, 1974), §§18–21. For further bibliography on the issue, see Calamari and Perillo, *The Law of Contracts*, §1.4 n. 23.

11. I wish to note here that many of the scholars whose works I will discuss utilize words such as "primitive" and "immature" to describe ancient or agriculturally based peoples, and use words such as "progressive," "mature," or "advanced" to describe modern or industrially based peoples. I think such word choices reflect Western industrial biases which can lead us astray. I will not, however, annotate every instance of such usage.

12. I also acknowledge the non-inclusive language of many of the scholars upon whom I rely. Again, I will not correct every instance of such.

13. Maine, *Ancient Law*, 172. Westbrook challenges even this notion that in "primitive" law, "law [only] exist[ed] between families, clans or tribes, not between individuals" ("What is the Covenant Code?" in *Theory and Method in Biblical and Cuneiform Law: Revision, Interpolation, and Development*, ed. Bernard M. Levinson, JSOTSup 181 [Sheffield: Sheffield Academic, 1994], 20).

Yet, I do not want to suggest here that I accept the evolutionary concept of the development of contract law as set forth by Maine. Let us look more closely at his thesis and that of his followers.

Maine argues that the ancient contract was "rudimentary" and required the presence of a solemn ceremony:

> At first, nothing is seen like the interposition of law to compel the performance of a promise. That which the law arms with its sanctions is not a promise, but a promise accompanied with a solemn ceremonial. Not only are the formalities of equal importance with the promise itself, but they are, if anything, of greater importance; for the delicate analysis which mature jurisprudence applies to the condition of mind under which a particular verbal assent is given appears, in ancient law, to be transferred to the words and gestures of the accompanying performance.... The transmutation of this ancient view into the familiar notion of a Contract is plainly seen in the history of jurisprudence.[14]

With respect to Roman law, he postulates a long developmental period by which the recognition factors for a contract shift from ceremony to formalized writing:

> First one or two steps in the ceremonial are dispensed with; then the others are simplified or permitted to be neglected on certain conditions; lastly, a few specific contracts are separated from the rest and allowed to be entered into without form, the selected contracts being those on which the activity and energy of social intercourse depend. Slowly, but most distinctly, the mental engagement isolates itself amid the technicalities, and gradually becomes the sole ingredient on which the interest of the jurisconsult is concentrated. Such a mental engagement, signified through external acts, the Romans called a Pact or Convention; and when the Convention has once been conceived as the nucleus of a Contract, it soon becomes the tendency of advancing jurisprudence to break away the external shell of form and ceremony. Forms are thenceforward only retained so far as they are guarantees of authenticity, and securities for caution and deliberation. The idea of a Contract is fully developed, or, to employ the Roman phrase, Contacts are absorbed in Pacts.[15]

Ancient Law first appeared in 1861.[16] Yet, scholars have continued, for the most part, to accept that the process of contract development is as

---

14. Maine, *Ancient Law*, 327.
15. Ibid., 327–8.
16. For an interesting study, placing Maine in his legal, historical, and philosophical context, see R. C. J. Cocks, *Sir Henry Maine: A Study in Victorian Jurisprudence* (Cambridge: Cambridge University Press, 1988).

Maine suggested, finding a significant turning point in the Roman period. For example, in 1907, Pol Collinet maintained that "most of the known forms, real and consensual, of contract are not prehistoric, nor even protohistoric, but are known to be of later date,—at Rome, specifically about the seventh century. This is true of sale (as a contract), letting, mandate, partnership, deposit, etc."[17] Burdick followed this view in 1938.[18] Even as late as 1988, we find discussions concerning the development of the recognition factors related to binding contracts that clearly represent the traditional position; Meir Malul offers a concise summary of the state of such thinking:

> Legal historians tend to view the development of the validation of contract along three consecutive stages of "real contract," "verbal contract," and "consensual contract." The first stage is characterized by what may be called symbolic ceremonialism, the employment of various acts and formal ceremonies as a means of concluding an agreement. The second stage consists of the recitation and declaration of specific words and formulae. The difference between the first two stages is not rigid, and scholars usually refer to the mingling of the performed act with the spoken word in legal ceremonies. In the third stage the contract is characterized by an element of consensus between the parties which by itself rendered the agreement valid and binding with writing used only to crystallize the specifics of the agreement. In the modern world, with the widespread use of the written contract, writing serves as the major proof of validation and thus has become the foremost instrument of validation. Historians of the law have long observed that the element of symbolic ceremonialism was widespread in immature law systems.[19]

Malul was relying on work written primarily between 1918 and 1953.[20] A. S. Diamond, writing in 1971, asserted that "in the law of the Late Codes, in England, Rome, Babylonia and Assyria, in India and China, in

---

17. Pol Collinet, "Sponsio and Primitive Contract," in *Evolution of Law: Primitive and Ancient Legal Institutions*, vol. 2 of *Evolution of Law: Select Readings on the Origin and Development of Legal Institutions*, ed. Albert Kocourek and John H. Wigmore, 3 vols. (Boston: Little, Brown, 1915), 514. 18.

18. Burdick, *The Principles of Roman Law*, 432–3.

19. Meir Malul, *Studies in Mesopotamian Legal Symbolism*, AOAT 221 (Kevelaer: Butzon & Bercker; Neukirchen-Vluyn: Neukirchener, 1988), 2–3.

20. Including Rudolf Huebner, *A History of Germanic Private Law*, Continental Legal History Series 4 (Boston: Little, Brown, 1918); Bernhard Rehefeldt, "Begriff und Wesen der Rechtssymbolik," *Studium Generale* 6 (1953): 288–95; Claudius Freiherr von Schwerin, "Rechtssymbole," *Reallexikon der germanischen Altertumskunde* 3:469–79; William Segal, *The Quest for Law* (New York: Alfred A. Knopf,

Hebrew and Islamic law, we must still talk not of contract but of transactions, that is to say transfers. The history of primitive contract is the history of primitive commerce, and the progress is small till the close of the primitive era."[21] He agrees with the common view that formalizing rites or language, or the presence of witnesses, were required to give legal effect to any transaction.[22] He expounds:

> We have seen enough to realize that there has been a large-scale development in this branch of law, and there are now a good many types of transactions, but there is not yet nearly enough of this in Babylon, Rome, England or elsewhere, to call for a general theory of contract: that, for example, a contract is made by an offer and an acceptance in the same terms, or that it must be carried out, or a breach compensated by the amount of the loss incurred. It is not that these peoples do not think that a promise should be performed, but that at this stage commerce does not proceed on that basis: no one relies on a mere agreement on both sides to do something in the future, and consequently no one can be damaged by a failure to carry it out. Law does not pretend to compensate where there is no loss, and there are few, if any, cases where the loss to the plaintiff is tried and estimated.[23]

Alan Watson agrees, stating that even highly formalized consensual contracts were a later development—"a great invention of Rome"[24]—possibly in the middle of the third century BCE.[25]

Thus, it is apparent that much of legal scholarship maintains that it took a great deal of time to move from ceremonial recognition factors to those accomplished by means of a written instrument with formalizing language, the presence of witnesses, or both—and then on to the recognition of a meeting of the minds in a bargained-for exchange of

---

1941); Segal, *Men of Law* (New York: Macmillan, 1947); R. Thurnwald, "Vertrag," *Reallexikon der Vorgeschichte* 14:135–42; and David M. Walker, "Formalities," in *The Oxford Companion to Law* (Oxford: Clarendon, 1980), 482.

21. A. S. Diamond, *Primitive Law: Past and Present* (London: Methuen, 1971), 379.

22. Ibid., 382–8.

23. Ibid., 387.

24. Alan Watson, "The Notion of Equivalence of Contractual Obligation and Classical Roman Partnership," in *Legal Origins and Legal Change* (London: Hambledon, 1991), 239.

25. Alan Watson, "The Origins of Consensual Sale: A Hypothesis," in *Legal Origins and Legal Change* (London: Hambledon, 1991), 165–74. Daube, however, dates the origin of the consensual sale to approximately 199 BCE (*Forms of Roman Legislation* [Oxford: Clarendon, 1956], 91–7).

valid consideration.²⁶ The claim is that, while there is evidence of oral or written, formal transactions (and, according to some, contracts) in the ancient world, there is no evidence of oral, informal contracts.

I argue, however, that evidence from the ancient Near East offers us an opportunity to rethink this position. In spite of the words of Diamond, scholars of the ancient Near East have long asserted that the many peoples of the ancient Near East participated in contract formation and had some mechanism of enforcement. Westbrook maintains: "The very earliest records [those extending back to the early third millennium]...already reveal a highly organized legal system, whose courts have full coercive power and whose individuals have the capacity to make contracts."²⁷

The presence of oral, formal contracts, those real or verbal contracts in the traditional evolutionary scheme, is strongly attested in the ancient Near East. Several scholars argue persuasively that contracts in the ancient Near East were usually made orally.²⁸ Such oral agreements were, indeed, typically formalized through the use of ceremonial rites or particularized speech acts.²⁹ Samuel Greengus writes:

> Our evidence indicates that the Old Babylonian marriage contract was an unwritten agreement. It is interesting to note that in the study of archaic legal systems, scholars have observed that unwritten agreements are usually formalized by mean of symbolic rites, or by *verba solemnia*, or by a combination of these elements.³⁰

---

26. There is a long-standing debate on the degree to which one should look at subjective as opposed to objective criteria when ascertaining whether a meeting of the minds has occurred. The objective criteria seem to still hold sway over contract law in Common Law systems (those of Britain and America). Thus, under our system, there must be some evidence of the formation of the contract to find a contract. Yet, that evidence need not be in writing. For bibliography on this issue, see Calamari and Perillo, *Law of Contracts*, §2.2.

27. Westbrook, "What is the Covenant Code?" 20.

28. Greengus, "Babylonian Marriage Contract," 512–13; Jonathan Paradise, "Marriage Contracts of Free Persons at Nuzi," *JCS* 39 (1987): 3–7; and Martha T. Roth, *Babylonian Marriage Agreements 7th–3rd Centuries B.C.*, AOAT 222 (Kevelaer: Butzon & Bercker; Neukirchen-Vluyn: Neukirchener, 1989), 26–8; cf. Neufeld, *Ancient Hebrew Marriage Laws*, 89–90, 94–112.

29. It is Tucker's position that all the contract forms of the ancient Near East have a "long, complicated and formalized oral ceremony" behind them ("Contracts in the Old Testament: A Form Critical Investigation" [PhD diss., Yale University, 1963], 3).

30. Greengus, "Old Babylonian Marriage Contract," 514.

Martha T. Roth similarly states, with respect to Neo-Babylonian contracts, "Marriage agreements normally were concluded orally, probably before witnesses, and perhaps were accompanied by ceremonies or rites of which we remain ignorant."[31] Jonathan Paradise arrives at a similar conclusion in his analysis of Nuzi marriage contracts.[32] The importance of legally symbolic acts in the formalization of oral contracts in the ancient Near East, including Israel, cannot be underestimated.[33]

As Roth asserts, the presence of witnesses as part of the formalization process of oral contracts is also attested, including within the biblical material. For instance, we find a story chronicling the formalization of an oral contract within Ruth 4. Here, Boaz requests transfer of the right of redemption from the nearest kinsman to himself before the elders at the gate. According to Gene M. Tucker, the formula that signifies such formalization is the address and response, "You are witnesses.... We are witnesses." He submits that these and similar formulae, involving a reference to witnesses, indicate that the Israelite law court, which was composed of the elders and/or people at the gate, had the power to formalize oral contracts.[34]

We find another example of an oral agreement solemnized by witnesses in Gen. 23:3-16, where Abraham acquires the cave of Machpelah for a burial place. Westbrook, in challenging the position of several commentators, namely, that the background of this narrative is to be found in certain Hittite business documents, argues that the narrative has greater affinity with Neo-Babylonian dialogue documents, even though a written document is not referenced in the story.[35] He notes the following:

31. Roth, *Babylonian Marriage Agreements*, 28.
32. Paradise, "Marriage Contracts of Free Persons at Nuzi," 3–6.
33. For two significant studies on symbolic acts, see Malul, *Studies in Mesopotamian Legal Symbolism*; and Åke Viberg, *Symbols of Law: A Contextual Analysis of the Legal Symbolic Acts in the Old Testament*, ConBOT 34 (Stockholm: Almqvist & Wiksell, 1992).
34. Tucker, "Contract in the Old Testament," 42–3; see also Hans J. Boecker, *Redeformen des Rechtslebens im Alten Testament*, 2nd ed., WMANT 14 (Neukirchen-Vluyn: Neukirchener Verlag, 1970), 160–2. Note Josh. 24:22, which attests to the witness formula in a different context.
35. Westbrook, *Property and Family in Biblical Law*, 24–35. For the view favoring a Hittite background, see Manfred R. Lehmann, "Abraham's Purchase of Machpelah and Hittite Law," *BASOR* 129 (1953): 17. For those who also point to a Neo-Babylonian background, see J. J. Rabinowitz, "Neo-Babylonian Legal Documents and Jewish Law," *JJP* 13 (1961): 131; Herbert P. H. Petschow, "Die neubabylonische Zwiegesprächsurkunde und Genesis 23," *JCS* 19 (1965): 103–20; and Gene M. Tucker, "The Legal Background of Genesis 23," *JBL* 85 (1966): 77–84.

A more direct parallel from the formal point of view has been suggested by several scholars in the "dialogue documents" of the neo-Babylonian period. This contract, as its name implies, described an interchange between buyer and seller.... It is not to be expected that the narrative form of Genesis 23, with the additional complexities of the situation, will conform to the tight juristic dialogue document; at most one might expect some similarity in structure and perhaps in certain terms and phrases. (Thus the absence of date, seal or scribe and only the vague mention of all those who came in at the gate of the city as witnesses.).... If one takes Ephron's statement of the price in v. 15 as an "offer," then the abrupt change from direct speech in Abraham's "acceptance" in v. 16, followed by the payment formula and clause stating transfer of the property (vv. 17-18), results in a remarkable affinity with the structure of a "dialogue document." The whole account of the purchase in Genesis 23, in spite of its detail, contains no mention of a written document (cf. Jer. 23:8-15), but describes the legally material steps as the dialogue document does.[36]

Westbrook advocates that what we have here is the description of the formulation and terms of an oral, formal contract lodged within a complex narrative. Even though some of the specific characteristics of a written legal document will be lost in a narrative concerning the formation of an oral contract, we can still see some of the important legal attributes of the contract.

In the above discussion, references have been made to the many attestations of formal, written contracts from the ancient Near East. The next step in the evolutionary chain, as described by Malul, is clearly present in this ancient world. First, there are numerous references to an international treaty or to a covenant in biblical and other ancient Near East materials.[37]

---

36. Westbrook, *Property and Family in Biblical Law*, 30–2.

37. See George E. Mendenhall, *Law and Covenant in Israel and the Ancient Near East* (Pittsburgh: Biblical Colloquium, 1955); Dennis J. McCarthy, *Treaty and Covenant: A Study in Form in the Ancient Oriental Documents and in the Old Testament*, AnBib 21 (Rome: Biblical Institute, 1963); Moshe Weinfeld, "The Covenant of Grant in the Old Testament and the Ancient Near East," *JAOS* 90 (1970): 184–203; Delbert R. Hillers, *Covenant: History of a Biblical Idea* (Baltimore: Johns Hopkins University Press, 1969); Ernest W. Nicholson, *God and His People: Covenant Theology in the Old Testament* (Oxford: Clarendon, 1986); Simo Parpola and Kazuko Watanabe, *Neo-Assyrian Treaties and Loyalty Oaths*, SAA 2 (Helsinki: Helsinki University Press, 1988); Christoph Koch, *Vertrag, Treueid und Bund: Studien zur Rezeption des altorientalischen Vertragsrechts im Deuteronomium und zur Ausbildung der Bundestheologie im Alten Testament*, BZAW 383 (Berlin: de Gruyter, 2008); and Kenneth A. Kitchen and Paul J. N. Lawrence, *Treaty, Law and Covenant in the Ancient Near East*, 3 vols. (Wiesbaden: Harrassowitz, 2012).

One can see the contractual elements in treaty stipulations.[38] Non-political, formal, written contracts between private parties have also been unearthed in great number. The societies of the Sumerians, Babylonians, Assyrians, and Egyptians, as well as those on the periphery of these areas, have all provided many examples of such contracts.[39] Unfortunately, we have virtually no examples of written contracts found in the area of ancient Israel.[40] The Hebrew Bible does, however, make reference to these types of contracts, but the references tend to be incomplete. Often the negotiation process is described in detail, but few phrases from the actual contract are provided. Furthermore, the contract may only be referenced, while its negotiation process and terms remain unrecorded. One illustration of this latter situation is the purchase of the field at Anathoth by Jeremiah: "I signed the deed, sealed it, got witnesses, and weighed the money on scales" (Jer. 32:10). Here, we find neither the language of an executory contract for land nor of the deed itself. Isaiah 8:1-2 also mentions a witnessed document: "Then the Lord said to me, 'Take a large tablet and write upon it in common characters, "Belonging to

---

38. The differences between covenants/treaties and private contracts are discussed at length by Tucker ("Covenant Form and Contract Forms," *VT* 15 [1965]: 500–503). It is, however, not clear that one should exclude the former from the larger category of agreements which one could label "contracts." While covenants rely upon a conditional self-curse and contracts use other means to effectuate the legal bond, both contracts and covenants entail the exchange of promises (even if one such promise be nothing more than loyalty) that can be enforced through some type of sanction. Westbrook asserts that treaties are a form of contract: "In the domestic legal systems of the ancient Near East, a contract between heads of household would bind their respective households. It is no accident that *rikiltu*, the term for 'contract' in Akkadian, the international lingua franca of the Amarna age, was used without discrimination for international treaties. A treaty between kings was simply a contract that would bind their 'households' in the same way.... [T]reaties were contracts on the domestic model, but gained their international character from two factors: the position of the contracting parties on the hierarchical scale, and their being purely within divine jurisdiction" ("International Law in the Amarna Age," in *Amarna Diplomacy: The Beginning of International Relations*, ed. Raymond Cohen and Raymond Westbrook [Baltimore: Johns Hopkins University Press, 1999], 36–7).

39. One has only to consult the different sections in Raymond Westbrook, ed., *A History of Ancient Near Eastern Law*, HdO 72 (Leiden: Brill, 2003) to see how thoroughly this is the case. Most chapters on the different regions and time periods have a full section (usually §7) devoted to contracts.

40. See Raymond Westbrook and Bruce Wells, *Everyday Law in Biblical Israel: An Introduction* (Louisville: Westminster John Knox, 2009), 15.

Mahershalal-hashbaz.'" And I got reliable witnesses, Uriah the priest and Zechariah the son of Jeberechiah, to attest for me." Moreover, 1 Macc. 14:43 contains the declaration that, when Simon became leader and high priest, "all contracts in the country should be written in his name...."[41] In this last example, however, we have no information concerning whether the contracts show the indices of formality, except possibly the language that contracts are to be "written in his name."

When it comes to marriage contracts more specifically, one may point to numerous written, formal examples from the ancient Near East, including those from Nuzi, Old Babylonian society, Neo-Babylonian society, and the Jewish colony at Elephantine.[42] Tobit 7:13 records a marriage contract, but we are not privy to its terms. The basic aspects of the contract negotiations are set forth in Tob. 7:9-12, but again the author provides precious few details. Here, too, we do not have sufficient detail to be absolutely certain that the contract is formal. Three times the text indicates that Sarah is to be given to Tobias as wife "in accordance with the decree in the book of Moses (v. 11; cf. the slightly altered versions in vv. 12 and 13)." This statement appears, however, to refer to Tobias's status as near kinsman rather than the formalities of marriage contracts.[43]

As Malul pointed out, the traditional schema maintains that in "the third stage of development the contract is characterized by an element of consensus between the parties which by itself rendered the agreement valid and binding with writing used only to crystallize the specifics of the agreement." I maintain that this sort of contract did indeed exist in the ancient world as well. Ancient Near Eastern scholars have long asserted that written contracts, when made, often simply codified a prior oral agreement. Mariano San Nicolò argued, in 1931, that many of the ancient

---

41. See further Tucker, "Contracts in the Old Testament," 42–5.

42. See, e.g., the discussion of marriage contracts in Paradise, "Marriage Contracts of Free Persons at Nuzi"; Westbrook, *Old Babylonian Marriage Law*; Roth, *Babylonian Marriage Agreements*; Cornelia Wunsch, *Urkunden zum Ehe-, Vermögens- und Erbrecht aus verschiedenen neubabylonischen Archiven*, BaAr 2 (Dresden: ISLET, 2003); and Alejandro Botta, *The Aramaic and Egyptian Legal Traditions at Elephantine: An Egyptological Approach*, LSTS 64 (New York: T&T Clark, 2009).

43. See, e.g., George W. E. Nickelsburg, "Tobit," *HBC*, 798–9. Commentators generally classify the bills of divorce mentioned at Isa. 50:1, Jer. 3:8, and Deut. 24:1, 3 as examples of written, formal contracts (see, e.g., Tucker, "Contacts in the Old Testament," 42). Yet, these are, of course, of quite a different nature from sale or marriage contracts, and they might not be contracts at all.

Mesopotamian written contracts were purely evidentiary.⁴⁴ The presence of the seals of parties and witnesses, which have often been found on the writings themselves or on their envelopes, do not necessarily reflect the formalization of the contract for the purpose of giving it legal effect, but rather are used to assist in any legal proceedings that might arise around the underlying oral contract.⁴⁵ Yet, often, the written records indicate that the underlying contract still found its legal force through the presence of formalizing acts or language. For example, Westbrook states in regard to the law of international diplomacy: "In contrast to modern law, treaties did not have to be in written form. They were frequently committed to writing, …but the legal core of a treaty was an oral agreement, of which the document was a record and of evidentiary value only. The legally binding element was the promissory oath sworn by the gods."⁴⁶ San Nicolò indicated that witnesses had to be present at the formation of the contract for it to have legal effect.⁴⁷ Moreover, in the passage discussed above, wherein Jeremiah purchases the field at Anathoth, we can note the process which was common in the ancient Near East for establishing a contract's evidentiary value: "I signed the deed, sealed it, got witnesses, and weighed the money on scales" (Jer. 32:10). But we do not have complete information about the formalization processes that any underlying oral contracts might have undergone. Greengus also agrees with the position that writings were not central to the contracts' formation, asserting, with respect to Old Babylonian marriage contracts, that any writing that occurred usually was a response to the need to have certain related matters, such as the bride-price, set forth in writing.⁴⁸ It is his view that the underlying oral agreement was already formalized by ceremonial acts or *verba solemnia*.⁴⁹ In the course of his argument, though, he collapses the marriage contract with the marriage itself, a move that Westbrook challenges.⁵⁰ Westbrook maintains that the *verba solemnia*, which Greengus suggests were part of the formalization of the marriage

---

44. Mariano San Nicolò, *Beiträge zur Rechtsgeschichte im Bereiche der keilschriftlichen Rechtsquellen* (Oslo: A. Aschehoug, 1931), 162–5.

45. Johannes Renger, "Legal Aspects of Sealing in Ancient Mesopotamia," in *Seals and Sealing in the Ancient Near East*, ed. McGuire Gibson and Robert D. Biggs, BMes 6 (Malibu: Undena, 1977), 75–6.

46. Tucker, "International Law in the Amarna Age," 21.

47. San Nicolò, *Beiträge*, 138. See also Renger, "Legal Aspects of Sealing," 79.

48. Greengus also asserts the purely evidentiary value of many of the written contracts of the ancient Near East ("Old Babylonian Marriage Contract," 519).

49. Ibid., 514.

50. Westbrook, *Old Babylonian Marriage Law*, 29–60, esp. 31–2, 48–50.

contract, were not actually a part of the contract but, instead, a part of the formation of the marriage itself.

Westbrook carefully distinguishes betrothal contracts, inchoate marriages, marriage contracts, and marriages in the Old Babylonian evidence. He reasons that a betrothal contract was an exchange of a promise to marry a woman in the future for the promise on the part of her parents to tender her hand in marriage at the later date.[51] The initiative for the contract usually lay with the groom, and the contract typically included a bride-price to be paid by the groom to the parents for relinquishment of their right to offer their daughter to another.[52] This contract was executory, it could be made orally or in writing, and damages could be had for breach. Once the bride-price had been paid, the bride and groom entered into an inchoate marriage that increased certain rights and duties between the parties.[53] For example, at this point, if the bride's family breached the contract, double the bride-price could be expected as damages.[54] A full marriage, at least in Old Babylonian society, required the following: (1) a contract, not merely informal negotiations with no legal significance as was asserted by Reuven Yaron;[55] (2) the consent of the parents, given through the actual tendering of the bride; and (3) a formality that seems to involve the drinking of beer, which attended a variety of contracts, but, in this case, accompanied the marriage itself.[56] The contract, while more than mere negotiations, did not need to be written, as was well established by Greengus. The marriage itself accomplished two things from a legal perspective. It served to "create the condition of marriage and to perform a principle obligation of the marriage [or betrothal] contract."[57] It is here that the contract and the marriage finally meet.[58] The marriage, according to Westbrook, was completed by either *in domum deductio*, whereby the bride was taken into the groom's domicile, or *copula carnalis*, consummation through sexual intercourse. In most instances, either act was

---

51. Ibid., 33, 48.
52. Ibid., 33, 60; see also 99–100. Pamela Barmash prefers to call the bride-price a "betrothal gift" (see the statement at n. 41 in "The Daughter Sold into Slavery and Marriage," Chapter 2 in this volume).
53. Westbrook, *Old Babylonian Marriage Law*, 30. Westbrook discriminates between the betrothal contract and the payment of the bride-price.
54. Ibid., 41–3.
55. Reuven Yaron, *The Laws of Eshnunna* (Jerusalem: Magnes, 1969), 110; cited by Westbrook, *Old Babylonian Marriage Law*, 29 n. 9.
56. Westbrook, *Old Babylonian Marriage Law*, 30–1.
57. Ibid., 32; cf. 48.
58. Ibid.

sufficient to exhibit that the groom had taken control of the bride sufficient for a finding of marriage.[59] It is only after marriage that all the rights and duties of the groom and bride fully accrue.[60] Marriage is not a contract right, but one of status, more in the nature of adoption than sale.[61]

The betrothal contract is a critical part of marriage in the ancient Near East. It can be oral. It is based on the exchange of mutual promises. This entices us to ponder a most critical question: can it also be informal? Might the underlying contract not have been required to have any formalizing ceremony, language, or witnesses to create its legal force as has been argued all these many years? In other words, might there have been contracts in the ancient Near East where the legal validity of such did not depend on the mode of expression, be it ceremonial rites, *verba solemnia*, or other formalizing acts, but rather upon the presence of two elements: (1) the manifestation of mutual assent to form a contract through an effective offer and acceptance; and (2) the exchange of legally sufficient consideration?[62] Westbrook never addresses this question. In seeking an answer, one first must ask: where would one look for information regarding an oral, informal contract? Certainly, any later writing would obscure the oral contract's informality due to its import as evidence. Consequently, we might best seek evidence of the existence of oral, informal contracts within the letters and literature at our disposal.[63] I submit that, because we can find the presence of oral, as well as written, formal contracts embedded in

---

59. Ibid., 50–3. The exception is the case where the groom's family chooses a young girl for eventual marriage to their son. In this situation, both elements would be required for a finding of marriage.

60. Ibid., 54.

61. Ibid., 60. For another overview of marriage in ancient Israel—one that defines marriage in more ambiguous terms—see the section, "Marriage and Divorce in the Hebrew Bible," in Barmash, "The Daughter Sold into Slavery and Marriage," Chapter 2 in this volume.

62. For more detailed discussions of the concepts of offer and acceptance in modern contract law, see generally Corbin, *Corbin on Contracts*, §§22–94; Calamari and Perillo, *The Law of Contracts*, §§2.1–10, 15–29; and Williston, *A Treatise on the Law of Contracts*, §§22–49, 94–8.

63. I acknowledge that Greengus rightly warns us: "literary sources may faithfully mirror the activities of life; …they may also contain invention and fantasy" ("Old Babylonian Marriage Contract," 517). He maintains that we should only accept such evidence to the extent that it "can be correlated with practices revealed in documents from daily life" (ibid.). Unfortunately, this is not always possible. Oral contracts that are not followed up with an evidentiary record, are, by nature, not set down in documents from daily life. We simply must turn to literature (and possibly letters) for confirmation of such. For further discussion of the issue, see Pamela Barmash, "The Narrative Quandary: Cases of Law in Literature," *VT* 54 (2004): 1–16.

the narratives of the Hebrew Bible, it is appropriate to test for the presence of oral, informal contracts within those same pages. Genesis 29:14-30 is where I propose to begin.

A Form-Critical Analysis of Genesis 29:14-30

Scholars only rarely consider Gen. 29:14-30 in terms of its contractual dimensions; furthermore, those who do tend to minimize them. Among those who ignore it are Georg Fohrer, Gerhard von Rad, Nahum M. Sarna, and Ephraim A. Speiser.[64] Those who acknowledge some business arrangement but are inclined to depreciate its import include Claus Westermann and George W. Coats.[65] Hans J. Boecker, Stephen K. Sherwood, and E. C. Stanton mention the contract as a contract but fail to discuss it.[66] Tucker acknowledges that this pericope has contractual elements of both one for hire and one for marriage but argues that "whatever expressions may have been used to signify agreement to the conditions of the marriage, the agreement would have to be solemnized formally."[67] Fortunately, David Daube gives serious attention to this provision as a contract. He maintains that it is an agreement for hire similar to that under Roman law, known as *locatio conductio operarum*.[68] Geoffrey P. Miller calls this both an employment agreement and a marriage contract, although his analysis focuses only upon the contractual aspects related to the marriage.[69] Westbrook, while never naming the contract a contract, implies it when he writes extensively on one of its terms, the dowry.[70] This range of views invites us to look closely at the pericope, first through a detailed analysis of its structure.

---

64. George Fohrer, *Introduction to the Old Testament* (London: SPCK, 1978), 71–3; von Rad, *Genesis: A Commentary*, 290–2; Sarna, *Genesis*, 201–6; and Speiser, *Genesis*, 225–7.

65. Westermann, *Genesis 12–36*, 466; and George W. Coats, *Genesis, with an Introduction to Narrative Literature*. Grand Rapids: Eerdmans, 1983.

66. Boecker, *Law and the Administration of Justice*, 109–10; Sherwood, *Examination of the Narrative Technique*, 81; and Elizabeth Cady Stanton, "Comments on Genesis: Genesis 29," in *A Feminist Companion to Genesis*, ed. Athalya Brenner, FCB 2 (Sheffield: Sheffield Academic, 1993), 296.

67. Tucker, "Contracts in the Old Testament," 137, 151–2.

68. David Daube, *Studies in Biblical Law* (Cambridge: Cambridge University Press, 1944), 17; although Watson submits that such a contract must involve an exchange of money ("The Prehistory of Contracts," 236).

69. Miller, "Contracts of Genesis," 15, 31–2.

70. Westbrook, *Property and Family in Biblical Law*, 145–56; cf. 149, where Westbrook acknowledges the existence of a marriage contract for Rebekah (Genesis 24).

I. Formation of kinship ties (14)
   A. Speech formula (14aα)
   B. Creation of kinship ties (14aβ)
   C. Recognition of status as co-heirs (14bα)
   D. Time notation (14bβ)
II. Disavowal of kinship ties and formation of contract (15-19)
   A. Disavowal of kinship ties and query to form contract (15)
      1. Speech formula (15aα)
      2. Speech (15aβ-15b)
         a. Rhetorical question disavowing kinship ties, suggesting need to form contract (15aβ^1)
         b. Rhetorical question inviting the making of an offer (15aβ^2)
         c. Request for specificity in offer (15b)
   B. Offer to make contract (16-18)
      1. Laban's legal consideration (16-17)
         a. Identification of daughters as consideration (16)
         b. Description of consideration through comparison (17)
      2. Jacob's legal consideration (18)
         a. Motivation for selection of the bargained-for exchange (18a)
         b. Speech formula (18bα)
         c. Speech: offer of bargained-for exchange of consideration (18bβ)
   C. Acceptance of offer—contract formed (19)
      1. Speech formula (19aα^1)
      2. Speech: acceptance (19aα^2-b)
         a. By acknowledgment of preference (19aα^2-β)
         b. By instruction to dwell permanently (19b)
III. Performance on contract (20-26)
   A. Report of Jacob's performance (20)
      1. Notation of performance with intent to receive bargain (20a)
      2. Effect of love on burden of performance (20b)
   B. Jacob's demand for Laban's performance (21)
      1. Speech formula (21aα^1)
      2. Speech (21aα^2-b)
         a. Demand to fulfill contract (21aα^2)
         b. Statement of intention to consummate marriage (21aβ)
         c. Basis of demand: report of performance (21b)
   C. Report of Laban's breach (22-25a)
      1. Performance initiated (22)
         a. Witnesses assembled (22a)
         b. Feast provided (22b)

        2. Breach: consideration switched (23a)
        3. Wrong marriage consummated (23b)
        4. Report of dowry item given for wrong marriage (24)
        5. Breach discovered (25a)
   IV. Conflict (25b-26)
        A. Accusation concerning breach (25b)
            1. Speech formula (25bα¹)
            2. Speech: accusation (25bα²-β)
                a. Rhetorical question imputing responsibility to Laban (25bα²)
                b. Rhetorical question identifying breach (25bβ¹)
                c. Formal accusation of breach (25bβ²)
        B. Defense against accusation of breach (26)
            1. Speech formula (26aα)
            2. Speech: defense offered (26aβ-b)
   V. Settlement (27-30)
        A. Offer of new contract (27)
            1. Suggestion to accept prior contract as satisfied; time of performance on new contract set (27a)
            2. Identification of new consideration of Laban (27bα)
            3. Bargained-for exchange; identification of Jacob's new consideration (27bβ)
        B. Acceptance shown by Jacob's partial performance (28a)
        C. Performance by Laban (28b-29)
            1. Consideration tendered (28b)
            2. Report of dowry item given for second marriage (29)
        D. Completion of performance by Jacob (30)
            1. Consummation of marriage (30aα)
            2. Comparison of two wives (30aβ)
            3. Completion of employment services (30b)

Let us explicate the above more fully.

In v. 14a, according to Daube and Yaron, Laban, after meeting Jacob and hearing his tale (v. 13), formally recognizes kinship ties with Jacob via the language, "Surely you are my bone and my flesh."[71] This speech creates a legal, familial relationship between the two men. The existence of this relationship is further supported and clarified by the language "and he dwelled with him a month" (v. 14b). Daube and Yaron argue that "to dwell together" is a technical term which would define Laban and Jacob as brothers or co-heirs; yet, the fact that Jacob stays with Laban indicates

---

71. David Daube and Reuven Yaron, "Jacob's Reception by Laban," *JSS* 1 (1956): 60–2.

some level of inequality.[72] Westbrook concurs, indicating that this is a "contractual partnership, an *adoptio in fratrem*, and not the natural partnership of undivided heirs."[73] Thus, he maintains: "Although the junior partner, Jacob can look forward to some share of the total estate."[74] One would expect that all would be well. Unfortunately, after the month runs, Laban repudiates the familial bond by stating, "Are you my kinsman?" (v. 15aβ) when one would expect him to say, "Are you not my kinsman?"[75] While Laban is already showing himself capable of reneging on his obligations, this is not a technical breach of the partnership contract pursuant to Westbrook's reasoning.[76] Still, this leaves Jacob in the lurch in terms of any inheritance. Laban, however, has a plan: he invites Jacob, through his rhetorical question, "Should you serve me for nothing?" (v. 15aβ2), to think about possible terms of a contract for hire. He continues, "Tell me what your wages should be" (v. 15b). This is, in modern parlance, a request for a bid, an invitation to make an offer,[77] with the second part of the communiqué demanding the requisite specificity. The fact that Laban makes a request for a bid rather than making the offer himself is consistent with the general practice, as disclosed by the dialogue documents of the ancient Near East, that the individual with the lower social standing and/or in need typically makes the offer while the person with the greater social standing accepts.[78] It is also consistent with the practice of expecting the groom to take the initiative in a betrothal contract as we found in Old Babylonian betrothal and marriage documents.

Jacob considers Laban's invitation. The narrator identifies (v. 16) and describes (v. 17) for us the possible consideration that Laban might decide to extend to Jacob, his daughters Leah and Rachel, and reports Jacob's preference for the younger (v. 18a). The consideration is made here with sufficient specificity to allow a contract to be struck. Now, Jacob is ready

72. Ibid., 61.
73. Westbrook, *Property and Family in Biblical Law*, 134.
74. Ibid.
75. Daube and Yaron, "Jacob's Reception by Laban," 61–2. The shift in status has received a great deal of attention from commentators generally. See, e.g., Sherwood, *Examination of the Narrative Technique*, 85–8; and J. P. Fokkelman, *Narrative Art in Genesis: Specimens of Stylistic and Structural Analysis*, 2nd ed., BibSem 12 (Eugene: Wipf & Stock, 2004), 126–7.
76. Westbrook, *Property and Family in Biblical Law*, 134.
77. See Corbin, *Corbin on Contracts*, §24; and Calamari and Perillo, *Law of Contracts* §2.6.
78. Westbrook, *Property and Family in Biblical Law*, 31, citing Petschow, "Die neubabylonische Zwiegesprächsurkunde," 117.

to make his offer: "I will serve you seven years for Rachel, your younger daughter" (v. 18bβ). This is not a "transaction" as Diamond might explain it. This is an offer to form an executory contract via the exchange of promises. One can hear the implicit promises in the offer: "I promise to work seven years for you, Laban, in exchange for your promise of your daughter's, Rachel's, hand in marriage seven years hence." With the offer on the table, Laban must make his move.

He accepts its terms (v. 19). It is unfortunate that the text does not include the language, "he agreed," which is often standard contractual acceptance language in the ancient Near East.[79] Yet, it does twice use the words, "I give." This language has its own significance. It constitutes a traditional acceptance within many of the written marriage contracts of the ancient Near East.[80] It is a curious acceptance, though, not in that it limits or changes the offer in any way, but, rather, in Laban's indirect acknowledgment that Jacob is not "an outsider." Laban once again says to Jacob, "Dwell with me." What are we to make of this? Is the partnership back on? We have to wait to discover our answer until separation occurs and matters are squared. It seems, in any case, that there has been an offer and an acceptance of the terms of an employment-betrothal contract.

One might still ask, however, is this really a contract? As Diamond declared: "It is not that these peoples do not think that a promise should be performed, but that at this stage commerce does not proceed on that basis: no one relies on a mere agreement on both sides to do something in the future, and consequently no one can be damaged by a failure to carry it out."[81] Thus, we must ask whether or not individuals are relying on the agreement. Will anyone be damaged by a failure to carry out the agreement? Is this even really about commerce? I would answer all those questions affirmatively. By his invitation to Jacob to dwell with him, Laban, at a minimum, invites Jacob to begin performance on the contract. In the exchange of promises, both parties put themselves at risk of a legal detriment, certainly. Yet, in staying, Jacob bears a still greater one. He offers his valuable labor in expectation that he will earn his bride. In v. 20, we learn that Jacob indeed relies on the promise. He serves for seven years. Even though the time passed quickly for him, it was due to his very great expectation of fulfillment (v. 20b) that he, in fact, served for those seven years. There is an oral, informal contract here. There is no indication in the text of any formalizing rites or language with regard to

---

79. Westbrook, *Property and Family in Biblical Law*, 32. See, e.g., Gen. 23:16.
80. Roth, *Babylonian Marriage Agreements*, 5.
81. See n. 23, above.

the original contract for marriage and hire. There is no indication of the presence of any witnesses to the exchange. We have a simple bargained-for exchange of promises, upon which one party relies and from which the other benefits. Jacob has tendered the bride-price, his long labor. We, too, await Laban's performance expectantly.

Moreover, this contract is very much about commerce. Most commentators have overly focused on the marital or familial side of the arrangement, hence ignoring the contract for hire.[82] What has not been said clearly to date is that this is the first agreement concerning employment that we have in the Hebrew Bible. We have noted real estate conveyances in Genesis 23. We have seen marriage negotiations at Gen. 24:34-61. We have not, however, heard of any prior employment arrangements. Some might suggest that the employment agreement first occurs when the flock allocations are negotiated in Gen. 30:28-34, but this is closer to a profit-sharing arrangement instituted after a substantial period of prior employment and is offered as an inducement to remain on the job.[83] In reality, an employment agreement first comes into play when Laban distances himself from Jacob, thus rendering such an agreement necessary. Furthermore, Laban does not open negotiations on the issue of a bride, as is the case in Gen. 24:31-61. Rather, the primary issue involves wages: "Tell me what your wages should be?" (v. 15b). It may be said that love and economics sit on opposite sides of this contract and this storyline. In the ancient world, however, where fertile wives were critical

---

82. Commentators have spent considerable effort on whether Jacob's servitude is that of an indentured servant or a slave working off a bridal debt (Davidson, *Genesis 12–50*, 153); whether it is a substitution whereby service takes the place of the bride-price and, if so, whether seven years was an appropriate length of time (August Dillmann, *Genesis*, 2 vols. [Edinburgh: T. & T. Clark, 1897], 2:237; Samuel R. Driver, *The Book of Genesis* [London: Methuen, 1907], 272; and Boecker, *Law and the Administration of Justice*, 109); or whether some form of adoption of Jacob by Laban has taken place, leaving Jacob as one in familial servitude (Westermann, *Genesis 12–36*, 466). While this work has important benefits, it also tends to keep the marriage aspects of the text in the fore to the detriment of the employment aspects (see Fokkelman, *Narrative Art in Genesis*, 126).

83. The text reads: "Jacob said to Laban, '…Give me my wives and my children for whom I have served you, and let me go; for you know the service which I have given you.' But Laban said to him, 'If you will allow me to say so, I have learned by divination that the LORD has blessed me because of you; name your wages, and I will give it'" (Gen 30:25-28). See also Miller, "Contracts of Genesis," 33–6. On Jacob and Laban's later confrontation regarding this contract, see J. J. Finkelstein, "An Old Babylonian Herding Contract and Genesis 31:38ff.," *JAOS* 88 (1968): 30–6.

to survival and economic prosperity, it may be better said that economics and economics balance this contract.[84] This is all about commerce. This is a contract.

Or, at least, Jacob thinks so. In v. 21, Jacob demands performance on the betrothal end of the contract from Laban: "Give me my wife for my days are fulfilled and let me go in to her." This is similar to the procedure known in Akkadian as, "claiming at the house of the father-in-law."[85] Jacob uses the critical language, "give me," to do so. He thereby makes his claim on the contract: he is the inchoate husband of Rachel and, as such, anticipates receiving her in marriage. He is fully entitled to make the demand upon Laban. Jacob indicates his intent to fulfill the obligations of the marriage through *copula carnalis*, since he is living, and may well remain, with his father-in-law. Jacob reminds Laban of his payment of the bride-price.

Laban seems to agree that the demand is reasonable, and initiates his performance by holding a wedding feast. He now brings in witnesses (v. 22a), and, presumably, if any additional ceremony needs to take place, he can accomplish that and thereby effectuate the formalization of the marriage during the ensuing feast (v. 22b). Yet, Laban breaches by switching brides (v. 23a), creating a failure in consideration, and giving a dowry gift to Leah (v. 24).[86] While commentators have suggested that all the elements are present for a valid marriage with Leah, that is not at all clear. For example, Miller states:

> The marriage story seems to endorse the proposition that Jacob's act of sleeping with Leah was sufficient to seal the marriage, even though he was misled as to the identity of his sexual partner. Thus, Laban complied with the terms of his contract with Jacob. It is significant that Jacob does not

---

84. On the economic status of women and their role in ancient Israelite society, see Carol L. Meyers, *Discovering Eve: Ancient Israelite Women in Context* (New York: Oxford University Press, 1988).

85. See Reuven Yaron, *Laws of Eshnunna*, 2nd ed. (Leiden: Brill, 1988), 191–5.

86. On the issue of the dowry and how it is implicated in the conflict around the separation of Jacob and Laban in Genesis 31, see Westbrook, *Property and Family in Biblical Law*, 142–64, esp. 145, 149–50, 156. It should also be noted that source critics have speculated that vv. 24 and 29, which narrate the gifts of the slaves to Leah and Rachel, respectively, are later insertions by P into a J text. See e.g., Westermann, *Genesis 12–36*, 467. The removal of these two verses for purposes of analysis in no way negatively impacts the finding of a contract in this pericope. Yet, Speiser, noting the similarity of these texts to the terms of a Nuzi marriage contract, wherein the bride receives a gift of a female slave upon marriage, suggests that they may not be later additions but, rather, insertions of older source material (*Genesis*, 227).

deny that Laban has fulfilled his contractual obligations, even though he has done so by trickery and in a way not consistent with the spirit of the original bargain.[87]

Quite to the contrary, however, there was no supporting betrothal contract for Leah, Laban did not act in good faith on the contract as drawn, and Jacob objects in the strongest of terms when he discovers that his bride is Leah (v. 25a).

The objection is not without legal significance. It is cast in words that form a legal accusation that would ordinarily initiate litigation in the ancient world. Jacob voices his protest with the formulaic imputation speech, "What is this that you have done to me?" (v. 25bα2), and then acknowledges that he served Laban for Rachel through posing a rhetorical question which plainly identifies the breach (v. 25bβ1).[88] The imputation speech is a more private accusation. Yet, Jacob is not finished with Laban. He then lodges his complaint publicly and formally, "So, why have you deceived me?" (v. 25bβ2).[89] Presumably, the witnesses to the wedding are still present to hear Jacob's complaint.[90] While such witnesses are not "at

---

87. Miller, "Contracts of Genesis," 31.

88. On the imputation speech (*Beschuldigungsrede*), see Boecker, *Redeformen des Rechtslebens*, 30; and Burke O. Long, *2 Kings*, FOTL 10 (Grand Rapids: Eerdmans, 1991), 302. See also Gen. 26:10. Here, we have a shortened form of the standard imputation speech (cf. Judg. 8:1; 2 Sam. 19:21; Neh. 13:17; Boecker, *Redeformen des Rechtslebens*, 26–9), which may well be a later development.

89. On the accusation formula, see Coats, *Genesis*, 320; Boecker, *Redeformen des Rechtslebens*, 42, 45 n. 1; and Long, *2 Kings*, 302. See also Josh. 9:22; 1 Sam. 19:17; 28:12.

90. There is some argument that v. 27 indicates the presence of witnesses who are involved in the dispute as a form of tribunal. The verse might be translated, "Fulfill the bridal week of this one, and *we will give* you this other one for the service that you will perform with me for yet another seven years." In this rendering, the verb is taken as a *qal* first person, plural cohortative. Numerous translations and commentators follow this view (e.g., NRSV, NIV, NJPS), as does Rashi (Abraham M. Silbermann, ed., *Pentateuch and Rashi's Commentary: Genesis*, trans. Morris Rosenbaum and Abraham M. Silbermann [London: Shapiro, Vallentine, 1946]). Hermann Gunkel also follows this view and states that the first-person plural pronoun refers to Laban and his kin (*Genesis übersetzt und erklärt*, 2nd ed. [Göttingen: Vandenhoeck & Ruprecht, 1902], 290). In a similar vein, Westermann designates them the "local people…[who] stand behind Laban" (*Genesis 12–36*, 468). Note that the Samaritan Pentateuch and the Septuagint have the first-person singular form, a reading accepted by almost no one, except the NJB. The other possibility is that the verb might be read as a *niphal* first person feminine singular, being used impersonally "with the object of the active construction still subordinated in the accusative, i.e., '*There shall be given* to you for

the gate," which would make it absolutely clear that they are sitting in judgment, the witnesses are available to give legal effect to the wedding. They may have an equal capacity to sit in judgment. Boecker indicates that there are instances when an assembly had legal authority without sitting at the gate.[91] It can happen when one of the parties proclaims, "Let them judge between the two of us," as in Gen. 31:37. It can happen when the individuals have taken an oath to abide by the decision of the group as in Jer. 42:5. We have neither event here. We do, however, see Laban defending himself by appealing to custom: "It is not done so in our area to give the younger before the firstborn" (v. 26). Is he asserting here a type of "illegal contract" defense?[92] Possibly. What is important to recognize, though, is that he does not simply dismiss the accusation. He responds to it, leading one to believe that he is taking the complaint seriously—so seriously, in fact, that he has another proposal to offer by way of resolution.

He offers Jacob yet another contract. If Jacob will accept the prior contract as satisfied by accepting the bride-week with Leah (v. 27a), Laban will offer the following bargained-for exchange: in one week's time, he will tender the hand of Rachel for yet another seven years of service (v. 27b).[93] Once again, we have an offer made for a betrothal contract with the exchange of promises, the consideration of which is clearly identified: seven years of service for the bride. This offer is not a bone thrown to an underdog who does not have the force of law behind him.[94] No, this is a most significant proposition. Laban is the one with the greater social standing. Laban is the father of the bride. It is not he who

the service'" (*GKC* §121a; cf. §121b). See further, Sherwood, *Examination of the Narrative Technique*, 126 n. 105.

91. Boecker, *Law and Administration*, 33–4.

92. In modern contract law, if performance on a contract constitutes an illegal act, it will not be enforced. If performance on a contract was legal at the time it was drawn up but becomes illegal in the intervening time, the contract is viewed as impossible to perform. Illegality and impossibility are legitimate defenses in a contract suit. See Corbin, *Corbin on Contracts*, §§1373–1540; Calamari and Perillo, *Law of Contracts*, §§22.2–9, 13–15.

93. Contesting the views of Miller that the groom has a general right to repudiate the bride during the week of festivities, "that sexual intercourse consummates the marriage for purposes of contracts for the purchase of a wife and that intercourse plus one week of nonrejection consummates the marriage for all purposes," and "that acceptance of goods by the buyer conclusively establishes performance by the seller" ("Contracts of Genesis," 32).

94. Contesting the more traditional position that Laban had the support of the witnesses behind him; see e.g., Westermann, *Genesis 12–36*, 468.

should be making such an offer; it is Jacob. The fact that Laban makes the offer indicates that he is no longer in the position of power. Jacob has won his case even without the decision of the people. Unfortunately, the situation is untenable. Jacob has served the seven years; Leah has been taken as bride. While monetary damages could be offered to restore Jacob's lost labor, Leah cannot be so easily restored to her former condition. The offer from Laban to give Rachel to Jacob, as well, seems the only appropriate solution. There is just one hitch. Jacob has to serve yet another seven years. It seems that the double indemnity for a breach of a betrothal contract on the part of the bride's family that we find in Old Babylonian marriage law does not hold here;[95] otherwise, Jacob would be able to walk away with two wives for the price of one.

Jacob accepts the terms of Laban's latest offer through his fulfillment of this bride-week with Leah, in partial performance on the contract (v. 28a).[96] The promise merges in the performance. Obligation and performance coalesce. The time has come for Laban once again to deliver, and he does so (v. 28b), finally! Moreover, Laban now gives a dowry gift to Rachel, equivalent to the one that he gave to Leah (v. 29). At long last, after much ado, Jacob takes Rachel as his bride and consummates the marriage through sexual relations (30aα). He then completes the terms of the contract by giving Laban yet another seven years of service (v. 30b).

One can see the fullness and sophistication of the contract development and maturation process at work within this unit. The structure suggests that Gen. 29:14-30 contains all the elements normally found in situations involving modern contracts. It is a superior description of the formation, partial performance, breach, suit for enforcement, settlement through renegotiation, and ultimate fulfillment of an oral, informal contract for marriage in exchange for services rendered. Upon the basis of this analysis, I submit that Gen. 29:14-30 contains an example of an ancient oral, informal contract. We should not ignore this in our discussions of this pericope. But more than that, we should not ignore this in our understanding of ancient contract law.

95. See n. 54, above.

96. In modern law, in the case of a breach, the aggrieved party may either enforce the contract or again enter negotiations to form another contract that is more likely to be fulfilled. In the latter case, however, a new contract will be found to exist only if new, distinctive, valuable consideration is given by the parties. See Corbin, *Corbin on Contracts*, §§171–92, 943–89; Williston, *Law of Contracts* §§130, 1288–1337A; and Calamari and Perillo, *Law of Contracts* §§5.14, 12.1–16.66. Acceptance of a contract through partial performance is also permissible under contemporary contract law. See Corbin, *Corbin on Contracts*, §63; and Williston, *Law of Contracts* §78A.

This pericope is not the only one within the Hebrew Bible that chronicles the development and maturation of an oral, informal contract. There are multiple attestations of such. For example, a detailed analysis would reveal similar chronicles in Gen. 24:31-61 (the negotiation by Abraham's servant with Laban and Bethuel for Rebekah's marriage to Isaac) and 30:25-34 (Jacob and Laban's profit-sharing arrangement). Hence, indications of the existence of oral, informal contracts can be found within the writings of ancient Israel. If we think of a contract only in terms of a piece of paper or a clay tablet, then Gen. 29:14-30 could not embody such a thing. If we hold preconceived notions that an ancient contract must be formalized, then we will never see what is before our eyes. Yet, the interaction recorded in Gen. 29:14-30 denotes that a series of operative acts occurred—an offer for the exchange of legally valid consideration was made and accepted—whereby the parties expressed their assent to the formation of a relationship that created reciprocal, legally enforceable rights and duties.[97] Moreover, the narrative records that the parties acted on the assumption that a contract of services in exchange for a bride was in effect. When the consideration of the contract was switched, a legal crisis arose that resulted in the institution of legal action. Settlement was had through the negotiation of yet another contract, which was, ultimately, performed upon properly. While the ancients did not use our vocabulary or categories to think about such things, the fact remains that what we have before us in this pericope is strikingly similar to our own world of contracts. Other biblical texts, while not as developed as the text here, reflect these points of similarity as well.

Finally, such oral, informal contracts are distinct from the chronicles of both the oral and written formal contracts of the Hebrew Bible. Consequently, it is no longer adequate to lump all contract chronicles together. As we have discovered in our survey of biblical references to contractual arrangements, the underlying contracts take varied forms both by way of structure and function. We need to become more precise in our discussions of biblical contract law if we hope to articulate the state of the art in ancient Israel. We need to sub-divide the genre. What we have here is an oral, informal contract chronicle.

Conclusions

Although modern contract law is not definitive in how it helps to explicate ancient contract law, it is a useful interpretive tool. When applied in combination with other traditional methodologies, new insights may be

---

97. Corbin, *Corbin on Contracts*, §3.

gleaned from familiar evidence. In the case at hand, both form criticism and legal terminology and categories were applied to the text. In so doing, we discovered that Gen. 29:14-30 and other texts are examples of an oral, informal contract chronicle. Such a piece of narrative describes with some particularity the formation and terms of an oral contract. This specific contract chronicle is based, not upon formalizing language or rites, or even the presence of witnesses, but, instead, upon an informal contract that is given legal effect due to a meeting of the minds, manifested through an offer and acceptance, to exchange valid and valuable consideration. The traditional theory of contract evolution is thereby undermined. The refinement that we see here in contract formation and maturation leads us to question the view that Rome is the home of the origins of the modern-day contract.

This analysis does not, however, lead us to question the role that women typically fulfilled in the arrangement of marriages in ancient Israel. The story of Jacob and Laban's agreement allows for virtually no role for Leah, Rachel, or their mother, and this does not appear to have been extraordinary in any way. As seen in this text, it was the groom that customarily approached the father of the woman whom he wanted to marry. We have no clear evidence that the wishes of the woman were consulted, and it is likely that they were not in most cases. Some evidence from other ancient Near Eastern societies suggests that mothers could negotiate on their daughters' behalf, but this would occur only if the father were deceased and there were no brothers available for this purpose. A widow could negotiate for herself, but other women almost never did. In an important sense, a daughter was viewed as a financial asset of her father's that had to be protected until a suitable offer was made. In the background of Laban's supposed concern about marrying off Leah before Rachel may have been the notion that Leah's financial value would be diminished if it appeared to other men that she had been passed over for Rachel by Jacob. Daughters were not merely a financial asset, but this aspect of their identity served to make them the object of the kinds of negotiations that we see in the story discussed above. They are passive observers and under the control of the men who negotiate over them and, in the end, decide their fate.[98]

For all that this study has attempted to accomplish, it is only a beginning. From a form-critical perspective, this essay focused more upon the subject and arrangement of one text. Other texts must be studied more carefully

---

98. See the discussion in M. L. Case, "The Inheritance Injunction of Numbers 36: Zelophehad's Daughters and the Intersection of Ancestral Land and Sex Regulation," Chapter 8 in this volume.

in a similar manner. Moreover, this text and others must be examined in order to identify, if possible, formal features of the text, including the presence of specific formulae, which would also serve to distinguish the particular contract chronicles from each other. Additionally, we must explore to what extent the various contract chronicles reflect different *Sitze im Leben*. We might well discover that the legal systems of the ancient world, particularly the ancient Near East, were far more intricate and sophisticated and impacted us far more than we ever imagined.

Bibliography

Barmash, Pamela. "The Narrative Quandary: Cases of Law in Literature." *VT* 54 (2004): 1–16.
Boecker, Hans J. *Law and the Administration of Justice in the Old Testament and Ancient East*. Translated by Jeremy Moiser. Minneapolis: Augsburg, 1980.
Boecker, Hans J. *Redeformen des Rechtslebens im Alten Testament*. 2nd ed. WMANT 14. Neukirchen-Vluyn: Neukirchener Verlag, 1970.
Botta, Alejandro. *The Aramaic and Egyptian Legal Traditions at Elephantine: An Egyptological Approach*. LSTS 64. New York: T&T Clark, 2009.
Burdick, William L. *The Principles of Roman Law and Their Relation to Modern Law*. Holmes Beach: Gaunt & Sons, 1989.
Burrows, Millar. *The Basis of Israelite Marriage*. AOS 15. New Haven: American Oriental Society, 1940.
Calamari, John D., and Joseph M. Perillo. *The Law of Contracts*. 3rd ed. St. Paul: West, 1987.
Coats, George W. *Genesis, with an Introduction to Narrative Literature*. Grand Rapids: Eerdmans, 1983.
Cocks, R. C. J. *Sir Henry Maine: A Study in Victorian Jurisprudence*. Cambridge: Cambridge University Press, 1988.
Collinet, Pol. "Sponsio and Primitive Contract." In *Evolution of Law: Primitive and Ancient Legal Institutions*. Volume 2 of *Evolution of Law: Select Readings on the Origin and Development of Legal Institutions*, edited by Albert Kocourek and John H. Wigmore, 512–17. Boston: Little, Brown, 1915.
Corbin, Arthur L. *Corbin on Contracts*. St. Paul: West, 1952.
Daube, David. *Forms of Roman Legislation*. Oxford: Clarendon, 1956.
Daube, David. *Studies in Biblical Law*. Cambridge: Cambridge University Press, 1944.
Daube, David, and Reuven Yaron. "Jacob's Reception by Laban." *JSS* 1 (1956): 60–2.
Davidson, Robert. *Genesis 12–50*. CBC. Cambridge: Cambridge University Press, 1979.
Diamond, A. S. *Primitive Law: Past and Present*. London: Methuen, 1971.
Dillmann, August. *Genesis*. 2 vols. Edinburgh: T. & T. Clark, 1897.
Driver, Samuel R. *The Book of Genesis*. London: Methuen, 1907.
Finkelstein, J. J. "An Old Babylonian Herding Contract and Genesis 31:38ff." *JAOS* 88 (1968): 30–6.
Fishbane, Michael. "Composition and Structure in the Jacob Cycle." *JJS* 26 (1975): 15–38.
Fohrer, George. *Introduction to the Old Testament*. London: SPCK, 1978.
Fokkelman, J. P. *Narrative Art in Genesis: Specimens of Stylistic and Structural Analysis*. 2nd ed. BibSem 12. Eugene: Wipf & Stock, 2004.

Gerstenberger, Erhard. "Psalms." In *Old Testament Form Criticism*, edited by John H. Hayes, 179–224. San Antonio: Trinity University Press, 1974.

Gordon, Cyrus H. "The Story of Jacob and Laban in Light of the Nuzi Tablets." *BASOR* 66 (1936–37): 25–7.

Gottwald, Norman K. *The Hebrew Bible: A Socio-Literary Introduction*. Philadelphia: Fortress, 1985.

Greengus, Samuel. "The Old Babylonian Marriage Contract." *JAOS* 89 (1969): 505–32.

Grotius, Hugo. *Grotius on the Rights of War and Peace: An Abridged Translation*. Edited and translated by William Whewell. Cambridge: Cambridge University Press, 1953.

Gunkel, Hermann. *Genesis übersetzt und erklärt*. 2nd ed. Göttingen: Vandenhoeck & Ruprecht, 1902.

Hillers, Delbert R. *Covenant: History of a Biblical Idea*. Baltimore: Johns Hopkins University Press, 1969.

Huebner, Rudolf. *A History of Germanic Private Law*. Continental Legal History Series 4. Boston: Little, Brown, 1918.

Jeansonne, Sharon P. *The Women of Genesis: From Sarah to Potiphar's Wife*. Minneapolis: Fortress, 1990.

Kant, Immanuel. *The Philosophy of Law: An Exposition of the Fundamental Principles of Jurisprudence as the Science of Right*. Translated by W. Hastie. Clifton: A. M. Kelly, 1974.

Kitchen, Kenneth A., and Paul J. N. Lawrence. *Treaty, Law and Covenant in the Ancient Near East*. 3 vols. Wiesbaden: Harrassowitz, 2012.

Koch, Christoph. *Vertrag, Treueid und Bund: Studien zur Rezeption des altorientalischen Vertragsrechts im Deuteronomium und zur Ausbildung der Bundestheologie im Alten Testament*. BZAW 383. Berlin: de Gruyter, 2008.

Kratz, Reinhard G. *The Composition of the Narrative Books of the Old Testament*. Translated by J. Bowden. New York: T&T Clark, 2005.

Lehmann, Manfred R. "Abraham's Purchase of Machpelah and Hittite Law." *BASOR* 129 (1953): 15–18.

Lemos, T. M. *Marriage Gifts and Social Change in Ancient Palestine 1200 BCE to 200 CE*. Cambridge: Cambridge University Press, 2010.

Levine, Etan. *Marital Relations in Ancient Judaism*. BZAR 10. Wiesbaden: Harrassowitz, 2009.

Long, Burke O. *2 Kings*. FOTL 10. Grand Rapids: Eerdmans, 1991.

Maine, Henry Sumner. *Ancient Law*. London: John Murray, 1920 (1861).

Malul, Meir. *Studies in Mesopotamian Legal Symbolism*. AOAT 221. Kevelaer: Butzon & Bercker; Neukirchen-Vluyn: Neukirchener, 1988.

McCarthy, Dennis J. *Treaty and Covenant: A Study in Form in the Ancient Oriental Documents and in the Old Testament*. AnBib 21. Rome: Biblical Institute, 1963.

Mendenhall, George E. *Law and Covenant in Israel and the Ancient Near East*. Pittsburgh: Biblical Colloquium, 1955.

Meyers, Carol L. *Discovering Eve: Ancient Israelite Women in Context*. New York: Oxford University Press, 1988.

Miller, Geoffrey P. "Contracts of Genesis." *Journal of Legal Studies* 22 (1993): 15–45.

Neufeld, Ephraim. *Ancient Hebrew Marriage Laws*. London: Longmans, Green, 1944.

Nicholson, Ernest W. *God and His People: Covenant Theology in the Old Testament*. Oxford: Clarendon, 1986.

Nickelsburg, George W. E. "Tobit." In *Harper's Bible Commentary*, edited by James L. Mays et al., 791–803. San Francisco: Harper & Row, 1988.

Paradise, Jonathan. "Marriage Contracts of Free Persons at Nuzi." *JCS* 39 (1987): 1–36.
Parpola, Simo, and Kazuko Watanabe. *Neo-Assyrian Treaties and Loyalty Oaths*. SAA 2. Helsinki: Helsinki University Press, 1988.
Perdue, Leo G., Joseph Blenkinsopp, John J. Collins, and Carol L. Meyers. *Families in Ancient Israel. The Family, Religion, and Culture*. Louisville: Westminster John Knox, 1997.
Petschow, Herbert P. H. "Die neubabylonische Zwiegesprächsurkunde und Genesis 23." *JCS* 19 (1965): 103–20.
Rabinowitz, J. J. "Neo-Babylonian Legal Documents and Jewish Law." *JJP* 13 (1961): 131–75.
Rad, Gerhard von. *Genesis: A Commentary*. 2nd ed. Philadelphia: Westminster, 1972.
Rehefeldt, Bernhard. "Begriff und Wesen der Rechtssymbolik." *Studium Generale* 6 (1953): 288–95.
Renger, Johannes. "Legal Aspects of Sealing in Ancient Mesopotamia." In *Seals and Sealing in the Ancient Near East*, edited by McGuire Gibson and Robert D. Biggs, 75–88. BMes 6. Malibu: Undena, 1977.
Roth, Martha T. *Babylonian Marriage Agreements 7th–3rd Centuries B.C.* AOAT 222. Kevelaer: Butzon & Bercker; Neukirchen-Vluyn: Neukirchener, 1989.
San Nicolò, Marian. *Beiträge zur Rechtsgeschichte im Bereiche der keilschriftlichen Rechtsquellen*. Oslo: A. Aschehoug, 1931.
Sarna, Nahum M. *Genesis: The Traditional Hebrew Text with the New JPS Translation*. Philadelphia: Jewish Publication Society of America, 1989.
Schwerin, Claudius Freiherr von. "Rechtssymbole." *Reallexikon der germanischen Altertumskunde* 3:469–79.
Segal, William. *Men of Law*. New York: Macmillan, 1947.
Segal, William. *The Quest for Law*. New York: Alfred A. Knopf, 1941.
Sherwood, Stephen K. *"Had God Not Been on My Side": An Examination of the Narrative Technique of the Story of Jacob and Laban, Genesis 29,1–32,2*. Frankfurt am Main: Peter Lang, 1990.
Silbermann, Abraham M., ed. *Pentateuch and Rashi's Commentary: Genesis*. Translated by Morris Rosenbaum and Abraham M. Silbermann. London: Shapiro, Vallentine, 1946.
Speiser, Ephraim A. *Genesis: A New Translation with Introduction and Commentary*. AB 1. New York: Doubleday, 1964.
Stanton, Elizabeth Cady. "Comments on Genesis: Genesis 29." In *A Feminist Companion to Genesis*, edited by Athalya Brenner, 296–7. FCB 2. Sheffield: Sheffield Academic, 1993.
Thurnwald, R. "Vertrag." *Reallexikon der Vorgeschichte* 14:135–42.
Tucker, Gene M. "Contracts in the Old Testament: A Form Critical Investigation." PhD diss., Yale University, 1963.
Tucker, Gene M. "Covenant Form and Contract Forms." *VT* 15 (1965): 500–503.
Tucker, Gene M. *Form Criticism of the Old Testament*. GBS. Philadelphia: Fortress, 1971.
Tucker, Gene M. "The Legal Background of Genesis 23." *JBL* 85 (1966): 77–84.
Van Seters, John. "Jacob's Marriages and Ancient Near East Customs: A Reexamination." *HTR* 62 (1969): 377–95.
Viberg, Åke. *Symbols of Law: A Contextual Analysis of the Legal Symbolic Acts in the Old Testament*. ConBOT 34. Stockholm: Almqvist & Wiksell, 1992.
Walker, David M. *The Oxford Companion to Law*. Oxford: Clarendon, 1980.

Watson, Alan. "The Notion of Equivalence of Contractual Obligation and Classical Roman Partnership." In *Legal Origins and Legal Change*, 239–50. London: Hambledon, 1991.

Watson, Alan. "The Origins of Consensual Sale: A Hypothesis." In *Legal Origins and Legal Change*, 165–74. London: Hambledon, 1991.

Weinfeld, Moshe. "The Covenant of Grant in the Old Testament and the Ancient Near East." *JAOS* 90 (1970): 184–203.

Wells, Bruce. "First Wives Club: Divorce, Demotion, and the Fate of Leah in Genesis 29." *Maarav* 18 (2011): 101–29.

Westbrook, Raymond. "The Character of Ancient Near Eastern Law." In *A History of Ancient Near Eastern Law*, edited by Raymond Westbrook, 1–90. 2 vols. HdO 72. Leiden: Brill, 2003.

Westbrook, Raymond, ed. *A History of Ancient Near Eastern Law*. HdO 72. Leiden: Brill, 2003.

Westbrook, Raymond. "International Law in the Amarna Age." In *Amarna Diplomacy: The Beginning of International Relations*, edited by Raymond Cohen and Raymond Westbrook, 28–41 and 239–42. Baltimore: Johns Hopkins University Press, 1999.

Westbrook, Raymond. *Old Babylonian Marriage Law*. AfO Beiheft 23. Horn, Austria: Berger & Söhne, 1988.

Westbrook, Raymond. *Property and the Family in Biblical Law*. JSOTSup 113. Sheffield: Sheffield Academic, 1991.

Westbrook, Raymond. "What is the Covenant Code?" In *Theory and Method in Biblical and Cuneiform Law: Revision, Interpolation, and Development*, edited by Bernard M. Levinson, 13–34. JSOTSup 181. Sheffield: Sheffield Academic, 1994.

Westbrook, Raymond, and Bruce Wells. *Everyday Law in Biblical Israel: An Introduction*. Louisville: Westminster John Knox, 2009.

Westermann, Claus. *Genesis 12–36: A Commentary*. Minneapolis: Augsburg, 1981.

Williston, Samuel. *A Treatise on the Law of Contracts*. 2nd ed. 9 vols. New York: Baker, Voorhis, 1936–38.

Wunsch, Cornelia. *Urkunden zum Ehe-, Vermögens- und Erbrecht aus verschiedenen neubabylonischen Archiven*. BaAr 2. Dresden: ISLET, 2003.

Yaron, Reuven. *The Laws of Eshnunna*. Jerusalem: Magnes, 1969.

Yaron, Reuven. *The Laws of Eshnunna*. 2nd ed. Leiden: Brill, 1988.

4

JUDAH, TAMAR, AND THE LAW OF LEVIRATE MARRIAGE

Eryl W. Davies

The story of Judah and Tamar in Genesis 38 has engaged the attention of numerous scholars for a variety of reasons. Its present location within the broader Joseph narrative of Genesis 37–50 has proved particularly perplexing, since it appears to be a digression with little connection either with what precedes or with what follows.[1] While debates continue

---

1. Cf. Gerhard von Rad, *Genesis: A Commentary*, trans. J. H. Marks, rev. ed. (London: SCM, 1972), 356–7; and George W. Coats, *Genesis, with an Introduction to Narrative Literature* (Grand Rapids: Eerdmans, 1983), 273. Other scholars, however, have argued that Genesis 38 is not entirely incongruous with the Joseph story in which it has been inserted, since certain structural and thematic elements connect it to the broader Joseph saga; see, e.g., Robert Alter, *The Art of Biblical Narrative* (New York: Basic Books, 1981), 3–22. For a discussion of the location of Genesis 38 in its present context, see Yairah Amit, "Narrative Analysis: Meaning, Context, and Origins of Genesis 38," in *Method Matters: Essays on the Interpretation of the Hebrew Bible in Honor of David L. Petersen*, ed. Joel M. LeMon and Kent Harold Richards (Atlanta: Society of Biblical Literature, 2009), 271–91 (esp. 279–83); Jonathan Kruschwitz, "The Type-Scene Connection between Genesis 38 and the Joseph Story," *JSOT* 36 (2012): 383–410; and Peter Bekins, "Tamar and Joseph in Genesis 38 and 39," *JSOT* 40 (2016): 375–97. As Judah Goldin reminds us, the present location of Genesis 38 was just as problematic for the midrashic-talmudic rabbis and the medieval commentators as it is for modern scholars ("The Youngest Son or Where Does Genesis 38 Belong," *JBL* 96 [1977]: 27–44 [esp. 27–9]).

about the composition, redaction, and literary features of the chapter,[2] the following discussion will focus on the legal background of the story and especially on its connection with the legislation concerning levirate marriage in Deut. 25:5-10.[3] The casuistic law of Deut. 25:5-10 states that "when brothers dwell together" and one brother dies childless, the surviving brother should marry the widow to provide the deceased with an heir. There are some similarities as well as differences between this law and the narrative of Genesis 38. The law appears to presuppose that there were only two brothers, one deceased and the other still alive, whereas Genesis 38 envisages a situation in which there are more surviving brothers and implies that the levirate obligation devolved on each of them in turn.[4] On the other hand, both the law and the narrative suggest that

---

2. For a source-critical and redactional discussion of Genesis 38, see J. A. Emerton, "Some Problems in Genesis XXXVIII," *VT* 25 (1975): 338–61; and for a discussion of the chapter's structure, see Martin O'Callaghan, "Structure and Meaning in Genesis 38: Judah and Tamar," *Proceedings of the Irish Biblical Association* 5 (1981): 72–88; and Anthony J. Lambe, "Genesis 38: Structure and Literary Design," in *The World of Genesis: Persons, Places, Perspectives*, ed. Phillip R. Davies and David J. A. Clines (Sheffield: Sheffield Academic, 1998), 102–20.

3. The custom of levirate marriage was widespread throughout the ancient world and appears to have been practised among the Hittites (cf. Paul Koschaker, "Zum Levirat nach hethitischem Recht," *RHA* 2 [1933]: 77–89; and O. R. Gurney, *The Hittites* [Harmondsworth: Penguin, 1952], 101–2), the Assyrians (cf. P. Cruveilhier, "Le lévirat chez les Hébreux et chez les Assyriens," *RB* 34 [1925]: 524–46; and Ephraim Neufeld, *Ancient Hebrew Marriage Laws* [London: Longmans, Green & Co., 1944], 51–2) and was possibly known also in Ugarit (cf. Matitiahu Tsevat, "Marriage and Monarchical Legitimacy in Ugarit and Israel," *JSS* 3 [1958]: 237–43). See, further, Millar Burrows, "The Ancient Oriental Background of Hebrew Levirate Marriage," *BASOR* 77 (1940): 2–15. For a discussion of the levirate institution as reflected in the Hebrew Bible, see Dvora E. Weisberg, *Levirate Marriage and the Family in Ancient Judaism* (Waltham: Brandeis University Press, 2009); Burrows, "Levirate Marriage in Israel," *JBL* 59 (1940): 23–33; Thomas Thompson and Dorothy Thompson, "Some Legal Problems in the Book of Ruth," *VT* 18 (1968): 79–99; Eryl W. Davies, "Inheritance Rights and the Hebrew Levirate Marriage," *VT* 31 (1981): 138–44, 257–68; and Donald A. Leggett, *The Levirate and Goel Institutions in the Old Testament with Special Attention to the Book of Ruth* (Cherry Hill: Mack, 1974). See, further, Steffan Mathias, "Reproducing Torah: Human and Divine Sexuality in the Book of Deuteronomy," Chapter 9 in this volume; and Mathias, *Paternity, Progeny, and Perpetuation: Creating Lives after Death in the Hebrew Bible* (London: Bloomsbury T&T Clark, forthcoming).

4. Genesis 38 gives the impression that the levirate requirements were imposed on the brothers in order of their seniority, an impression which might be corroborated by the Gospel accounts of the challenge of the Sadducees to Jesus concerning the case of

the primary aim of the institution was to provide a son for the childless widow. The points of similarity and difference between the two texts require further explication, and the discussion that follows will attempt to address three basic questions. First, did the levirate custom, even from earliest times, contemplate marriage between the brother-in-law and the widow? Second, was the levirate duty optional or obligatory? Finally, did the levirate obligation at one time extend to the widow's father-in-law? Each question will be considered in turn.

Did the Levirate Custom Contemplate Marriage between the Brother- in-Law and the Widow?

The narrative of Genesis 38 records that Judah gave his eldest son, Er, to Tamar as a wife. However, Er dies before Tamar could conceive a child, and so Judah instructs his second son, Onan, to "perform the duty of a brother-in-law to her," thus ensuring that she could have offspring (v. 8). But Onan fails to fulfill his fraternal responsibility, and since his refusal "was displeasing in the sight of the LORD," he is put to death (v. 10). Judah informs Tamar that he is unwilling to allow his third son, Shelah, to perform the levirate duty, claiming that he is too young, though the narrator reveals that his real reason was his fear that Shelah will die like his brothers (v. 11). The legal interest of the story hinges on Tamar's rights within the levirate custom. Clearly, she had the right to expect to conceive a child, but did she also have the right to expect marriage?

Some scholars have argued that, at least in early times, the sole purpose of the levirate was to raise up a son for the deceased brother and that, when this object had been accomplished, the obligation was regarded as having been fulfilled and the relationship would thereby have ceased.[5] George W. Coats, for example, on the basis of the narrative in Genesis 38,

---

a woman who had been widowed and was married to each of her deceased husband's six younger brothers in succession (cf. Mt. 22:25-27; Mk 12:20-22; Lk. 20:27-32). However, as Frederick E. Greenspahn has observed, the absence of such principles of seniority in Deuteronomy, and parallel provisions from other Near Eastern cultures, suggest that the sequence with which the brothers are mentioned in the Genesis and Deuteronomic texts "may be a literary feature rather than a legal requirement" (*When Brothers Dwell Together: The Preeminence of Younger Siblings in the Hebrew Bible* [Oxford: Oxford University Press, 1994], 52).

5. Cf. H. H. Rowley, "The Marriage of Ruth," in *The Servant of the Lord and Other Essays on the Old Testament*, rev. ed. (Oxford: Blackwell, 1965), 177 n. 3, who states that the "sole *raison d'être* of levirate marriage that appears in the Old Testament is the provision of an heir for the deceased."

has argued that marriage between the brother-in-law and the widow was not necessarily required by the levirate obligation, for the widow had the right to expect only conception of a child.[6] Coats concedes that a widow might seek marriage from her brother-in-law and that he, in turn, might be prepared to grant her request, but he was under no obligation to do so, and consequently she had the right only to have a child by him. Coats points out that Judah's command to Onan to go into his brother's wife (Gen. 38:8) does not mention marriage; his duty was merely to "perform the duty of a brother-in-law to her" (v. 8), which merely meant producing a male heir for the widow. In fact, the text makes clear that she remained the wife of the dead brother ("go in to your brother's wife," v. 8a). Moreover, when Judah himself later performed the levirate duty (albeit unwittingly), the question of marriage between him and Tamar did not arise. Indeed, Coats argues that this would seem to be specifically precluded by the narrative, for there is a suggestion that Judah had no further sexual relations with her ("he did not lie with her again," Gen. 38:26b). Coats's final point is based on an argument from silence: if it was normal for the widow to marry the brother-in-law, then it must be concluded that the narrative of Genesis 38 ends somewhat unsatisfactorily, since it fails to mention whose wife Tamar eventually became. Had she eventually been given in marriage to Judah's son, Shelah, this would surely have been mentioned, especially since Tamar was judged by Judah to be in the right. Thus, Coats concludes: "If one assumes that the levirate custom demands not only conception of a child but marriage of the widow, then the story has an unsatisfactory ending. Tamar remains a widow. But if one assumes that the levirate custom, at least at this stage in history, concerns only the widow's right to conceive a child, the ending fits."[7]

Despite these arguments, however, it is probable that the levirate duty, from the beginning, did normally involve a marriage between the widow and the brother of the deceased. It is true that the narrative of Genesis 38 does not mention marriage between Tamar and Onan, but it certainly does not preclude the possibility that such a marriage may have taken place. Moreover, it indicates that Tamar had decided to "play the harlot" precisely because Judah's youngest son, Shelah, had by then grown up but had still not been given to her "in marriage" (Gen. 38:14).[8] The fact

---

6. George W. Coats, "Widow's Rights: A Crux in the Structure of Genesis 38," *CBQ* 34 (1972): 461–6. Coats's argument has been accepted by Claus Westermann, *Genesis 37–50*, trans. J. J. Scullion (London: SPCK, 1987), 52, 56.

7. Coats, "Widow's Rights," 465–6.

8. For a detailed discussion of זנה, see Hilary Lipka, "The Offense, Its Consequences, and the Meaning of זנה in Leviticus 19:29," Chapter 6 in this volume.

that no marriage was mentioned between Tamar and Judah may be due to the unusual circumstances in which the levirate duty was performed. In any case, as Gerhard von Rad has observed, since the duty of the levirate probably extended beyond the brother-in-law (see below), Tamar may "well have reckoned with Judah's taking her in marriage."[9] Furthermore, other references to the levirate institution in the Hebrew Bible suggest that marriage was, indeed, contemplated between the widow and her brother-in-law. For example, it is clear from the provision of Deut. 25:5 that the brother of the deceased was urged to take the widow "in marriage" and perform the levirate duty. Moreover, the levirate obligation as depicted in the book of Ruth seems to involve the marriage of the widow.[10] In sending Ruth to Boaz, Naomi was probably seeking to arrange for a marriage based on Boaz's relationship as kinsman (Ruth 2:20), and Ruth's request to Boaz to "spread your skirt over your maidservant" (3:9) is usually interpreted by commentators as a request for marriage (cf. Ezek. 16:8).[11]

Was the Levirate Duty Optional or Obligatory?

It is clear from the law of Deut. 25:5-10 that the levirate custom was not regarded as binding in the strict sense, for the brother-in-law who refused to undertake the obligation suffered no punishment save that of the indignity of being exposed to public humiliation.[12] The widow might bring a

---

9. Cf. von Rad, *Genesis*, 359.

10. Although some scholars have questioned whether the book of Ruth provides evidence for the institution of levirate marriage, the balance of probability is that the book does, indeed, reflect the levirate custom as described in Deut. 25:5-10. See Eryl W. Davies, "Ruth IV 5 and the Duties of the Gō'ēl," *VT* 33 (1983): 231–4. Murray D. Gow (*The Book of Ruth: Its Structure, Theme and Purpose* [Leicester: Apollos, 1992], 143–82) provides a detailed discussion of the issue and concludes that the overall evidence of the book of Ruth "weighs heavily in favour of a leviratic interpretation" (ibid., 181). For a different perspective, cf. the extensive discussion in Edward Allen Jones III, *Reading Ruth in the Restoration Period: A Call for Inclusion* (London: Bloomsbury T & T Clark, 2016).

11. Cf. Leggett, *The Levirate*, 192–201; William McKane, "Ruth and Boaz," *TGUOS* 19 (1961–2): 37–8. Other scholars, however, have argued that Ruth's words in this context are merely an invitation to sexual relations and need not necessarily suggest marriage (so, e.g., D. R. G. Beattie, "Ruth III," *JSOT* 5 [1978]: 42–3; and Coats, "Widow's Rights," 465).

12. It is interesting to observe that the levirate custom mentioned in Hittite Laws §193 contains the clause *ul ḫaratar*, "no punishment"; these words, however, may be a later addition (cf. Koschaker, "Zum Levirat," 79).

reluctant brother-in-law before the elders of the town, and they, in turn, might persuade him to perform his duty; however, they had no authority to compel him to do so, and the brother-in-law was not even obliged to give a reason for his refusal. Indeed, the law even provided a ceremony by which the levir could formally renounce his obligation of providing the widow with a son.[13] While he would no doubt have incurred a measure of social opprobrium in doing so,[14] he would at least have been spared what may have been regarded by him as an onerous and unwelcome task.

While possible reasons for the brother-in-law's refusal to perform the levirate duty are not mentioned in the text, it is clear that he would have had nothing to gain and possibly a great deal to lose by providing his sister-in-law with an heir, for the child born of the union would inherit the property which he would otherwise have possessed, since the deceased's estate normally passed to the surviving brothers. The laws in ancient Israel concerning inheritance encountered in Num. 27:8-11 suggest that when a man died without leaving a son, the inheritance usually passed to the dead man's brother; thus, by performing the levirate duty and providing the widow with a son who would have prior claim to the inheritance of the deceased, the levir would clearly have been acting contrary to his own interests. As Dvora E. Weisberg notes, the brother-in-law would effectively have been "disinherited through his own actions."[15] Admittedly, the levir

---

13. The ceremony consisted of the removal of the brother-in-law's shoe, and although the significance of this symbolic action is not explained, it is usually understood to symbolize his renunciation of the right to take the widow as his wife. For a discussion of this symbolic action, see Calum M. Carmichael, "A Ceremonial Crux: Removing a Man's Sandal as a Female Gesture of Contempt," *JBL* 96 (1977): 321–36. Some scholars have noted parallels between the custom recorded in Deut. 25:9 and similar practices mentioned in texts from Nuzi; see, e.g., Ernest R. Lacheman, "Note on Ruth 4: 7–8," *JBL* 56 (1937): 53–6; and Ephraim A. Speiser, "Of Shoes and Shekels," *BASOR* 77 (1940): 15–20.

14. Lyn M. Bechtel ("Shame as a Sanction of Social Control in Biblical Israel: Judicial, Political, and Social Shaming," *JSOT* 49 [1991]: 57–61) regards the widow's action of removing the shoe of the brother-in-law and spitting in his face as a particularly good example of a shaming sanction within the judicial system which indicated the importance of public humiliation and public opinion as a means of social control. As if to add to his humiliation, the brother-in-law and his family would henceforth be publicly labelled by the community as "the house of him whose sandal was pulled off" (Deut. 25:10).

15. Weisberg, *Levirate Marriage*, 27. A similar point is made by David Daube, who comments, "The temptation to leave the widow alone and thus remain in sole possession must be considerable, and the indications are that many succumbed" ("The

who performed the obligation may well have enjoyed certain economic advantages, for in addition to his own land he would now become the administrator of his dead brother's estate and would presumably have had full enjoyment of its produce. Besides, there was always the possibility that no son would be born of the levirate union and that the land would consequently have remained permanently in the possession of the brother-in-law.[16] Nevertheless, in many cases the brother-in-law would probably have concluded that any advantages which might accrue from performing the levirate duty would have been offset by the disadvantages, and in such cases he may well have sought to evade his obligation.

Some scholars have argued that the narrative in Genesis 38 confirms the non-obligatory nature of the levirate custom, for here, too, the duty was not regarded as strictly binding. Judah's refusal to give his third son to Tamar because he was too young to perform the obligation would seem to indicate that the duty could be disregarded. Moreover, the fact that Tamar was forced to resort to disguising herself as a harlot to induce Judah to perform his duty would seem to confirm that performance of the duty was optional; had the levirate been binding, she would simply have sought the support of public opinion to compel him to fulfill his obligation.[17]

However, these arguments favoring the non-obligatory nature of the levirate in Genesis 38 are open to question. In the first place, Judah's refusal to give Shelah to Tamar need not be taken to imply that the levirate custom was not compulsory, since the reason he gave—that Shelah was too young—may have been perfectly valid and legitimate. In this regard it is interesting to observe that Middle Assyrian Laws §43 (which deals with a case where a woman's husband dies or suddenly disappears) stipulates that the father can give his daughter-in-law one of his remaining sons on the condition that the son was at least ten years old. That Judah still refused to give Shelah to Tamar even after he had grown up simply indicates his fear that Shelah, too, would be slain, in which case the hereditary line would be threatened with complete destruction. It was due

---

Culture of Deuteronomy," *Orita* 3 [1969]: 35). For a discussion of the relevance of Numbers 27 and 36 for the issue of inheritance, see Megan L. Case, "The Inheritance Injunction of Numbers 36: Zelophehad's Daughters and the Intersection of Land Inheritance and Sex Regulation," Chapter 8 in this volume.

16. David R. Mace, *Hebrew Marriage: A Sociological Study* (London: Epworth, 1953), 107, notes that this must have been a real possibility since, "if the woman was sterile with one husband, there was an even chance that she would be so with another."

17. Cf. Rowley, "The Marriage of Ruth," 181.

to this fear that Judah opted out of his duty to see to it that the levirate custom was upheld. Moreover, Tamar's refusal to appeal to public opinion may simply reflect the embarrassment and humiliation felt by every widow who was forced to make formal and public what must have been a matter of the greatest delicacy.

Furthermore, some aspects of the narrative in Genesis 38 imply that the custom was, indeed, regarded as an unavoidable obligation. Judah's command to Onan to take his brother's wife to provide her with offspring, and Onan's placid acceptance, suggests that he had no option but to perform his duty towards the widow of the deceased brother.[18] Moreover, the fact that Onan had to resort to a secret act of defiance (Gen. 38:9) implies that there was no other way for him to avoid his responsibility. The narrative of Genesis 38 may thus be taken to underscore the authority of the *paterfamilias* who could command his sons to perform the levirate duty, and this duty would have been regarded as compulsory.

Did the Levirate Obligation at One Time Extend to the Widow's Father-in-Law?

While the levirate law of Deut. 25:5-10 limited the obligation of marrying the widow to the brothers of the deceased alone, the narrative of Genesis 38 implies that the levirate duty devolved not only upon the brothers of the deceased but also upon his father. Roland de Vaux appears to dismiss this possibility, arguing instead that Tamar's action should rather be viewed as "the desperate act of a woman who desires children of the same stock as her husband."[19] However, the evidence concerning the levirate institution as practiced elsewhere in the ancient Near East would seem to suggest that the obligation did, indeed, at one time extend to the father-in-law of the widow.[20] The levirate custom practiced by the Hittites, for example, indicates that the obligation to marry the widow of the deceased falls successively upon his brother, his father, and his paternal nephew (HL §193). Similarly, in the Middle Assyrian Laws (§33) the marriage of

---

18. Cf. Jeffrey H. Tigay, *The JPS Commentary on Deuteronomy* (Philadelphia: Jewish Publication Society, 1996), 483, who observes that "the fact that Onan does not simply refuse to marry Tamar may mean that the law at that time denied him the option of refusing."

19. Roland de Vaux, *Ancient Israel: Its Life and Institutions*, trans. J. McHugh (London: Darton, Longman & Todd, 1961), 37–8.

20. So, e.g., Anthony Phillips, *Deuteronomy* (Cambridge: Cambridge University Press, 1973), 168–9; and Tigay, *Deuteronomy*, 483.

the childless widow to the father-in-law is permitted. These ancient Near Eastern laws support the view that Tamar was quite within her rights in forcing Judah to fulfill his levirate duty; indeed, her actions are rewarded with male progeny, and it is significant that Judah himself declares Tamar to be righteous and readily acknowledges the legitimacy of her conduct: "She is more in the right than I am" (Gen. 38:26).[21] Indeed, she is the only character who emerges with any credit in the story and is the only one who is unmistakably praised by the narrator.

Finally, it remains to be considered how the narratives of Genesis 38 and the book of Ruth are to be related to the law in Deut. 25:5-10, since neither of these narrative texts strictly correspond with the Deuteronomic legislation. While Deut. 25:5-10 appears to limit the levirate obligation to the brothers of the deceased, Genesis 38 implies that the levirate duty devolved also upon his father, and the book of Ruth seems to extend the duty to all male members of the family according to the proximity of their relationship to the deceased. According to Rowley, the narrative in the book of Ruth preserves a tradition of the levirate custom as it existed prior to the Deuteronomic legislation, and he views the evolution of the levirate practice in terms of a developing tendency to limit those obligated under the levirate scheme from more distant relatives (Genesis 38; Ruth) to the later Deuteronomic law of "brothers dwelling together."[22] The difficulty with his argument, however, is that if both Genesis 38 and the book of Ruth reflect pre-Deuteronomic conditions, it is difficult to explain why the levirate obligation is compulsory in one (Genesis 38) and optional in the other (Ruth). It seems more probable that Genesis 38 reflects the earliest stage in the levirate custom, when it was regarded as an unavoidable obligation. By the time of the Deuteronomic legislation it was possible to evade the duty, although a certain stigma would have attached to the brother who refused. The latest stage is represented by the book of Ruth, for here the duty is no longer regarded as obligatory and refusal evidently carried no shame.[23] It is doubtful, however, whether, as some scholars

---

21. Tamar's actions were also viewed positively in later Jewish tradition; see Michael James Williams, *Deception in Genesis: An Investigation into the Morality of a Unique Biblical Phenomenon* (New York: Peter Lang, 2001), 108, 121, 128.

22. Rowley, "The Marriage of Ruth," 179–80.

23. When it is considered that in the book of Ruth the brother-in-law was required not only to marry the widow but also to undertake the additional burden of redeeming the property, it seems almost inevitable that the provision of Deut. 25:5-10 would have been regarded as too restrictive, and that recourse would sometimes have to be made to other relatives in order of proximity to the deceased so that both obligations would be dutifully accomplished. Cf. Davies, "Inheritance Rights," 266–7.

have argued,[24] this development culminates in the complete abrogation of the levirate law by the provisions enacted in Lev. 18:16 and 20:21, for while Lev. 20:21 does seem to prohibit marriage with a brother's wife, and Lev. 18:16 appears to forbid any sexual relations between them, it is probable that these laws applied only during the lifetime of the brother,[25] whereas levirate marriage was operative after his death.[26]

Conclusion

We are now able to suggest an answer to each of the questions posed at the beginning of this chapter. Even from earliest times, the levirate custom did, indeed, involve marriage between the widow and her brother-in-law. Moreover, even at the earliest stage, as reflected in Genesis 38, it was regarded as an unavoidable obligation, though by the time of the later Deuteronomic provision it was possible to evade the duty (although a certain stigma attached to the brother-in-law who refused). The Deuteronomic law effectively made optional a duty that was once regarded as compulsory. In the period when the narrative of Ruth was composed, the kinsman could decline his duty without blame (Ruth 4:8-9). Also, at the earliest stage, the levirate obligation devolved not only upon the brothers of the deceased but on his father; the later Deuteronomic law, however, limited the custom to the brothers of the deceased, and it

---

24. Cf., e.g., Anthony Phillips, "Some Aspects of Family Law in Pre-exilic Israel," *VT* 23 (1973): 356; and Julian Morgenstern, "The Book of the Covenant, Part II," *HUCA* 7 (1930): 183 n. 235.

25. For a different perspective, see the brief comments at n. 100 in Bruce Wells, "On the Beds of a Woman: The Leviticus Texts on Same-Sex Relations Reconsidered," Chapter 5 in this volume.

26. Some have suggested that the liaison between Judah and Tamar in Genesis 38 appears to constitute a breach of the law of Lev. 18:15: "you must not have intercourse with your daughter-in-law, because she is your son's wife; you must not bring shame on her." However, the ancient rabbis were probably correct in supposing that the law of Leviticus was intended to state the general principle prohibiting an incestuous relationship between a father and daughter-in-law, whereas the law in Deuteronomy applied only to the specific case where a married man died without leaving male progeny. Johanna Stiebert argues that the account in Genesis 38 constituted a special case, since Judah was unaware of Tamar's identity; once her identity is revealed, Judah acknowledges his remiss conduct and refrains from having sex with her again (*Fathers and Daughters in the Hebrew Bible* [Oxford: Oxford University Press, 2013], 146). As Susan Niditch has observed, "an unusual adherence to the law of the levirate takes precedence over an incest law" ("The Wrong Woman Righted: An Analysis of Genesis 38," *HTR* 72 [1979]: 148).

applied to them only if they lived on the unpartitioned family estate. By the time of the book of Ruth, the law of Deut. 25:5-10 was felt to be too restrictive, and it was therefore widened in its application to include other, more distant, family members.

Bibliography

Alter, Robert. *The Art of Biblical Narrative*. New York: Basic Books, 1981.
Amit, Yairah. "Narrative Analysis: Meaning, Context, and Origins of Genesis 38." In *Method Matters: Essays on the Interpretation of the Hebrew Bible in Honor of David L. Petersen*, edited by Joel M. LeMon and Kent Harold Richards, 271–91. Atlanta: Society of Biblical Literature, 2009.
Beattie, D. R. G. "Ruth III." *JSOT* 5 (1978): 39–51.
Bechtel, Lyn M. "Shame as a Sanction of Social Control in Biblical Israel: Judicial, Political, and Social Shaming." *JSOT* 49 (1991): 57–61.
Bekins, Peter. "Tamar and Joseph in Genesis 38 and 39." *JSOT* 40 (2016): 375–97.
Burrows, Millar. "The Ancient Oriental Background of Hebrew Levirate Marriage." *BASOR* 77 (1940): 2–15.
Burrows, Millar. "Levirate Marriage in Israel." *JBL* 59 (1940): 23–33.
Carmichael, Calum M. "A Ceremonial Crux: Removing a Man's Sandal as a Female Gesture of Contempt." *JBL* 96 (1977): 321–36.
Coats, George W. *Genesis, with an Introduction to Narrative Literature*. Grand Rapids: Eerdmans, 1983.
Coats, George W. "Widow's Rights: A Crux in the Structure of Genesis 38." *CBQ* 34 (1972): 461–6.
Cruveilhier, P. "Le lévirat chez les Hébreux et chez les Assyriens." *RB* 34 (1925): 524–46.
Daube, David. "The Culture of Deuteronomy." *Orita* 3 (1969): 30–42.
Davies, Eryl W. "Inheritance Rights and the Hebrew Levirate Marriage." *VT* 31 (1981): 138–44, 257–68.
Davies, Eryl W. "Ruth IV 5 and the Duties of the *Gōʾēl*." *VT* 33 (1983): 231–4.
Emerton, J. A. "Some Problems in Genesis XXXVIII." *VT* 25 (1975): 338–61.
Goldin, Judah. "The Youngest Son or Where Does Genesis 38 Belong." *JBL* 96 (1977): 27–44.
Gow, Murray D. *The Book of Ruth: Its Structure, Theme and Purpose*. Leicester: Apollos, 1992.
Greenspahn, Frederick E. *When Brothers Dwell Together: The Preeminence of Younger Siblings in the Hebrew Bible*. Oxford: Oxford University Press, 1994.
Gurney, O. R. *The Hittites*. Harmondsworth: Penguin, 1952.
Jones, Edward Allen III. *Reading Ruth in the Restoration Period: A Call for Inclusion*. London: Bloomsbury T & T Clark, 2016.
Koschaker, Paul. "Zum Levirat nach hethitischem Recht." *RHA* 2 (1933): 77–89.
Kruschwitz, Jonathan. "The Type-Scene Connection between Genesis 38 and the Joseph Story." *JSOT* 36 (2012): 383–410.
Lacheman, Ernest R. "Note on Ruth 4: 7–8." *JBL* 56 (1937): 53–6.
Lambe, Anthony J. "Genesis 38: Structure and Literary Design." In *The World of Genesis: Persons, Places, Perspectives*, edited by Phillip R. Davies and David J. A. Clines, 102–20. Sheffield: Sheffield Academic, 1998.

Leggett, Donald A. *The Levirate and Goel Institutions in the Old Testament with Special Attention to the Book of Ruth*. Cherry Hill: Mack Publishing, 1974.

Mace, David R. *Hebrew Marriage: A Sociological Study*. London: Epworth, 1953.

Mathias, Steffan. *Paternity, Progeny, and Perpetuation: Creating Lives after Death in the Hebrew Bible*. London: Bloomsbury T&T Clark, forthcoming.

McKane, William. "Ruth and Boaz." *TGUOS* 19 (1961–2): 29–40.

Morgenstern, Julian. "The Book of the Covenant, Part II." *HUCA* 7 (1930): 19–258.

Neufeld, Ephraim. *Ancient Hebrew Marriage Laws*. London: Longmans, Green & Co., 1944.

Niditch, Susan. "The Wrong Woman Righted: An Analysis of Genesis 38." *HTR* 72 (1979): 143–9.

O'Callaghan, Martin. "Structure and Meaning in Genesis 38: Judah and Tamar." *Proceedings of the Irish Biblical Association* 5 (1981): 72–88.

Phillips, Anthony. *Deuteronomy*. Cambridge: Cambridge University Press, 1973.

Phillips, Anthony. "Some Aspects of Family Law in Pre-exilic Israel." *VT* 23 (1973): 349–61.

Rad, Gerhard von. *Genesis: A Commentary*. Translated by J. H. Marks. Rev. ed. London: SCM, 1972.

Rowley, H. H. "The Marriage of Ruth." In *The Servant of the Lord and Other Essays on the Old Testament*, 169–94. Rev. ed. Oxford: Blackwell, 1965.

Speiser, Ephraim A. "Of Shoes and Shekels." *BASOR* 77 (1940): 15–20.

Stiebert, Johanna. *Fathers and Daughters in the Hebrew Bible*. Oxford: Oxford University Press, 2013.

Thompson, Thomas, and Dorothy Thompson. "Some Legal Problems in the Book of Ruth." *VT* 18 (1968): 79–99.

Tigay, Jeffrey H. *The JPS Commentary on Deuteronomy*. Philadelphia: Jewish Publication Society, 1996.

Tsevat, Matitiahu. "Marriage and Monarchical Legitimacy in Ugarit and Israel." *JSS* 3 (1958): 237–43.

Vaux, Roland de. *Ancient Israel: Its Life and Institutions*. Translated by J. McHugh. London: Darton, Longman & Todd, 1961.

Weisberg, Dvora E. *Levirate Marriage and the Family in Ancient Judaism*. Waltham: Brandeis University Press, 2009.

Westermann, Claus. *Genesis 37–50*. Translated by J. J. Scullion. London: SPCK, 1987.

Williams, Michael James. *Deception in Genesis: An Investigation into the Morality of a Unique Biblical Phenomenon*. New York: Peter Lang, 2001.

5

ON THE BEDS OF A WOMAN:
THE LEVITICUS TEXTS ON SAME-SEX RELATIONS
RECONSIDERED

Bruce Wells

Introduction

The Hebrew Bible has little to say about homosexuality. Scholars and general readers of the Bible typically identify just two verses—Lev. 18:22 and 20:13—as containing explicit prohibitions on same-sex relations, and they address only the matter of male homosexual relations.[1] These two prohibitions in Leviticus occur in what virtually all scholars describe as priestly literature. Substantial portions of the Pentateuch were written from the perspective of the priestly classes in ancient Israel and Judah, or some portion thereof, and highlight matters and concerns of special interest to them. Many scholars identify the broad pericope in which these texts appear, Leviticus 17–26, as the Holiness Legislation/Source (H), which is usually considered a subset of the larger collection of priestly writings in the Pentateuch.[2] The statements take the form of rules or laws

---

1. Other biblical texts, such as Genesis 19, Judges 19, and Ezek. 16:48-52 lie outside the scope of this article.
2. A great deal of debate exists with respect to the date of H. For a summary of the view that H is early or pre-exilic, see Jacob Milgrom, *Leviticus 17–22: A New Translation with Introduction and Commentary*, AB 3A (New York: Doubleday, 2000), 1361-4. I accept a later, exilic or post-exilic date for H. On this view, see the arguments in Christophe Nihan, *From Priestly Torah to Pentateuch: A Study in the Composition of the Book of Leviticus*, FAT 2/25 (Tübingen: Mohr Siebeck,

and appear within lists of sexual prohibitions mostly, but not exclusively, having to do with incest. They have been interpreted by most readers as blanket prohibitions on sex between men. The translation of the New Revised Standard Version exemplifies the most common interpretation of these statements.[3]

Lev. 18:22:

ואת זכר לא תשכב משכבי אשה תועבה הוא

You shall not lie with a male as with a woman; it is an abomination.

Lev. 20:13:

ואיש אשר ישכב את זכר משכבי אשה תועבה עשו שניהם מות יומתו דמיהם בם

If a man lies with a male as with a woman, both of them have committed an abomination; they shall be put to death; their blood is on them.

While many seem to assume that the meaning of these texts is perfectly clear, they are not without their difficulties. Most importantly, both contain the phrase משכבי אשה (vocalized as *miškəbê 'iššâ*), a longstanding crux for interpreters. In fact, Jacques Berlinerblau finds this phrase so unintelligible that he believes scholars should "admit defeat" in light of the perplexities it presents and forgo further attempts to arrive at a sensible interpretation of these biblical texts.[4] Like the NRSV, most English translations render the phrase along the lines of "as (one lies) with a woman," although justifications for such a rendering have been far from numerous. My intention here is to contest the standard translation of this particular phrase and the usual interpretation that accompanies it. I will do so on both philological and contextual grounds. I will argue that, in these verses, the phrase משכבי אשה functions as an adverbial accusative of location and should be translated as "on the beds of a woman," in keeping with the most common denotation of משכב. I will also argue that, apart from this

---

2007), 545–59; see also Eckart Otto, "Das Heiligkeitsgesetz Leviticus 17–26 in der Pentateuchredaktion," in *Altes Testament: Forschung und Wirkung; Festschrift für Henning Graf Reventlow*, ed. Peter Mommer and Winfried Thiel (Frankfurt a.M.: Peter Lang, 1994), 65–80.

3. For other English versions that present very similar translations, see K. Renato Lings, *Love Lost in Translation: Homosexuality and the Bible* (Bloomington: Trafford, 2013), 200–201.

4. Jacques Berlinerblau, *The Secular Bible: Why Nonbelievers Must Take Religion Seriously* (New York: Cambridge University Press, 2005), 104. See also the comments in Lings, *Love Lost*, 203–5.

basic denotation, the connotation of "beds" in this context has to do with other Judean men who are married and also with younger males who are under the authority of a Judean woman (אשה). I begin with several philological arguments related primarily to the syntactic structure of the main clause in these verses and then move to a consideration of the general meaning of the prohibition and its context.

The Grammar of משכבי אשה

Missing Elements

Some of the most noticeable features of Lev. 18:22 and 20:13 have to do with what is missing. First, neither verse qualifies the term זכר ("male") with the use of כל ("all, any, every"). It remains unclear to what degree this should affect the interpretation of these texts, but the fact is worth noting. In contrast, the statement in 18:23 incorporates כל in its prohibition on bestiality: "with any (כל) animal you shall not have sexual intercourse and thereby become unclean with it" (Lev. 18:23).[5] This suggests that the author of ch. 18 could have included כל in 18:22 but chose not to.

A particular strategy may have motivated the decision not to include it. All of the sexual prohibitions in Leviticus 18 begin by identifying the illicit sexual partner; the noun referencing the partner is typically preceded by only one other word such as ערוה ("nakedness") or a preposition. If the prohibition on male-with-male sex in 18:22 is excluded for now, each of these identifications, except for the reference to כל בהמה ("any animal") in 18:23, includes a qualification that restricts the scope of the prohibition.[6] For example, there is no law that prevents a man from having sex simply with an אשה (woman/wife). The word אשה is always qualified, and the prohibition is thereby limited to a certain woman or a certain situation. The list below illustrates this, with the underlined words indicating the qualification.[7]

---

5. If one takes שכבת (šəkōbet) as "penis," as some scholars do, then a literal translation of this prohibition would be: "into any animal you shall not put your penis to become unclean with it." See Milgrom, *Leviticus 17–22*, 1550; and Roy E. Gane, "Didactic Logic and the Authorship of Leviticus," in *Current Issues in Priestly and Related Literature: The Legacy of Jacob Milgrom and Beyond*, ed. Roy E. Gane and Ada Taggar-Cohen, SBLRBS 82 (Atlanta: SBL, 2015), 206.

6. For how the prohibition on child sacrifice fits with this, see further below at n. 8.

7. The laws in ch. 20 contain identical or similar qualifications.

18:8 "the wife of your father"

18:9 "your sister"

18:10 "the daughter of your son or the daughter of your daughter"

18:11 "the daughter of your father's wife"

18:12 "the sister of your father"

18:13 "the sister of your mother"

18:14 "the brother of your father … his wife"

18:15 "your daughter-in-law"

18:16 "the wife of your brother"

18:17 "a woman and her daughter…the daughter of her son…the daughter of her daughter"

18:18 "a woman as a rival to her sister"

18:19 "a woman in her menstrual uncleanness"

18:20 "the wife of your fellow"

The consistent use of limiting qualifications in this way creates the presumption that every illicit sexual partner in ch. 18, including the זכר (male) in 18:22, is qualified unless the text includes a marker signifying an all-encompassing reference, as it does with the prohibition on bestiality. Even with the prohibition on child sacrifice in 18:21, the text employs a particular use of the preposition מן that often carries the same semantic force as כל.[8] It should be noted that כל is missing from the prohibition in 18:23b on copulation between a woman and an animal, but כל does in fact appear in ch. 20's counterpart to this law in 20:16: ואשה אשר תקרב אל כל בהמה לרבעה ("and a woman who draws near to any animal for copulation"). It is hard to imagine that, at some point, chs. 18 and 20 were

---

8. The partitive use of מן that expresses the idea "(taken) from among" (*GKC* §119w) is well known. When this use occurs in a statement with a prohibitive sense, as it does here, its force is equivalent to that of the expression "any of" in English. In 1 Sam. 30:22, for instance, men from David's militia assert that they will "not give to them [other men] any of the loot that we have taken" (מהשלל אשר הצלנו). See also Exod. 12:9; 30:33; and Lev. 5:15. In addition, the second-person suffix on מזרעך ("from your offspring") should not be taken to imply that one could sacrifice another person's children. Individuals had legal control over their own children, but to do anything harmful with someone else's child would have already been considered a violation of legal and social norms.

not meant to be read together, given that the punishments for most of the prohibitions in ch. 18 come in ch. 20. One can infer, therefore, that, when taken together, these texts include a limiting qualifier in every prohibition except when it inserts כל or a similar indicator.[9] This means that qualifying language may occur in 18:22 and 20:13 as well, and I argue that such language comes in the phrase משכבי אשה. Exactly how the phrase fulfills this limiting function will be explained in due course.

Second, the phrase משכבי אשה is missing a particle of comparison. Were the phrase meant to convey the meaning "as (one lies) with a woman," we would expect a construction utilizing either כ ("like, as")[10] or כאשר ("just as"). These are the terms in Biblical Hebrew that typically introduce this type of comparison ("as one..."). In such constructions, the particle כ is prefixed to an infinitive construct. The text of Judg. 14:6, for example, states "and he tore it [a lion] apart as one tears apart a kid" (וישסעהו כשסע הגדי). Here, the particle is attached to the infinitive construct of שסע to form the comparison.[11] When the subordinator כאשר is used, it is followed by a finite verb. This construction is found in Jer. 19:11: "I will break this people and this city as one breaks a potter's vessel" (אשבר את העם הזה ואת העיר הזאת כאשר ישבר את כלי היוצר). In this case, the subordinator כאשר is followed by an imperfect form of the root שבר ("to break").[12] Neither of these constructions occurs in the texts from Leviticus.

What we have instead is the phrase משכבי אשה—a plural form of the word משכב ("bed") in construct to the singular form of אשה ("woman/

---

9. A possible analogy can be found in Neh. 13:15. Alex P. Jassen argues that this text reformulates part of Jer. 17:21, which states: "you shall not carry a burden on the Sabbath day" (אל תשאו משא ביום השבת). In Neh. 13:15, according to Jassen, the word כל has been inserted before משה ("burden") to ensure that the prohibition there clearly applies to all items; Jassen also points to two passages in *Jubilees* that have reformulated the Jeremiah text similarly (*Scripture and Law in the Dead Sea Scrolls* [Cambridge: Cambridge University Press, 2014], 214–15). Scribes were clearly not averse to making such additions. Regardless of whether one takes the material in Leviticus 18 to be earlier than that of ch. 20 or vice versa, one of the two prohibitions under discussion could easily have been adjusted to include the word כל in like fashion to Neh. 13:15. But this is not the case.

10. Also noted by Lings, *Love Lost*, 203–4.

11. For similar constructions, see also 2 Sam. 6:20; Isa. 10:14; Zech. 12:10; 13:9; Job 2:10. Lings (ibid., 204) notes Prov. 23:34 as well, which contains כ prefixed to a participial form of שכב: והיית כשכב בלב ים וכשכב בראש חבל, "and you will be like one lying (or who lies) in the heart of the sea and like one lying at the top of a mast."

12. See also 2 Kgs 21:13; Amos 9:9.

wife"). Scholars agree that the phrase functions as an accusative complementing the particular form of the intransitive verb שכב ("to lie") used in each verse—תשכב in Lev. 18:22 and ישכב in Lev. 20:13. We are thus dealing here with an adverbial accusative, and the key question then becomes what kind of adverbial function the phrase fulfills.[13] If one were to accept the conventional understanding, one would say that the phrase describes the *manner* or *mode* of the act of lying.[14] An analysis of the use of שכב in the Hebrew Bible, however, shows that it can be associated with two types of adverbial accusatives: those of manner and those of location.[15] I believe that it also shows that the adverbial function of the phrase משכבי אשה in these texts is not to indicate manner but location.

Adverbial Accusative of Location

Of the more than two hundred uses of the verb שכב in the Hebrew Bible, the vast majority occur in the *qal* stem and have no direct object or other type of accusative. Only thirteen uses of שכב occur with an adverbial accusative or what is more or less the equivalent thereof. A few of these texts (Mic. 7:5; Ps. 88:6; Ruth 3:8) present the verb שכב as a participle in construct to nouns that would, if the verb had a finite form, function as adverbial accusatives, and I analyze them below as if they are performing that function.[16] Two of these thirteen uses come in the Leviticus texts under analysis here. That leaves eleven occurrences of the verb to examine. In eight of these occurrences, the function of the adverbial accusative is to indicate location.

---

13. According to *GKC* §118a, adverbial accusatives specify "some more immediate circumstance under which an action or an event takes place. Of such circumstances the most common are those of place, time, measure, cause, and finally the manner of performing the action."

14. On adverbial accusatives of manner or instrumental accusatives, see *GKC* §118m.

15. This will be demonstrated in the section directly below. On adverbial accusatives of location, see *GKC* §118d–h. The subtype most relevant for this discussion contains those accusatives that provide an "answer to the question *where?* after verbs of being, dwelling, resting" (*GKC* §118d). For this subtype, *GKC* notes that, "as observed by Driver on 1 [Sam] 229, accusatives of this kind are almost without exception…connected with a noun in the genitive" (§118g). This is indeed the case with משכבי אשה.

16. In these situations, participles may be analyzed as being in construct to their accusatives; see *GKC* §116g.

2 Sam. 4:5	והוא שכב את משכב הצהרים	And he (Ishbosheth) was lying (on) a bed at noon
2 Sam. 11:9	וישכב אוריה פתח בית המלך את כל עבדי אדניו	And Uriah lay (at) the door of the house of the king with all the servants of his lord.
2 Sam. 12:16	וישכב ארצה	And he lay (on) the ground.
2 Sam. 13:31	וישכב ארצה	And he lay (on) the ground.
Mic. 7:5	משכבת חיקך שמר פתחי פיך	From the female one lying (in) your lap guard the doors of your mouth.
Ps. 88:6	כמו חללים שכבי קבר	like the slain, those lying (in) the grave
Ruth 3:8	והנה אשה שכבת מרגלתיו	And, behold, a woman was lying (at) his feet.
Ruth 3:14	ותשכב מרגלתיו עד הבקר	And she lay (at) his feet until morning.

Some of the accusatives in the table above signal a sexual act rather than merely a location. In addition to Mic. 7:5, which refers to the "female one lying in your lap," the actions that Ruth takes, lying at Boaz's feet (a word that can serve as a euphemism for sexual organs), are likely meant to be sexual in nature.[17] But the meaning of these expressions at the surface level of the text is strictly about location. We might say, in our vernacular, "I found the two of them in bed together." The surface-level or semantic denotation has only to do with location; it is at a deeper level where one finds a sexual connotation. From a syntactic point of view, therefore, these texts still contain adverbial accusatives of location. The deeper-level connotation would have to be determined on a case-by-case basis.

The other three texts are Lev. 15:18, Lev. 19:20, and Num. 5:13, and all come from priestly literature. In each of these, the accusative associated with שכב is שכבת זרע, literally "a lying of seed." The accusative functions in these instances to indicate the manner or nature of the lying down.[18] The act of lying down is sexual in nature because it results in the emission of seed or semen. This use of שכבת זרע shows that the priestly authors—including the authors of H, given the occurrence of שכבת זרע in Lev. 19:20—already had an expression at hand that they could use to convey the sexual nature of an act, and this expression does not occur in the two

---

17. See Jeremy Schipper, *Ruth: A New Translation with Introduction and Commentary*, AB 7D (New Haven: Yale University Press, 2016), 143–4.

18. This is precisely how Lev. 15:18 is classified in *GKC* §118q.

texts under discussion. Moreover, the surrounding context of both verses plainly relates to sexual pairings, and to specify this particular lying down as sexual in nature would have been superfluous. All of this evidence points to the conclusion that the adverbial accusative in Lev. 18:22 and 20:13 is not one of manner but location.

One of the most significant challenges that could be raised against my claim that the phrase functions in this way comes from the work of Jerome T. Walsh.[19] In his view, the noun משכבי is not part of a phrase with a locative function but is instead a cognate accusative.[20] Biblical Hebrew frequently employs cognate accusatives: to dream a dream (e.g., Gen. 37:5), to sacrifice sacrifices (e.g., 1 Sam. 6:15), and similar constructions.[21] For Walsh, the combination of the action of the verb שכב together with a noun derived from that verb indicates the performance of the act of lying down.[22] Because משכבי is in construct to אשה, Walsh concludes that the main clause in these two verses refers to one who "lies…the lying down of a woman"—that is, one who lies down as a woman would lie down.[23] Thus, Walsh argues that these laws are addressed to the male who is the receiving (penetrated) partner in a male-with-male sexual relationship, and the prohibition seeks to prevent him from lying down in such a way as to be penetrated by another male. Walsh's interpretation is creative, but he, like others, still takes the key phrase in question as specifying an act (not a place) of lying down and as performing the function of an adverbial accusative of manner.

As I argue throughout this study, the basic denotation of משכב, in all of its uses, should be understood as "bed(s)" (i.e., place[s] of lying down), and it is not necessary to posit the separate meaning of "act of lying down."[24] Walsh is certainly correct that the noun משכב derives from the verbal root שכב, but this does not mean that the noun has to perform the function of a cognate accusative when it is paired with שכב.[25] First,

---

19. Jerome T. Walsh, "Leviticus 18:22 and 20:13: Who Is Doing What to Whom?" *JBL* 120 (2001): 201–9.
20. Ibid., 205.
21. See *GKC* §117p–r.
22. Walsh, "Leviticus 18:22 and 20:13," 205. 23.
23. Ibid.
24. Unlike other Biblical Hebrew lexicons, *HALOT* 646 does not list "act of lying down" as a possible meaning for משכב. The occurrences in Leviticus 18 and 20 come under the gloss "marriage bed."
25. The usual cognate accusative of שכב is שכבה; see BDB 1012. The evidence from other words suggests that derived nouns that take a *miqtāl/maqtāl* form often do not function as cognate accusatives if other cognate forms are available; on the

if Walsh's understanding of the text's intent is correct, there is another formulation that would have been expected. In the text of Lev. 15:18, a woman is spoken of as being lain with by a man: "(As for) a woman with whom a man lies" (ואשה אשר ישכב איש אתה). The author of Lev. 20:13, which contains a casuistic formulation like Lev. 15:18, could have worded the verse in a similar fashion: "(As for) a male with whom a man lies" (וזכר אשר ישכב איש אתו). This would have clearly made the penetrated partner the subject of the law. That 20:13 employs a different formulation from Lev. 15:18 suggests that it conveys a different meaning.

Second, Walsh compares Lev. 18:22 and 20:13 with 2 Sam. 4:5 where he also believes that משכב functions as a cognate accusative of שכב. His translation reads: "they came to Ishbosheth's house in the heat of the day, while he was lying the lying down of noontime (משכב הצהרים)."[26] This comparison is a key component of Walsh's attempt to ground his claim concerning the use of משכב in Leviticus. It is not evident, however, that, when used with an indicator of time, משכב must necessarily refer to an act of lying down. The main Akkadian term for bed, *mayyālu*, occurs frequently in construct with *mūši/mušīti* ("night") and, when it does so, consistently indicates a place rather than an act of lying down.[27] This calls Walsh's particular comparison of 2 Sam. 4:5 with the texts in Leviticus into question. The regular reference of *mayyālu* to a place or bed, when connected to a temporal indicator, favors taking משכב in 2 Sam. 4:5 as identifying the place—not the act—of lying down at noontime. In light of these considerations, Walsh's argument seems to be insufficient to establish the meaning of "act of lying down" for משכב, in either its

---

connection between *miqtāl* and *maqtāl* forms, see Wolfram von Soden, "Bedeutungsgruppen unter den Substantiven nach der Nominalform *ma/iqtāl* mit Pluralformen nach *ma/iqtallīm/*ôt im Althebräischen," *ZAH* 1 (1988): 103–6 (I thank John Huehnergard for this reference). For example, the verbal root זבח ("to sacrifice") yields the derived nouns מזבח ("altar") and זבח ("sacrifice"). The latter is the cognate accusative, while the former always identifies a place of sacrifice. The same can be said for the verbal roots בטח ("to trust"), זרע ("to sow"), טבח ("to slaughter"), and ספר ("to count"). That is, the *miqtāl/maqtāl* nouns derived from these roots do not perform the function of a cognate accusative. If we understand the root שכב on this model, then שכבה is indeed the cognate accusative, and משכב refers to a location (a place of lying down).

26. Walsh, "Leviticus 18:22 and 20:13," 205.

27. For example, the second tablet of the Epic of Gilgamesh contains a line that reads: "for Išḫara a bed for the night (*mayyāl mušītu*) is given" (col. ii, line 44). This plainly cannot be understood as referring to preparing for Išḫara the act of lying down at night. For similar examples, see *CAD* M/1 119–20 (s.v. majālu 1 i).

singular or plural form. Rather, משכב should be uniformly interpreted as a place of lying down and its plural usage in Lev. 18:22 and 20:13 as indicative of location.

Interpreting משכבי אשה

The Plural Form

That משכבי אשה indicates location seems sensible in light of the basic meaning of the term משכב—"bed." A straightforward translation of משכבי אשה would be, taking into account its adverbial function, "on the beds of a woman." In this case, Lev. 18:22 would read, "And with a male you shall not lie on the beds of a woman; it is an abomination." Scholars have generally avoided this interpretation without saying exactly why. One possible reason is that the term משכב appears with two different plural forms in the Hebrew Bible: one with the ending -*ê* in the construct state, which presumes an -*îm* ending in the absolute state, and one with the ending -*ôt*. It is the -*ôt* form that conveys the plural notion of the term's most basic meaning, "beds" (Isa. 57:2; Hos. 7:14; Mic. 2:1; and Ps. 149:5).[28] The -*îm/ê* form occurs in the Leviticus texts and Gen. 49:4. If it is the -*ôt* form that carries the straightforward meaning "beds," then the -*îm/ê* form may imply a different connotation.

There are, in fact, a number of nouns in the Hebrew Bible that exhibit both plural forms. Several reasons can account for this.[29] First, some nouns, such as the term היכל ("palace"), tend to take one form in the absolute state and the other form in the construct state. Second, particular biblical books or texts from particular time periods or even particular genres can prefer one plural form over the other.[30] Third, some nouns

---

28. The Ugaritic term for "bed" may be rendered as *mškb* (as in *KTU* 4.195), and the plural form thereof may take the form *mškbt*; see Josef Tropper, *Ugaritisch: Kurzgefasste Grammatik mit Übungstexten und Glossar*, Elementa Linguarum Orientis 1 (Münster: Ugarit-Verlag, 2002), 144. In addition, *mškbt* should perhaps be understood as an alternate singular form, given its use in *KTU* 4.385: 10; see Robert R. Stieglitz, "A Physician's Equipment List from Ugarit," *JCS* 33 (1981): 52–5. In either case, the regular plural of the term appears to take the plural ending typically associated with feminine nouns. A form of Semitic *mškb* is used at Mari, where it also occurs in a feminine plural form (*AHw* II 626). This evidence supports the idea that the basic plural meaning of the term in Hebrew would have taken the -*ôt* ending.

29. See Meirav Tubul, "Nouns with Double Plural Forms in Biblical Hebrew," *JSS* 52 (2007): 189–210.

30. With the term בכור ("firstborn"), for example, writings from the Second Temple period seem to prefer the -*îm/ê* form, while earlier texts prefer the -*ôt* form.

differ semantically in their plural forms. The term חצר, for example, typically denotes the outside area around a house in the *-ôt* form but small, unwalled settlements in the *-îm* form. It would not be unusual, therefore, for the *-îm/ê* form of משכב to have a somewhat different meaning from the *-ôt* form. My argument is that the difference between the two plural forms of משכב is indeed semantic but obtains at the level of connotation. The surface-level denotation of both forms can still be accurately captured by the word "beds." The connotation of the *-ôt* form remains "beds," whereas that of the *-îm/ê* form goes beyond this basic meaning.

Before explaining my own view on the difference between the *-ôt* and *-îm/ê* plural forms of משכב, I want to look at what I think are the two most substantive attempts in recent scholarship to deal with the connotation of משכבי אשה in these texts. They come from the work of Saul Olyan and David Tabb Stewart. As we will see, Olyan's interpretation has proved very influential since its publication over two decades ago.[31] He concurs with the generally accepted notion that משכבי indicates the act (as opposed to the place) of lying down, although he qualifies that conclusion somewhat. Stewart contests Olyan's understanding and argues that משכבי serves as a figure of speech for the purpose of identifying a particular set of men with whom one should not have sex. Stewart's view, the fullest presentation of which comes in his 2000 dissertation, has not been considered sufficiently by recent scholarship.[32]

Olyan's Analogical Interpretation

A number of studies of Lev. 18:22 and 20:13 have taken as their starting point one of the main conclusions drawn by Saul Olyan in his 1994 article.[33] That conclusion is essentially this: the specific act referenced by the two verses is sexual intercourse that entails anal penetration by

---

31. Saul Olyan, "'And with a Male You Shall Not Lie the Lying Down of a Woman': On the Meaning and Significance of Leviticus 18:22 and 20:13," *Journal of the History of Sexuality* 5 (1994): 179–206.

32. David Tabb Stewart, "Ancient Sexual Laws: Text and Intertext of the Biblical Holiness Code and Hittite Law," PhD diss., University of California, Berkeley, 2000. An abbreviated version of Stewart's views on these texts can be found in "Leviticus," in *The Queer Bible Commentary*, ed. Deryn Guest (London: SCM, 2006), 77–104, esp. 96–9. Stewart is followed in part by Milgrom, *Leviticus 17–22*, 1569.

33. Olyan, "Meaning and Significance." Scholars who have followed Olyan's lead include Martti Nissinen, *Homoeroticism in the Biblical World*, trans. Kirsi Stjerna (Minneapolis: Fortress, 1998), 44; Robert A. J. Gagnon, *The Bible and Homosexual Practice: Texts and Hermeneutics* (Nashville: Abingdon, 2001), 111–17;

a male Israelite of any other male Israelite. "Other sexual acts" between two men, says Olyan, lie outside the scope of these prohibitions.[34] Olyan's interpretation is analogical in that he bases his understanding of the male-with-male sex referred to in Leviticus on an analogy with sex between a man and a woman.

The focus of his analysis is the phrase in question, משכבי אשה, which he translates as "the lying down of a woman." Olyan appears to assume a semantic differentiation in the term משכב— a difference that manifests itself across both the singular and plural uses of the word. In some cases, the term clearly refers to a bed; in others, however, Olyan believes that it identifies an action or an experience rather than a place. Olyan presents a comparison of משכבי אשה and a similar phrase— משכב זכר—found in Numbers 31 and in Judges 21, where virgin women are described as those who "have not known the משכב זכר" and other women are described as those who have.[35]

> Num. 31:17: כל אשה ידעת איש למשכב זכר ("any woman who has known a man with respect to the משכב of a male")[36]
>
> Num. 31:18 and 35: אשר לא ידעו משכב זכר ("who have not known the משכב of a male")
>
> Judg. 21:11: כל אשה ידעת משכב זכר ("any woman who has known the משכב of a male")
>
> Judg. 21:12: אשר לא ידעה איש למשכב זכר ("who has not known a man with respect to the משכב of a male")

Walsh, who claims that Olyan lays out "a convincing philological analysis that the laws refer specifically to male–male intercourse" ("Leviticus 18:22 and 20:13," 201); David M. Carr, who calls Olyan's work "a pivotal article" and agrees that the texts refer "specifically to one man's sexual penetration of another male" (*The Erotic Word: Sexuality, Spirituality, and the Bible* [New York: Oxford University Press, 2003], 52); and Lesleigh Cushing Stahlberg, who also cites Olyan, albeit less enthusiastically than others, but prefers to see these texts as "explicit prohibitions on any same-sex sexual behavior" ("Modern Day Moabites: The Bible and the Debate about Same-Sex Marriage," *BibInt* 16 [2008]: 463).

34. Olyan, "Meaning and Significance," 204. For a brief critique of this particular claim, see Eve Levavi Feinstein, *Sexual Pollution in the Hebrew Bible* (Oxford: Oxford University Press, 2014), 174–6.

35. Olyan, "Meaning and Significance," 184.

36. On the translation of ל as "with respect to," see ibid., 184 n. 12, citing *GKC* §133d.

Given its use in these texts concerning virginity, Olyan argues that the phrase משכב זכר refers to what the lying-down experience with a man would ordinarily entail for a woman. Olyan terms this "vaginal penetration."[37]

According to Olyan, the phrase in our two texts—משכבי אשה—must identify the converse of vaginal penetration. In other words, it connotes what a man experiences during intercourse, namely, the receiving of him by a woman. Olyan calls this "vaginal receptivity."[38] Olyan goes on to argue that the phrases משכב זכר and משכבי אשה form a pair.[39] The former, based on the texts from Numbers and Judges, is restricted to vaginal penetration, since any other sort of sexual experience would not affect a woman's virginity. The latter, concludes Olyan, is also restricted—in this case, to vaginal receptivity.[40] But what does vaginal receptivity look like when it occurs between two men? Olyan explains his reasoning as follows:

> The male-male sex laws of the Holiness Source appear to be circumscribed in their meaning; they seem to refer specifically to intercourse and suggest that anal penetration was seen as analogous to vaginal penetration on some level, since "the lying down of a woman" seems to mean vaginal receptivity.[41]

For Olyan, then, the two texts from Leviticus are directing their comments primarily at the man who experiences "the lying of a woman" with another man—i.e., he experiences the receptivity of the other man. He is the addressee of the law, and it is his act that the texts primarily prohibit.

Stewart's Metonymic Interpretation

Stewart's main criticism of Olyan's analysis has to do with Olyan's apparent decision not to make any distinction between those phrases that use a singular form of משכב and those that use a plural form.[42] In Olyan's

---

37. Ibid., 184.
38. Ibid., 185.
39. Ibid., 184–5. For Olyan, the verb that occurs in the clause along with the expressions under discussion is not of great significance (ibid., 185).
40. Ibid., 184–6.
41. Ibid., 185–6.
42. Stewart, "Ancient Sexual Laws," 72. Previous attempts to explain the difference between the singular and plural forms of משכב include those of Daniel Boyarin, who says that the use of the plural form with אשה occurs because there are multiple ways—vaginally and anally—to penetrate a woman ("Are There Any Jews

understanding, the phrase in Leviticus with the plural form of משכב is simply the counterpart to the phrase from Numbers and Judges with the singular form. Stewart, however, points to a text, not mentioned by Olyan, that complicates the straightforward connection that Olyan makes between the two phrases.[43] The text occurs in Gen. 49:4, where Jacob says to Reuben,

> Reckless like water, you will not excel,
> for you went up (onto) the beds of your father (משכבי אביך); then you defiled (them); you went up (onto) my couch.[44]

The reference here is to Reuben's having been sexually involved with one of Jacob's women and may specifically have in view the tradition that Reuben slept with Bilhah, recorded in Genesis 35. The phrase "(onto) the beds of your father" (משכבי אביך) is clearly an adverbial accusative indicating location.[45]

This verse does not fit Olyan's understanding. According to Olyan, what a man experiences—vaginal receptivity—is normally described in

in the 'History of Sexuality'?" *Journal of the History of Sexuality* 5 [1995]: 346–7); Milgrom, who, like Stewart, claims that the plural stands for illicit intercourse and the singular for licit (*Leviticus 17–22*, 1569); and Walsh, who speculates that the distinction may have to do with the multiple positions that a receptive partner can take during intercourse ("Leviticus 18:22 and 20:13," 204 n. 9). In the same way as Olyan, Gagnon seems to assume that any distinction between the singular and the plural of משכב is unimportant for interpreting these particular texts in Leviticus ("A Critique of Jacob Milgrom's Views on Leviticus 18:22 and 20:13," *Dr. Robert A. J. Gagnon*, January 2005, http://www.robgagnon.net/articles/homoMilgrom.pdf).

43. Stewart, "Ancient Sexual Laws," 72.

44. My translation of the last two words follows the Septuagint and other versions. The Masoretic text has יצועי עלה ("he went up onto my couch"), which requires an awkward shift from the second to the third person. Some scholars have suggested that the word עלה (at the end of the verse) relates to the Arabic root ʿlh, which can yield the meaning "concubine"; see Raymond de Hoop, *Genesis 49 and Its Literary and Historical Context*, Oudtestamentische Studiën 29 (Leiden: Brill, 1999), 86–91. The translation that de Hoop opts for is "then you defiled the concubine's couch" (ibid., 86); he repoints יצועי as a plural but translates it as a singular. One problem with this interpretation is that 1 Chron. 5:1 seems to recall this verse or something similar to it and gives a rendering different from de Hoop's: "in his defiling the couches of his father" (ובחללו יצועי אביו). Interestingly, יצועי is pointed as a plural here, but the text takes the couch(es) as belonging to Jacob and not to a concubine.

45. See also Isa. 57:8: "you have uncovered, you have gone up (onto), you have made wide your bed." As in Gen. 49:4, the word משכב functions here as an adverbial accusative for the verb עלה ("to go up").

terms of the משכבים* of a woman.[46] In Gen. 49:4, however, what Reuben experiences is described in terms of the משכבים* of a man, namely, Reuben's father. This appears to weaken Olyan's fundamental claim. It is also, in part, what leads Stewart to the conclusion that the singular–plural distinction between the different forms of משכב is an important part of a larger distinction between "licit and illicit sexual relations," with the plural identifying illicit relations.[47] These expressions with משכבי, for Stewart, are about a particular kind of illicit sex, namely, incest. Reuben committed incest with a female relative, and it was described in terms of the משכבים* of a male. Thus, Stewart infers, incest with a male would likely be described in terms of the משכבים* of a female. In other words, if the Genesis text is about incest, then the Leviticus texts are as well—but, more specifically, homosexual incest between men. Stewart explains his conclusion:

> Just as the plural construct משכבי אביך (*mišk^ebê ʾābîkā*) speaks of incest, so also משכבי אשה (*mišk^ebê ʾiššâ*) speaks of incest. The former speaks of incest with a female relative in terms of a male relative; the latter speaks of incest with male kin in terms of female kin. What female kin? Kin of all the same degrees of relation already spoken of in Lev. 18:7-18.[48]

Stewart's interpretation of the key phrase in Lev. 18:22 and 20:13, then, is not analogical but metonymic. Just as he believes that the term אב in Gen. 49:4 serves as a specific metonym for Bilhah, so he believes that the term אשה functions as a generic metonym for male relatives with whom the male addressee of the laws is not allowed to have sex. The plural form of משכב signals the illicit nature of the sex act, and the gender switch—from Bilhah to אב in Genesis and from male relative to אשה in Leviticus—provides the connotation of incest. Hence, Stewart's metonymic interpretation identifies homosexual incest as the prohibited sex act in Lev. 18:22 and 20:13.

Critique of Olyan and Stewart

Regarding Olyan's interpretation, it seems to me that he eliminates *a priori* the possibility that משכב in the texts from Numbers and Judges can denote "bed." There is little doubt, though, that the word can represent a location and still refer to sexual activity. In Isa. 57:8, the bed represents

---

46. The asterisk (*) indicates that the specific form, משכבים, does not actually occur in the Hebrew Bible or the Dead Sea Scrolls and is, thus, a hypothetical form.
47. Stewart, "Ancient Sexual Laws," 73. 48.
48. Ibid., 74.

a place for having sex in an allegory where illicit sexual activity stands in for religious apostasy. A sexual association comes through strongly as well in Prov. 7:17, where the wayward wife tells the target of her seduction that she has perfumed her bed with myrrh. It seems unnecessary for Olyan to insist on understanding משכב in Numbers and Judges as an act as opposed to a place of lying down. To know the bed of a male would seem to be a rather intelligible euphemism for sex and in keeping with the already euphemistic employment of the verb ידע ("to know"). Akkadian *mayyālu* functions similarly. A handful of references reveal that it, too, can convey the sense of a place for sex.[49] Furthermore, it always refers to a location, and I see no reason why Hebrew משכב should not be taken in the same way.

More importantly, however, a disadvantage of the views of both Olyan and Stewart is that each scholar omits discussion of a relevant text that the other addresses.[50] For his part, Olyan omits any reference to Gen. 49:4, and Stewart's criticism of Olyan in this regard carries weight. Stewart, on the other hand, overlooks a Qumran text (1QSa) that Olyan references. Although this sectarian text is considerably later than the biblical texts, it may manifest the continued use of biblical language and idiom as a variety of Qumran texts tend to do. The following section occurs in 1QSa I, 8-11 (1Q28a; also known as "The Rule of the Congregation"):

וב[ן] עשרים שנ[ה] יעבר על[] הפקודים לבוא בגורל בתוך משפ[ח]תו ליחד בעד[ת]
קודש ולוא י[קרב] אל אשה לדעתה למשכבי זכר כיאם לפי מילואת לו עש[רי]ם שנה
בדעתו [טוב] ורע

> At the age of twenty yea[rs, he will be transferred to] those appointed to enter the lot among his clan and join the holy congregation. He will not [approach] a woman to know her with respect to the משכבי of a male until he is fully twenty years old and knows [good] and evil.[51]

A young man, who intends to follow "the rule for all the armies of the congregation, for all native Israelites" (1QSa I, 6), is not to approach a

---

49. See the texts cited in *CAD* M/1 119 (s.v. majālu 1 f).

50. To be fair, I should say that, without the analysis that Stewart provides in his work, I never would have considered the line of thinking that I am pursuing.

51. See Florentino García Martínez, *The Dead Sea Scrolls Translated: The Qumran Texts in English*, trans. Wilfred G. E. Watson (Leiden: Brill, 1994), 126. Geza Vermes entitles the document "The Messianic Rule" and translates the relevant section thus: "He shall not [approach] a woman to know her by lying with her before he is fully twenty years old, when he shall know [good] and evil" (*The Dead Sea Scrolls in English*, 4th ed. [New York: Penguin Books, 1995], 119–20).

woman before he is twenty years old. The prohibition literally says that he may not "approach a woman to know her with respect to (ל) the beds of a male (משכבי זכר)."

This text would have been difficult for Stewart to reconcile with his interpretation of the phrase משכבי אשה in Leviticus, since the act it prohibits is not restricted to incest. According to the pattern that Stewart lays out, the use of the plural of משכב with a male noun should signal incest with a female relative. The text presents a broader scope than incest. Olyan also cannot fit the text into his interpretation. Within Olyan's scheme, it would refer to a young man, who sleeps with a woman, as experiencing the משכבי זכר or vaginal penetration—the very thing that a woman is supposed to experience when she sleeps with a man. Olyan recognizes this and concludes, "A solution is elusive."[52]

If we focus on those texts that employ the -îm/ê form of משכב, we find only four, all of which present the form in a construct state. They are:

Gen. 49:4: משכבי אביך "the beds of your father" (when Reuben has sex with a woman)

Lev. 18:22: משכבי אשה "the beds of a woman" (when a man has sex with a man)

Lev. 20:13: משכבי אשה "the beds of a woman" (when a man has sex with a man)

1QSa I, 10: משכבי זכר "the beds of a male" (when a man has sex with a woman)

Two features of this collection of texts stand out. First, each instance happens to refer to a sexual act that is illicit.[53] Second, in each case, the plural form is in construct to a noun that represents the opposite gender of the sexual partner. In contrast to this, the occurrences of singular construct

---

52. Olyan, "Meaning and Significance," 185 n. 14.

53. As noted above, some scholars do not see any significant distinction between the meaning of the singular and plural uses of משכב. I am not arguing that any use of the -îm/ê plural form of משכב would necessarily have indicated illicit sexual activity, but the four uses we do have clearly refer to such. Whether or not the -îm/ê plural form of משכב was intended to mark illicit activity is unclear, but making use of a plural form in this way would not be unprecedented. Another example of using a plural form, in certain situations, to signal unlawfulness comes with the word אלהים. Several biblical texts employ "plural forms [of אלהים] for a singular deity in the context of heterodox worship, including both wrong worship practice and worship of the wrong deity" (Michael B. Hundley, "What Is the Golden Calf?" *CBQ* 79 [2017]: 577).

forms of משכב that are used in the context of sexual activity (i.e., those in Numbers 31 and Judges 21) are in construct to a noun that has the same gender as the sexual partner. This makes the use of the -îm/ê plural form distinct from that of the singular; therefore, readers should not assume that the two uses carry the same connotation.[54]

משכבי *as an Abstract Plural*

What does the -îm form of משכב connote? Let us start with the only biblical occurrence of this form outside Leviticus—the reference in Gen. 49:4 to Reuben's actions with respect to his father. There, Jacob says of Reuben that "you went up (onto) the משכבים* of your father; then you defiled (them); you went up (onto) my couch." What seems quite clear is that, regardless of the term's meaning, the משכבים* at issue belong to Jacob, and, by going up onto Jacob's משכבים* Reuben has wronged his father. Does the author want us to imagine that Reuben lay directly on Jacob's personal bed when he committed this transgression? Although the surface level of the text recounts that Reuben went up onto Jacob's beds, the deeper meaning is that he "went up onto" one of the women who belonged to Jacob. It is the woman herself who functions as Jacob's משכבים* or, at least, falls within that category. The term משכבים* is being used here to identify women that belong to Jacob such that other men are not allowed to sleep with them. They are Jacob's "beds," as it were. In short, Reuben accessed משכבים* that were not his to access.[55]

Further, the word משכבי is plural, of course, but the word in parallel with it is singular—יצוע (yāṣûaʿ; "couch"). It seems much more likely that משכבי is meant to convey a singular idea than that יצוע is intended to convey plurality.[56] We can now combine these two aspects of how משכבי is used: a) that it represents women who belong, sexually speaking, to Jacob and b) that it conveys a singular as opposed to a plural concept. In this way, I arrive at my proposal that משכבי/משכבים* is an abstract plural that communicates the notion of someone's lying-down area or zone. We might even say that it stands for an individual's sexual domain. Reuben's

---

54. To be sure, the difference between the singular and plural is one letter, since the -îm/ê plural form of משכב only occurs in the construct state. Nevertheless, the data presented above should caution against casually dismissing the use of the plural as unimportant and as indistinguishable in meaning from the use of the singular form.

55. Lings takes the right approach when he says that "Jacob's 'sleeping places,' plural, were his private territory invaded by a rebellious son" (*Love Lost*, 211–12).

56. The word יצוע is a term that can convey a similar connotation in the sense that what it identifies—"bed of wedlock" (BDB 426–7)—belongs only to Jacob.

transgression, therefore, lay in the act of crossing over into his father's sexual domain and lying with a woman who belonged to that domain.⁵⁷

The expression of abstract concepts in Biblical Hebrew can take various forms. Words such as גאון ("pride") and חמון ("noise") retain the ending -ān, which was originally associated in Proto-Semitic with abstracts and collectives and eventually began to function as a plural marker in some Semitic languages.⁵⁸ Other words use the feminine singular form to express abstracts—e.g., נקמה ("vengeance") and גדולה ("greatness").⁵⁹ Others, still, employ feminine plural forms to convey abstract concepts: ידידת ("love"), מררת ("bitterness"), מדות ("measurement"), and סליחות ("forgiveness"). Less common abstract endings include -ūt (e.g., ילדות ["youth"]) and -īt (e.g., שארית ["remainder"]).⁶⁰ Abstracts can also take the form of a masculine plural—for example, זקנים ("old age") and נעורים ("youth").⁶¹ But I am positing an abstract plural that derives from a *miqṭāl* singular (משכב) and would take the form *miqṭālîm* in the absolute state and *miqṭəlê* (משכבי) in the construct. I am also assuming that an abstract concept can be derived from a noun that ordinarily refers to a concrete location. Are there philological grounds for these claims?

I contend that there are, but the evidence in this regard is more suggestive than decisive. A few other words that generally follow the same pattern as משכב do indeed appear to express abstract concepts. For example, מאמצי

---

57. An omen text seems to make use of Akkadian *mayyālu* ("bed") in a similar fashion, albeit in its singular form. One of the so-called Venus omens reads, "If Ištar shows (herself) at the beginning of the year and disappears: slaves will ascend to their masters' bed and marry the women who hired them" (translation from Erica Reiner, in collaboration with David Pingree, *Babylonian Planetary Omens: Part Three*, CM 11 [Groningen: Styx, 1998], 183). A commentary on the text equates "the women who hired them" with the masters' wives (see Eckart Frahm, *Babylonian and Assyrian Text Commentaries: Origins of Interpretation*, GMTR 5 [Münster: Ugarit-Verlag, 2011], 61–2). The thrust of the apodosis is that the slaves will take (*aḫāzu*, probably meaning "to marry" here but with a plainly sexual connotation) the wives of their masters and have sex with them. Whether the act occurs on a particular bed is beside the point. The slaves will be occupying their masters' sexual domain.

58. Rebecca Hasselbach, "External Plural Markers in Semitic: A New Assessment," in *Studies in Semitic and Afroasiatic Linguistics Presented to Gene B. Gragg*, ed. Cynthia L. Miller, SAOC 60 (Chicago: The Oriental Institute of the University of Chicago, 2007), 125–8.

59. *GKC* §122q. See also Hasselbach, "External Plural Markers," 130.

60. *GKC* §86k. See also Hasselbach, "External Plural Markers," 130 n. 40.

61. Other examples include בחרים ("youth"), גלואים ("redemption"), כפרים ("atonement"); and עשוקים ("oppression").

is a *hapax legomenon* that occurs in Job 36:19 and conveys the concept of "force." מהלכים is found in Zech. 3:7 and may express the notion of "access." A better example comes from מבטחים, which occurs in Isa. 32:18 as an abstract plural for "security."[62] The best example, though, may be מישרים (*mêšārîm*). This term appears exclusively in the Hebrew Bible as a plural and conveys the abstract concept of justice. Its hypothetical singular form would be מישר* (*mêšār), which seems to fit the *miqtāl/ maqtāl* pattern and add support to the idea that the -*îm/ê* form of a *miqtāl/ maqtāl* noun can indeed function as an abstract noun.

The noun מחנה (*maḥănê*, "encampment") is also relevant to this discussion. According to Meirav Tubul, the absolute plural form of this word with the ending -*îm* refers to "a place to camp," whereas the plural form with the ending -*ôt* denotes "a large group of people or soldiers."[63] She also claims that the -*îm/ê* form, when connected to a pronominal suffix, carries the same meaning as the absolute form with -*ôt*. Tubul appears to be partially correct, but a few references do not coincide directly with her assessment. The -*îm/ê* forms with pronominal suffixes in Deuteronomy (23:15; 29:10) and in 1 Sam. 17:53 could be interpreted as identifying a single encampment (the meaning that Tubul ascribes to the -*îm* form in the absolute state); and the usages of the -*ôt* form in the absolute state in 1 and 2 Chronicles (1 Chron. 9:18; 2 Chron. 31:2) also appear to refer to an encampment rather than groups of people or soldiers. What is important to note is that, like משכב, מחנה typically refers to a concrete location and occurs in both plural forms. Moreover, the -*îm/ê* form can be used to designate a singularity—that is, an encampment area—while the -*ôt* form typically conveys true plurality, although the distinction is not as consistent as what I am positing for the different plural forms of משכב. In any case, the evidence set forth above provides plausibility to the interpretation of משכבי in Lev. 18:22 and 20:13 as an abstract plural, even if it does not establish that interpretation in a conclusive fashion.[64]

---

62. Bruce K. Waltke and Michael O'Connor, *An Introduction to Biblical Hebrew Syntax* (Winona Lake: Eisenbrauns, 1990), 121.

63. Tubul, "Nouns with Double Plural Forms," 198.

64. Waltke and O'Connor put this form of the word into the category of "complex inanimate nouns" as opposed to that of abstract plurals (ibid., 120). *GKC* also does not see it as an abstract plural but instead classifies it with "plurals of local extension" (§124b), a category under the collective use of the plural form. I think that both assessments show the difficulty of determining the precise function of the -*îm/ê* form of משכב.

I wish to proceed, then, on the assumption that the word משכבי expresses, at the connotative level, an abstract concept that should be understood as sexual domain. This sexual domain, it seems, can be one of two types. The first type may be called an ownership domain. It is one where the person who owns the domain possesses exclusively the right to have sex with the individuals who fall within that domain, This is the type of domain referred to in Gen. 49:4. I call the second type a guardianship domain. This occurs, for example, in a father–daughter relationship. The father does not possess the right to have sex with his daughter. But her sexual activity is under his control, and he is the one to decide who is allowed into the sexual domain that she inhabits. Other texts in Leviticus (e.g., Lev. 19:29) show that the authors of H took seriously the responsibility of fathers, in particular, to supervise the sexuality of their daughters.[65] Moreover, any illegitimate trespass in the domain supervised by a father is not a violation of the daughter but a violation of the rights of the father.

I base this understanding of the second type of sexual domain on how the term משכבי is used in 1QSa. The text forbids a young man from approaching (קרב) a woman "to know her" (לדעתה) "with respect to the משכבים* of a male."[66] Just as the משכבים* mentioned in Genesis 49 did not belong to Reuben or to the woman but to Jacob, so the משכבים* here in 1QSa belong neither to the young man nor to the woman with whom he might sleep but to another male. For the young man to have sex with the woman, whether forced or consensual, would not be a violation of her as much as it would be of whichever male figure in her life had the authority to say with whom she could and could not have sex.[67] The young man would thus be trespassing in someone else's sexual domain. The woman in question is restricted territory, and access to this territory is governed by a male. This male could be her husband, but, in this context, it seems more likely that the male would be her father or, perhaps, even her brother or another male relative, should her father be deceased. Thus, the use of the term משכבי does not necessarily mean that this male to whom the

---

65. See Hilary Lipka, "The Offense, Its Consequences, and the Meaning of זנה in Leviticus 19:29," Chapter 6 in this volume.

66. For a survey of the scholarly literature on this text, see William Loader, *The Dead Sea Scrolls on Sexuality: Attitudes towards Sexuality in Sectarian and Related Literature at Qumran* (Grand Rapids: Eerdmans, 2009), 201–11. Loader takes the phrase למשכבי זכר as simply clarifying the nature of the act of approaching (קרב) a woman.

67. See the discussion in M. L. Case, "The Inheritance Injunction of Numbers 36: Zelophehad's Daughters and the Intersection of Ancestral Land and Sex Regulation," Chapter 8 in this volume, especially the material at nn. 28–32.

משכבי belong has the right to lie down with the woman himself; rather, it communicates that this woman is in a sexual domain under his control. Only when the young man has reached the age of twenty may he approach a woman under the supervision of another male, and only by the process of marriage will she be transferred to his sexual domain, at which point he may have sexual relations with her.

In the Leviticus texts under examination, the prohibition has to do with the משכבים* of a woman or wife. If we apply the understanding of משכבי just described to these texts, the command that they set forth is not to lie down with a male in the sexual domain of a woman. Is this domain one of ownership or guardianship? I maintain that both types of domain are involved here and function similarly to those at issue when the sexual domain of a man is in view.

The Notion of Sexual Domain in Leviticus 18:22 and 20:13

Women in Leviticus 18 and 20

Using the concept of sexual domain in a discussion of Lev. 18:22 and 20:13 could encounter a significant problem. The difficulty emerges from the fact that the construct chain in both texts ends with אשה. According to my reasoning, the person whose rights are violated by the male-with-male sex envisioned by the verses is a woman. In what sort of situation would a woman be violated, should two men sleep together? Throughout the ancient Near East, including the societies of Israel and Judah, it is not at all clear that women—whether married or unmarried—were viewed in this way.[68] Generally speaking, women did not possess rights to or over a man's, even their own husband's, sexuality.

Nevertheless, I wish to highlight three considerations pointing to the idea that women were taken into consideration by H's authors more than one might have assumed for an ancient patriarchal society. First, Leviticus 20 contains unusual indications of sexual agency on the part of some women. In other words, the rhetoric of the text accords to these women the ability to choose sexual activity in ways that other biblical texts tend not to do. For example, In Lev. 20:17, where a man is said to take or marry (לקח is the customary word for "to marry") his sister, the text says that "he sees her nakedness and she sees his nakedness." The text includes the pronoun היא ("she"), most likely to emphasize the woman's

---

68. See Raymond Westbrook, "Adultery in Ancient Near Eastern Law," *RB* 97 (1990): 542–80.

involvement in the action described.⁶⁹ Nowhere else in the Hebrew Bible does one find reference to a woman seeing the nakedness of a man.⁷⁰ In the very next verse (Lev. 20:18), when a man lies with a woman during her menstrual period, the text states that "he has laid bare her flow and she has uncovered the flow of her blood"; again, the pronoun היא is included. The woman here, as well, is described as having agency in the execution of the act in question.⁷¹ The ascription of proactive participation to these particular women runs counter to how biblical texts typically speak of women's engagement in sexual activity. This allowance of agency reflects an unusual strategy on the part of H's authors vis-à-vis other biblical authors, for taking women into account as they construct their rules.

Second, in both Leviticus 18 and 20, it is the relationship that some individuals have with a woman rather than a man that renders them unavailable sexually. In Lev. 18:13, the sister of one's mother is a prohibited sexual partner, because she is the blood relative (שאר) of one's mother. Leviticus 20:19 contains a similar prohibition. In Lev. 18:17, one is not to have sex with the daughter of one's wife (presumably, one's stepdaughter) nor with the daughter of her son or daughter, and in Lev. 20:14, it is the mother of one's wife who is off limits. Both prohibitions occur due to the relationships that these women have with one's wife. The same is true for the prohibition in Lev. 18:18, where the sister of one's wife is forbidden. It is not only certain relationships with men, therefore, that play a role in the reasoning presented in Leviticus 18 and 20; particular relationships with women are also highly significant.⁷²

---

69. For similar interpretations of this text, see Deborah L. Ellens, *Women in the Sex Texts of Leviticus and Deuteronomy: A Comparative Conceptual Analysis*, LHBOTS 458 (London: T&T Clark, 2008), 122, and the literature cited there.

70. Other biblical texts refer only to men seeing someone else's nakedness. In addition to the references in Leviticus, Ham is said to see the nakedness of his father in Genesis 9, and it is men who see the nakedness of personified Jerusalem in Ezek. 16:37 and Lam. 1:8.

71. Ellens argues that Leviticus 20 treats women generally as having agency: "The woman is focalized, in the chapter as a whole, as agent. She is responsible to the laws" (*Women in the Sex Texts*, 147).

72. In fact, in commenting on Lev. 18:17, Madeline Gay McClenney-Sadler claims that "the focus of this verse in on the rights of the wife in relation to her daughters and granddaughters" (*Recovering the Daughter's Nakedness: A Formal Analysis of Israelite Kinship Terminology and the Internal Logic of Leviticus 18*, LBHOTS 476 [London: T&T Clark, 2007], 86). Whether or not "rights" is the proper term to capture the thrust of the text is unclear, but it helps to underline the importance of some individuals' relationships to certain women within this set of prohibitions.

Third, evidence external to the Bible suggests that women were able to control some aspects of their husband's sexual activity through contract if not through established law. A Neo-Assyrian marriage contract, for instance, includes a clause preventing the husband from marrying a second wife, implying that, should he ever wish to, he would have to obtain the permission of his first wife.[73] In addition, several marriage contracts from the Neo-Babylonian and Persian periods include clauses making it prohibitively expensive for the husband to take a second wife without, presumably, having received permission from the first.[74] These documents signal greater influence for some wives in these periods over their husband's sexual pursuits.

What the priestly authors have done is to allow the consideration of women's relationships and agency to influence their laws.[75] They do so by taking women into consideration in new ways. In essence, the priestly authors are looking at the relationships that some women have with other individuals and including those relationships among the important factors that determine their list of sexual prohibitions.

In light of these considerations, a more precise way to understand the import of the phrase משכבי אשה is to say that it conveys the idea that certain males are, sexually speaking, off limits because of their relationship to a woman. As we have seen, Bilhah was off limits to Reuben by virtue of her relationship to Jacob, and the woman imagined in the Qumran text is off limits to the young man by virtue of her relationship to the male who controls access to her sexual activity. Importantly, it was a משכבי-phrase that marked their status as such. By the same token, the male-with-male relationships mentioned in Leviticus are also qualified by means of a משכבי-phrase; the males referenced by these texts, therefore, are considered forbidden territory by virtue of their relationship to a woman.

---

73. The text is CTN 2 247—that is, no. 247 in J. N. Postgate, *The Governor's Palace Archive*, Cuneiform Texts from Nimrud 2 (London: British School of Archaeology in Iraq, 1973). See the discussion of the document in Karen Radner, *Die neuassyrischen Privatrechtsurkunden als Quelle für Mensch und Umwelt*, SAAS 6 (Helsinki: The Neo-Assyrian Text Corpus Project, 1997), 160.

74. See the documents with penalties of 5 minas or 6 minas of silver cited in Bruce Wells, "First Wives Club: Divorce, Demotion, and the Fate of Leah in Genesis 29," *Maarav* 18 (2011): 126–8.

75. This approach on the part of the priestly authors does not reflect an egalitarian move on their part but rather a concern about the effects of women on purity; see Sarah Shectman, *Women in the Pentateuch: A Feminist and Source-critical Analysis*, Hebrew Bible Monographs 23 (Sheffield: Sheffield Phoenix, 2009), 48–9.

The Forbidden Relationships

What sorts of women and what sorts of relationships might be envisioned? Initial clues to answer this question come in the sexual taboos that precede the prohibition in Lev. 18:22 and in those that surround the prohibition in Lev. 20:13. Many of the women in these chapters are off limits due to the relationship that they have to a particular man. To begin with, then, the men with whom one is prevented from having sex in Lev. 18:22 are likely to include the very men who are in these relationships. They are off limits due to the relationship that they have with the women identified in the prohibitions. One's neighbor is off limits due to the fact that he is married and falls into the category of the משכבים* of his wife. One's father, uncle, and brother are off limits for the same basic reason: they are married men.[76] Such a line of reasoning might suggest that the prohibitions on male-with-male sex are intended to forbid sex simply with married men. The domain in these cases would essentially be that of ownership. The fact that the prohibitions use the term זכר, however, points to the idea that other males, unmarried males to be specific, are also included. Such males could include, for example, one's stepson, the son of one's wife who was born to her in a different marriage. This stepson would be the male counterpart to the stepdaughter mentioned in Lev. 18:17. He has a particular relationship to a particular woman, namely, one's own wife, and he is off limits sexually due to this relationship.[77] The domain into which these males fall would be that of guardianship. In short, the prohibitions forbid sex with other married men and with any unmarried males who fall under the guardianship of a Judean woman.

The Structure of Leviticus 20

If the prohibitions in Lev. 18:22 and 20:13 are understood in this way, many of the men within the community of a Judean man would be removed from being possible sexual partners for him. What would mostly be left

---

76. To some degree, I am following Stewart's reasoning, when he argues that the men who are off limits are those husbands who correspond to "all the same degrees of relation" mentioned elsewhere in the lists in Leviticus 18 and 20. But I do not think that Stewart went far enough in terms of the males included in the prohibition.

77. I would argue that the oversight of this stepson's sexual activity is the responsibility of his mother and not that of his stepfather. He probably does not stand to inherit from the stepfather and so would not be under the latter's supervision in the same way as a legitimate heir. For example, §§12–15 in the Neo-Babylonian Laws strongly imply that a stepson in this situation will receive an inheritance only out of his mother's property or dowry.

would include male slaves, foreign travelers (not resident foreigners, like the גר), and possibly male prostitutes. This focus on regulating sexual relations within the community seems to be in keeping with the majority of the other prohibitions in Leviticus 18 and 20. Most of the individuals who are declared sexually off limits for the laws' addressees are such because of their relationship to another person within the community.

This is especially clear in ch. 20, where the prohibitions are grouped together quite differently from what one finds in ch. 18.[78] The latter arranges the laws according to the relationship that the forbidden person (e.g., father's wife, sister, granddaughter) has with the addressee of the laws.[79] The laws in ch. 20, by contrast, begin with infractions that require the death penalty and then move to those with a penalty that stops short of execution. After the prohibition in v. 9 that appears to head the entire list of laws, two sections stand out: vv. 10-14 and vv. 17-21. Between the sections come the prohibitions on bestiality; those within the sections just identified refer to sexual violations committed with other persons. Each section begins with a prohibition that sets the tone for the laws following it. The death penalty section begins with a prohibition on adultery: "A man who commits adultery (נאף) with the wife of a man, who commits adultery with the wife of his fellow (רעה), shall be put to death—the adulterer and the adulteress."[80] This section appears to deal with sexual transgressions that violate accepted social hierarchies. Sex with another man's wife violates the hierarchy in which this other man has exclusive rights to and control over his wife and her sexuality.[81] The laws that follow

---

78. Several scholars maintain that the provisions of ch. 20 were written after those of ch. 18 and reformulated the latter for a variety of reasons. See, e.g., Olyan, "Meaning and Significance," 186–8; Nissinen, *Homoeroticism*, 37; and Phyllis Bird, "The Bible in Christian Ethical Deliberation concerning Homosexuality: Old Testament Contributions," in *Homosexuality, Science, and the "Plain Sense" of Scripture*, ed. David L. Balch (Grand Rapids: Eerdmans, 2000), 152, 155.

79. Ellens, *Women in the Sex Texts*, 96–9.

80. On the possible text-critical issues in Lev. 20:10, see Milgrom, *Leviticus 17–22*, 1747. Milgrom himself does not believe that the MT of this text is corrupt.

81. One might surmise that, in cases where incest takes place with the wife of a relative, the prohibition against adultery (Lev. 20:10) would be sufficient to cover and ban such acts. As I see it, however, the list in Leviticus 20 evidently assumes that it does not. There are at least two explanations for this. First, Westbrook argues that, by including separate laws on incest, the authors are seeking to prevent collusion on the part of a married couple (e.g., one's aunt and uncle), whereby the husband gives his wife permission to sleep with the law's addressee (Westbrook, "Adultery," 568 n. 97). Second, the repetition in the protasis of Lev. 20:10 ("A man who commits adultery

also involve hierarchical relationships—with one's father in v. 11 (his wife is forbidden), with one's son in v. 12 (his wife is also forbidden), and with the mother of one's wife in v. 14 (she is forbidden). The next section (laws without the death penalty) begins with a prohibition on sex/marriage with one's sister.[82] The subsequent laws all relate to sibling relationships: the sister of a parent in v. 19 (she is forbidden), the brother of a parent in v. 20 (his wife is forbidden), and one's own brother in v. 21 (his wife is also forbidden). This second section focuses on lateral rather than hierarchical relationships.[83]

Further, each section manifests a similar literary structure. After the opening law in each (v. 10 and v. 17), one finds three laws that begin with ואיש אשר ישכב (vv. 11-13 and vv. 18-20),[84] followed by one law that begins with ואיש אשר יקח (v. 14 and v. 21). The prohibition on male-with-male sex in Lev. 20:13 is part of the first set of three laws that begin with ואיש אשר ישכב. Each one contains the same basic elements along with a similar formulation. One can identify five elements in each verse: (1) the initial ואיש אשר ישכב ("and a man who lies..."); (2) the identity of the individual being lain with, preceded by the preposition את; (3) a word or phrase that captures the wrongfulness of the act; (4) the death sentence;

---

with the wife of a man, who commits adultery with the wife of his fellow [רעהו]...") may be meant to indicate that this prohibition applies only to sex with the wife of a רע, who would then be a man outside the circle of one's close male relatives. If that is the case, then the prohibitions on incest would be necessary. On the repetition in 20:10, cf. the comments of Michael Fishbane (*Biblical Interpretation in Ancient Israel* [Oxford: Clarendon, 1985], 169–70).

82. The text says not to "take" (לקח) one's sister and, thus, most likely has marriage in view. Most of the prohibitions in Leviticus 20 use other verbs to denote sexual intercourse: נאף in 20:10; שכב in 20:11, 12, 13, 18, and 20; נתן (with שכבת) in 20:15; and רבע in 20:16. See Milgrom, *Leviticus 17–22*, 1750.

83. The one law that stands out as a likely exception is v. 18, which forbids sex with a menstruating wife. The possible connection here to sibling relationships is that, during the menstrual period of one's wife, she is to be treated as a sister: a woman within one's family who is off limits to one sexually.

84. Verse 19, in the surviving manuscripts, clearly does not begin this way. I maintain, though, that it did originally and that a copyist was affected by the formulation of the corresponding commandments from ch. 18 (vv. 12-13) and introduced an unintended emendation. Milgrom believes that the altering—he admits that something has indeed been altered—of the beginning of Lev. 20:19 was intentional on the part of the "H redactor" in order to "distinguish this prohibition from all the others" (Milgrom, *Leviticus 17–22*, 1756). Milgrom does not, however, say exactly why the redactor wanted this provision to stand out.

and (5) the statement that "their blood is on them" (דמיהם בם).[85] I present the verses below with each element identified. Verse 12 switches the order of elements 3 and 4 when compared with vv. 11 and 13.

5	4	3		2	1
דמיהם בם	מות יומתו שניהם	ערות אביו גלה		את אשת אביו	ואיש אשר ישכב (11
דמיהם בם	מות יומתו שניהם	תבל עשו		את כלתו	ואיש אשר ישכב (12
דמיהם בם	מות מות שניהם יומתו	תועבה עשו	משכבי אשה	את זכר	ואיש אשר ישכב (13

I have not included the phrase משכבי אשה in any of the elements in v. 13 because it may not be immediately apparent to which element it belongs. A consideration of element 2 in each of the other two verses, however, reveals that something is missing from v. 13's element 2 as it is currently demarcated, and this harks back to the discussion earlier in this study regarding how illicit sexual partners are qualified in the text. In both of the other verses, the identity of the person being lain with is limited or qualified in some way. It is not just any wife with whom one may not lie in v. 11 but the wife of one's father. It not just any daughter-in-law with whom one may not lie in v. 12 but one's own daughter-in-law. If these verses are as carefully structured as they appear to be, then it stands to reason that the identity of the person being lain with in v. 13 is also qualified. This qualification can only be found in the phrase משכבי אשה, and, thus, it seems evident that this phrase does indeed belong in element 2 of v. 13. It is not just any male with whom one may not lie, but it is a male who is qualified as the lying-down territory or sexual domain of a woman. The formulation of the prohibition and its placement within the list of laws in ch. 20 highlight this qualification.[86]

---

85. This is similar to what Hartley does in his analysis (John E. Hartley, *Leviticus*, WBC 4 [Dallas: Word, 1992], 360).

86. As noted, the literary structure of Leviticus 18 differs from that of chapter It is worth asking whether its structure should affect the interpretation of משכבי אשה in 18:22 in ways that are similar to how I think ch. 20's structure should influence our understanding of the phrase in 20:13. In my view, the nature of the influence in each chapter is different. In Leviticus 18, all of the laws having to do with uncovering nakedness come first. These incest laws are then followed by other types of infractions: marrying two sisters, sex with a menstruating woman, adultery, child sacrifice, male-with-male sex, and bestiality. It seems evident that the last three deal with partners other than women and do so in a descending hierarchical order: gods,

The Purpose of Leviticus 18 and 20

The laws of Leviticus 18 and 20 are addressed principally to men, especially given the second-person masculine forms of address in ch. 18 and the reference to a woman in the third person in 18:23.[87] According to my reading of Lev. 18:22 and 20:13, these texts were intended to prevent men in the authors' community from sleeping with another male (זכר) who had a particular relationship to a woman (אשה) within the community.[88] Any married male was forbidden, as well as younger males who were under the guardianship of such a woman. Should a man have sex, for example, with a male slave, he would not violate these prohibitions because the slave is neither married nor under a woman's guardianship.[89] Furthermore, one should not necessarily assume that the man who slept with the slave has violated the rights of his own wife. Just as a husband who sleeps with a female slave or a female prostitute did not, according to ancient Near Eastern standards, commit adultery and violate the rights of his wife in any way, so a man who sleeps with a male slave would not be deemed to have transgressed against his wife. Moreover, the slave

---

men, animals. Since the law in 18:22 is not, in terms of its language and syntax, as closely connected with the prohibitions surrounding it as is the case with 20:13, I do not think that the elements of 18:22 should be expected to match closely with the elements of the laws next to it.

87. See Feinstein, *Sexual Pollution*, 122–4.

88. There may be a parallel in the Middle Assyrian Laws (§§19–20). The first provision, §19, has to do with false accusations of male-with-male sex. The second, §20, states: "If a man sodomizes his comrade (*tappā'u*) and they prove the charges against him and find him guilty, they shall sodomize him and they shall turn him into a eunuch" (translation from Martha T. Roth, *Law Collections from Mesopotamia and Asia Minor*, ed. Piotr Michalowski, SBLWAW 6 [Atlanta: Scholars Press, 1997], 160). Nissinen makes the argument that ancient societies did not consider "homosexual acts nor heterosexual acts...as being done by two equals" (*Homoeroticism*, 26). Thus, in his view, even consensual sex between a man (*aīlu*) and his social equal (*tappā'u*) would have been forbidden by this provision. If Nissinen is right about this, then §20 would be similar, though not identical, in import to Lev. 18:22 and 20:13 as I have interpreted them. That is, all three rules seek to prevent sex between men of equal status in a given community; the main difference is that the texts in Leviticus prohibit sex with additional males.

89. Compare how Lev. 19:20-22 handles sex with a female debt slave. The usual rules do not apply when a person with slave status is involved and, I would venture to say, anyone who does not belong to someone else's sexual domain or is not one of the laws' addressees.

would not be considered a violator because the laws were not addressed to slaves, and any such slave would be subject to whatever punishment his master deemed suitable.

What is especially noteworthy about the rhetoric of Leviticus 18 is that it attributes impurity or uncleanness (see the forms of טמא in v. 24) to the men who transgress the sexual taboos listed there. Eve Levavi Feinstein has shown that, apart from Leviticus 18, biblical texts typically speak of illicit sexual relations as causing women to be unclean, not men.[90] Men do the polluting, and women are the passive recipients thereof.[91] "Leviticus 18," writes Feinstein, "represents a turning point in the development of the concept of sexual pollution."[92] It also appears to reflect a shift, in some quarters, in the conception of women's relationship to men. Rather than assuming the ownership of women's sexuality by men, the authors of Leviticus 18 express it in different terms. A married woman's sexuality is, in some cases, the "nakedness" (ערוה) of her husband. This may still convey a notion of ownership, but the authors feel compelled to make this explicit.[93] The term "nakedness," however, communicates a somewhat different concept in Lev. 18:10 where sexual relations with one's granddaughters are forbidden because "they are your nakedness" (ערותך הנה). This cannot refer to ownership in the same sense as other uses of ערוה in Leviticus 18, but it may identify the kind of guardianship that I have described above—the guardianship that a man would have over the women and girls in his household. In any event, every illicit uncovering of nakedness in Leviticus 18 is now presented as a purity concern.

For Feinstein, this emphasis on the purity of men fits well with H's notion of Israel as a nation of holy men: holiness is applied to lay males as well as priests, and it is elevated to the status of a mandate for these men.[94] Their avoidance of uncleanness or impurity was critical in marking their community as distinct ("holy") from those of other groups. It remains to

---

90. Feinstein, *Sexual Pollution*, 42–99, 123.

91. In Leviticus 18, not only do the men become unclean, but they then impart that uncleanness to the land (ibid., 124–6).

92. Ibid., 160. The change represented by Leviticus 18 did not succeed in all quarters, since some older ideas continued to persist.

93. I am speaking of how the notion of revealing nakedness is used in the form of Leviticus as we have it today. On possible changes in what this meant to authors in ancient Israel and Judah, see Idan Dershowitz, "Revealing Nakedness and Concealing Homosexual Intercourse: Legal and Lexical Evolution in Leviticus 18," *HBAI* 6 (2017): 510–26.

94. Feinstein, *Sexual Pollution*, 123.

be asked, though, why the particular prohibitions set forth in Leviticus 18 and 20 were deemed so crucial that they predominate within H's rules for behavior by non-priests.

Scholars have offered a variety of answers to this question with little consensus. That is, they have tried to identify one overarching rationale that can explain the motivation for including all of the rules set forth in Leviticus 18 and 20. The proposals for what these rules were meant to achieve have ranged from presenting an expanded commentary on the Ten Commandments[95] to limiting individual defilement[96] to preventing the misuse of semen[97] to maintaining familial and social stability.[98] One idea with several proponents is that these provisions sought to reinforce the gender boundaries and functions that H's authors believed were right and proper and that would meet with favor from YHWH. This has led to the argument that "sexual contact between two men was prohibited because the passive party assumed the role of a woman and his manly honor was thus disgraced."[99] This may be accurate, but one does not find a great deal of evidence in Leviticus 18 and 20 to support the notion that H's authors were concerned with manly honor.

It may well be that no one single rationale underlies all of the rules as we have them in these two chapters. As an alternative to seeking such a rationale, I wish to highlight one particular aspect of the prohibitions in Leviticus 18 and 20 that may be helpful at this point. It is widely acknowledged that some of the prohibitions appear to be in conflict with traditions known from elsewhere in the Hebrew Bible. For example, Lev. 18:9 and

---

95. Gagnon, *Bible and Homosexual Practice*, 121.
96. Olyan, "Meaning and Significance," 205.
97. Martin Samuel Cohen, "The Biblical Prohibition of Homosexual Intercourse," in *Biblical Studies Alternatively: An Introductory Reader*, ed. Suzanne Scholz (Upper Saddle River: Prentice Hall, 2002), 153–64; see also Milgrom, *Leviticus 17–22*, 1567.
98. Adrian Schenker, "What Connects the Incest Prohibitions with the Other Prohibitions Listed in Leviticus 18 and 20?" in *The Book of Leviticus: Composition and Reception*, ed. Rolf Rendtorff and Robert A. Kugler (Leiden: Brill, 2003), 162–85.
99. Nissinen, *Homoeroticism*, 44. See also the arguments in Ronald Hendel, Chana Kronfeld, and Ilana Pardes, "Gender and Sexuality," in *Reading Genesis: Ten Methods*, ed. Ronald Hendel (Cambridge: Cambridge University Press, 2010), 71–91. Gagnon takes a similar view but rejects the identification of gender stratification and male dominance as one of the main concerns of the authors behind the Leviticus texts. For him, it is strictly gender differentiation that is the driving force behind the prohibition: male-with-male sex is "wrongly putting a person gendered by God as a male in the category of female so far as sexual interaction is concerned" ("Critique," 4).

20:17 forbid sexual relations and marriage, respectively, with one's sister. This conflicts with the narrative in Genesis 20, which speaks of Sarah as the half-sister of Abraham and condones their marital relationship. The text of Lev. 18:16 and 20:21 prohibit relations with the wife of one's brother, a stipulation that challenges the law of levirate marriage in Deuteronomy 25.[100] Another point of tension lies between Lev. 18:18, which forbids marriage to two sisters, and Jacob's marriages to Leah and Rachel. I infer from this evidence that the authors of Leviticus 18 and 20 may have been interested in distinguishing their community not only from non-Judean groups around them (a clear point of emphasis in the rhetoric of these texts) but also from Judean groups who did not fully accept the same traditions and rules advocated by these authors. Thus, a handful of the prohibitions in Leviticus 18 and 20, such as the ones just cited, may have been new relative to the traditions and customs that other Judeans were generally familiar with.

It is not unreasonable to consider the prohibition on male-with-male sex (whether qualified according to my arguments above or not) to be part of the set of comparatively new regulations added by the authors of these texts.[101] The only legal material elsewhere in the Pentateuch that comes close to speaking to the issue of homosexual activity occurs in Deuteronomy, where the text appears to prohibit very specific kinds (such as sex with male prostitutes) and to leave open the distinct possibility that other types were permitted.[102] What one finds in Deuteronomy, then, may have been one of the perspectives or traditions that H's authors were interested in countering. They may have, therefore, included the prohibitions in Lev. 18:22 and 20:13 as one of the rules that would make their community distinctive and, in their view, more acceptable to YHWH.

The theology of H's authors, if one may call it that, was certainly centered around the rubric of purity at the level of rhetoric. If we could discern the historical circumstances in which the authors were composing

---

100. See the argument in Milgrom, *Leviticus 17–22*, 1758.

101. For the claim that this prohibition was indeed added later, see Dershowitz, "Revealing Nakedness." In addition, no clear evidence of a widespread ban on male-with-male sex has survived from other parts of the ancient Near East. The best evidence for any sort of ban comes in §20 of the Middle Assyrian Laws, discussed above (see n. 88 above). On the general lack of evidence in this regard, see Olyan, "Meaning and Significance," 192–4; and Donald J. Wold, *Out of Order: Homosexuality in the Bible and the Ancient Near East* (Grand Rapids: Baker, 1998), 44.

102. See the arguments outlined in Isaac S. D. Sassoon, "What Does Deuteronomy Say about Homosexuality?" *TheTorah.com*, 30 August 2017, http://thetorah.com/what-does-deuteronomy-say-about-homosexuality.

and compiling their texts, however, we might discover other motivations at work. I suspect we would find the authors and their community in a struggle to preserve their identity and the traditions that they believed formed a critical ingredient thereof. This may be why the rules in Leviticus 18 and 20 seem to deemphasize the understanding of women as the sexual property of men in favor of an emphasis on the preservation of particular sexual boundaries within the community.[103] Some social-scientific evidence suggests that, when small groups feel that their identity is under threat from external forces, they tend not only to reinforce and harden the boundaries separating them from external groups but also to increase the number and rigidity of internal boundaries among their own members.[104] It is, admittedly, difficult to discern if this is the precise dynamic at work with respect to H's laws governing sexual relations. What is fairly evident, though, is that these texts stress the importance of sexual boundaries among community members and concentrate less on ensuring male control of women's sexuality. Thus, the authors' efforts to ground their theology in matters of purity may ultimately be motivated by concerns related to group identity and distinctiveness. The rhetoric itself speaks of distinguishing the community from the Egyptians and the Canaanites—a combination that, at this point in the overall story, represents the archetypal "other" from Israel's past and in Israel's future.[105]

Conclusion

Throughout this discussion, I have attempted to demonstrate that the phrase משכבי אשה refers to the sexual domain of a woman and to compile a set of arguments that build toward this conclusion. First, the phrase occurs in Lev. 18:22 and 20:13 as an adverbial accusative with a locative function and thus indicates the place where or the space in which the law's addressee may not lie down with another male. Second, because the *-îm/ê* plural form is used, the term likely connotes something other than simply beds. I have argued that there is no compelling evidence to attribute the meaning "act of lying down" to the word משכב and that its fundamental

---

103. See Ellens, *Women in the Sex Texts*, 121, 132, 135–6.
104. See, e.g., Christie Davies, "Sexual Taboos and Social Boundaries," *American Journal of Sociology* 87 (1982): 1032–63. The concern in H (in Leviticus 21) regarding the kind of woman that a priest should be allowed to marry may also be a symptom of this intense interest in group distinctiveness and the concomitant desire to clarify and stabilize internal boundaries and distinctions. See the discussion of that issue in Sarah Shectman, "Priestly Marriage Restrictions," Chapter 7 in this volume.
105. See Lev. 18:3, 24-28, and 20:22-24.

denotation remains "place of lying down" on a consistent basis, even if its connotation may extend beyond that. Third, it seems reasonable to propose that the *-îm/ê* plural form of משכב conveys an abstract meaning in the sense of sexual zone or domain. This meaning comes in part from how the form is used in Gen. 49:4 and 1QSa I, 10. Fourth, these latter two texts show that a person can belong to another's sexual domain in one of two senses. Either the person can be slept with only by the other individual, or the person's sexual activity is guarded and managed by the other, who has the right to say who may and may not sleep with that person. Fifth, when this notion is applied to the Leviticus texts, it means that the men with whom the law's addressees may not have sex are qualified as males who are off limits by virtue of a relationship that they have with a particular woman. Sex with married men, therefore, would be forbidden as well as sex with any males who are under the guardianship of a woman within the community.

Whether or not this reasoning is congruent with the rationale(s) behind the other sexual taboos in chs. 18 and 20 remains to be answered. I have suggested that the emphasis in H on sexual boundaries may stem from concerns about group solidarity and distinctiveness. The rhetoric of the text emphasizes purity concerns, but the language regarding the need to behave differently from particular groups of foreigners may signal that additional considerations are motivating the authors to connect these rules with purity requirements. In any event, H seeks to establish strict boundaries around the sexual activity of its community's members and is specific about the individuals with whom a man may not engage sexually. Every person who is considered off limits is qualified in some way by the text, and, for male individuals who are taboo, that qualification comes with the phrase משכבי אשה.

Bibliography

Berlinerblau, Jacques. *The Secular Bible: Why Nonbelievers Must Take Religion Seriously.* New York: Cambridge University Press, 2005.

Bird, Phyllis. "The Bible in Christian Ethical Deliberation concerning Homosexuality: Old Testament Contributions." In *Homosexuality, Science, and the "Plain Sense" of Scripture*, edited by David L. Balch, 142–76. Grand Rapids: Eerdmans, 2000.

Boyarin, Daniel. "Are There Any Jews in the 'History of Sexuality'?" *Journal of the History of Sexuality* 5 (1995): 333–55.

Carr, David M. *The Erotic Word: Sexuality, Spirituality, and the Bible.* New York: Oxford University Press, 2003.

Cohen, Martin Samuel. "The Biblical Prohibition of Homosexual Intercourse." In *Biblical Studies Alternatively: An Introductory Reader*, edited by Suzanne Scholz, 153–64. Upper Saddle River: Prentice Hall, 2002.

Cushing (Stahlberg), Lesleigh. "Modern Day Moabites: The Bible and the Debate about Same-Sex Marriage." *BibInt* 16 (2008): 442–75.
Davies, Christie. "Sexual Taboos and Social Boundaries." *American Journal of Sociology* 87 (1982): 1032–63.
Dershowitz, Idan. "Revealing Nakedness and Concealing Homosexual Intercourse: Legal and Lexical Evolution in Leviticus 18." *HBAI* 6 (2017): 510–26.
Ellens, Deborah L. *Women in the Sex Texts of Leviticus and Deuteronomy: A Comparative Conceptual Analysis*. LHBOTS 458. London: T&T Clark, 2008.
Feinstein, Eve Levavi. *Sexual Pollution in the Hebrew Bible*. Oxford: Oxford University Press, 2014.
Fishbane, Michael. *Biblical Interpretation in Ancient Israel*. Oxford: Clarendon, 1985.
Frahm, Eckart. *Babylonian and Assyrian Text Commentaries: Origins of Interpretation*. GMTR 5. Münster: Ugarit-Verlag, 2011.
Gagnon, Robert A. J. *The Bible and Homosexual Practice: Texts and Hermeneutics*. Nashville: Abingdon, 2001.
Gagnon, Robert A. J. "A Critique of Jacob Milgrom's Views on Leviticus 18:22 and 20:13." *Dr. Robert A. J. Gagnon*, January 2005, http://www.robgagnon.net/articles/homoMilgrom.pdf.
Gane, Roy E. "Didactic Logic and the Authorship of Leviticus." In *Current Issues in Priestly and Related Literature: The Legacy of Jacob Milgrom and Beyond*, edited by Roy E. Gane and Ada Taggar-Cohen, 197–221. SBLRBS 82. Atlanta: SBL, 2015.
García Martínez, Florentino. *The Dead Sea Scrolls Translated: The Qumran Texts in English*. Translated by Wilfred G. E. Watson. Leiden: Brill, 1994.
Hartley, John E. *Leviticus*. WBC 4. Dallas: Word, 1992.
Hasselbach, Rebecca. "External Plural Markers in Semitic: A New Assessment." In *Studies in Semitic and Afroasiatic Linguistics Presented to Gene B. Gragg*, edited by Cynthia L. Miller, 123–38. SAOC 60. Chicago: The Oriental Institute of the University of Chicago, 2007.
Hendel, Ronald, Chana Kronfeld, and Ilana Pardes. "Gender and Sexuality." In *Reading Genesis: Ten Methods*, edited by Ronald Hendel, 71–91. Cambridge: Cambridge University Press, 2010.
Hoop, Raymond de. *Genesis 49 and Its Literary and Historical Context*. Oudtestamentische Studiën 29. Leiden: Brill, 1999.
Hundley, Michael B. "What Is the Golden Calf?" *CBQ* 79 (2017): 559–79.
Jassen, Alex P. *Scripture and Law in the Dead Sea Scrolls*. Cambridge: Cambridge University Press, 2014.
Lings, K. Renato. *Love Lost in Translation: Homosexuality and the Bible*. Bloomington: Trafford, 2013.
Loader, William. *The Dead Sea Scrolls on Sexuality: Attitudes towards Sexuality in Sectarian and Related Literature at Qumran*. Grand Rapids: Eerdmans, 2009.
McClenney-Sadler, Madeline Gay. *Recovering the Daughter's Nakedness: A Formal Analysis of Israelite Kinship Terminology and the Internal Logic of Leviticus 18*. LBHOTS 476. London: T&T Clark, 2007.
Milgrom, Jacob. *Leviticus 17–22: A New Translation with Introduction and Commentary*. AB 3A. New York: Doubleday, 2000.
Nihan, Christophe, *From Priestly Torah to Pentateuch: A Study in the Composition of the Book of Leviticus*. FAT 2/25. Tübingen: Mohr Siebeck, 2007.
Nissinen, Martti. *Homoeroticism in the Biblical World*. Translated by Kirsi Stjerna. Minneapolis: Fortress, 1998.

Olyan, Saul. "'And with a Male You Shall Not Lie the Lying Down of a Woman': On the Meaning and Significance of Leviticus 18:22 and 20:13." *Journal of the History of Sexuality* 5 (1994): 179–206.

Otto, Eckart. "Das Heiligkeitsgesetz Leviticus 17–26 in der Pentateuchredaktion." In *Altes Testament - Forschung und Wirkung: Festschrift für Henning Graf Reventlow*, edited by Peter Mommer and Winfried Thiel, 65–80. Frankfurt a.M.: Peter Lang, 1994.

Postgate, J. N. *The Governor's Palace Archive*. Cuneiform Texts from Nimrud 2. London: British School of Archaeology in Iraq, 1973.

Radner, Karen. *Die neuassyrischen Privatrechtsurkunden als Quelle für Mensch und Umwelt*. SAAS 6. Helsinki: The Neo-Assyrian Text Corpus Project, 1997.

Reiner, Erica, in collaboration with David Pingree. *Babylonian Planetary Omens: Part Three*. CM 11. Groningen: Styx, 1998.

Roth, Martha T. *Law Collections from Mesopotamia and Asia Minor*. Edited by Piotr Michalowski. 2nd ed. SBLWAW 6. Atlanta: Scholars Press, 1997.

Sassoon, Isaac S. D. "What Does Deuteronomy Say about Homosexuality?" *TheTorah.com*, 30August 2017, http://thetorah.com/what-does-deuteronomy-say-about-homosexuality.

Schenker, Adrian. "What Connects the Incest Prohibitions with the Other Prohibitions Listed in Leviticus 18 and 20?" In *The Book of Leviticus: Composition and Reception*, edited by Rolf Rendtorff and Robert A. Kugler, 162–85. Leiden: Brill, 2003.

Schipper, Jeremy. *Ruth: A New Translation with Introduction and Commentary*. AB 7D. New Haven: Yale University Press, 2016.

Shectman. Sarah. *Women in the Pentateuch: A Feminist and Source-critical Analysis*. Hebrew Bible Monographs 23. Sheffield: Sheffield Phoenix, 2009.

Soden, Wolfram von. "Bedeutungsgruppen unter den Substantiven nach der Nominalform *ma/iqṭāl* mit Pluralformen nach *ma/iqtallîm/ôt* im Althebräischen." *ZAH* 1 (1988): 103–6.

Stewart, David Tabb. "Ancient Sexual Laws: Text and Intertext of the Biblical Holiness Code and Hittite Law." PhD diss., University of California, Berkeley, 2000.

Stewart, David Tabb. "Leviticus." In *The Queer Bible Commentary*, edited by Deryn Guest, 77–104. London: SCM, 2006.

Stieglitz, Robert R. "A Physician's Equipment List from Ugarit." *JCS* 33 (1981): 52–5.

Tropper, Josef. *Ugaritisch: Kurzgefasste Grammatik mit* Übungstexten *und Glossar*. Elementa Linguarum Orientis. Münster: Ugarit-Verlag, 2002.

Tubul, Meirav. "Nouns with Double Plural Forms in Biblical Hebrew." *JSS* 52 (2007): 189–210.

Vermes, Geza. *The Dead Sea Scrolls in English*. 4th ed. New York: Penguin, 1995.

Walsh, Jerome T. "Leviticus 18:22 and 20:13: Who Is Doing What to Whom?" *JBL* 120 (2001): 201–9.

Waltke, Bruce K., and Michael O'Connor. *An Introduction to Biblical Hebrew Syntax*. Winona Lake: Eisenbrauns, 1990.

Wells, Bruce. "First Wives Club: Divorce, Demotion, and the Fate of Leah in Genesis 29." *Maarav* 18 (2011): 101–29.

Westbrook, Raymond. "Adultery in Ancient Near Eastern Law." *RB* 97 (1990): 542–80.

Wold, Donald J. *Out of Order: Homosexuality in the Bible and the Ancient Near East*. Grand Rapids: Baker, 1998.

6

The Offense, Its Consequences, and the Meaning of זנה in Leviticus 19:29

Hilary Lipka

Introduction

Leviticus 19 opens with a call upon all of Israel to be holy (Lev. 19:2).[1] The rest of the chapter provides guidance on how this can be achieved. The areas covered are diverse and wide-ranging and include matters related to proper worship and sacrificial practice, ethical conduct in business and in the courts, and how one should behave towards those in need.[2] While the two chapters framing it, Leviticus 18 and 20, both largely concern themselves with various kinds of prohibited sexual unions,[3] only two of the laws in Leviticus 19 relate to sexual behavior, and both are unique to this chapter. One, Lev. 19:20-22, dictates what to do if a man has sexual

---

1. This call to holiness is a recurring motif in the Holiness Collection (from this point referred to as H). See, e.g., in addition to Lev. 19:2, 11:44-45; 20:7, 26.

2. The question of whether Leviticus 19 has a discernible structure has been the subject of some debate. For a discussion of the various approaches that have been taken, see Christophe Nihan, *From Priestly Torah to Pentateuch: A Study in the Composition of the Book of Leviticus*, FAT 2/25 (Tübingen: Mohr Siebeck, 2007), 460–7.

3. For a discussion of the prohibitions against certain sexual unions in Leviticus 18 and 20, and the possible purpose and motivation behind them, see Bruce Wells, "On the Beds of a Woman: The Leviticus Texts on Same-Sex Relations Reconsidered," Chapter 5 in this volume.

relations with a female slave who has been designated for another man.[4] The other, Lev. 19:29, is the subject of this study.

Leviticus 19:29 admonishes each male member of the community, "Do not desecrate (אל־תחלל) your daughter להזנותה lest the land תזנה and the land be filled with depravity (זמה)." Generally, this is understood as a warning to fathers not to desecrate their daughters by making them prostitutes.[5] Yet is the issue really about prostitution, or does the stem

---

4. Because of the woman's status as a slave, the case is technically not considered one of adultery with a betrothed woman, and yet the man must still bring to the temple an אשם (guilt) offering in expiation for the sin he has committed. On Lev. 19:20-22, see Baruch J. Schwartz, "A Literary Study of the Slave-Girl Pericope— Leviticus 19:20-22," in *Studies in Bible*, ed. Sara Japhet, ScrHier 31 (Jerusalem: Magnes, 1986), 241–55; Jacob Milgrom, *Leviticus 17–22: A New Translation with Introduction and Commentary*, AB 3A (New York: Doubleday, 2000), 1665–77; and Deborah L. Ellens, *Women in the Sex Texts of Leviticus and Deuteronomy: A Comparative Conceptual Analysis*, LHBOTS 458 (New York: T & T Clark, 2008), 100–113.

5. A survey of translations, commentaries, and scholarship that touches upon this verse reveals that this interpretation has largely gone unquestioned. Almost every modern Bible translation interprets the *hiphil* of זנה in להזנותה as relating to prostitution. English variations include "making her a prostitute" (e.g., ESV, HCSB, NET, NIV, NLT, NRSV), "make/making her a harlot" (e.g., ASV, JPS Tanakh, NASB, RSV), "cause her to be a whore" (e.g., KJV), and "cause her to be a harlot" (e.g., The Webster Bible). There are some exceptions. The *Bible in Basic English* renders להזנותה "by letting her become a loose woman." The CEB translates it as "by making her sexually promiscuous," though it also includes a note that an alternative translation is "by making her a prostitute." *The Jubilee Bible* also appears to straddle both interpretations, rendering להזנותה as "causing her to commit fornication" and rendering ולא תזנה הארץ as "lest the land be prostituted." A survey of commentaries on Leviticus finds that they, too, generally see this verse as a warning to fathers not to desecrate their daughters by making them prostitutes. See, e.g., Milgrom, *Leviticus 17–22*, 1298, 1696–7; Gordon J. Wenham, *The Book of Leviticus*, NICOT (Grand Rapids: Eerdmans, 1979), 263 and 272; Baruch A. Levine, *Leviticus: The Traditional Hebrew Text with the New JPS Translation* (Philadelphia: Jewish Publication Society, 1989), 133; John E. Hartley, *Leviticus*, WBC 4 (Nashville: Nelson, 1992), 303 and 308–9; Jay Sklar, *Leviticus*, TOTC 3 (Downers Grove, IL: InterVarsity, 2014), 250–1; and S. Tamar Kamionkowski, "K'doshim," in *The Torah: A Women's Commentary*, ed. Tamara Cohn Eskenazi and Andrea L. Weiss (New York: URJ, 2008), 709. General works on sex in the Bible also tend to interpret this verse as addressing prostitution (e.g., Michael Coogan, *God and Sex: What the Bible Really Says* [New York: Twelve, 2010], 151–2; J. Harold Ellens, *Sex in the Bible: A New Consideration* [Westport: Praeger, 2006]; 78, Gerald Larue, *Sex and the Bible* [Buffalo: Prometheus, 1983]; 111–13, and Ilona N. Rashkow, *Taboo or not Taboo: Sexuality and Family*

זנה denote something else? A close examination of the semantic range of זנה can help answer this question by determining how likely it is that it denotes prostitution in this verse. If it seems likely that זנה does not denote the act of prostitution, then other options will be considered, to determine what זנה most likely does mean in this context.

Once the nature of the desecrating behavior has been determined, several other issues raised by this text will be addressed. In what way is the daughter desecrated? How much blame is attached to the daughter, and how much to the father? What threat does such behavior pose to the land, and what are the consequences? Lastly, this chapter will address the question of how this admonition fits into the larger context of Leviticus 19 and its concern with achieving holiness.

זנה: *Prostitution, Promiscuity, or Apostasy?*

Since how one understands the nature of the daughter's desecrating behavior hinges on how one interprets the *hiphil* and *qal* of זנה as it is used in this verse, we will begin with an extensive examination of the stem זנה. As Phyllis Bird has demonstrated in her article, "To Play the Harlot: An Inquiry into an Old Testament Metaphor," the basic meaning of the stem זנה is "to engage in sexual relations outside of or apart from marriage."[6]

---

in the Hebrew Bible [Minneapolis: Fortress, 2000], 29–30), as do works focusing on the nature of holiness and desecration in biblical texts (e.g., David P. Wright, "Holiness [OT]," *ABD* 3:246; Jan Joosten, *People and Land in the Holiness Code: An Exegetical Study of the Ideational Framework of the Law in Leviticus 17–26*, VTSup 67 [Leiden: E. J. Brill, 1996], 32; W. Dommershausen, "חלל," *TDOT* 4:414–15; and Philip Jenson, *Graded Holiness: A Key to the Priestly Conception of the* World, JSOTSup 106 [Sheffield: Sheffield Academic, 1992], 123). Noteworthy exceptions will be discussed below.

6. Phyllis Bird, "To Play the Harlot: An Inquiry into an Old Testament Metaphor," in *Gender and Difference in Ancient Israel*, ed. Peggy Day (Minneapolis: Fortress, 1989), 76–9. Among those who agree with or follow Bird are Francis I. Andersen and David Noel Freedman, *Hosea: A New Translation with Introduction and Commentary*, AB 24 (Garden City: Doubleday, 1980), 224; Gale Yee, "Hosea," in *The Women's Bible Commentary, Revised and Updated*, ed. Carol A. Newsom, Sharon H. Ringe, and Jacqueline E. Lapsley, 3rd ed. (Louisville: Westminster John Knox, 2012), 301; Timothy R. Ashley, *The Book of Numbers*, NICOT (Grand Rapids: Eerdmans, 1993), 266; Carolyn Pressler, *The View of Women Found in the Deuteronomic Family Laws*, BZAW 216 (Berlin: de Gruyter, 1993), 30–1; Athalya Brenner, *The Intercourse of Knowledge: On Gendering Desire and 'Sexuality' in the Hebrew Bible*, Biblical Interpretation Series 26 (Leiden: E.J. Brill, 1997), 147–51; Alice A. Keefe, *Women's*

While נאף, sometimes paired with זנה, specifically refers to adultery, that is, the violation of a husband's exclusive sexual right to his wife (e.g., Exod. 20:14 [= Deut. 5:18]; Lev. 20:10; Ps. 50:18; and Job 24:15), זנה is a more general and inclusive term, covering all instances of sexual intercourse in which there is an absence of a marriage bond between otherwise acceptable partners. This includes adultery, premarital sex by a daughter who is still part of her father's household, and the sexual activities of a prostitute.[7]

זנה is used both literally and figuratively in biblical texts. When used literally, זנה refers to sexually promiscuous behavior. In these instances, the subject is always female[8] and the verb generally does not take an object. When used figuratively, the subject is those who engage in religious or political infidelity against God, worshipping other gods (e.g., Lev. 17:7; 20:5; Num. 15:39; Deut. 31:16; Judg. 2:17; 1 Chron. 5:25) or seeking the help of other nations (e.g., Ezek. 16:26, 28-34; 23:1-21), and the verb is usually (though not always) followed by an object or, most commonly, a prepositional phrase.[9] Those who engage in such behavior

---

Body and the Social Body in Hosea (Sheffield: Sheffield Academic, 2001), 18–20; Ellens, *Women in the Sex Texts of Leviticus and Deuteronomy*, 115; and Eve Levavi Feinstein, *Sexual Pollution in the Hebrew Bible* (New York: Oxford University Press, 2014), 76 and 211 n. 43.

7. Bird, "To Play the Harlot," 76–7. Bird (90 n. 13) observes that incest, bestiality, and homosexuality are not covered by זנה.

8. There are two cases, Num. 25:1 and Ezek. 23:14, where a form of זנה appears to be used in the literal sense with men as the subject, but both verses conflate the literal and figurative uses of זנה, and are much more about infidelity to Yahweh than sexual promiscuity.

9. The most common preposition used with זנה in these cases is אחרי. See, for example, Exod. 34:15-16; Lev. 17:7; 20:5-6; Deut. 31:16; Judg. 2:17; 8:27; Ezek. 6:9; 20:30; 1 Chron. 5:25. For a discussion of the syntactical distinction between the literal and figurative uses of זנה, see Baruch A. Levine, *Numbers 21–36: A New Translation with Introduction and Commentary*, AB 4A (New York: Doubleday, 2000), 282–3. While most scholars view engaging in sex outside of or apart from marriage as the primary meaning of זנה, and religious and/or political infidelity to Yahweh as a figurative usage derived from the primary sexual meaning (e.g., Bird, "To Play the Harlot," 80–9; S. Erlandsson, "זנה," *TDOT* 4:99–104; Milgrom, *Leviticus 17–22*, 1462; Levine, *Leviticus*, 114; Walther Zimmerli, *Ezekiel 1–20: A Commentary on the Book of the Prophet Ezekiel, Chapters 1–24*, trans. Ronald E. Clements, Hermeneia [Philadelphia: Fortress, 1979], 297–9; and Feinstein, *Sexual Pollution*, 211 n. 43), Irene E. Riegner, *The Vanishing Hebrew Harlot: The Adventures of the Hebrew Stem* זנה, StBibLit 73 (New York: Lang, 2009), 63–216, makes an intriguing case for a זנה

are often depicted metaphorically in prophetic texts as God's promiscuous, unfaithful wife.¹⁰

The *qal* feminine participle form of זנה, זונה, when used as a noun, either alone or in combination with אשה, denotes an occupation, that of a prostitute, a woman who engages in sex outside of marriage as a profession.¹¹ The biblical texts that mention prostitutes reflect a society in which prostitution is licit and tolerated, though a rather marginalized and stigmatized profession. In the case of זונות in the Hebrew Bible, the women appear to be without husbands or male guardians, and thus they are not violating the rights or honor of any male by having sexual relations outside the bounds of marriage.¹² All other nominal forms derived from

stem meaning "to engage in non-Yahwistic cultic practice" that was independent of any sexual meaning. She points out that there are many cases in which זנה is used and in which there is no hint of a sexual context, and based on this she contends that there is no reason to assume that the usage of זנה in a religious context derives from the sexual meaning of זנה. It is possible that originally there were two independent זנה stems, one denoting sexual relations outside of marriage and the other meaning to engage in non-Yahwistic religious practices, and that at some point the two became conflated, perhaps when the former began to be used as a metaphor for the latter. However, Riegner's argument for a third independent זנה stem meaning "to feed, nourish" (resulting in an additional meaning of זונה as "innkeeper") is less convincing.

10. See, for example, Jer. 3:1-5; Ezek. 16:15-34; 23:1-21; Hosea 1–3. נאף is used in a similar way in Isa. 57:3 and Jer. 23:10. נאף and זנה are paired in such metaphors in Jer. 3:8-9; 13:27; Hos. 2:4; 4:13-14. In these prophetic metaphors, when זנה is used to describe the actions of God's promiscuous, unfaithful wife, the subject is always female (which makes sense, given the dictates of the metaphor), and it sometimes takes an object and sometimes does not.

11. See, for example, Gen. 38:15; Lev. 21:7, 14; Deut. 23:19; Josh. 2:1; 6:17, 22, 25; Judg. 11:1; 16:1; 1 Kgs 3:16; 22:38; Prov. 6:26; 7:10; 29:3. The nominal construction is the same as שומר ("guard"), רועה ("shepherd"), and כוהן ("priest"). For more on the usage of this nominal pattern in Biblical Hebrew to denote occupations, see Benjamin Kedar-Kopfstein, "Semantic Aspects of the Pattern *qôṭēl*," *HAR* 1 (1977): 158, 164–5. For more on prostitutes in the Hebrew Bible, see Bird, "The Harlot As Heroine: Narrative Art and Social Presupposition in Three Old Testament Texts," in *Women in the Hebrew Bible: A Reader*, ed. Alice Bach (New York: Routledge, 1999), 99–118; Bird, "To Play the Harlot," 77–8; and Coogan, *God and Sex*, 151–60. It is important to note that the nominal form זונה derives from the verb זנה, not the other way around. On this see Bird, "To Play the Harlot," 78; and Keefe, *Women's Body and the Social Body in Hosea*, 19–20.

12. Niditch, "The Wronged Woman Righted," 147, observes that Rahab has her own house, apart from her family, and that the two prostitutes who come to King

the root זנה, such as זנות, זנונים, and תזנות, refer to sexual or religious promiscuity, as do all verbal forms of זנה.[13]

The distinction between a זונה, a woman who is a prostitute, and all other uses of the stem זנה is an important one, since the two are treated very differently in biblical texts. The occupation of a זונה is tolerated and licit. In contrast, whenever any other nominal or any verbal form of זנה is used, the activity is condemned and is treated as highly illicit.[14] In order to avoid confusion between the licit occupation of a זונה and the illicit sexual activities of women denoted by all other forms of the stem זנה when it is being used literally, it is probably best to avoid translating the verb זנה as "to play the harlot" or "to whore around," since both harlot and whore are terms in English which have double meanings, denoting both professional prostitutes and sexually promiscuous women. A preferable translation of זנה to denote illicit sexual activity on the part of women would be "to be sexually promiscuous" or "to commit fornication." For this same reason, translating זנה in contexts in which it is used figuratively as "whore after" or "play the harlot after" is equally problematic, since it conflates prostitution and religious and/or political infidelity against Yahweh. Thus I propose that when the stem זנה is used figuratively, one can translate as "go astray after," to convey the basic sense of the term while still keeping the figurative sense, and eliminating any confusion between prostitution and either of these forms of promiscuity and infidelity.

Now we can turn to the question of how likely it is that זנה in Lev. 19:29 denotes the act of prostitution.[15] As we have seen, the basic meaning

---

Solomon in 1 Kings 3 also appear to form a household together, independent of male authority over them. Similarly, Keefe, *Women's Body and the Social Body in Hosea*, 20.

13. See, for example, the usage of the nominal forms זנונים (in Gen. 38:24; 2 Kgs 9:22; Ezek. 23:11, 29; Hos. 1:2; 2:4), זנות (in Ezek. 23:27; Hos. 4:11; 6:10), and תזנות (in Ezek. 16:20; 23:8, 17). For examples of the usage of verbal forms, see Gen. 38:24; Lev. 21:9; Deut. 22:21; and Amos 7:17. The usage of verbal forms of זנה in Lev. 21:9 and Gen. 38:24, both of which are often interpreted as involving prostitution, will be discussed below.

14. Similarly, Bird, "The Harlot As Heroine," 103; and Keefe, *Women's Body and the Social Body in Hosea*, 20. Yee, "Hosea," 301, notes how the scholarly tendency to conflate the two has resulted in the misunderstanding of Gomer as a prostitute in Hosea 1–3. Gomer is never labeled a זונה. Rather, she is called an אשת זנונים, a "wife of promiscuity" or "promiscuous wife."

15. An option that will not be seriously considered is that this verse concerns "sacred" or "cultic" prostitution, since a large body of scholarship has been produced in the past few decades that has cast serious doubt on the practice of cultic prostitution,

of זנה is "to engage in sexual relations outside of or apart from marriage," not "to be a prostitute," and the usage of the stem זנה in the context of prostitution is limited to the nominal form זונה. While it is possible that in Lev. 19:29 we have the one case in a biblical text where verbal forms of זנה denote the activities of a prostitute, with the *qal* form meaning "to be a prostitute" or "prostitute oneself" and the *hiphil* meaning "to make someone a prostitute," this reading seems unlikely to be the correct one.[16]

both in ancient Israel and in neighboring cultures. See, e.g., Eugene Fisher, "Cultic Prostitution in the Ancient Near East? A Reassessment," *BTB* 6 (1976): 225–3; Joan Goodnick Westenholz, "Tamar, Qĕdēšā, Qadištu, and Sacred Prostitution in Mesopotamia," *HTR* 82 (1989): 245–65; Julia Assante, "From Whores to Hierodules: The Historiographic Invention of Mesopotamian Female Sex Professionals," in *Ancient Art and Its Historiography*, ed. A. A. Donahue and M. D. Fullerton (Cambridge: Cambridge University Press, 2003), 13–47; Christine Stark, *"Kultprostitution" im Alten Testament? Die Qedeschen der Hebräischen Bibel und das Motiv der Hurerei*, OBO 221 (Fribourg: Academic Press; Göttingen: Vandenhoeck & Ruprecht, 2006); Christl Maier, "Myth and Truth in Socio-Historical Reconstruction of Ancient Societies: Hosea 4:11-14 as a Test Case," in *Thus Says the Lord: Essays on the Former and Latter Prophets in Honor of Robert R. Wilson*, ed. J. J. Ahn and S. L. Cook, LHBOTS 502 (New York: T&T Clark, 2009), 256–72; and Marie-Theres Wacker, "'Kultprostitution' im Alten Israel? Forschungsmythen, Spuren, Thesen," in *Tempelprostitution im Altertum: Fakten und Fiktionen,* ed. Tanja Scheer and Martin Lindner, Oikumene, Studien zur antiken Weltgeschichte 6 (Berlin: Verlag Antike, 2009), 55–84.

16. Many scholars also understand the stem זנה as denoting prostitution in Gen. 38:24 and Lev. 21:9. When we consider these two texts, both of which involve a woman sentenced to death by burning for זנה, several problems arise if one takes זנה as denoting prostitution. First, there is no biblical evidence that prostitution was considered a crime in ancient Israel. It is not prohibited in any of the legal collections, and it is also not prohibited or condemned in any of the narrative texts. Second, the context in which זנה is used in each of these texts makes such a translation unlikely. In Genesis 38, the one time Tamar disguised herself as a prostitute, she was so heavily veiled that Judah did not recognize her. Immediately after their sexual encounter, she went back home and returned to her widow's garments. It seems highly unlikely that anyone else would have recognized Tamar during the very brief interlude when she disguised herself as a prostitute, if her own father-in-law didn't recognize her. Central to the accusation against Tamar in Gen. 38:24 is her pregnancy. One need not be a prostitute to get pregnant. One does, however, need to have sex. Tamar's pregnancy revealed that she engaged in illicit sexual activity by having sexual relations while awaiting levirate marriage to Shelah. Tamar's crime is thus somewhat similar to that addressed by Deut. 22:23-25, sexual relations by a betrothed woman. Lev. 21:9 is discussed below.

The *hiphil* of זנה is used eight other times in the Hebrew Bible. In none of these cases does it appear to mean "make someone a prostitute," nor do any of the occurrences have anything to do with prostitution.[17]

Since the verb זנה here does not seem to denote the act of prostitution, we must now determine how it is being used in this verse. Given that several of the other occurrences of זנה in the *hiphil* involve the figurative use of the term, it is quite possible that זנה is used in Lev. 19:29 in the figurative sense: fathers are warned not to lead their daughters astray by encouraging them to engage in worshipping other gods or other prohibited religious practices. Such behavior would lead to the land going astray, in the sense that others might be influenced into engaging in such illicit activity, as well. In support of this interpretation, there is some biblical evidence that worshipping other gods was viewed as a disease that had to be eradicated lest it spread to the rest of the population (see, e.g., Deuteronomy 13). Moreover, since Lev. 19:29 is both preceded and followed (in v. 31) by laws having to do with forbidden religious practices, it would make sense if it also concerned forbidden religious practices.

Yet there is reason to question whether this is the most likely meaning of זנה in this verse. In Lev. 19:29 and again in 21:9, which addresses the case of a priest's daughter who engages in זנה, it seems odd that daughters alone would be singled out if worship of other gods is what is intended. Is worship of other gods by wives, sons, or other members of the household less problematic than by daughters? One would also expect more severe consequences, not only for the daughter but for the father, if the metaphoric usage is intended here and the daughter, with her father's encouragement, is worshipping other gods or engaging in some other form of apostasy. It seems more likely, given that fathers were considered responsible for maintaining control over their daughters' sexual behavior,[18] that זנה in both Lev. 19:29 and 21:9 refers to a young woman's sexual promiscuity, rather than worship of other gods.

---

17. In four of these occurrences, Exod. 34:16 and 2 Chron. 21:11 and 13 (twice), the *hiphil* of זנה takes an object. All four involve leading people astray into religious infidelity against YHWH. The other usages of זנה in the *hiphil* are in Hosea (Hos. 4:10, 18 [twice]; 5:3), where the *hiphil* is used intransitively. The passage in Hosea 4–5 uses sexual promiscuity as a metaphor for religious infidelity to YHWH, in some cases conflating the two.

18. See, e.g., Deut. 22:20-21, where the bride proven not to have been a virgin when she got married is to be stoned in front of her father's house. The reason given (v. 21): "Because she committed an outrage (נבלה) against Israel by being sexually promiscuous in the house of her father (לזנות בית אביה)." See also M. L.

There are some other indications that the literal meaning of זנה is intended. Generally, when the subject of זנה is an actual woman or women, as it is here, the verb denotes sexually promiscuous behavior. Moreover, זנה and הזנה in this verse are not followed by an object or a preposition, while they are in most cases where the figurative usage is intended.

Since fathers are being addressed regarding their daughters' sexual behavior and there is no reference to husbands, the daughters in question are likely unmarried young women still living at home. זנה in this context thus refers to sexual promiscuity in the form of engaging in premarital sexual relations. While the *hiphil* usually has a causative sense, it also occasionally has a modal sense, denoting the permitting or allowing of an action designated by the *qal*.[19] Since it is difficult to imagine how a father could cause (or make) his daughter engage in sexually promiscuous behavior, the modal sense of זנה is probably the one intended. Each father is charged with preventing his daughter from engaging in premarital sex.[20]

In What Way Is the Daughter Desecrated?

Now that the nature of the daughter's desecrating behavior has been identified, we can turn to the question of how she is desecrated. In what way does a father desecrate his daughter by allowing her to engage in sexually promiscuous behavior, and what is the significance of this form of desecration? To answer this question, we must consider how חלל is used in this context.

Case's discussion of the role that paternal control over premarital female sexuality plays in biblical legal material related to women in "The Inheritance Injunction of Numbers 36: Zelophehad's Daughters and the Intersection of Ancestral Land and Sex Regulation," Chapter 8 in this volume, 204–6.

19. See Bruce K. Waltke and Michael O'Connor, *Biblical Hebrew Syntax* (Winona Lake: Eisenbrauns, 1990), 445–6.

20. The *lamed* is best understood as serving an explanatory function with the *hiphil* infinitive construct, and thus the term can best be translated "by letting her be sexually promiscuous." O. E. Collins, "The Stem ZNH and Prostitution in the Hebrew Bible" (PhD diss., Brandeis University, 1977), 94–5, also interprets the *hiphil* here as having a modal function, translating הזנה as "by allowing her to become unchaste" (94), though he says זנה in this context may refer to either lack of chastity or prostitution, since the result, loss of virginity out of wedlock, would be the same.

The term חלל, to *profane* or *desecrate*, is used in Biblical Hebrew to express negative,[21] involuntary loss of holiness.[22] In contrast to defilement, denoted by טמא, where the person or object becomes impure and, as such, is in a state of opposition to holiness,[23] the object of desecration simply

21. In biblical texts, there is both positive and negative loss of holiness. Positive loss of holiness, best expressed by a neutral English term such as *desanctification* or *desacralization*, involves a voluntary and necessary transition from the realm of the sacred to the realm of the profane. Examples of positive loss of holiness include the rites undergone by someone who has taken a Nazirite vow after the vow has been fulfilled (Num. 6:13-20), the ritual in which the high priest changes clothes and washes after he has fulfilled his responsibilities on the Day of Atonement (Lev. 16:23-24), and the scouring of the metal vessels used to cook holy sacrificial meat (Lev. 6:21). On positive loss of holiness, see Nilton Dutra Amorim, "Desecration and Defilement in the Old Testament" (PhD diss., Andrews University, 1985), 164–77; Jenson, *Graded Holiness*, 51–2; Jacob Milgrom, "Desecration," *Encyclopedia Judaica* 5:1559; and Wright, "Holiness (OT)," 244–5. The vast majority of cases involving loss of holiness are negative, which might explain why there is no specific Hebrew term used to express positive loss of holiness.

22. On the nature of holiness in biblical literature, see (among many others) Wenham, *The Book of Leviticus*, 18–25; Baruch A. Levine, "The Language of Holiness: Perceptions of the Sacred in the Hebrew Bible," in *Backgrounds for the Bible*, ed. Michael Patrick O'Connor and David Noel Freedman (Winona Lake: Eisenbrauns, 1987), 241–55; Levine, *Leviticus*, 256–7; Jenson, *Graded Holiness*, 40–55; Joosten, *People and Land in the Holiness Code*, 123–36; David Wright, "Holiness in Leviticus and Beyond," *Interpretation* 53 (1999): 351–63; Wright, "Holiness (OT)," 237–49; Milgrom, *Leviticus 17–22*, 1711–26; and Baruch J. Schwartz, "Israel's Holiness: The Torah Traditions," in *Purity and Holiness: The Heritage of Leviticus*, ed. M. J. H. M. Poorthuis and Joshua J. Schwartz (Leiden: Brill, 2000), 47–59. On חלל as to profane or desecrate (cause to lose holiness), see *HALOT* 2:319–20; Dommershausen, *TDOT* 4:409–21; Amorim, "Desecration and Defilement in the Old Testament," 164–236; Jenson, *Graded Holiness*, 51–2; Milgrom, "Desecration," 1559; and Wright, "Holiness (OT)," 244–6. While חלל is used almost exclusively to denote negative loss of holiness (and is always used as such in H and Ezekiel, where it occurs most frequently), it is used in one particular context to denote a positive loss of holiness: the point at which vineyards cease to be holy and the grapes can be harvested (see Deut. 20:6; 28:30; and Jer. 31:5). In all other contexts, חלל is used to denote negative loss of holiness.

23. While חלל and טמא may sometimes appear to be used interchangeably, they represent two very different concepts. חלל belongs to the realm of the holy–profane, while טמא belongs to the realm of the clean–unclean. Just as holiness and purity cannot be equated, desecration and defilement cannot be equated. Holiness and impurity are dynamic qualities, while profanity and purity are static qualities, states in which these respective dynamic qualities of holiness and impurity are absent.

loses holiness, becoming profane, or common (חול).²⁴ Some of the things that can be profaned are the name of God (e.g., Lev. 18:21; 19:12; 20:3; 21:6; 22:2; and 22:32; Ezek. 20:39; and Amos 2:7), holy or sacred objects, such as the sacrificial offerings (e.g., Lev. 19:8 and 22:9, 15), sacred times, such as the Sabbath (e.g., Exod. 31:14; Ezek. 20:13, 16, 21, 24; 22:8; 23:38; Isa. 56:2 and 6; and Neh. 13:15-22), sacred places, such as the sanctuary (e.g., Lev. 21:23 and Ezek. 44:7), and, as is the case here, people.

Leviticus 19:29 is one of four instances in H where people profane themselves and/or others. The other three cases are found in the first half of Leviticus 21, which contains instructions intended to safeguard the holiness of priests, mostly by providing restrictions against certain behaviors. Priestly contact with corpses of those who are not close blood kin (v. 4), sexual misbehavior of a priest's daughter (v. 9), and failure of the high priest to marry a suitable bride (vv. 13-15) all result in the loss of holiness on the part of priests and/or their offspring. While there are a few instances outside of H where חלל is used figuratively, with the meaning of debase or degrade,²⁵ in H it appears to always denote literal

---

Thus desecration is the loss of holiness, leading to profanity (חול), and purity is the lack of impurity. On the relationship between the holy and the profane, and the pure and the impure, see Amorim, *Desecration and Defilement in the Old Testament*, 9–10, 246–52, and 338–45; Wenham, *The Book of Leviticus*, 18–25; Jenson, *Graded Holiness*, 40–55; Jacob Milgrom, *Leviticus 1–16: A New Translation with Introduction and Commentary*, AB 3 (New York: Doubleday, 1991), 729–32; Joosten, *People and Land in the Holiness Code*, 124; Walter Houston, *Purity and Monotheism: Clean and Unclean Animals in Biblical Law*, JSOTSup 140 (Sheffield: JSOT Press, 1993), 221–3; Wright, "Holiness (OT)," 246–7; and Donald J. Wold, "The *Kareth* Penalty in P: Rationale and Cases," in *Society of Biblical Literature 1979 Seminar Papers*, ed. Paul J. Achtemeier, 2 vols., SBLSP 16–17 (Missoula: Scholars Press, 1979), 1:1–3.

24. Or, in some cases, the holiness of the object of desecration is diminished. Amorim, *Desecration and Defilement in the Old Testament*, 159 and 345, draws a distinction between tangible and intangible objects of חלל. Tangible objects, such as people, the sanctuary, the land, and holy objects, lose holiness and become profane when they are desecrated, and thus must be consecrated anew, when possible, in order to regain holiness. In contrast, intangible objects, such as the name of God and holy times such as the Sabbath, perhaps suffer a diminishment of holiness to some degree when they are subject to חלל, but never suffer a complete loss of holiness. Amorim suggests that part of the reason for this distinction is that they are intrinsically holy and thus enjoy a higher degree of holiness, the kind that cannot be lost.

25. In Gen. 49:4 and 1 Chron. 5:1, חלל is best understood as "desecrate" or "profane" in this figurative sense. Reuben does not literally desecrate his father's

loss of holiness, and given the overall concern with holiness in Leviticus 19, the literal understanding in this context makes the most sense. The father, by allowing his daughter to engage in such behavior, causes her to lose holiness.[26]

As to the matter of who is blamed for the daughter's loss of holiness, the exhortation is addressed to the father, not the daughter, which seems to indicate that the authors hold each father responsible for his daughter's sexual behavior. When a daughter does manage to desecrate herself through sexually promiscuous behavior, the blame falls upon the father who failed in his responsibility to properly control her sexuality. Yet while the father is to blame if his daughter's sexuality gets out of control, the only one to suffer the consequences would apparently be his daughter. The father did nothing to profane himself. His negligence causes his daughter to fail in her obligatory duty to pursue holiness, and thus she is desecrated, but she is the only one affected.

There is no indication that the daughter in Lev. 19:29 is subject to any additional consequences other than loss of holiness. While adultery, as well as a host of other sexual acts not under the scope of זנה such as incest, bestiality, and male–male sexual relations, is considered punishable by *kareth* (the cutting off of one's line), childlessness, or death elsewhere in H (Lev. 18:29; 20:10-21), sexual promiscuity on the part of an unmarried, non-betrothed woman is apparently not perceived by H as a punishable crime,[27] as long as the one engaging in it is not the daughter of a priest.

---

couch through adulterous sexual relations with his father's concubine Bilhah. The couch was not holy; hence it could not literally have been desecrated. חלל is also used figuratively in Isa. 23:9, in a pronouncement against Tyre.

26. It should be noted that the concept of personal holiness that we find in H is different from that in D. Holiness is never described in H as something the lay population of Israelites already possesses, but rather something they must strive for and that they can lose. This stands in contrast with D, where the people are considered to be already holy through their election by God (see Deut. 7:6; 14:2, 21). On the conception of personal holiness in D, see Moshe Weinfeld, *Deuteronomy and the Deuteronomic School* (Oxford: Clarendon, 1972), 227–8; and Schwartz, "Israel's Holiness," 51–2.

27. This is not necessarily the case outside of H. Exod. 22:15-16 treats (likely consensual) sex with an unmarried, non-betrothed woman as an offense against her father. The perpetrator must pay the father a bride-price and marry the woman, unless the father refuses (in which case he still receives the bride-price). In Deut. 22:20-21, premarital sexual promiscuity is considered a capital crime. If a newly married woman is found guilty of having lost her virginity before marriage (the assumption is that it was through consensual sex, since זנה is used), she is stoned in front of her father's house, which seems to implicate the father to some extent. On these

Leviticus 19:29 and 21:9: A Comparison

Leviticus 21:9 addresses what happens if the daughter of a priest, rather than that of a layman, engages in זנה: "The daughter of a priest, when she desecrates herself (תֵּחֵל)[28] through sexual promiscuity (לזנות)[29]—it is her father she desecrates; she shall be put to the fire." The nature of the daughter's deviant behavior is the same as Lev. 19:29: sexual promiscuity, and given that there is no indication that she is married, we can assume that the daughter is guilty of engaging in premarital sex. The nature of the consequences are to an extent the same as in Lev. 19:29. The daughter suffers loss of holiness. However, this is where the similarity between the two texts ends. While the layman's daughter suffers serious, but not life-threatening consequences, the priest's daughter is sentenced to death by burning. Why the difference in punishment? The key is who is impacted by the daughter's behavior. In Lev. 19:29, the only one who suffers a loss of holiness is the daughter. But in Lev. 21:9, the priest's daughter, through her illicit sexual behavior, desecrates not only herself, but also her father. Why does the priest's daughter's sexual misbehavior profane her father? There must be something about the position of the father as priest that causes his daughter's actions to have such an effect on him.

If we consider Lev. 21:9 within the larger context of instruction directed towards the priests in Leviticus 21, we can see how this verse fits into the regulations intended to safeguard priests' holiness and limit their exposure to impurity. Leviticus 21:4 limits priestly contact with defiling corpses. Leviticus 21:7 instructs priests on the kinds of women they can marry, and the restrictions essentially limit priests to marrying only a virgin or, presumably, a widow. A reason is given for the restriction: each

---

texts, see Alexander Rofé, "Family and Sex Laws in Deuteronomy and the Book of the Covenant," *Henoch* 9 (1987): 131–59; Pressler, *View of Women*; Tikva Frymer-Kensky, "Virginity in the Bible," in *Gender and Law in the Hebrew Bible and the Ancient Near East*, ed. Victor H. Matthews, Bernard M. Levinson, and Tikva Frymer-Kensky, JSOTSup 262 (Sheffield: Sheffield Academic, 1998), 79–96; Hilary Lipka, *Sexual Transgression in the Hebrew Bible*, Hebrew Bible Monographs 7 (Sheffield: Sheffield Phoenix, 2006), 97–102 and 170–84; and Adele Berlin, "Sex and the Single Girl in Deuteronomy 22," in *Mishneh Todah: Studies in Deuteronomy and Its Cultural Environment in Honor of Jeffrey H. Tigay*, ed. Nili Sacher Fox, David A. Glatt-Gilad, and Michael J. Williams (Winona Lake: Eisenbrauns, 2009), 95–112.

28. חלל here is in the *niphal* imperfect feminine singular, with a reflexive force.

29. The form of זנה used, לזנות, is the *qal* infinitive construct preceded by a *lamed*. The *lamed* is best understood as serving an explanatory function with the infinitive, and thus לזנות can best be translated as "by being sexually promiscuous" or "through sexual promiscuity."

priest is holy to his God. Since priests need to preserve a higher level of holiness than that of the lay population in order to perform their priestly functions, restrictions on the classes of women whom a priest might marry are necessary. The restrictions reflect a concern with protection of both priestly lineage (priests must be assured that their offspring are really their own) and reputation. The members of a priest's family, partaking of his portion of the holy sacrifices and living in his household, are expected to conduct themselves with a certain level of propriety. Thus only women of good repute and assumed high moral character, such as widows and virgins, are considered appropriate marital candidates,[30] while prostitutes,[31] divorcées,[32] and women who lost their virginity out

30. With a virgin there is no concern, either regarding paternity of her children or reputation. Widows are also generally above suspicion so far as reputation goes, and one's children with a widow can be presumed to be one's own so long as she waited at least several months to remarry.

31. The reason for the disqualification of prostitutes is likely because prostitution was stigmatized as a profession (see the discussion on pp. 163–4), and having a prostitute for a wife (even if she "retired" upon marriage) would have been considered highly inappropriate, given the level of propriety expected of a priest's family.

32. The disqualification of divorcées is likely also related to negative stigma. There are only a few references to men divorcing their wives in biblical texts, but each of them (Deut. 22:13-14; 24:1; and, in prophetic metaphors in which God "divorces" Israel, Isa. 50:1; Jer. 3:8; Hos. 2:4-7) involves improper behavior or false charges of improper behavior on the part of the wife, and in several, the impropriety is of a sexual nature. Another indication that there was likely a stigma against divorcées is their absence from social welfare provisions. Both widows and divorcées were likely living under the same conditions, often left with no adult male to protect them and see to their welfare. Yet while widows are included among those groups in need of protection, support, and compassion from the community (cf., Exod. 22:21-23; Deut. 14:29; 16:9-15; 24:17-22; 26:12-15; Isa. 1:17; Jer. 22:3), divorcées apparently are left to fend for themselves. This may be a reflection of an attitude that divorced women held some responsibility for their situation, since they must have done something to offend their husband, while widows are viewed as blameless for their circumstances. On the stigma against divorcees, see Milgrom, *Leviticus 17–22*, 1808; and Feinstein, *Sexual Pollution*, 95. Also worth mentioning are two cases in the legal collections which address situations in which women who are enslaved for the purpose of marriage are to be freed: Exod. 21:7-8 (or at least the master/husband must allow her to be redeemed; see Pamela Barmash, "The Daughter Sold Into Slavery and Marriage," Chapter 2 in this volume), and Deut. 21:10-14 (in which a man takes a captive woman as a wife; if at some point he no longer wants her, he must set her free). The circumstances in these two cases are quite different from regular divorce, though, since they involve liberating a female slave from a master/husband who perhaps does not want to free her, and it is done out of concern for the best interest of

of wedlock[33] are designated as off limits.[34] The restrictions imposed on the high priest are even greater, both in terms of avoidance of activities that would expose him to impurity (for example, the high priest must remain within the bounds of the sanctuary, and he is prohibited from being anywhere near a corpse [v. 11]), and in terms of whom he can marry. The high priest is limited in his choice of wife to a virgin of his own kin (vv. 13-14), lest he "profane his seed (זרעו) among his kin" (v. 15).[35]

These verses reflect a belief that priests pass down at least some degree of holiness to their offspring.[36] Yet the inheritance of priestly holiness is not absolute. The high priest (and possibly any priest) can profane

the woman (better to be a free woman with a divorced or semi-divorced status than in her current situation). For a contrasting view, see Sarah Shectman's argument in "Priestly Marriage Restrictions," Chapter 7 in this volume, 183–87 against there being any stigma attached to divorced women.

33. It is not entirely clear what חללה in Lev. 21:7 (and also in v. 14) means. One option is that the term derives from a stem identified by Dommershausen as חלל II that means "to pierce," in which case it could be a descriptive term: "a pierced woman," that is, a woman who has lost her virginity (thus pierced, or penetrated) out of wedlock (see Dommershausen, *TDOT* 4:421; similarly, Hayim Tawil, "The Semantic Range of the Biblical Hebrew חלל: Lexicographical Note X," *ZAW* 117 (2005): 94; *HALOT* 2:320; and Wenham, *Leviticus*, 288). Amorim, *Desecration and Defilement in the Old Testament*, 180–3, reaches a similar conclusion, even though he takes חללה as deriving from the חלל stem meaning "to profane, desecrate" (usually designated as חלל I). Similarly, Feinstein, *Sexual Pollution*, 93–4. The woman is desecrated through losing her virginity out of wedlock. A חללה may not have been considered an appropriate wife for a priest because of presumed past sexual impropriety.

34. These categories of women are only off-limits for priests. We know from Deut. 24:1-4 that divorcées could and did remarry members of the lay population, and presumably prostitutes and חללות could also be married by members of the lay population. While the stigma associated with these categories of women is one possible explanation for the priestly marital restrictions in Lev. 21:7, it is not the only one. For an intriguing, innovative, and completely different explanation for these restrictions, see the discussion in Shectman, "Priestly Marriage Restrictions," 188–92 in this volume.

35. See Shectman, "Priestly Marriage Restrictions," 286–9 in this volume for a detailed discussion of the marital restrictions applied to the high priest.

36. Jenson, *Graded Holiness*, 115, sees a hierarchy of holiness, with the high priest at the top of the hierarchy, followed by the priests, then their families (thus the special rules regarding not only the behavior of priests but also their families), then the Levites, then the clean lay population, then the unclean. This inherited holiness also explains why in Lev. 21:17-23 a physically "defective" male born of the priestly line is prohibited from performing sacrifices at the altar and must stay away from certain sacred spaces in the temple, yet may eat of the most holy offerings.

his children by marrying the wrong woman. If he chooses an inappropriate vessel for his children, his holiness will not be passed down to them. The holiness that should be their birthright will be nullified.[37] It is this inheritance of holiness from the priestly father to his children that might explain why the priest's daughter profanes her father. It may be analogous to the way that the priests and lay population can profane God's name through their misbehavior. God's name sanctifies the people, yet it is also profaned (at least in some sense) by the actions of those it sanctifies.[38] Because of the two-way holiness connection between priests and their children, the high priest who marries inappropriately profanes his offspring, and priestly offspring who profane themselves through their behavior also profane their fathers.[39]

Holiness is achieved and maintained by members of the general population on an individual basis, and it is also lost on an individual basis. But when it comes to the families of priests, because holiness is trans- mitted at least to some extent through the family line, behavior that results in desecration can have a cross-generational impact. While the layman's daughter suffers no punishment other than desecration, the priest's daughter is put to the fire because the loss of holiness that is the

---

37. The requirement that the high priest's wife be a virgin may have to do with a purity restriction, perhaps reflecting a belief that only a woman who has never had another man's seed in her could be pure enough to bear the high priest's offspring. The further restriction to one from his own kin (מעמיו), meaning in this case from the priestly line, indicates something else: that it is not only the father's lineage that is important, but also the mother's. This emphasis on the mother's lineage in vv. 13-15, along with the fact that it is all of the priest's offspring who will be profaned, indicates that daughters, not only sons, inherited some degree of holiness from the priestly line. Similarly, Dommershausen, *TDOT* 4:414–15; and Milgrom, *Leviticus 17–22*, 1820.

38. The desecration of God's name has a negative impact on its power to sanctify (see, for example, Lev. 18:21; 19:12; 20:3; 21:6; 22:2; and 22:32). While sanctification of the divine name increases the power of God (represented by his name) to sanctify, profaning God's name has the opposite effect: the name loses some of its power to sanctify. In Lev. 22:32, this connection is made explicit (see Amorim, *Desecration and Defilement in the Old Testament*, 196–206; Dommershausen, *TDOT* 4:410–12; Milgrom, *Leviticus 17–22*, 1634–6; and Wright, "Holiness [OT]," 246). Thus it appears that sources of sanctification are vulnerable to loss of holiness, at least to some extent, through the negative actions of those they sanctify.

39. Somewhat similarly, Dommershausen, *TDOT* 4:414–15. On the nature of priestly holiness, see Joosten, *People and Land in the Holiness Code*, 128–30; Israel Knohl, *The Sanctuary of Silence: The Priestly Torah and the Holiness School* (Minneapolis: Fortress, 1995), 190–2; Jenson, *Graded Holiness*, 49; and Dommershausen, *TDOT* 4:413–15.

consequence of her behavior goes beyond her to affect her father. Her holiness, intrinsically linked to the holiness of her father, must be maintained, lest she profane her father while profaning herself.

Filling the Land with זמה *(Depravity)*

While the only consequences suffered by the promiscuous layman's daughter herself is loss of holiness, such behavior still poses a very serious threat to the community. Society as a whole is endangered when a father neglects to control his daughter's sexuality, as expressed by the explanation provided in the second part of the verse: "lest the land fall into promiscuity (תזנה) and the land be filled with זמה." The authors of this text seem to view sexual promiscuity as contagious (just as apostasy is contagious). It is especially dangerous to the community because it creates a domino effect: once one young woman engages in illicit sexual behavior, the others will follow, and without warning, people will begin engaging in all sorts of illicit sexual behavior. For this reason, the onus is put on fathers to keep close watch over their daughters, lest there be an outbreak of such behavior among the community.

The result of all of this promiscuity among the inhabitants of the land is that the land will be filled with זמה. The term זמה is part of the vocabulary of deviance, used to label behaviors, often sexual (and always sexual in H and Ezekiel), that appear to be considered particularly intolerable to the community and/or God.[40] The term is used two other times in H, in both cases involving sex with two generations of directly related women. Leviticus 18:17 prohibits a man from having sexual relations with both a woman and her daughter or granddaughter, labeling such behavior זמה. No punishment is cited, but it is part of a group of sexual acts (including adultery, incest, and bestiality) that lead not only to the defilement of those involved, but to the defilement of the land (Lev. 18:24-30). In Lev. 20:14, marriage to a woman and her mother simultaneously is labeled זמה, and a sentence is given: all three are sentenced to death by fire, reflecting

---

40. On זמה, see S. Steingrimsson, "זמם," *TDOT* 4:89–90; Levine, *Leviticus*, 122; Milgrom, *Leviticus 17–22*, 1548 and 1698; and Zimmerli, *Ezekiel 1–20*, 283. Sexual behavior described as זמה includes marital infidelity, both literal (Job 31:11) and metaphoric (by God's metaphoric wife in Jer. 13:27; Ezek. 16:27, 58; 23:21, 27, 29, 35, 44, 48, and 49), sex with a woman who is ritually impure (Ezek. 22:10), various forms of incest (Lev. 18:17; 20:14; Ezek. 22:11), and acts of sexual violence (Judg. 20:6). זמ is used in non-sexual contexts, as well. Examples of non-sexual uses of זמה, which usually involve plotting or scheming, include Deut. 19:19; Isa. 32:7; Ps. 26:10; and Prov. 24:9.

the gravity of the offense. Given that the term seems to be used to label behavior (usually sexual) that the authors find particularly egregious, an appropriate translation of זמה when used in sexual contexts would be *depravity*.

Leviticus 19:29 within the Larger Context of Leviticus 19

The final question that must be addressed is how this admonition fits into the larger context of Leviticus 19 and its concern with achieving holiness. While the men are the only ones in attendance, the call to holiness is addressed to everyone: it is imperative that every member of the community strive for holiness by following the commandments. If the people actively pursue holiness in this way, they will continue to be sanctified by God, who will remain among them in his dwelling place in the sanctuary, and all will go well for them (see Lev. 26:11-12).[41] However, if the population as a collective fails to pursue and achieve holiness, then presumably God will depart from their midst, and everyone will suffer the consequences (cf. Lev. 26:31).[42]

The danger presented by fathers who do not control their daughter's sexual behavior in Lev. 19:29 is two-fold. First, the problem with individuals backsliding in their pursuit of holiness is that there is no way of knowing the limits of God's threshold for tolerating human failure in this endeavor. Because of this uncertainty, every human act that causes loss of personal holiness puts the community at risk of God leaving. Yet the repercussions of allowing such behavior within the community go beyond that. The authors of H see sexual promiscuity on the part of young women not only as contagious, but also as a gateway behavior that will lead to other illicit sexual behaviors among the population. The result will be that the land will be filled with זמה (depravity), which involves not only acts that profane, but, significantly, also acts that defile. In Lev. 18:24-30 and 20:22-24, illicit sexual acts that defile individuals also defile the land, and if the land becomes so polluted with defilement that it

---

41. On how the lay population can achieve holiness according to Leviticus 19 (as well as in H, more generally), see Wright, "Holiness in Leviticus and Beyond," 353–4; Joosten, *People and Land in the Holiness Code*, 123–32; Knohl, *The Sanctuary of Silence*, 180–6; Jenson, *Graded Holiness*, 119; Houston, *Purity and Monotheism*, 248–9; Milgrom, *Leviticus 17–22*, 1602–8; and Schwartz, "Israel's Holiness," 55–9.

42. On the risk that God will leave if the people do not do enough to strive for holiness, see Joosten, *People and Land in the Holiness Code*, 117–18; Levine, "The Language of Holiness," 249–50; Wright, "Holiness in Leviticus and Beyond," 358; and Schwartz, "Israel's Holiness," 48–9.

cannot withstand it any more, it will spit out the people who are defiling it so it can rest.[43] Thus, if fathers fail to properly control their daughters' sexuality, then, in H's worldview, the ultimate result will be exile.[44]

Bibliography

Amorim, Nilton Dutra. "Desecration and Defilement in the Old Testament." PhD diss., Andrews University, 1985.
Andersen, Francis I. and David Noel Freedman. *Hosea: A New Translation with Introduction and Commentary*. AB 24. Garden City: Doubleday, 1980.
Ashley, Timothy R. *The Book of Numbers*. NICOT. Grand Rapids: Eerdmans, 1993.
Assante, Julia. "From Whores to Hierodules: The Historiographic Invention of Mesopotamian Female Sex Professionals." In *Ancient Art and Its Historiography*, edited by A. A. Donahue and M. D. Fullerton, 13–47. Cambridge: Cambridge University Press, 2003.
Berlin, Adele. "Sex and the Single Girl in Deuteronomy 22." In *Mishneh Todah: Studies in Deuteronomy and Its Cultural Environment in Honor of Jeffrey H. Tigay*, edited by Nili Sacher Fox, David A. Glatt-Gilad, and Michael J. Williams, 95–112. Winona Lake: Eisenbrauns, 2009.
Bird, Phyllis. "The Harlot as Heroine: Narrative Art and Social Presupposition in Three Old Testament Texts." In *Women in the Hebrew Bible: A Reader*, edited by Alice Bach, 99–118. New York: Routledge, 1999.
Bird, Phyllis. "To Play the Harlot: An Inquiry into an Old Testament Metaphor." In *Gender and Difference in Ancient Israel*, edited by Peggy Day, 75–94. Minneapolis: Fortress, 1989.
Brenner, Athalya. *The Intercourse of Knowledge: On Gendering Desire and "Sexuality" in the Hebrew Bible*. BibInt 26. Leiden: Brill, 1997.
Collins, O. E. "The Stem ZNH and Prostitution in the Hebrew Bible." PhD diss., Brandeis University, 1977.
Coogan, Michael. *God and Sex: What the Bible Really Says*. New York: Twelve, 2010.
Ellens, Deborah L. *Women in the Sex Texts of Leviticus and Deuteronomy: A Comparative Conceptual Analysis*. LHBOTS 458. New York: T&T Clark, 2008.
Ellens, J. Harold. *Sex in the Bible: A New Consideration*. Westport; Praeger, 2006.
Feinstein, Eve Levavi. *Sexual Pollution in the Hebrew Bible*. New York: Oxford University Press, 2014.
Fisher, Eugene. "Cultic Prostitution in the Ancient Near East? A Reassessment." *BTB* 6 (1976): 225–36.

---

43. Ezekiel 22:9-16 similarly asserts that the consequences of illicit sexual behaviors such as adultery, sex with a woman who is ritually impure, and various forms of incest, which Ezekiel labels as זמה in 22:9 and 11 (in addition to several non-sexual behaviors deemed unacceptable by Yahweh that are listed in 22:1-8) are going to result in exile.

44. Milgrom, *Leviticus 17–22*, 1698, comes to a similar conclusion in terms of the ultimate repercussion of such behavior being exile, though he understands the verse as being about prostitution.

Frymer-Kensky, Tikva. "Virginity in the Bible." In *Gender and Law in the Hebrew Bible and the Ancient Near East*, edited by Victor H. Matthews, Bernard M. Levinson, and Tikva Frymer-Kensky, 79–96. JSOTSup 262. Sheffield: Sheffield Academic, 1998.
Hartley, John E. *Leviticus*. WBC. Nashville: Nelson, 1992.
Houston, Walter. *Purity and Monotheism: Clean and Unclean Animals in Biblical Law*. JSOTSup 140. Sheffield: JSOT Press, 1993.
Jenson, Phillip Peter. *Graded Holiness: A Key to the Priestly Conception of the World*. JSOTSup 106. Sheffield: Sheffield Academic, 1992.
Joosten, Jan. *People and Land in the Holiness Code: An Exegetical Study of the Ideational Framework of the Law in Leviticus 17–26*. VTSup 67. Leiden: Brill, 1996.
Kamionkowski, S. Tamar. "K'doshim." In *The Torah: A Women's Commentary*, edited by Tamara Cohn Eskenazi and Andrea L. Weiss, 701–15. New York: URJ Press, 2008.
Kedar-Kopfstein, Benjamin. "Semantic Aspects of the Pattern *qôṭēl*." *HAR* 1 (1977): 155–76.
Keefe, Alice A. *Women's Body and the Social Body in Hosea*. Sheffield: Sheffield Academic, 2001.
Knohl, Israel. *The Sanctuary of Silence: The Priestly Torah and the Holiness School*. Minneapolis: Fortress, 1995.
Larue, Gerald. *Sex and the Bible*. Buffalo: Prometheus, 1983.
Levine, Baruch A. "The Language of Holiness: Perceptions of the Sacred in the Hebrew Bible." In *Backgrounds for the Bible*, edited by Michael Patrick O'Connor and David Noel Freedman, 241–55. Winona Lake: Eisenbrauns, 1987.
Levine, Baruch A. *Leviticus: The Traditional Hebrew Text with the New JPS Translation*. Philadelphia: Jewish Publication Society, 1989.
Levine, Baruch A. *Numbers 21–36: A New Translation with Introduction and Commentary*. AB 4A. New York: Doubleday, 2000.
Lipka, Hilary. *Sexual Transgression in the Hebrew Bible*. Hebrew Bible Monographs 7. Sheffield: Sheffield Phoenix, 2006.
Maier, Christl. "Myth and Truth in Socio-Historical Reconstruction of Ancient Societies: Hosea 4:11–14 as a Test Case." In *Thus Says the Lord: Essays on the Former and Latter Prophets in Honor of Robert R. Wilson*, edited by J. J. Ahn and S. L. Cook, 256–72. LHBOTS 502. New York: T & T Clark, 2009.
Milgrom, Jacob. "Desecration." *Encyclopedia Judaica* 5:1559–60.
Milgrom, Jacob. *Leviticus 1–16: A New Translation with Introduction and Commentary*. AB 3. New York: Doubleday, 1991.
Milgrom, Jacob. *Leviticus 17–22: A New Translation with Introduction and Commentary*. AB 3A. New York: Doubleday, 2000.
Niditch, Susan. "The Wronged Woman Righted: An Analysis of Genesis 38." *HTR* 72 (1979): 143–9.
Nihan, Christophe. *From Priestly Torah to Pentateuch: A Study in the Composition of the Book of Leviticus*. FAT 2/25. Tübingen: Mohr Siebeck, 2007.
Pressler, Carolyn. *The View of Women Found in the Deuteronomic Family Laws*. BZAW 216. Berlin: de Gruyter, 1993.
Rashkow, Ilona N. *Taboo or not Taboo: Sexuality and Family in the Hebrew Bible*. Minneapolis: Fortress, 2000.
Riegner, Irene E. *The Vanishing Hebrew Harlot: The Adventures of the Hebrew Stem* זנה. StBibLit 73. New York: Lang, 2009.
Rofé, Alexander. "Family and Sex Laws in Deuteronomy and the Book of the Covenant." *Henoch* 9 (1987): 131–59.

Schwartz, Baruch J. "Israel's Holiness: The Torah Traditions." In *Purity and Holiness: The Heritage of Leviticus*, edited by M. J. H. M. Poorthuis and Joshua J. Schwartz, 47–59. Leiden: Brill, 2000.

Schwartz, Baruch J. "A Literary Study of the Slave-girl Pericope—Leviticus 19:20–22." In *Studies in Bible*, edited by Sara Japhet, 241–55. *ScrHier 31*. Jerusalem: Magnes, 1986.

Sklar, Jay. *Leviticus*. TOTC 3. Downers Grove, IL: InterVarsity Press, 2014.

Stark, Christine. *"Kultprostitution" im Alten Testament? Die Qedeschen der Hebräischen Bibel und das Motiv der Hurerei*. OBO 221. Fribourg: Academic Press; Göttingen: Vandenhoeck & Ruprecht, 2006.

Tawil, Hayim. "The Semantic Range of the Biblical Hebrew חלל: Lexicographical Note X." *ZAW* 117 (2005): 91–4.

Wacker, Marie-Theres. "'Kultprostitution' im Alten Israel? Forschungsmythen, Spuren, Thesen." In *Tempelprostitution im Altertum: Fakten und Fiktionen*, edited by Tanja Scheer and Martin Lindner, 55–84. Oikumene; Studien zur antiken Weltgeschichte 6. Berlin: Verlag Antike, 2009.

Waltke, Bruce K., and Michael O'Conner. *Biblical Hebrew Syntax*. Winona Lake: Eisenbrauns, 1990.

Weinfeld, Moshe. *Deuteronomy and the Deuteronomic School*. Oxford: Clarendon, 1972.

Wenham, Gordon J. *The Book of Leviticus*. NICOT. Grand Rapids: Eerdmans, 1979.

Westenholz, Joan Goodnick. "Tamar, Qĕdēšā, Qadištu, and Sacred Prostitution in Mesopotamia." *HTR* 82 (1989): 245–65.

Wold, Donald J. "The *Kareth* Penalty in P: Rationale and Cases." In *Society of Biblical Literature 1979 Seminar Papers*, edited by Paul J. Achtemeier, 1–45. 2 vols. SBLSP 16–17. Missoula: Scholars Press, 1979.

Wright, David. "Holiness in Leviticus and Beyond." *Interpretation* 53 (1999): 351–64.

Wright, David. Holiness (OT)." *ABD* 3:237–49.

Yee, Gale. "Hosea." In *The Women's Bible Commentary, Revised and Updated*, edited by Carol A. Newsom, Sharon H. Ringe, and Jacqueline E. Lapsley, 299–308. 3rd ed. Louisville: Westminster John Knox, 2012.

Zimmerli, Walther. *Ezekiel 1: A Commentary on the Book of the Prophet Ezekiel, Chapters 1–24*. Translated by Ronald E. Clements. Hermeneia. Philadelphia: Fortress, 1979.

7

Priestly Marriage Restrictions*

Sarah Shectman

Leviticus 21 contains various rules related to the behavior of priests, intended to ensure that the priests maintain their purity—and the purity of the sancta—while in cultic service. The rules cover contact with corpses, marriage restrictions, and physical requirements for priests in active service in the temple. I will focus here on the laws about marriage and especially on the exclusion of divorced women from marriage with priests. Interpretations of this rule have failed to provide an explanation that fits with biblical evidence about divorce; indeed, biblical marriage and divorce are poorly understood due to the limited evidence, despite the popular valorization of the institution of "biblical marriage." I will thus attempt to develop an understanding of how biblical marriage and divorce were understood and what it was about divorce specifically that rendered a divorced woman ineligible for marriage to a priest.

Leviticus 21:7 and 13-14 list the types of women a regular priest and the high priest, respectively, are allowed to marry. Forbidden for the regular priest are a prostitute (זנה), a "defiled" woman (חללה), and a

---

* This paper was presented in the Priests and Levites in History and Tradition program unit at the Society of Biblical Literature Annual Meeting in Baltimore, Maryland, in November 2013. Thanks to Claudia Camp, Eve Feinstein, and Annette Schellenberg for feedback on that draft. It was also presented at a meeting of the Bay Area Bible Scholars in January 2017; additional thanks to the members present then, including Aaron Brody, Eve Feinstein, Ron Hendel, Kyong-Jin Lee, Ingrid Lilly, and Jenna Stover-Kemp.

divorced woman (גרושה).[1] The high priest is also forbidden from marrying a widow (אלמנה); he is to marry a virgin (בתולה) "of his own kin" (מעמיו). Ezekiel, because he does not acknowledge a high priest, extends the restriction on widows to all priests. According to Ezek. 44:22, all priests must marry virgin Israelite women, though with the exception that they may marry the widows of other priests. Ezekiel has nothing to say about defiled women and prostitutes, perhaps because this exclusion is covered by the virgin stipulation.

The High Priest

For the high priest in Leviticus 21, and for all priests in Ezekiel to a slightly lesser extent, the rules seem fairly straightforward: a virgin is required, in order to safeguard the sexual and genealogical purity of the priestly line. Leviticus 21:15 makes this explicit: the high priest is not to "profane his offspring among his kin, because I, Yahweh, sanctify him."[2] Making sure the woman is a virgin ensures that there is no possibility that she could have been impregnated by another man, thus maintaining the purity of the priestly genetic line. It also ensures that the woman does not bear what Eve Feinstein has termed the sexual "marking essence" of another man, a quasi-physical residue left behind by sexual intercourse, which might infiltrate her partner and, thereby, his offspring.[3] In Ezekiel, too, allowing the widow only of another priest may be aimed at

---

1. On the range of meanings and nuances for these terms, see, e.g., Eve Levavi Feinstein, *Sexual Pollution in the Hebrew Bible* (New York: Oxford University Press, 2014), 76, 93–4; Hilary Lipka, *Sexual Transgression in the Hebrew Bible*, Hebrew Bible Monographs 7 (Sheffield: Sheffield Phoenix, 2006), 249–50; and Lipka, "The Offense, Its Consequences, and the Meaning of זנה in Leviticus," Chapter 6 in this volume, 161–7.

2. The wording here may also reflect a literary attempt to provide structure, linking this verse to v. 9, where it is the daughter who defiles her father; see Jacob Milgrom, *Leviticus 17–22: A New Translation with Introduction and Commentary*, AB 3A (New York: Doubleday, 2000), 1820, 1836.

3. See Feinstein, *Sexual Pollution*, 94–5. Feinstein also notes the similarity between marriage and mourning restrictions for the high priest: "The high priest is required to remain absolutely free of such pollution" (95). The priestly author here refers to the idea of genealogical purity, an idea also reflected in Ezek. 44:22 and Ezra 9 (see ibid., 95–7, 154). As Feinstein also notes, "lineal purity does not seem to be the central concern" (ibid., 97). See also Feinstein, "Purity of Priests: Contamination through Marriage," *TheTorah.com*, 10 May 2017, http://thetorah.com/purity-of-priests-contamination-through-marriage/.

genealogical matters: if the woman is the widow of another priest, there is no possibility of entanglements with non-priestly lines.[4]

Though the marriage restrictions for the high priest in Leviticus 21 seem fairly clear, one aspect remains unclear: the precise meaning of מעמיו applied to the woman the high priest is allowed to marry. Does this refer to a woman from a priestly family only, or is it a broader, even pan-Israelite designation? Scholars disagree on this question,[5] though elsewhere in Leviticus 21 עם is used to refer to closer, that is, priestly, kin.[6] But Ezek. 44:22 also permits priests to marry any Israelite virgin, not only virgins of priestly families. Though Ezekiel may simply have a looser restriction than Leviticus, Ezekiel's limitation of all priests to virgins or widows of priests also suggests that he tends, if anything, to be more restrictive, not less so. However, because Ezekiel does not distinguish between regular priests and the high priest, he may have adopted the lesser restriction on clan or family membership for all priests.

If מעמיו in Leviticus 21 does refer only to a woman from a priestly family, as opposed to just any Israelite woman, then there would seem to be some redundancy here: the daughter of a priest who prostitutes or sexually defiles herself is, according to Lev. 21:9, to be burned.[7] In theory, then, there should not *be* a זנה or a חללה of a priestly family (מעמיו) available for marriage, rendering the restriction on marrying such a woman unnecessary. If the high priest is indeed restricted by Leviticus 21 to marrying a woman from a priestly family,[8] the repetition of the list of forbidden women in v. 14 may therefore be something of a formality, echoing the list for the regular priest in v. 7, as is suggested by the inverted

---

4. As Feinstein, *Sexual Pollution*, 96, notes, Ezekiel's allowance of a priest's widow "reveals [the rule's] inner logic: A woman who has had sex with another priest remains an acceptable partner because the essence with which she has been marked comes from a holy source." Why the divorced wife of another priest would not be allowed is less clear; Feinstein argues that it is because "she has been rejected."

5. Milgrom, for example, takes it to mean that the woman must be from a priestly family; Milgrom, *Leviticus 17–22*, 1819.

6. See Feinstein, *Sexual Pollution*, 95. Feinstein argues that the עם of the priest probably means a very close kin group, namely, the priest's extended family. See Lev. 21:1, 4, 15. Elsewhere in the H corpus (Leviticus 17–26), however, it seems to refer to the broader community of priests or even of Israelites. See Milgrom, *Leviticus 17–22*, 1471–2; Lev. 17:4, 9, 10; 18:29; 19:8, 16, 18; 20:3, etc.

7. See Lipka, "The Offense, Its Consequences, and the Meaning of זנה in Leviticus," in this volume, esp. 171, on this verse.

8. See Sarah Shectman, "The Social Status of Priestly and Levite Women," in *Levites and Priests in History and Tradition*, ed. Mark A. Leuchter and Jeremy M. Hutton, SBLAIIL 9 (Atlanta: SBL, 2011), 88–9.

word order, with the additional prohibition of the widow foregrounded at the beginning of the list.⁹ In the case of the regular priest, who is not limited to a wife from a priestly family, there is no redundancy in forbidding the defiled woman or the prostitute. The redundancy in the case of the high priest is a result of the author's formal use of inverted literary structure. But the message is nevertheless clear: the high priest must marry a virgin, probably one from another priestly family, restrictions that are intended to safeguard the genealogical purity of the high priest's line.

The Ordinary Priest

The reasoning behind the rules for the regular priest is less clear than is the case for the high priest. He is neither required to marry a woman from a particular family or line nor is he explicitly required to marry a virgin. The omission of the widow from the list of excluded women in v. 7 (and Ezekiel's middle position on marrying widows) also suggests that he could marry a widow.¹⁰ And whereas the rule for the high priest focused on genealogical purity, the motive clause in Lev. 21:8 states that the restrictions in v. 7 are meant to safeguard the purity of the priest in his service to Yahweh and his proximity to the holy, in particular the sacred offerings (some of which would have gone home for the priest's wife and children to eat).¹¹ Thus, in the case of the regular priest, the concern seems to be with the purity of the priest and his wife themselves. As Feinstein argues, a חללה, likely meaning an unmarried woman who has had sex,¹² and a זנה, or prostitute, are forbidden because they have had sex outside of marriage, habitually in the case of the latter, and are therefore perceived as unfit for marriage to a priest,¹³ though both forms of sexual activity, unlike adultery, are technically licit.

The question in which I am really interested, however, is why the priest may marry a widow but not a divorced woman. At first glance it might seem logical that a divorced woman is not deemed a suitable wife for a priest, and indeed this tends to be the scholarly conclusion.¹⁴ Explanations

---

9. See Feinstein, *Sexual Pollution*, 232–3 n. 297. See also the discussion of literary structure by Christine Hayes in Milgrom, *Leviticus 17–22*, 1834–6.
10. See Milgrom, *Leviticus 17–22*, 1819.
11. See Shectman, "Social Status," 93–5.
12. Feinstein, *Sexual Pollution*, 93–4.
13. Ibid., 94.
14. See, e.g., Milgrom, *Leviticus 17–22*, 1808; Feinstein, *Sexual Purity*, 95; Jonathan Klawans, *Impurity and Sin in Ancient Judaism* (New York: Oxford University Press, 2000), 29, suggests that a divorced woman also suffers from a moral

focus on reasons that are considered to be obvious: the woman is not a virgin, the status of potential sons may therefore come into question, or there is a stigma attached to divorce. However, none of these explanations are satisfactory. Though the woman cannot be a prostitute (זנה) or defiled (חללה), she need not be a virgin specifically. Likewise, if offspring (the woman's hypothetical non-priestly sons by her former husband, in particular) were the concern, they would be a problem for a widow as well, and yet she is permitted. A potentially pregnant widow is the same as a divorced woman in this regard, and in either case there is a simple solution: just wait a few months. Ezekiel's restriction allowing only widows of priests might be an effort to deal with the problem of offspring, especially sons, from non-priestly lineages being brought into a priestly household by a widow with children—though if that is the case, then the divorced wife of a priest should also be allowed.[15] Moreover, Lev. 21:8 itself makes clear that cultic purity (for offering sacrifices) rather than genealogical purity is the issue.[16] Thus the offspring argument, too, falls down.

This leaves the final argument: the alleged stigma attached to divorce, in some way analogous to the stigma attached to harlotry and prostitution. This is the argument used by Jacob Milgrom, who claims that "the prohibition focuses on reputation," in particular on the possibility that the divorced woman may also be an adulteress.[17] But this explanation,

impurity that leads to her exclusion as a wife for a priest. The notes for this text in Tamara Cohn Eskenazi and Andrea L. Weiss, eds., *The Torah: A Women's Commentary* (New York: URJ, 2008), 727–8, argue that certain passages seem to connect divorce with some kind of impropriety, ignoring those texts that do not.

15. Possibly the widow could have come with some property that she owned as a result of her husband's death, especially if she had no sons to inherit or if those sons were minors, making her more appealing than the divorced woman as a wife. However, the problems this might have caused could just as easily have rendered it a strike against her as a potential wife.

16. Feinstein, *Sexual Pollution*, 95. The concept of genealogical purity is introduced only for the high priest's line, in v. 15. On the concerns with priestly purity in these verses, see also Lipka, "The Offense, Its Consequences, and the Meaning of זנה in Leviticus," in this volume, esp. 171–2.

17. Milgrom, *Leviticus 17–22*, 1808; see also Feinstein, *Sexual Pollution*, 95: "Most likely, the issue here is one of status: The divorcée has been rejected by another man, while the widow is simply a victim of circumstance.... [A] divorcée was in some way defective, and accepting another man's 'reject' would ill-befit a priest." According to Feinstein, there is a qualitative difference between a widow and a divorced woman, despite the fact that their marking essences should be conceived of identically because they came about in the context of licit marital relations.

too, is inadequate, primarily because there is no evidence that a social stigma was attached to divorce in ancient Israel. The legal texts that refer directly to divorce generally take it as a matter of course without attaching a negative valuation to the action or impugning the woman's behavior.[18] A divorced woman is allowed to remarry; the only restriction on remarriage, in Deuteronomy 24, is on her marrying a previous husband after she has married someone else and been divorced or widowed from that husband.[19]

In addition, according to Lev. 22:13, the divorced or widowed childless daughter of a priest is allowed to return to her father's house and eat sacred portions, suggesting that any effects of divorce are minimal and do not influence the woman's purity status.[20] According to Deut. 21:14, the captive woman taken as a wife is explicitly permitted a divorce and is protected from being treated as a slave and sold should her husband not be pleased with her. The specific word used of her release, ושלחתה, is divorce terminology.[21] Similarly, the enslaved wife in Exod. 21:7-11 may not be sold if her husband no longer wishes to support her, indicated by his failure to fulfill her marital rights; instead, she is to be released and

---

Feinstein argues on the analogy to corpse contamination being permissible for regular priests for certain close family members; since all corpses are equally polluting, this is a "qualitative" judgment about which settings allow for some slippage of the more-stringent rules that apply to the high priest. More than this qualitative judgment, though, I would argue that these differences are relational—that is, they have to do with particular relationships and social bonds (see below). In the case of the divorced woman, the former husband is likely still alive, whereas the widow's former husband is dead. Though cultic/purity distinctions and qualitative judgments may play some role, the importance of social relationships should not be ignored.

18. Even Deuteronomy 24, which allows for the husband's finding something repellent in his wife, does not seem to stigmatize the woman for anyone other than her first husband. Some texts might even suggest that it is the right of a woman whose husband is not providing for her adequately. See Yair Zakovitch, "The Woman's Rights in the Biblical Law of Divorce," *JLA* 4 (1977): 35–6, who argues that women did have some right to divorce. See also Bernard S. Jackson, "The 'Institutions' of Marriage and Divorce in the Hebrew Bible," *JSS* 56 (2011): 221–51. On texts dealing with divorce, see Kenneth Bergland, "Divorce Instruction and Covenantal Unfaithfulness: A New Examination of the Reuse of Deuteronomy 24:1-4 as Metaphor in Jeremiah 3:1-10," Chapter 11 in this volume.

19. See the discussion of this passage in Feinstein, *Sexual Pollution*, 53–65.

20. Shectman, "Social Status," 94.

21. Though the term can refer simply to sending someone away, it is often used in the context of ending a marriage; see Deut. 22:19, 29; 24:1, 4. On divorce terminology, see Zakovitch, "Woman's Rights," 35.

restored to free status. Though in this case specifically divorce-related terms are not used, if she is a wife and she is being released rather than sold, it is hard to see what to call this if not divorce.[22] The perception in Deuteronomy 21 and Exodus 21 of divorce as a protection, perhaps even a right, also argues against a stigma being attached to it.

Some argue that the divorced woman is stigmatized because divorce is connected to adultery—that adultery is even assumed in cases of divorce. However, the texts that make a connection between divorce and adultery appear primarily in prophetic literature, in the prophetic marriage metaphor.[23] And there is a striking difference between the prophetic and the legal handling of divorce. Though the prophetic literature connects divorce to adultery, this is all it does. That is, it depicts divorce as the usual consequence of adultery.[24] In contrast, the legal literature requires that the confirmed adulteress and her partner be put to death.[25] Thus, in

22. As Pamela Barmash notes ("The Daughter Sold into Slavery and Marriage," Chapter 2 in this volume), there is no single definition of *marriage* or *wife* in the Hebrew Bible, and a variety of relationships seem to be covered loosely under the umbrella of what we call *marriage*. Nevertheless, the text of Exod. 21:7-11 sees the release of the woman from this sexual relationship as a protection and as a *right* to which she was entitled. See also Sarah Shectman, "What Do We Know about Marriage in Ancient Israel?" in *Reading a Tendentious Bible: Essays in Honor of Robert B. Coote*, ed. Marvin L. Chaney, Uriah Y. Kim, and Annette Schellenberg, Hebrew Bible Monographs 66 (Sheffield: Sheffield Phoenix, 2014), 166–75.

23. See, e.g., Naomi Graetz, "God Is to Israel as Husband Is to Wife: The Metaphoric Battering of Hosea's Wife," in *A Feminist Companion to the Latter Prophets*, ed. Athalya Brenner, FCB 8 (Sheffield: Sheffield Academic, 1995), 126–45.

24. See, e.g., Hos. 2:1-9; Ezekiel 16; 23. Even in Ezekiel, where the metaphor is far more graphic and troubling, the adulterous Israel ultimately lives. This is not to say that there is no connection between the legal and the prophetic use of divorce or that the latter did not draw in some ways on the former; see Bergland, "Divorce Instruction and Covenantal Unfaithfulness."

25. See Feinstein, *Sexual Pollution*, 62. The death penalty in legal literature pertains to anyone caught in the act; when there is no eyewitness, then it is not treated as confirmed adultery, and the death penalty does not apply (as in Deut 22:25-27, where the woman is given the benefit of the doubt and not killed, though the man is, and in the case of the suspected adulteress in Num. 5:11-31). Likewise, the prohibition on adultery in Lev. 18:20 does not address the circumstances or the existence of witnesses. The penalty (Lev. 18:29) for the man is that he will be "cut off" (כרת); the text does not specify what happens to the woman. This case also seems to be akin to suspicion of adultery, rather than a confirmed case with witnesses; Lipka, *Sexual Transgression*, 52–8, 104, 120, notes the similarity in the penalties in Lev. 18:29 and Num. 5:11-31. Furthermore, the legal literature nowhere connects divorce to adultery; see Feinstein, *Sexual Pollution*, 61–2, for a rebuttal to Eckart Otto's argument that the

the legal literature, with which we are concerned here, a divorced woman *cannot be* an adulteress.

Why Is Divorce Problematic?

What is it, then, about divorce that renders a divorced woman an unfit wife for a priest? Feinstein argues, rightly, that in the ancient Israelite understanding, sexual intercourse left a sort of invisible but very real residue of pollution on a woman—what she terms a *marking essence*. This marking essence was not problematic if it took place within the licit confines of a marriage; in this case, the woman was sexually pure. But problems arose if sexual relations took place outside of marriage; then, the marking essence might become negative and polluting.[26] The primary effect of sexual intercourse was to mark the woman as her husband's sexual property and therefore off limits to other men. Feinstein notes, "A wife, as her husband's sexual property, can be described as pure so long as he alone has sexual access to her. Having his essence as part of her is an aspect of her rightful status as wife. When another man enters her, she becomes contaminated with his essence, which ruins her for her husband."[27] Feinstein's model is particularly useful in understanding adultery: the adulteress is characterized as polluted,[28] and, in the legal material, her death is required as a result. Feinstein's explanation is also useful for the case of the divorced woman in Deuteronomy 24: divorce spoils the relationship for the woman and her first husband. The woman is called *defiled* (הֻטַּמָּאָה), but her defilement is *relational*—it exists only in relation to her first husband and not anyone else.[29] She may go on to have as many subsequent marriages, one at a time, as she likes. It is only prior husbands who become forbidden.

Neither the divorced woman nor the widow, then, was inherently spoiled as a spouse and appropriate sexual partner by virtue of the fact that she had been marked by a prior husband's sexual essence. The common

---

divorce in Deut. 24:1-4 is a result of the wife's adultery. For a summary of views on adultery and its punishment, see Eckart Otto, *Deuteronomium 12–34*, Erster Teilband: 12, 1-23, 15, HTKAT (Freiburg: Herder, 2016), 1715–17.

26. Feinstein, *Sexual Pollution*, 91.
27. Ibid., 49.
28. Ibid., 50.
29. Ibid., 64. For a detailed discussion of the meaning of the term ערות דבר and why it does not indicate a stigma or illicit behavior as grounds for divorce (the woman does remarry, after all, so it cannot be not a mark against her having a future husband), see ibid., 54–64.

element is that both the divorced woman and the widow had intercourse within the confines of marriage; thus, according to Feinstein's model, they both contracted sexual pollution of the licit kind, which would permit future marriages to men they had not been married to previously. The same women were excluded from marrying the high priest, whose heightened holiness required a virgin wife, a woman who was entirely sexually unmarked.[30] But as Feinstein notes, sexual purity cannot explain the distinction between the widow and the divorced woman for the regular priest, or the allowance of a priest's widow, but not his divorced wife, in Ezekiel. Thus Feinstein, too, argues that the stigma of the divorced woman's rejection by another man explains her exclusion, but not the widow's, as a suitable wife for a priest.[31]

None of these explanations make sense of the distinction between the widow and the divorced woman because in the end, they all require a special understanding of divorce that is not attested elsewhere in the Hebrew Bible. Instead of looking to understand how divorce itself might have been perceived, then, it will be more useful to approach divorce through the lens of marriage: how did divorce end a marriage, and how did it differ from widowhood in doing so?

The Cord Analogy

Here, Feinstein's point that the purity of the woman in Deuteronomy 24 is relational—that her sexual experience, and especially her divorce, marks her in relationship to other men, though it is not in and of itself problematic—is instructive. A woman's status in ancient Israel was determined by her primary male bond—that is, her relationship to a man.[32] At birth, this bond was with the woman's father, and her father's social status determined her own. This explains the apparent requirement that the high priest marry the daughter of a priestly family. Upon marriage, a woman formed a new primary bond with her husband. This bond effectively replaced the bond with the father, though in the event that the marriage

---

30. Ibid., 93–4.
31. Ibid., 95.
32. On women's legal and economic dependence on male relatives, see Phyllis Bird, *Missing Persons and Mistaken Identities: Women and Gender in Ancient Israel*, OBT (Minneapolis: Fortress, 1997), 21–31, esp. 31; Jennie Ebeling, *Women's Lives in Biblical Times* (London: T&T Clark, 2011), 27; Saul Olyan, *Rites and Rank: Hierarchy in Biblical Representations of Cult* (Princeton: Princeton University Press, 2000), 31.

was dissolved without children, the daughter might return to her father's house—so some element of the bond remained permanent. We see this in the example of the priest's childless widowed or divorced daughter, who is allowed to return to her father's house and resume eating sacrificial portions.[33] The bond with the husband, of course, was sexual and involved sexual pollution (of a licit and therefore harmless nature). But as we have seen, sexual pollution is not determinative for all aspects of the woman's identity—it only affects her relationship to her husband. It is not carried over into her relationships with future husbands, since remarriage after divorce or widowhood is possible. Thus, there must be something about the marriage bond itself that is significant.[34] Here, I think it is helpful to analogize the bond in physical terms, as a sort of cord connecting the husband and wife. When a marriage ends, what happens to this cord? In the case of the husband's death, the cord dissolves and disappears, but in the case of divorce, the cord is cut, leaving a length attached to the woman.

Of course, though the cord connects both husband and wife, the restrictions it creates are primarily relevant for the woman: she can only have a single connected cord at a time, whereas a man can have multiples. A woman can have multiple *cut* cords, though—or, perhaps better, she can retie her cord to another husband after it has been cut. The divorced woman's cut cord limits her options for remarriage in two ways, however: she cannot retie her cord to her prior husband if she has married someone else in the meantime. And she cannot tie her cord to a priestly cord. The priest, in other words, requires a woman with no cord.

A widow's cord, unlike a divorced woman's, dissolves completely, leaving her somewhat freer in her options: she may marry a regular priest. However, the cord appears to leave some sort of trace—something like a pressure mark, to extend the analogy—that prevents her from marrying the high priest. In this regard, the cord is similar to the sexual essence, which leaves a kind of residue. Perhaps the concern was with virginity,

---

33. Apparently having a son also affects her primary male bond—perhaps permanently connecting her to her husband. Again, though, if concerns of children, property, or inheritance were at issue, we might expect to see stipulations about the woman's parental status here, as we see in the laws about priestly daughters returning to their fathers' households and eating sacrificial portions.

34. As Feinstein also points out, these Priestly (H) laws focus on women's sexuality from the perspective of purity, not only from that of the father's or husband's property rights (as is the case, e.g., in Exodus 22 and Deuteronomy 22; 24); Feinstein, *Sexual Pollution*, 49–50, 64.

not with the cord, but again, the shift in the law in Ezekiel suggests that virginity (or another man's sexual essence, to use Feinstein's model) is not the only issue. Ezekiel's ruling that a priest may marry a widow of another priest—meaning that her cord was previously tied to a priest—indicates that despite his broadening of the restriction on widows in comparison to Leviticus 21, Ezekiel nevertheless considered the mark left by the cord acceptable in this case. And as in Leviticus, a woman with a cut cord is unacceptable for a priest in Ezekiel.

The cord analogy highlights the key difference between the divorced woman and the widow: the divorced woman's husband is still alive and her primary male bond is therefore not entirely clear. Though divorce severs that bond, it does not completely erase it and thereby resolve the question of the woman's primary male affiliation. In most cases this is not a problem, but for priests, where clarity of categorization is particularly important, it renders the woman unfit as a wife. And for the high priest, the existence of the prior bond, though it is severed or dissolved, is even more problematic. The cord analogy also explains why divorced *men* are never a topic of discussion in the Hebrew Bible and why priests, despite the prohibition against marrying divorced women, are never restricted from getting divorced themselves. The cord has almost no effect on a man, the one exception being the law barring remarriage in Deuteronomy 24.[35] The bond affects the woman uniquely because women, unlike men, are defined socially in relation to this bond.

The cord analogy also explains the status of prostitutes. Though frowned upon in a "not my daughter" kind of way, prostitution is never explicitly forbidden, and men—even priests, presumably—are not prohibited from visiting prostitutes (though a priest may not marry one). Moreover, men are not prohibited from visiting the same prostitute more than once, even if she has had intercourse with another man in the meantime (which surely could have happened).[36] If revisiting a prostitute was not considered a defiling act (any more so than any other licit act of sexual

---

35. It is not entirely clear that the category of "divorced man" existed in ancient Israel. Divorce was a man's prerogative and pertained to his ability to divorce his wife if he desired. Men, unlike women, were not defined or limited by their marital status; men did not move into and out of different kin groups as women did when they married—they were the patriline. Thus male divorce may simply not have been a concept.

36. Nor is there any prohibition against a lay Israelite marrying a prostitute, as long as she discontinues her activities after the marriage, since that would constitute adultery.

intercourse was), then the issue in Deuteronomy 24 must not only be sexual pollution.[37] There is something more going on because the couples were married. The marriage bond—the cord itself—creates the problem of entanglement after the bond is broken.[38] A prostitute, unlike a married woman, has no primary male bond—she has no cord at all—and therefore there is nothing to get tangled.[39]

This aspect of the cord analogy also helps make sense of the priestly prohibition against marrying a זנה or a חללה. These women belong to a problematic category of women who have had sex but who have no cord. If sex is supposed to take place only within the confines of marriage, then a woman with no cord who has had sex is an anomaly.[40] Feinstein's marking essence may also apply here, but it is the marital status of the woman that is particularly relevant. These women have unclear primary male bonds, and they are therefore unfit as wives for priests. Imagined physically, sexual essence acquired without a cord is just as problematic as sexual essence with a cut cord, where marrying a priest is concerned.

This cord analogy on its own does not explain why marrying a divorced woman would be a concern for priests but not for non-priests. But the rules about whom a priest may marry take for granted that their priestly status requires different standards for partners by virtue of the very fact that they are priests. Just as laypeople are not forbidden from marrying other types of women (including a prostitute), the author of Leviticus 21 seems simply to take for granted that there are different rules for priests. Though premarital sex did not necessarily preclude a woman from marrying either the man she had premarital sex with or another man, she

---

37. Or perhaps prostitutes cannot be sexually polluted.
38. The fact that adultery laws also applied to betrothed women (Deut. 22:23-27), meaning that intercourse had not yet taken place, also suggests that the issue was one of relationship bond, not only of physical pollution.
39. In theory, a (former) prostitute could get married, and then she would have a cord. At that point, adultery would result in her death. However, this seems like an unlikely scenario.
40. Feinstein, *Sexual Pollution*, 87, notes, "Sex outside wedlock taints a female in some way that can apparently not be fully remedied." Though the focus is often on adultery, it is noteworthy that this principle applied to non-marital sex of any kind, including premarital sex (see ibid., 86–7). Feinstein, "Purity of Priests," also notes, "Because the husband of a divorcée might still be alive, her sexual connection with him would be felt more keenly than in the case of a widow, whose husband was deceased." This connection can best be understood conceptually through the cord analogy.

could not marry a priest. In that regard, it must surely be about the priest's purity—as the text suggests. That is, the marital cord and the question of the woman's primary bond also fall under the rubric of purity in this case, as does Feinstein's sexual essence. The sexual essence alone also does not provide a complete explanation, since the widow is permissible. Both the cord and the essence explanations are needed. Only with both does the difference between the widow and the divorced woman become clear: both have another man's essence, but in the case of the widow, the previous husband is deceased and the cord is dissolved, which renders the sexual essence unproblematic.

Conclusions

At a very basic level, the women a priest is not allowed to marry—the חללה, the זנה, and the divorced woman—have in common that their past sexual partners are still alive. Though it is possible that this is what lies behind the prohibition of these three kinds of women for the priest, I suspect that there is more to it. Not only does the death of the husband not solve the problem of pollution in Deuteronomy 24, but there is also no suggestion that a defiled woman or prostitute would become an acceptable wife if all her former sexual partners were to die. There is some significance to the proper formation and dissolution of sexual connections—that is, the way in which the woman acquired the sexual essence, the context, inside or outside of marriage. The nature of the woman's relationship(s) to the men who are her sexual partners matters, just as it does for the divorced and remarried woman in Deuteronomy 24.

The restrictions on whom a priest may marry, then, are not focused only on sexual purity: the sexual bond (Feinstein's marking essence) and the marriage bond are not the same thing, despite the fact that they frequently overlap. Rather, the marriage bond has a quasi-physical nature of its own, transferring a woman's primary male bond from one man to another. Because divorce severed this bond but did not dissolve it completely, the woman was left in an ambiguous state that rendered her unfit for marriage (the transfer of her bond) to a priest. A woman must have a cord when she acquires another man's sexual essence in order to later be eligible to marry a priest. To marry other men, the cord may be cut (divorce), but to marry a priest, the cord must have dissolved, a result of the husband's death. And for the high priest, the woman must be a virgin—she can have no sexual essence and no cord at all.

Bibliography

Bird, Phyllis. *Missing Persons and Mistaken Identities: Women and Gender in Ancient Israel*. OBT. Minneapolis: Fortress, 1997.
Ebeling, Jennie. *Women's Lives in Biblical Times*. London: T&T Clark, 2011.
Eskenazi, Tamara Cohn, and Andrea L. Weiss, eds. *The Torah: A Women's Commentary*. New York: URJ, 2008.
Feinstein, Eve Levavi. "Purity of Priests: Contamination through Marriage." *TheTorah.com*, 10 May 2017, http://thetorah.com/purity-of-priests-contamination-through-marriage/.
Feinstein, Eve Levavi. *Sexual Pollution in the Hebrew Bible*. New York: Oxford University Press, 2014.
Graetz, Naomi. "God Is to Israel as Husband Is to Wife: The Metaphoric Battering of Hosea's Wife." In *A Feminist Companion to the Latter Prophets*, edited by Athalya Brenner, 126–45. FCB 8. Sheffield: Sheffield Academic, 1995.
Jackson, Bernard S. "The 'Institutions' of Marriage and Divorce in the Hebrew Bible." *JSS* 56 (2011): 221–51.
Klawans, Jonathan. *Impurity and Sin in Ancient Judaism*. New York: Oxford University Press, 2000.
Lipka, Hilary. *Sexual Transgression in the Hebrew Bible*. Hebrew Bible Monographs 7. Sheffield: Sheffield Phoenix, 2006.
Milgrom, Jacob. *Leviticus 17–22: A New Translation with Introduction and Commentary*. AB 3A. New York: Doubleday, 2000.
Olyan, Saul. *Rites and Rank: Hierarchy in Biblical Representations of Cult*. Princeton: Princeton University Press, 2000.
Otto, Eckart. *Deuteronomium 12–34, Erster Teilband: 12, 1–23, 15*. HTKAT. Freiburg: Herder, 2016.
Shectman, Sarah. "The Social Status of Priestly and Levite Women." In *Levites and Priests in History and Tradition*, edited by Mark A. Leuchter and Jeremy M. Hutton, 83–99. SBLAIIL 9. Atlanta: Society of Biblical Literature, 2011.
Shectman, Sarah. "What Do We Know about Marriage in Ancient Israel?" In *Reading a Tendentious Bible: Essays in Honor of Robert B. Coote*, edited by Marvin L. Chaney, Uriah Y. Kim, and Annette Schellenberg, 166–75. Hebrew Bible Monographs 66. Sheffield: Sheffield Phoenix, 2014.
Zakovitch, Yair. "The Woman's Rights in the Biblical Law of Divorce," *JLA* 4 (1977): 28–46.

8

THE INHERITANCE INJUNCTION OF NUMBERS 36: ZELOPHEHAD'S DAUGHTERS AND THE INTERSECTION OF ANCESTRAL LAND AND SEX REGULATION

M. L. Case

After a census of the households (בית אבת) of the Israelites in Numbers 26, the text of Num. 27:1-11 contains the request of the daughters of Zelophehad—Mahlah, Noah, Hoglah, Milcah, and Tirzah—before Moses, Eleazar the priest, the leaders, and all the Israelites. It also contains the law of inheritance decreed by YHWH as a result of their request.[1] The daughters note that their father died in the wilderness "by his own sin"

---

1. Scholars debate the historicity of this account. David Aaron views the story not as history but as "reality" which must have some plausibility for the reader (see David H. Aaron, "The Ruse of Zelophehad's Daughters," *HUCA* 80 [2009]: 1–38). That does not detract from the usefulness of this narrative. Even if fictive, the fact that it was preserved suggests it had some importance for the Israelites. In addition, both parts of this pericope can be attributed to the Priestly source and so have an exilic or post-exilic date. Thus, these later authors are presenting a story of what life was like in the pre-monarchic period. Aaron also suggests that all the daughters are prepubescent because they are all unmarried. If, however, the story is fictional, but plausible, why must that be the case? This is not the only instance of there being more unmarried women of marriageable age than expected in the Hebrew Bible. See, for instance, the virgins at Jabesh-Gilead in Judg. 21:12. See also Baruch A. Levine, *Numbers 21–36: A New Translation with Introduction and Commentary*, AB 4A (New York: Doubleday, 2000), 46–59. Finally, I do not use the daughters' individual names throughout this essay. The fact that they are named on more than one occasion (Num. 26:33; 27:1; 36:11; Josh. 17:3) is striking, but for ease of reading, I simply refer to them as the daughters.

(Num. 27:3) but had no sons.² They express their concern that their father's name (שם) will not be preserved due to his lack of sons. To ensure the continuance of his name, they wish to possess the property that would have come to Zelophehad during the Israelites' allotment of the land (Num. 27:4). Moses consults God and returns with an inheritance law, presented as new, which allows daughters to inherit in the absence of sons (Num. 27:8).³

The narrative moves forward, leaving readers to assume the matter has been settled. At the end of Numbers, however, members of the Manassite tribe, the tribe of Zelophehad and his daughters, complain to Moses and the leaders about this decision (Numbers 36). They argue that if the daughters marry outside the tribe of Manasseh, the daughters' land, the land originally allotted for Zelophehad, would be transferred to the tribes of their husbands (Num. 36:3-4). Moses, without consulting God this time, at least according to the biblical text, places an injunction on these heiresses: they must marry within Manasseh, in order to keep land from being transferred between tribes.⁴

Because of this attention to the land in both parts of the pericope, most scholars have concluded that the concern the Manassites raise is strictly about maintaining the proper, and divine, allotment of the land. Such a reading, however, ignores another fundamental aspect: the restraint placed upon the daughters' agency in choosing their own husbands. I argue that the daughters threaten the social order of the Israelites due to the combination of their lack of a male head of household (*paterfamilias*) to control their actions and their potential economic independence with the possession of their own land. To make this point, I first briefly summarize three common interpretations that miss this crucial element concerning the daughters' sexuality and independence and that each present a particular focus: on the land, on the boldness of the daughters, and on the legal innovation in this narrative. I then outline the social order of the ancient Israelites depicted at this time in order to illustrate how the daughters could be seen as a threat. Finally, I consider the treatment of women in biblical law more generally before turning to the dangers presented by the daughters specifically.

---

2. All translations are my own.
3. As discussed below, scholars debate whether there was a time when Israel did not allow for female inheritance. If they did not, that would make them unique among ancient Near Eastern societies.
4. See the discussion below on the debate about whether the daughters must marry within their tribe or within their clan.

Three Interpretations: Land, Boldness, Legal Innovation

The most common interpretations of the account of Zelophehad's daughters revolve around the issue of land, which is prominent throughout Numbers. For example, Baruch Levine avers that the daughters seek "to be declared their father's heirs in the upcoming apportionment of the land of Canaan."[5] He suggests that their distress over preserving the "name" (שם) of their father in Num. 27:4 is actually about the "title to his land," or making sure the land is registered in their father's name among his family.[6] Likewise, Martin Noth argues that Zelophehad's name can only be perpetuated "in association with the inheritance of the land by his descendants."[7] Given the location of Numbers 27 directly after the census in Numbers 26—in which the names of Zelophehad's daughters appear—and that of Numbers 36 after the description of the boundaries of the land in Num. 34:1-15 and the appointment of cities for the Levites and cities of refuge in Numbers 35, we would be incorrect to completely divorce this story from apprehension over the division of the land.[8] As Horst Seebass notes, "the holy land is a main theme underlying the whole book of Numbers."[9] Despite this concentration, interpreting Numbers 27 and 36 as merely deciding the fate of allotted land misses the underlying anxiety about women who are not under the control of a *paterfamilias*.

While proper apportionment is the most typical reading, some interpreters combine the centrality of the land in this passage with the boldness or insightfulness of Zelophehad's daughters in making their request. Dennis Olson, for example, repeatedly notes the importance of the land in this passage, both in the organization of the Israelites as

---

5. Levine, *Numbers 21–36*, 341.

6. Ibid., 346. Levine notes that both Hoglah and Noah are place names found in the Samaria Ostraca (eighth century BCE), and this suggests that the legal innovation of this episode must be understood in the context of the settlement plan (ibid., 344). See also Zafrira Ben-Barak, *Inheritance by Daughters in Israel and the Ancient Near East: A Social, Legal and Ideological Revolution* (Jaffa: Archaeological Center Publications, 2006), 52–7.

7. Martin Noth, *Numbers*, OTL (Philadelphia: Westminster, 1968), 211. See also Mary Douglas, *In the Wilderness: The Doctrine of Defilement in the Book of Numbers* (Oxford: Oxford University Press, 1993), 87, 236–8.

8. The text has YHWH specifically reference the allotment of the land as the reason for the census in Numbers 26. According to the provision in Num. 26:52-56, the census determines how much property each tribe will receive: larger tribes receive larger portions to divide, while smaller tribes receive smaller portions.

9. Horst Seebass, "'Holy' Land in the Old Testament: Numbers and Joshua," *VT* 56 (2006): 93.

a whole, and within the concept of patrilineal inheritance. At the same time, he refers to the daughters as "five bold women" who "challenge their tradition of male only inheritance."[10] They base their challenge, of course, on the importance of the correct allotment of the land. Despite this, Olson sees this story as "one small step toward enhancing the status of women in the world of the biblical narrative."[11] Dora Rudo Mbuwayesango, while noting the imperialist nature of the daughters' demand for property already occupied by other peoples, suggests they want to be understood as Zelophehad's heirs and sons, in order that they can pass the land to their own sons.[12]

Other scholars, including many feminist scholars, concentrate primarily on the women in Numbers 27 and 36, relegating discussion of the land to a relatively minor position. For example, in a pair of short notes best read in tandem, Josiah Derby and Zvi Ron both suggest that the daughters of Zelophehad are the earliest feminists in Israel and that early rabbis sensed this about them.[13] Juliana Claassens adheres to this feminist interpretation of Zelophehad's daughters, stating that the women "emerge as a symbol of the powerless standing up for what is right," yet she also acknowledges post-colonial critiques of the women's role in the Israelite conquest project, such as Mbuwayesango's, mentioned above.[14] In her *Women's Bible Commentary* entry on the daughters, Katherine Doob Sakenfeld refers to them as "incredibly daring." She concludes by stating, however, that while this account could have been comforting for women who would now not be left destitute, "it was preserved primarily as a story of comfort for men who had the misfortune not to bear any male heirs."[15]

---

10. Dennis T. Olson, *Numbers*, IBC (Louisville: John Knox, 1996), 166.
11. Ibid., 167.
12. Dora Rudo Mbuwayesango, "Can Daughters Be Sons? The Daughters of Zelophehad in Patriarchal and Imperial Society," in *Relating to the Text: Interdisciplinary and Form-Critical Insights on the Bible*, ed. Timothy J. Sandoval, Carleen Mandolfo, and Martin J. Buss (London: T&T Clark, 2003), 251–62.
13. Josiah Derby, "The Daughters of Zelophehad Revisited," *JBQ* 25 (1997): 169–71; and Zvi Ron, "The Daughters of Zelophehad," *JBQ* 26 (1998): 260–2.
14. Juliana Claassens, "'Give Us a Portion among our Father's Brothers': The Daughters of Zelophehad, Land, and the Quest for Human Dignity," *JSOT* 37 (2013): 321.
15. Katherine Doob Sakenfeld, "Numbers," in *The Women's Bible Commentary*, ed. Carol Ann Newsom and Sharon H. Ringe (Louisville: Westminster John Knox, 1998), 85. See also Claassens, "'Give Us a Portion among our Father's Brothers,'" 321.

Finally, another interpretation focuses neither on the role of the women nor the land, but rather on the legal innovation presented in these texts.[16] David H. Aaron interprets Numbers 27 and 36 as a single account designed to reform standard practices in the post-exilic period. In his view, the author emphasizes Numbers 36 and its attempt at undermining the daughters' inheritance claim, juxtaposing the current law of inheritance in Numbers 27 with the revised law in Numbers 36.[17] Emmanuel O. Nwaoru, in his comparison of Numbers 27 to inheritance practices in Africa, argues that "never before the time of the petition of Zelophehad's daughters had there been any provision in the existing laws for the recognition of daughters as lawful heirs, even when there were no sons."[18] However, while a law of inheritance for daughters does not appear in the biblical text before this pericope, we should restrain from claiming, like Nwaoru, that no such practice existed in ancient Israel; lack of legal material does not automatically preclude the practice.[19] Regardless, Numbers 27 and 36 present a legal precedent for future generations, if not also a substantial legal innovation.

All of these interpretations bring valuable insight into this intriguing narrative. As mentioned above, in light of this story's location in the book of Numbers, concern over the proper division of land—and that this property remain with its divinely assigned caretakers—certainly is highlighted. Moreover, in an androcentric biblical text that rarely mentions any but the most extraordinary of women, we can correctly read Zelophehad's daughters as brave and insightful. Finally, whether or not women could inherit before this point, and I agree with Aaron that

16. Sakenfeld offers a brief explanation of all three of these interpretations. See Katherine Doob Sakenfeld, "Feminist Biblical Interpretation," *ThTo* 46 (1989): 154–68.

17. Aaron, "The Ruse of Zelophehad's Daughters." Aaron argues that the same author or an author from the same school/generation as the author of Numbers 27 wrote Numbers 36. See also Dean R. Ulrich, "The Framing Function of the Narratives about Zelophehad's Daughters," *JETS* 41 (1998): 529–38. In contrast, Levine calls Numbers 36 "an addendum to the Book of Numbers." See Levine, *Numbers 21–36*, 575.

18. Emmanuel O. Nwaoru, "The Case of the Daughters of Zelophehad (Num 27:1-11) and African Inheritance Rights," *AsJT* 16 (2002): 55.

19. See, for instance, Aaron, "The Ruse of Zelophehad's Daughters," 8. In contrast, Jacob Milgrom notes that the Hebrew Bible is anomalous in the ancient Near East because of its lack of inheritance rights for daughters, thereby making the addition of this story necessary. See Jacob Milgrom, *Numbers: The Traditional Hebrew Text with the New JPS Translation* (Philadelphia: Jewish Publication Society, 2003), 482–4.

it is likely they could, Numbers 27 and 36 provide official legislation and a legal precedent on this issue. Despite these worthy interpretations, however, one crucial piece of the puzzle is missing. The women as landowners pose a threat to society because they lack a *paterfamilias* yet have the potential for economic independence. A closer look at the social ordering depicted in the Hebrew Bible for the Israelites before the time of the monarchy illustrates the danger posed by these daughters.[20]

The בית אב and the Control of Women[21]

In the form of ancient Israelite society before the rise of the monarchy, which the authors of this account recreate here, most everyday activities and decisions occur at the level of the בית אב ("father's house").[22] The larger kinship groups, the משפחה ("clan"), שבט or מטה ("tribe"), and בני־ישראל ("Israelites"), rarely participate but instead function for

---

20. As stated in n. 1 above, while not historical, this text is understood as set in the pre-monarchic period. Though likely dated to the exilic or post-exilic period, the authors present it as a representation of life before the monarchy. That being said, the interest in maintaining possession of the divinely given land also fits with the exilic and post-exilic communities' similar concerns, as seen in the intermarriage warnings in Ezra 9–10.

21. Much research has been done on the social order of pre-monarchic Israel. Here I provide an overview of some of the more pertinent points for this current study. For detailed discussions, see Norman K. Gottwald, *The Tribes of Yahweh: A Sociology of the Religion of Liberated Israel, 1250–1050 B.C.E.* (Maryknoll: Orbis, 1979); Lawrence E. Stager, "The Archaeology of the Family in Ancient Israel," *BASOR* 260 (1985): 1–35; and Robert Wilson, *Sociological Approaches to the Old Testament* (Philadelphia: Fortress, 1984). Carol Meyers uses archaeological and ethnographic evidence to offer an analysis of women's social roles in ancient Israel, which challenges traditional notions of patriarchal societies, discussed in n. 28 below (*Rediscovering Eve: Ancient Israelite Women in Context* [Oxford: Oxford University Press, 2013]). See also the discussion of the בית אב and the status of men and women in biblical texts in Pamela Barmash, "The Daughter Sold into Slavery and Marriage," Chapter 2 in this volume.

22. Stager, "The Archaeology of the Family," 19–20. Wilson calls this a lineage. Though their terminology differs, Stager's and Wilson's kinship models complement each other and are both useful in discussing the possible social organization of the Israelites during the pre-monarchic period presented. See Wilson, *Sociological Approaches*, 40–7; and Wilson, *Genealogy and History in the Biblical World* (New Haven: Yale University Press, 1977), 18–37. The בית אב continues to function as the most basic unit of society in the monarchic period; see Philip J. King and Lawrence E. Stager, *Life in Biblical Israel* (Louisville: Westminster John Knox, 2001), 36–40.

military purposes at times when smaller units cannot sufficiently defend themselves; they also are important for some ritual practices or to dispense inter-tribal justice. All these different groupings, from the father's house to the people of Israel, can adjudicate internal disputes depending on the individuals or groups involved. Within a single בית אב, the senior male member, the *paterfamilias*, acts as leader and so settles conflicts within his own household. When quarrels occur across households, clans, or tribes, a single person does not have authority over all the individuals involved, and a satisfactory replacement for the *paterfamilias* must be found. Typically, a group of elders from the various clans or tribes suffice, depending on the level of the conflict.[23] Thus, in Num. 36:1 the heads of the clans in Manasseh take their complaint against Zelophehad's daughters to Moses and the leaders (הנשאים), the heads of the families of the Israelites (ראשי אבות לבני ישראל). Though the daughters belong to a tribe, because the law set forth in Numbers 27 allows for the potential of marriage outside the tribe, the Manassites cannot adjudicate this issue themselves.[24] Also, since they seek, and receive, a legal innovation that changes the marriage rights of all Israelite heiresses, the elders in charge of all the Israelites must be consulted.

In their popular overview of ancient Israelite society, Philip King and Lawrence Stager list six features of the biblical בית אב, this most basic unit of society: endogamous, patrilineal, patriarchal, patrilocal, joint, and polygynous.[25] The feature of endogamy indicates the preference for marriage within a specified social group, yet the difference between endogamy and exogamy is a matter of degree and definition. For the ancient Israelites, the extreme limit for endogamy is within the Israelites, though as Numbers 36 suggests, preferences for intra-tribal, or even intra-clan, marriages appear.[26] The patrilineal aspect of ancient Israel, inheritance through the male line, is the force behind the law and its

---

23. Wilson, *Sociological Approaches*, 41–3.
24. Remember also that Numbers 27 depicts the law as coming directly from YHWH.
25. King and Stager, *Life in Biblical Israel*, 38.
26. Derby notes that the biblical text depicts the tribes as being isolated, so this concern over the daughters marrying outside the tribe is perhaps unwarranted ("The Daughters of Zelophehad Revisited," 171). Indeed, the book of Judges, also said to portray pre-monarchic Israelite society, rarely presents more than one tribe cooperating even to fight an enemy, with the exception of Judges 19–21, often considered an idealized example of the pre-monarchic social order, the poetic account of Deborah's judgeship in Judges 5, and Gideon's judgeship in Judges 6–7. See, for example, Jo Ann Hackett, "In the Days of Jael: Reclaiming the History of Women

revision in Numbers 27 and 36.²⁷ The patrilocal and joint characteristics are less important for this study, as they indicate residence of a married couple within the husband's בית אב with more than one generation in residence. Likewise polygyny, having more than one wife, has no effect on our interpretation of Numbers 27 and 36.

In a patriarchal society, the males, especially the *paterfamilias*, have control over and are the primary actors in political and social institutions.²⁸ Women live under the authority of men—first their father and

in Ancient Israel," in *Immaculate and Powerful: The Female in Sacred Image and Social Reality*, ed. Clarissa Atkinson, Margaret Miles, and Constance Buchanan (Boston: Beacon, 1985), 24.

On the other hand, we see serious apprehension over intermarriages in the Hebrew Bible, especially in the post-exilic texts of Ezra and Nehemiah. Hannah Harrington addresses this topic at length in "Sexual Relations and the Transition from Holy People to Human Sanctuary in Second Temple Times," Chapter 12 in this volume. See also, Tamara C. Eskenazi, "Out from the Shadows: Biblical Women in the Postexilic Era," *JSOT* 54 (1992): 25–43. If we place the composition of Numbers 27 and 36 in an exilic or post-exilic setting, then the Manassite concern about whom the daughters marry could also reflect this larger anxiety about post-exilic intermarriage. Katherine Southwood places the composition of Judges 21 in the post-exilic period, though it depicts pre-monarchic Israel, and interprets it as an ethnic narrative warning against intermarriage. See Katherine E. Southwood, *Marriage by Capture in the Book of Judges: An Anthropological Approach* (Cambridge: Cambridge University Press, 2017), 189–231.

27. See also Barmash's discussion of the patrilineal inheritance outlined in the biblical text ("The Daughter Sold into Slavery and Marriage").

28. Debate has arisen recently as to the accurateness of labeling ancient Israel a patriarchal society. Carol Meyers argues instead for the term "heterarchy," Carole L. Crumley's anthropological concept, asserting that it better illustrates the fluctuation of social relations in pre-modern societies. Women maintain power within the household and, due to their movement from the household of their father to that of their husband, are better positioned than men to mediate between communities. Meyers additionally warns that because the household is the fundamental economic unit in ancient Israel, we should not underestimate the power, both economic and social, of women within the household. Vrushali Patil also argues against the term patriarchy as it contributes to homogenous accounts of gender oppression. Despite these valuable critiques, I am not convinced that patriarchy is inappropriate in describing life in tribal Israel. While women have power within the family, and occasionally outside the household, men dominate public life, including the governance of the people. Given the elite male authorship of the Hebrew Bible, we cannot overlook the overarching power exercised by men in their depiction of ancient Israelite society. On all of this discussion, see Carole L. Crumley, "Three Locational Models: An Epistemological Assessment of Anthropology and Archaeology," in *Advances in Archaeological Method and Theory*,

then their husband.²⁹ Only in cases of being orphaned, like Zelophehad's daughters, divorced, or widowed (see below) would a woman ever live outside the authority of a *paterfamilias*.³⁰ We can understand this control, among other things, as power over these women's sexuality, or better yet, power to determine who has sexual access to their bodies. In the case of daughters, a father wants to ensure their virginity to receive the best economic compensation for them in marriage—the bride-price.³¹ As for wives, restricting sexual access to their bodies to the husbands alone safeguards the line of succession—especially important in a patrilineal society. If a son is to inherit his father's land, wealth, etc., the father wants to be certain the son is his. In each case, however, the *paterfamilias*

II, ed. Michael B. Schiffer (New York: Academic Press, 1979), 141–73; Carol Meyers, "Having Their Space and Eating There Too: Bread Production and Female Power in Ancient Israelite Households," *Nashim: A Journal of Jewish Women's Studies and Gender Issues* 5 (2002): 14–44; Meyers, "Engendering Syro-Palestinian Archaeology: Reasons and Resources," *NEA* 66 (2003): 185–97; Meyers, "Hierarchy or Heterarchy? Archaeology and the Theorizing of Israelite Society," in *Confronting the Past: Archaeological and Historical Essays on Ancient Israel in Honor of William G. Dever*, ed. Seymour Gitin, J. Edward Wright, and J. P. Dessel (Winona Lake: Eisenbrauns, 2006), 245–55; Meyers, "Was Ancient Israel a Patriarchal Society?" *JBL* 133 (2014): 8–27; and Vrushali Patil, "From Patriarchy to Intersectionality: A Transnational Feminist Assessment of How Far We've Really Come," *Signs: Journal of Women in Culture and Society* 38 (2013): 847–67.

29. See, for example, Ada Tagger-Cohen, "Law and Family in the Book of Numbers: The Levites and the *Tidennūtu* Documents from Nuzi," *VT* 48 (1998): 74–94; and Robert S. Kawashima, "Could a Woman Say 'No' in Biblical Israel? On the Genealogy of Legal Status in Biblical Law and Literature," *AJSR* 35 (2011): 9–10.

30. The ancient Israelite definition of both orphans and widows depends on the complete absence of supporting family. Therefore, a widow with a son to support her is not technically understood as a widow. For a discussion of widows, see Paula S. Hiebert, "'Whence Shall Help Come to Me?' The Biblical Widow," in *Gender and Difference in Ancient Israel*, ed. Peggy L. Day (Minneapolis: Fortress, 1989), 125–41.

31. See, for example, laws about a man giving money to the father of a virgin he has had sexual intercourse with in Exod. 22:15-16 and Deut. 22:28-29. In both instances, the man is to marry the woman. In Exodus, the money given is specifically called a bride-price (מהר). According to Exod. 22:16, even if the father refuses to let his violated daughter marry the man, the man will still pay the father the equivalent amount of the bride-price for virgins. See Barmash's discussion of the economic value of daughters sold into slavery for sexual use ("The Daughter Sold into Slavery and Marriage," Chapter 2 in this volume). See also F. Rachel Magdalene, "Rachel's Betrothal Contract and the Origins of Contract Law," Chapter 3 in this volume, for a discussion of the oral nature of betrothal contracts and the father's role in such contracts, where the woman's interests are not typically considered.

regulates the sexuality of the women under his control in order to lessen the potential threat of these female bodies to his household.[32]

Women not under the control of a *paterfamilias* present a grave threat to a society founded upon the household. For example, in the ancient Near East more broadly, including in Israel, special attention is paid to widows. While living without the protection of a man places widows in a precarious situation, they are also seen as a danger to society because they live away from the control of the *paterfamilias*.[33] Karel van der Toorn argues that ancient Near Eastern texts depict widows as poor and chaste because that image poses less of a social threat, not because all widows actually were poor and chaste.[34] A poor widow who relies on charity for survival can be controlled economically by individuals or institutions. A chaste widow will not exert her sexual agency, and so her lack of a *paterfamilias* to regulate her sexuality does not jeopardize the social order.[35] In a similar vein, Zelophehad's daughters, lacking both father and husbands, threaten the order of society because of the self-determination they now have when it comes to sexual access to their own bodies.

If we affirm that each *paterfamilias* in ancient Israel maintains power and authority over the women, children, and subordinate men in his household (בית אב), we must question what that means legally for women. Robert Kawashima argues that ancient Israelite women, and subordinate men, achieve moral agency as adults, but do not obtain full legal status. Thus, women can be found guilty of a crime, but can never be the victims of a crime.[36] Notably, given this assertion, the Hebrew Bible has no term for rape; as discussed below, sexual crimes against a woman are

---

32. Bryan S. Turner, *The Body and Society*, 3rd ed. (Los Angeles: Sage, 2008), 103. See Hilary Lipka's argument that a priest's control of his daughter's sexuality suggests reading זנה literally as sexual promiscuity, not as apostasy ("The Offense, Its Consequences, and the Meaning of זנה in Leviticus," Chapter 6 in this volume).

33. See, for example, Karel van der Toorn, "Torn Between Vice and Virtue: Stereotypes of the Widow in Israel and Mesopotamia," in *Female Stereotypes in Religious Traditions*, ed. Ria Kloppenborg and Wouter J. Hanegraaff (Leiden: Brill, 1995), 2.

34. Ibid., 3–5, 10–12.

35. For a discussion of depictions of widows as non-threatening in the biblical material, see Lipka, "The Offense, Its Consequences, and the Meaning of זנה in Leviticus," Chapter 6 in this volume, especially the material around n. 32.

36. Kawashima, "Could a Woman Say 'No' in Biblical Israel?" 9–10. In the same vein, women can also be found not guilty of the crime. See, for example, the difference between presumably consensual and nonconsensual sex in determining the woman's guilt in Deut. 22:23-27.

actually crimes against her *paterfamilias*.³⁷ Likewise, in his discussion of biblical inheritance laws, Calum Carmichael argues that the male head of household lives on after death through the preservation of his name (שם), meaning his status and reputation. The actions of children and other subordinates reflect on the *paterfamilias*, not the other way around. In this way, "the head of house is the focus of reward and its members are but the subjects."³⁸ The subordinates are not understood as persons in their own right, and in the case of Zelophehad's daughters, they never will be. As Carmichael suggests, the daughters show concern about their father's name and frame their request in terms of how it benefits their father, the deceased *paterfamilias*, and not themselves. The mere fact that the law added in Numbers 36 determines the fate of these women's marriages suggests a need for male control over their sexuality and, consequently, how they can perpetuate their father's line. In addition, this reading of the regulation of women's bodies in Numbers 36 is bolstered by the fact that most laws about women in the biblical legal material attend to regulating their sexuality.

Women in the Biblical Legal Material

Women are not frequently discussed in the Israelite legal codes found in Exodus–Deuteronomy, nor is much of the legal material intended for them. For example, the most famous collection from the legal material, the Decalogue (Exod. 20:1-17; Deut. 5:6-21), does not address women. "You" are commanded to honor both fathers and mothers (Exod. 20:12), but the apodictic laws address only adult male Israelites. Not only are the laws addressed to the second masculine singular person, but in preparation for receiving the law, the Israelites are told not to go near a woman (Exod. 19:15), and included in the Decalogue is a command not to covet a neighbor's wife (Exod. 20:17).³⁹ The instances where laws deal with

---

37. Bruce Wells argues that the lone sexual activity made illegal, as compared to simply a sin, is adultery. See, for example, Bruce Wells, "Sex, Lies, and Virginal Rape: The Slandered Bride and False Accusation in Deuteronomy," *JBL* 124 (2005): 41–72; and idem, "Sex Crimes in the Laws of the Hebrew Bible," *NEA* 78 (2015): 294–300.

38. Calum Carmichael, "Inheritance in Biblical Sources," *Law & Literature* 20 (2008): 238.

39. While we could argue that the second masculine singular usage in these laws is a general "you," meant to refer to all Israelites, male and female, the specific prohibition against sexual intercourse with a woman before receiving the law suggests that only men are included. Jewish feminists have long noticed this comment and

women typically involve controlling the women's bodies and/or sexuality in some way, indicating that the interest of the law is still in the man behind, or rather above, a given woman—namely, the *paterfamilias*.

Two primary categories regarding women appear in the biblical legal code: purity laws and sex/marriage laws. Among laws about the former, Leviticus 12 addresses the purification of women after giving birth, while Lev. 15:19-33 covers their impurity following regular and irregular menstruation.[40] These menstruation laws focus both on the impurity of the woman and how she can pass that impurity on to others, including through sexual intercourse with a man (Lev. 15:24). In the latter category of laws, Leviticus 18 contains a list of prohibited sexual partners, again addressing only male Israelites.[41] These laws signify that the victim in such cases is often not the woman, but rather her *paterfamilias*: her husband (e.g., Lev. 18:8), her grandfather (e.g., Lev. 18:10), or her brother (e.g., Lev. 18:11).[42] The laws in Deut. 22:22-29 discuss other sexual offenses, specifically various scenarios when a man has sex with a woman not his wife. Once again, the victim of such actions remains the *paterfamilias*, either husband/fiancé (Deut. 22:22-27) or father (Deut. 22:28-29).[43] Numbers 5 contains an extensive legal treatise directed at marital discord, where either a woman has sexual relations with a man not her husband or her husband is jealous and makes false claims against her.[44]

Other sporadic references to women in the laws continue in this pattern. In the Covenant Code (Exod. 20:22–23:19), for example, laws about

---

have used it to question their inclusion in the biblical text and modern Judaism. See, for example, Rachel Adler, "I've Had Nothing Yet So I Can't Take More," *Moment* 8 (1983): 22–6. In addition, comparisons to other ancient Near Eastern law codes support reading differences based on gender or social status.

40. The first half of this latter chapter deals with the impurity of men following a seminal discharge. While he can make a woman impure (Lev. 15:18), much like a woman can make a man impure (Lev. 15:24), the fact remains that laws involving men cover a wide range of topics, while those concerning women are limited.

41. The commands switch between second masculine plural (e.g., Lev. 18:3) and second masculine singular (e.g., Lev. 18:6).

42. See also Lev. 20:17-21.

43. Cf. Lev. 20:10-12.

44. We should note the unevenness between the marital fidelity requirements of the wife versus the husband, but in a society where polygyny and male dominance are practiced, such inequality should not be surprising. See, for instance, the law permitting a man to marry a virgin he "rapes" in Deut. 22:28-29, mentioned above. See also Barmash's discussion of the lack of a wife's right to an exclusive sexual relationship with her husband ("The Daughter Sold into Slavery and Marriage," Chapter 2 in this volume).

women occasionally appear amongst other laws, yet attention frequently remains on the control the *paterfamilias* has over the female's body and actions. This includes slave women (Exod. 21:2-11), pregnant women (Exod. 21:22-25), and unmarried women (Exod. 22:15-16).[45] Similar to Num. 5:11-31, Deut. 22:13-21 provides legal guidelines for a man making false claims against his wife in hopes of divorcing her. Finally, Numbers 30 clarifies that only women without a *paterfamilias*, such as a widow or divorcée, have the power and ability to make binding vows (v. 10); otherwise, the male heads of household are permitted to void a woman's vows.[46]

Through this short survey, we see that most laws about women revolve around their domination by the men in their lives.[47] In the patriarchal tribal period depicted in this text, when the בית אב is the primary unit of society, the *paterfamilias* controlled the women, children, and subordinate males within his household. For women—wives, daughters, sisters, even female slaves—this meant the regulation of their bodies and who had sexual access to said bodies. We should not take the idea of a woman being under control of her father until marriage, at which point she is under control of her husband, as a mere literary device. The presence of laws dedicated to the proper regulation of female bodies suggests it was a legal obligation of the *paterfamilias* and an essential part of being female for the ancient Israelites.

The Danger of the Daughters

The daughters of Zelophehad, particularly after ensuring that their father's allotment of land will be given to them, thus pose the greatest threat to ancient Israelite society: they are single women not under the control of a *paterfamilias* who potentially have the means to support themselves. Given the focus on regulating women's bodies and sexuality in the Israelite legal code, placing restrictions upon the daughters' eligible marriage partners through a new legal precedent allows for the men of Israel to reassert their power over the daughters—and over any other

---

45. The law forbidding female sorcerers to live (Exod. 22:1) is one of the rare laws that do not explicitly focus on a woman's sexuality or body. However, like the widow without a *paterfamilias* (Exod. 22:21-23), the female sorcerer is presented as a threat to the social order and so must be neutralized.

46. Kawashima, "Could a Woman Say 'No' in Biblical Israel?" 9–10. See also Barmash, "The Daughter Sold into Slavery and Marriage," Chapter 2 in this volume.

47. Carmichael suggests that women play a central role in all inheritance laws in the biblical text. See Carmichael, "Inheritance in Biblical Source," 229.

women in the future who find themselves in a similar position. Certainly, the placement of this pericope in the midst of the Israelite census and allotment of the land highlights the importance of keeping property within the assigned clan, but ultimately the purpose of this legal material is to reestablish control over the daughters' sexuality in order to negate the threat these unattached women pose to the social order.

Due to the marital limitations in Num. 36:6, we could surmise that Zelophehad's daughters in Num. 27:3-4 are simply asking for their rightful dowry, not to become sons and/or heirs.[48] But nothing in the text suggests such a reading. When presenting their request to Moses, Eleazar, and the leaders, they state:

> Our father died in the wilderness, but he was not among the group that gathered themselves together against YHWH in the company of Korah. For he died by his [own] sin, and he had no sons. Why should the name of our father be taken away from the midst of his clan because he did not have a son? Give to us a possession among the brothers of our father. (Num. 27:3-4)

The notice that their father did not participate in Korah's rebellion legitimates their father's claim to an allotment of the land being divided by the Israelites. Remarking that Zelophehad had no sons legitimates *their* claim to his land as heirs.[49] The daughters' question in v. 4 supports this assertion that they see the land more as an inheritance than a dowry: Like a male heir, they wish to perpetuate their father's name through possession of his land. Their request, however, is less for an inheritance from their father than for the right to legally obtain the land allocated to him, which he never himself possessed.

---

48. Jay Caballero, "The Inheritance of the Daughters of Zelophehad" (paper presented at the Annual Meeting of the Society of Biblical Literature, San Antonio, TX, November 22, 2016). Joseph Fleishman, in his examination of Caleb and Achsah in Josh. 15:16-19 and Judg. 1:12-15, compares ancient Near Eastern law codes and ancient Jewish law found in Tannaitic sources to understand the use of immovable property as a dowry in biblical texts ("A Daughter's Demand and a Father's Compliance: The Legal Background to Achsah's Claim and Caleb's Agreement," *ZAW* 118 [2006]: 357–73). While such dowries occur, in the case of Zelophehad's daughters, we have little evidence to support this interpretation.

49. Presumably Zelophehad's wife is also dead; otherwise, we might expect her to either request inheritance or, following the levirate custom, marry one of her brothers-in-law in hopes of producing a male heir. See, for example, Noth, *Numbers*, 212; Levine, *Numbers 21–36*, 358; and Ben-Barak, *Inheritance by Daughters*, 19.

The language the daughters use in their request differs from YHWH's response. They ask for a possession, אחזה, while the legal decision primarily uses the term נחלה. Although we could translate both as "possession" or "inheritance," a closer look at their usage suggests a difference between the request and its legal interpretation.[50] In his lexicographic study of the term אחזה, Levine maintains that the term indicates "the legal acquisition of land."[51] Though the related verb, אחז, frequently refers to physical conquest, Levine traces the link between physical conquest or seizure and legal acquisition and contractual possession.[52] In Genesis, for example, אחזה refers to land either legally purchased or given. Its first appearance, in Gen. 17:8, is in the context of the promise of land given by God to Abraham and his descendants. Genesis 23:4, 9, 20; 49:30; and 50:13 all refer to the land purchased by Abraham as a burying place, first for Sarah, and later for himself. Other usages include numerous references in Leviticus 25 in the Jubilee year provisions, in Numbers 32 when the tribes of Reuben and Gad ask for land in the Transjordan region, and in Numbers 35 which allocates cities for both the Levites and for refuge. The occurrences of the term in Numbers 32 come the closest to the idea of land attained through conquest, but at the time the Reubenites and Gadites ask for the land, it has already been conquered, as they themselves note in v. 4. Therefore, the tribes ask Moses, Eleazar, and the leaders for the land as a grant given to them as a legal possession.[53] Thus, Zelophehad's daughters ask to receive their father's rightful portion of the land through legal acquisition or grant.

Levine argues that in the biblical text, נחלה frequently refers to land which is conquered.[54] While he uses comparative evidence, particularly

---

50. BDB 28 lists the main definition of אחזה as "possession," with specialized definitions of "land possessed" and "possession by right of inheritance." The latter definition includes Num. 27:7 as an example. נחלה, in contrast, has three primary definitions: "possession," "property," and "inheritance" (BDB 635). Since נחלה is the more widely used term, does this definition suggest a more common meaning of inheritance for נחלה? See BDB 28, 635.

51. Baruch A. Levine, "On the Semantics of Land Tenure and the Hebrew Bible," in *The Tablet and the Scroll: Near Eastern Studies in Honor of William W. Hallo*, ed. Mark E. Cohen, Daniel C. Snell, and David B. Weisberg (Bethesda: CDL, 1993), 139. See also, Levine, *Numbers 21–36*, 346.

52. Levine, "On the Semantics of Land Tenure in the Hebrew Bible," 135.

53. On the other hand, in the same chapter, the Reubenites and Gadites also refer to their land as "our inheritance" נחלתנו (v. 19) and "the possession of our inheritance" אחזת נחלתנו (v. 32); so perhaps the distinction is not as strong in this case.

54. Ibid., 134–5.

the Mari texts, to make this claim, the main support for such interpretation in the biblical texts themselves appears in discussions about the land of Canaan, promised by YHWH and conquered by the people, such as the land allotment in Joshua 13–21, or in Numbers 26 when the census is taken in preparation for dividing the land.[55] In addition, נחלה is used to indicate the inheritance given from father to child, and in some instances, specifically to a female child. For example, in Gen. 31:14, Rachel and Leah ask Jacob, "Is there yet a portion or inheritance (נחלה) for us in our father's house?" When discussing the land inheritance that comes with marriage to Ruth, Boaz twice designates that land as נחלה (Ruth 4:5, 10). While the land is understood as the property of Ruth's father-in-law, Elimelech (Ruth 4:9), Boaz can only possess it through marriage to Ruth.[56] The most interesting case comes from the book of Job. After being restored to his good fortune (42:10), Job has seven sons and three daughters (42:13). Not only are the daughters named (42:14), like the daughters of Zelophehad, but Job gives his daughters an inheritance (42:15): "And there were no women found as beautiful as Job's daughters in all the land, and their father gave to them an inheritance (נחלה) among their brothers." While women do not typically inherit in ancient Israel, at least according to the Hebrew Bible, in this extraordinary case, their inheritance is marked by the term נחלה.

Levine notes that נחלה appears in early biblical texts and אחזה in later texts, perhaps in the early post-exilic period.[57] Yet the terms also occur in the same pericopes, even at times in the same verse, such as in Num. 27:7. Unless we choose to divide and subdivide the biblical text into miniscule portions, we need to seek an alternative to source divisions.[58]

---

55. Of course, that means the use of אחזה in Num. 35:5, 22, 29, and 32, in reference to the Transjordan land given to the Reubenites and the Gadites, could also refer to land originally conquered, calling into question Levine's concluding thesis that אחזה indicates legal acquisition.

56. In the tradition of levirate marriage, Boaz notes in v. 10 that he marries Ruth "to revive the name of the dead upon his inheritance." As noted above, this does not appear to be an option for Zelophehad. On the other hand, it could be that the daughters are proposing an alternative to levirate marriage in Numbers 27 by inheriting their father's land. See Aaron, "The Ruse of Zelophehad's Daughters," 11–12 n. 24.

57. Levine, "On the Semantics of Land Tenure in Biblical Literature."

58. Richard Elliott Friedman, for example, notes that "[t]he term 'possession' (ʾăḥuzzāh) is characteristic of P," and he divides Num. 32:5 into three portions. Surprisingly, in Num. 32:32, one of the verses containing both נחלה and אחזה, he does not divide the verse, but simply attributes it all to the Priestly source (*The Bible with Sources Revealed: A New View into the Five Books of Moses* [New York: Harper, 2003], 301–2).

In a literarily unified passage, such as we have here with the text concerning Zelophehad's daughters in Num. 27:1-11 and 36:1-12, we do not need to create complicated source partitions. When we read the story as a whole, the difference in terminology is perhaps significant for interpretation, or happenstance and irrelevant for interpretation, but not an indication of multiple sources.[59] Since נחלה is used six times in the census of Numbers 26, which includes a reference to Zelophehad and his daughters in v. 33, we have to wonder if the switch to אחזה in Num. 27:4 is deliberate, as is the switch back to נחלה in v. 7.[60] I contend that the women are presented as not asking for a dowry, understood as a daughter's inheritance from her father, but rather for legal acquisition of the land which would have been allotted to their father in the division of the land among the Israelites upon their arrival in Canaan, if he were still alive. Though promised to them by YHWH, the Israelites receive the land primarily through conquest, as the frequent use of נחלה, such as in Numbers 26, suggests. The daughters, who do not take active part in the conquest, nevertheless seek a legal claim to the land (אחזה).[61]

YHWH's response, which transforms this request into a legal precedent for use in future cases, changes the focus from the acquisition of land (אחזה) to a law of inheritance (נחלה). On the one hand, this change legally permits Israelite women to inherit in the absence of sons; on the other hand, it allows for the objections of the Manassites and Moses' subsequent ruling in Numbers 36 which places limitations on the agency of the daughters. The biblical text presents Zelophehad's daughters as accepting the marriage injunction placed upon them: they do as Moses commands and marry within the tribe of Manasseh.[62] Later, when the daughters

---

59. For an overview of the Neo-Documentarian approach to the Pentateuch, see Joel S. Baden, *The Composition of the Pentateuch: Renewing the Documentary Hypothesis* (New Haven: Yale University Press, 2012).

60. Despite his lexicographic study, Levine argues that the two terms have "implicit synonymity" in this pericope. See Levine, *Numbers 21–36*, 346.

61. The joining of the two terms in Num. 27:7 perhaps indicates that both interepretations of their right to the land are considered in the legal decision.

62. It is unclear whether they must marry within their father's tribe or their father's clan. Numbers 36:6 restricts the daughters to marry "in the clan of the tribe of their father" and Num. 36:8 instructs heiresses in general to do the same. The explanation for this restriction, however, is so that "no inheritance from the Israelites moves from tribe to tribe," not clan to clan (Num. 36:7, 9). Zelophehad's daughters marry men "of the clans of the Manassites," and their inheritance remains "in the tribe of the clan of their father" (Num. 36:12). In all cases, the word for clan, משפחה, appears in the construct, משפחת. Because of this, the difference between the singular and plural, which would both appear as משפחת, can only be found in the vowel

demand that Eleazar, Joshua, and the leaders honor the legal stipulation of land, the text has them use the term נחלה, the term which signified the change from legal acquisition to inheritance (Josh. 17:3-6).

Since YHWH's interpretation of the daughters' request as a matter of inheritance opened the door for the Manassites' objections to their freedom to choose a husband, a closer look at their claims is warranted. In the three verses of their complaint, Num. 36:2-4, the "heads of the families of the clan of the descendants of Gilead, the son of Machir, the son of Manasseh, of the Josephite clans" (Num. 36:1) reference the land promised to the daughters as נחלה no fewer than ten times—twice in v. 2, four times each in vv. 3 and 4. Clearly, the Manassites understand the law in Num. 27:8-11 as one involving inheritance. As is typical in patriarchal and patrilineal societies, they are distressed that the daughters' property would be transferred into the ownership of their husbands upon marriage. If they marry outside the tribe, the divine allotment of the land would be compromised (Num. 36:3).

I translate the opening phrase of Num. 36:1 ראשי האבות as "heads of the families," but it literally means "heads of the fathers." This phrase, with or without the definite article (ה), rarely appears in the Pentateuch and elsewhere appears primarily in other late biblical texts, such as Chronicles, Ezra, and Nehemiah. Numbers 36:1 contains the phrase twice: once, quoted above, introducing the plaintiffs from Manasseh, and once to introduce the individuals hearing the case—Moses, the leaders, and the heads of the families of the Israelites (ראשי אבות לבני ישראל). This phrase brings to mind the בית אב, the basic unit of society, as discussed above. Common English translations of this phrase include "the heads of the ancestral houses" (NRSV) and "the heads of the fathers' houses" (JPS). We also see similar phrases that include the term בית ("house") elsewhere in Numbers: נשיא בית־אב in Num. 3:27, 30, 35 and Num. 25:14; and ראש אמות בית־אב in Num. 25:15.[63]

Invoking the idea of the בית אב suggests to the reader the secondary reason behind the Manassite request. Yes, they are worried about the land remaining in their tribe (Num. 36:3-4), as Moses' response indicates (vv. 7, 9). But, as discussed above, these women represent a threat to the (male) order of society. Thus, the Manassite men regard the daughters' mere presence as a threat to the existence of their tribe, now that they both lack a *paterfamilias* and have the potential of economic viability.

---

pointing. Is it possible that heiresses have slightly more freedom over their choice of husband and only need to remain within the tribe?

63. See Levine, *Numbers 21–36*, 576–7 for his discussion of this phrase in Num. 36:1.

The heads of the ancestral houses want these daughters to once again be under the control of a *paterfamilias*, even if the regulating authority stands at the highest, tribal level. The Manassites are forcing the daughters to marry within a specific marriageable community, limiting those who can have sexual access to their bodies.[64] In both the specific case of the Manassites' control over the daughters and the general role of the *paterfamilias* over women in his household, the concern is to ensure the proper line of succession in this patrilineal society.

In a way, the Manassites, and the marriage restriction placed upon all future daughters who inherit, negate the line of inheritance described in Num. 27:8-11. Remember that the daughters ask for "a possession (אחזה) among the brothers of our father" (Num. 27:4). YHWH first responds by saying, "The daughters of Zelophehad speak correctly. Give to them a possession (אחזה) of an inheritance (נחלה) among the brothers of their father, and you will let the inheritance (נחלה) of their father pass to them" (Num. 27:7). In the accompanying inheritance law, when a man dies childless, "you will let his inheritance (נחלה) pass to his daughter" (Num. 27:8). Here the daughter is understood as the heir, and while she is perhaps not understood as a son, as one finds in some other ancient Near Eastern wills, the law suggests she has the same legal rights to the inheritance as any other male heir.[65] Perhaps the Israelites imagine this inheritance as an alternative to levirate marriage, a way to continue the man's name.[66]

---

64. Is it merely the narrative's pace that has the daughters marry before receiving their land? Or do they not even receive an allotment until their husbands can immediately gain control over it?

65. For example, in wills from Nuzi, it appears that a son-less father had two main choices: make his daughter(s) the sole heir, sometimes even making her a son, or adopting a son to marry her. See Jonathan Paradise, "A Daughter and Her Father's Property at Nuzi," *JCS* 32 (1980): 189–207. We have evidence from Ugarit that a daughter could inherit family goods, though, once again, she could be passed over in favor of an adopted son. See Wilfred G. E. Watson, "Daily Life in Ancient Ugarit (Syria)," in *Life and Culture in the Ancient Near East*, ed. Richard E. Averbeck, Mark W. Chavalas, and David B. Weisberg (Potomac: CDL, 2003), 134–5. Using biblical and extra-biblical evidence, Ben-Barak argues for a core Canaanite custom that allowed for the inheritance of daughters in the absence of sons, which was eventually adopted by the Israelites. See Ben-Barak, *Inheritance by Daughters*, 61–2. See also Milgrom, *Numbers*, 482–4.

66. Ben-Barak references the daughters of Barzillai in Ezra 2:61 and Neh. 7:63 as evidence of a husband who adopted his father-in-law's name, in essence preserving the name of Barzillai. This is thin evidence, but it at least raises this possibility with Zelophehad's daughters. See Ben-Barak, *Inheritance by Daughters*, 86–7.

As for Zelophehad's daughters specifically, by exerting control over whom they can marry, the leaders of the Manassites effectually take them out of the line of inheritance. The daughters do not inherit; their husbands do. The daughters also no longer have the option of continuing their father's name, the reasoning behind their entire claim in the first place (Num. 27:4). They now can perpetuate only the name of their husband.

Conclusion

As discussed throughout this essay, daughters as landowners present a threat to the social order of the Israelites. Through the injunction placed on Mahlah, Noah, Hoglah, Milcah, and Tirzah—and on all future heiresses—in Numbers 36, the men mitigate this threat. While I agree with feminist scholars who note the bravery and daring of the daughters in Numbers 27, I do not conclude that the entire pericope benefits women by the end of Numbers 36.[67] In contrast to scholars who interpret this passage solely about the proper allotment of land, I argue that the control of the women's sexuality, together with the concomitant concern over the proper line of succession, underlies the Manassites' complaint in Numbers 36—and Moses' quick agreement.[68] Some scholars have noted that the daughters' original request makes no sense in a patrilineal system; since the land will be transferred to their husbands, the daughters cannot actually perpetuate their father's name.[69] Whether or not the daughters understand that limitation, or whether they propose possessing the land in lieu of their future husbands as a sort of alternate to levirate marriage, the danger remains the same. In terms of the sexual control of women, either of these options threatens the social order, at least during the lifetime of Zelophehad's daughters.

---

67. Sakenfeld, for example, understands the marriage restrictions as protection for the daughters, as unscrupulous men might try to marry them for their land—and their family members might sell them off for the bride-price that would come for such an heiress ("Numbers," 87).

68. Seebass, for example, scoffs, "Was it really an urgent necessity to narrow down the possibilities of marriage for women with a land inheritance?" ("'Holy' Land in the Old Testament," 103 n. 37). In the context of the ancient Israelite social order, yes, it was an urgent necessity.

69. See, for example Levine, *Numbers 21–36*, 357; and Aaron, "The Ruse of Zelophehad's Daughters," 12.

Bibliography

Aaron, David H. "The Ruse of Zelophehad's Daughters." *HUCA* 80 (2009): 1–38.
Adler, Rachel. "I've Had Nothing Yet So I Can't Take More." *Moment* 8 (1983): 22–6.
Baden, Joel S. *The Composition of the Pentateuch: Renewing the Documentary Hypothesis*. New Haven: Yale University Press, 2012.
Ben-Barak, Zafrira. *Inheritance by Daughters in Israel and the Ancient Near East: A Social, Legal and Ideological Revolution*. Jaffa: Archaeological Center Publications, 2006.
Caballero, Jay. "The Inheritance of the Daughters of Zelophehad." Paper presented at the Annual Meeting of the Society of Biblical Literature. San Antonio, TX, 22 November 2016.
Carmichael, Calum. "Inheritance in Biblical Sources." *Law & Literature* 20 (2008): 229–42.
Claassens, Juliana. "'Give Us a Portion among our Father's Brothers': The Daughters of Zelophehad, Land, and the Quest for Human Dignity." *JSOT* 37 (2013): 319–37.
Crumley, Carole L. "Three Locational Models: An Epistemological Assessment of Anthropology and Archaeology." In *Advances in Archaeological Method and Theory, II*. Edited by Michael B. Schiffer, 141–73. New York: Academic Press, 1979.
Derby, Josiah. "The Daughters of Zelophehad Revisited." *JBS* 25 (1997): 169–71.
Douglas, Mary. *In the Wilderness: The Doctrine of Defilement in the Book of Numbers*. Oxford: Oxford University Press, 1993.
Eskenazi, Tamara C. "Out from the Shadows: Biblical Women in the Postexilic Era." *JSOT* 54 (1992): 25–43.
Fleishman, Joseph. "A Daughter's Demand and a Father's Compliance: The Legal Background to Achsah's Claim and Caleb's Agreement." *ZAW* 118 (2006): 357–73.
Friedman, Richard Elliott. *The Bible with Sources Revealed: A New View into the Five Books of Moses*. San Francisco: Harper, 2003.
Gottwald, Norman K. *The Tribes of Yahweh: A Sociology of the Religion of Liberated Israel, 1250–1050 B.C.E.* Maryknoll: Orbis, 1979.
Hackett, Jo Ann. "In the Days of Jael: Reclaiming the History of Women in Ancient Israel." In *Immaculate and Powerful: The Female in Sacred Image and Social Reality*, edited by Clarissa Atkinson, Margaret Miles, and Constance Buchanan, 15–38. Boston: Beacon, 1985.
Hiebert, Paula S. "'Whence Shall Help Come to Me?' The Biblical Widow." In *Gender and Difference in Ancient Israel*, edited by Peggy L. Day, 125–41. Minneapolis: Fortress, 1989.
Kawashima, Robert S. "Could a Woman Say 'No' in Biblical Israel? On the Genealogy of Legal Status in Biblical Law and Literature." *AJSR* 35 (2011): 1–22.
King, Philip J., and Lawrence E. Stager. *Life in Biblical Israel*. Louisville: Westminster John Knox, 2001.
Levine, Baruch A. *Numbers 21–36: A New Translation with Introduction and Commentary*. AB 4A. New York: Doubleday, 2000.
Levine, Baruch A. "On the Semantics of Land Tenure and the Hebrew Bible." In *The Tablet and the Scroll: Near Eastern Studies in Honor of William W. Hallo*, edited by Mark E. Cohen, Daniel C. Snell, and David B. Weisberg, 134–9. Bethesda: CDL, 1993.

Mbuwayesango, Dora Rudo. "Can Daughters Be Sons? The Daughters of Zelophehad in Patriarchal and Imperial Society." In *Relating to the Text: Interdisciplinary and Form-Critical Insights on the Bible*, edited by Timothy J. Sandoval, Carleen Mandolfo, and Martin J. Buss, 251–62. London: T&T Clark, 2003.

Meyers, Carol A. "Engendering Syro-Palestinian Archaeology: Reasons and Resources." *NEA* 66 (2003): 185–97.

Meyers, Carol A. "Having Their Space and Eating There Too: Bread Production and Female Power in Ancient Israelite Households." *Nashim: A Journal of Jewish Women's Studies and Gender Issues* 5 (2002): 14–44.

Meyers, Carol A. "Hierarchy or Heterarchy? Archaeology and the Theorizing of Israelite Society." In *Confronting the Past: Archaeological and Historical Essays on Ancient Israel in Honor of William G. Dever*, edited by Seymour Gitin, J. Edward Wright, and J. P. Dessel, 245–54. Winona Lake: Eisenbrauns, 2006.

Meyers, Carol A. *Rediscovering Eve: Ancient Israelite Women in Context*. Oxford: Oxford University Press, 2013.

Meyers, Carol A. "Was Ancient Israel a Patriarchal Society?" *JBL* 133 (2014): 8–27.

Milgrom, Jacob. *Numbers: The Traditional Hebrew Text with the New JPS Translation*. Philadelphia: Jewish Publication Society, 2003.

Noth, Martin. *Numbers*. OTL. Philadelphia: Westminster, 1968.

Nwaoru, Emmanuel O. "The Case of the Daughters of Zelophehad (Num 27:1-11) and African Inheritance Rights." *AsJT* 16 (2002): 49–65.

Olson, Dennis T. *Numbers*. IBC. Louisville: John Knox, 1996.

Paradise, Jonathan. "A Daughter and Her Father's Property at Nuzi." *JCS* 32 (1980): 189–207.

Patil, Vrushali. "From Patriarchy to Intersectionality: A Transnational Feminist Assessment of How Far We've Really Come." *Signs: Journal of Women in Culture and Society* 38 (2013): 847–67.

Ron, Zvi. "The Daughters of Zelophehad." *JBQ* 26 (1998): 260–2.

Sakenfeld, Katharine Doob. "Feminist Biblical Interpretation." *ThTo* 46 (1989): 154–68.

Sakenfeld, Katharine Doob. "Numbers." In *The Women's Bible Commentary*, edited by Carol A. Newsom and Sharon H. Ringe, 49–56. 2nd ed. Louisville: Westminster John Knox, 1998.

Sakenfeld, Katharine Doob. "Zelophehad's Daughters." *PRSt* 15, no. 4 (1988): 37–47.

Seebass, Horst. "'Holy' Land in the Old Testament: Numbers and Joshua." *VT* 56 (2006): 92–104.

Snaith, N. H. "The Daughters of Zelophehad." *VT* 16 (1966): 124–7.

Southwood, Katherine E. *Marriage by Capture in the Book of Judges: An Anthropological Approach*. Cambridge: Cambridge University Press, 2017.

Stager, Lawrence E. "The Archaeology of the Family in Ancient Israel." *BASOR* 260 (1985): 1–35.

Taggar-Cohen, Ada. "Law and Family in the Book of Numbers: The Levites and the *Tidennūtu* Documents from Nuzi." *VT* 48 (1998): 74–94.

Tucker, W. Dennis. "Women in the Old Testament: Issues of Authority, Power, and Justice." *ExpTim* 119 (2008): 481–6.

Turner, Bryan S. *The Body and Society: Explorations in Social Theory*. 3rd ed. London: Sage, 2008.

Ulrich, Dean R. "The Framing Function of the Narratives about Zelophehad's Daughters." *JETS* 41 (1998): 529–38.

Van der Toorn, Karel. "Torn between Vice and Virtue: Stereotypes of the Widow in Israel and Mesopotamia." In *Female Stereotypes in Religious Traditions*, edited by Ria Kloppenborg and Wouter J. Hanegraaff, 1–13. Leiden: Brill, 1995.

Watson, Wilfred G. E. "Daily Life in Ancient Ugarit (Syria)." In *Life and Culture in the Ancient Near East*, edited by Richard E. Averbeck, Mark W. Chavalas, and David B. Weisberg, 121–52. Potomac: CDL, 2003.

Weingreen, Jacob. "The Case of the Daughters of Zelophehad." *VT* 16 (1966): 518–22.

Wells, Bruce. "Sex Crimes in the Laws of the Hebrew Bible." *NEA* 78 (2015): 294–300.

Wells, Bruce. "Sex, Lies, and Virginal Rape: The Slandered Bride and False Accusation in Deuteronomy." *JBL* 124 (2005): 41–72.

Westbrook, Raymond. "Biblical and Cuneiform Law Codes." *Revue Biblique* 92 (1985): 247–64.

Wilson, Robert. *Genealogy and History in the Biblical World*. New Haven: Yale University Press, 1977.

Wilson, Robert. *Sociological Approaches to the Old Testament*. Philadelphia: Fortress, 1984.

9

Reproducing Torah: Human and Divine Sexuality in the Book of Deuteronomy

Steffan Mathias

He who teaches Torah to the son of his friend, it is as though he has begotten him. Babylonian Talmud, *Sanhedrin* 19B

Your corpses shall be food for every bird of the air; your wife shall lie with another man; you will eat the fruit of your womb, the flesh of your sons and daughters, which you will not even share with your remaining children; even your wife will not share her afterbirth for food. It all sounds pretty bleak, does it not? These warnings could be mistaken as jumping from the darkest depths of Jeremiah or Lamentations, from prophetic texts and judgments. Yet they are found in that most seemingly enlightened of legal documents, Deuteronomy.[1] Deuteronomy, considered by many the pinnacle of biblical law, a kind of model for contemporary human rights, gender equality, and the U.S. Constitution, is a text of two halves. Bookending the legal material is substantial narrative and poetic material.

---

1. Specifically, Deuteronomy 28. While there is "evident stratification" through Deuteronomy, particularly in the introduction and conclusion, we will look at the final redacted text, particularly since, despite stratification, "the D document is a cohesive and coherent whole, with a defined agenda, consistent themes and language, and a recognizable structure" (Joel S. Baden, *The Composition of the Pentateuch: Renewing the Documentary Hypothesis*, AYBRL [New Haven: Yale University Press, 2012], 138).

This chapter will argue that by reading it as a single text, as opposed to two separate and distinct parts, Deuteronomy produces particular kinds of knowledge (following Michel Foucault) of sexuality. Significant work looking at gender, sexuality, and reproduction in the legal material has been done by Deborah L. Ellens and Carolyn Pressler,[2] particularly the regimentation of women's bodies in Deuteronomy; in addition, a short but comprehensive essay by Mark George outlines a starting point for looking at masculinity in Deuteronomy.[3] This chapter will build on their work in important ways by reading the legal and non-legal material together, and extending the discussion away from simply human sexuality to explore divine sexuality in Deuteronomy.[4]

The kinds of knowledge that Deuteronomy produces involve men who are highly sexualized and reproducing, for whom paternity is legislated and progeny are produced; conversely, it constructs women whose bodies are for reproduction and serve as the sexual possession of father and husband. But rather than arguing for uninhibited male sexual autonomy, I will argue that Deuteronomy constructs YHWH as non-sexual but highly reproductive—a kind of *paterfamilias*, who not only regulates highly reproducing households, but also holds the keys to their fruitfulness. In doing so, Torah becomes a kind of divine seed, ensuring fertility. But YHWH is also depicted as posing the threat of reproductive destruction, which will ensue upon the people's failure to follow the Torah of Deuteronomy. This undoes the promise of blessing and destroys the type of reproducing family units that the legal material requires.

Foucault and Knowledge

This project is primarily concerned with *discourse*, and for Foucault discourse is about power; power, however, is conceived of not as a kind of Marxist top-down force, but as something exercised through relation.

---

2. Deborah L. Ellens, *Women in the Sex Texts of Leviticus and Deuteronomy: A Comparative Conceptual Analysis*, LHBOTS 458 (New York: T&T Clark, 2008); Carolyn Pressler, *The View of Women Found in the Deuteronomic Family Laws*, BZAW 216 (Berlin: de Gruyter, 1993).

3. Mark George, "Masculinity and Its Regimentation in Deuteronomy," in *Men and Masculinity in the Hebrew Bible and Beyond*, ed. Ovidiu Creangă (Sheffield: Sheffield Phoenix, 2010).

4. This chapter is partly building on my forthcoming manuscript, *Paternity, Progeny, and Perpetuation: Creating Lives after Death in the Hebrew Bible* (London: Bloomsbury T&T Clark, forthcoming), which looks specifically at Deut. 25:5-10, the so-called "Law of Levirate Marriage."

In this way power is creative and creates knowledge about the world[5]—which forms personhood, sexuality, gender difference, and divine/human difference. So, for example, Foucault examines how different disciples of philosophical masters developed certain understandings of sexuality and, through exercising power, created a particular kind of knowledge, which governs the way we think about sexuality. This dynamic between power and knowledge manifests itself in the form of discourses, the traces of ways of understanding things that are left behind in the primary sources we probe. The traces of discourse demonstrate different epistemes, periods in which knowledge is organized in a particular way, and so Foucault understood his work as a kind of *archaeology* or *genealogy*: by digging down and uncovering layers of meaning, we uncover particular epistemes. Following this, Deuteronomy is isolated as a fragment of a particular episteme, in which it is possible to talk about sexuality in a particular way.[6]

This should lead to extremely close readings of texts, taking into account language and plot, but also the way language is used to express ideas to the exclusion of other modes of thinking, rather than flattening biblical texts into a single cultural remain. Foucault, while not doing "history" as it stood in academic disciplines at the time, was still working with historical questions. Gina Hans-Piazza suggests:

> Foucault views texts within very broad, unbridled categories—as part of a larger framework of texts, customs, practices, and institutions. This enlarged notion of texts complicates interpretation. It attends to the many connections between a given text and other texts—cultural texts, material contexts, and intellectual contexts—and thus invites intertextual readings and interpretations.[7]

For example, in his work on sexuality, Foucault demonstrates how Christian acts of confession created a certain kind of understanding of desire and the interiority of a soul. In the nineteenth century, this is taken up

---

5. Michel Foucault, *The History of Sexuality, vol. 1: An Introduction*, trans. Robert Hurley, 5th ed. (New York: Vintage, 1990), 59.

6. Foucault outlines this kind of archaeology in Michel Foucault, *The Archaeology of Knowledge*, trans. Alan Sheridan (London: Tavistock, 1972). However, when we come to Michel Foucault, *Discipline and Punish: The Birth of the Prison*, trans. Alan Sheridan (New York: Vintage, 1977), in which he outlines the development of modern methods of punishment and the prison system, he changes preference to the term "genealogy." Genealogy has a greater focus on accounting for shifts in knowledge, which he suggests are a result of contingent developments, not grand rational projects.

7. Gina Hens-Piazza, *The New Historicism* (Minneapolis: Fortress, 2002), 11.

by psychology, psychiatry, and medical practitioners, who transform "desire" into an organizing principle around which identities (homosexual, heterosexual, etc.) can be organized. In this way, what were previously understood as perversions now become "a personage, a past, a case history, and a childhood." And through this kind of organization of knowledge, we learn how to regulate ourselves.[8] However, because power is relational, not top down, it can offer modes of resistance as well as coercion.[9]

This will be important for this project for two reasons. First, it enables us to "dig away" beneath the layers and consider how different aspects of culture are interconnected (for instance, law, reproduction, and land, as will be discussed below). Second, it takes into account that, when looking at cultural remains such as Deuteronomy, these are not just objective accounts of a particular belief but exercise power (for example, by being included in a revered text) and thus coerce us into different roles. That is, "discourses of knowledge conspire to produce that which they purport to describe."[10] Through its reading and practice, Deuteronomy creates that which it legislates, and by this we can begin to understand its self-perception as Torah. Robert Hodge suggests a methodology that "emphasize[s] literature as a process rather than simply a set of products; a process which is intrinsically social, connected at every point with mechanisms and the institutions that mediate and control the flow of knowledge and power in a community."[11]

These social functions are, arguably, all the more tied up with biblical texts, which have been in dialogue with culture throughout history, culture that is then worked back onto the texts through modern critical scholarship's dialogue with the Bible. Hens-Piazza suggests a mode of reading that

> crosses boundaries separating the different disciplinary specializations and ignores the boundaries separating the world of the text and the world of the reader. It invites critics to address the political consequences, economic ramifications, social functions, and ethical import of the texts in their historical *and* in their contemporary contexts.[12]

---

8. Foucault, *History of Sexuality*, 1:43.
9. Ibid., 94–5.
10. The Bible and Culture Collective, *The Postmodern Bible*, ed. George Aichele et al. (New Haven: Yale University Press, 1995), 139.
11. Robert Hodge, *Literature as Discourse: Textual Strategies in English and History* (Cambridge: Polity, 1990), viii.
12. Hens-Piazza, *The New Historicism*, 19.

This crossover is productive and can help us understand the dynamic relationship between text, context, and co-text. Therefore, when looking at social practice in a biblical text we can be both aware that texts are not necessarily reflections of historical reality but may also "be an attempt to subvert current social practice."[13] We do this through close scrutiny of the "statement," and by interrogating texts for what they say and leave unsaid. According to Foucault,

> We must grasp the statement in the exact specificity of its occurrence... determine its conditions of existence, fix at least its limits, establish its correlations with other statements that may be connected with it, and show what other forms of statement it excludes. We don't seek below what is manifest in the half silent murmur of another discourse; we must show why it could not be other than it was, in what respect it is exclusive of any other, how it assumes, in the midst of others and in relation to them, a place that no other could occupy. The question proper to such an analysis might be formulated in this way: what is this specific existence that emerges from what is said and nowhere else?[14]

For Foucault, "power is tolerable only on the condition that it masks a substantial part of itself. Its success is proportional to its ability to hide its own mechanisms."[15] Some of the ways the Hebrew Bible constructs knowledge of gender and sexuality are well rehearsed—whether by the etymological construction of bodies as male/female, זכר/נקבה, "remembered one"/"pierced one,"[16] or by foundational narratives that differentiate between sexes (Genesis 1–3). This study will look specifically at how Deuteronomy constructs sexuality as gendered, as powered, and as fundamentally reproductive. This construction of knowledge is not some sort of crude propaganda, however; according to Foucault, power masks itself by producing knowledge of the world. It is therefore not simply about how law constructs sexuality (although law is not imposed externally but arises within a discourse), but how the law is framed within narratives and admonitions to produce knowledge about the world and YHWH, even if the laws are not put into practice.

---

13. Robert P. Carroll, "Poststructuralist Approaches: New Historicism and Postmodernism," in *The Cambridge Companion to Biblical Interpretation*, ed. John Barton (Cambridge: Cambridge University Press, 1998), 40.
14. Foucault, *The Archaeology of Knowledge*, 28.
15. Foucault, *History of Sexuality*, 1:86.
16. Athalya Brenner, *The Intercourse of Knowledge: On Gendering Desire and "Sexuality" in the Hebrew Bible*, BibInt 26 (Leiden: Brill, 1997), 11–12.

Deuteronomy and Social Life

Deuteronomy 1:1 places the text firmly in the mouth of Moses; Moses proceeds to demand obedience from the people (Deut. 4:1-40). Deuteronomy "establishes itself as sole sovereign authority," subordinating public life to the "textual authority of deuteronomic Torah (Deut. xvi 18-xviii 22)";[17] moreover, the text of Deuteronomy 12–26 is the "one potent authority," even replacing the normal role of the monarch and the cultic center in administering justice found elsewhere in the Hebrew Bible (and surrounding ancient West Asia).[18] Bernard M. Levinson goes as far as to argue that the text transfers royal ideology from king to nation. So where God adopts the monarchy in 2 Sam. 7:14—"I will be a father to him, and he shall be a son to me" (אני אהיה לו לאב והוא יהיה לי לבן)[19]—in Deut. 17:14-20 this sentiment is suppressed. Instead, the idea of adoption in Deuteronomy is applied to the people: "you are children of the Lord your God" (בנים אתם ליהוה אלהיכם, Deut. 14:1). Through this reworking of power, "Yahweh here formally adopts Israel."[20] While Levinson's study is more directed at political institutions and powers, George demonstrates from a social and familial level the way Deuteronomy acts as "*the* Torah of Yhwh, or, more precisely, the *Torah* of Yhwh,"[21] asserting itself over the assembly (קהל) and regimenting their social lives, bodies, and gender.[22]

We will look at how Deuteronomy constructs knowledge of gendered sexual relationships and reproduction, and then examine how this relates to wider discourses of reproduction, particularly YHWH's adoption of the people as a whole.

---

17. Bernard M. Levinson, "The Reconceptualization of Kingship in Deuteronomy and the Deuteronomistic History's Transformation of Torah," *VT* 51 (2001): 511–12.

18. Ibid., 522–3.

19. Unless otherwise noted, all quotations of biblical texts follow the NRSV.

20. Levinson, "Reconceptualization," 513.

21. George, "Masculinity," 65.

22. The relationship between Deuteronomy and other legal texts in the Hebrew Bible is complex and contested. If we accept Levinson's influential thesis, then this only strengthens George's description of Deuteronomy acting as *the* Torah of YHWH. See Bernard M. Levinson, *Deuteronomy and the Hermeneutics of Legal Innovation* (New York: Oxford University Press, 1997).

Sexual Dynamics in Legal Material

The following is a series of laws from Deuteronomy that construct knowledge of men and women as sexual actors. They will be dealt with here briefly, only in relation to the discussion at hand; wider discussion can be found elsewhere.[23]

The Ten Commandments on Adultery and Coveting (5:18, 21)

The text is not particularly descriptive in v. 18 (ולא תנאף) or v. 21 (ולא תחמד אשת רעך), although v. 18 sets a general standard for sexual corruption, and v. 21 does demonstrate what will be seen through the rest of the law: the desire for another woman is understood in terms of male desire (as opposed to female), and the appropriateness of a woman being sexually desired relates to her being the woman of another man.[24]

Taking Women in War (20:14)

The taking of women as booty in war is specifically allowed, which presumably includes sexual use.

Beautiful Woman Captured in War Whom a Man Wishes to Take as a Wife (21:10-14)

The law, despite placing restrictions on the man (the woman is to undergo a period of mourning, including shaving her hair), appears to give the man sexual ownership of a woman he came to desire while engaged in war. Its highlighting of her beautiful form (יפת תאר) is particularly noteworthy: her desirability is the significant factor and connected with her sexuality. Moreover, the period of waiting (a month) may be at least partially to ensure she is not pregnant.[25]

---

23. See, specifically, for a much further ranging discussion of the laws: Ellens, *Sex Texts*; Cheryl Anderson, *Women, Ideology and Violence: Critical Theory and the Construction of Gender in the Book of the Covenant and the Deuteronomic Law*, JSOTSup 394 (London: T&T Clark, 2004); Cynthia Edenburg, "Ideology and Social Context of the Deuteronomic Women's Sex Laws (Deuteronomy 22:13-29)," *JBL* 128 (2009): 43–60; and Pressler, *The View of Women*.

24. While תחמד could be understood in terms of a woman desiring the woman of another man, the fact the law is not addressed to her desire for another woman's husband suggests that the law is framed in terms of male listeners.

25. Ellens, *Sex Texts*, 175.

Law of the Rights of the Firstborn Son, Even if the Man Should Prefer the Son of a Different Wife (21:15-17)

This law indirectly allows for men to have multiple wives (though polyandry is never considered); it does, however, countenance competition and preferences between the man and the women and, thus, the possibility for sexual preference. It also legislates for the proper transfer *between* generations, constructing reproduction in terms of social stability, reflecting a discourse in which communal integrity overrides male autonomy.

The Rebellious Son (21:18-21)

While not specifically about sexual acts, it places the fruit of a sexual union firmly under the authority of those who have created it. Interestingly, the mother plays an explicit judicial role here.

Prohibition Against Cross-dressing (22:5)

While some have argued that this verse is specifically related to sexual crimes (cultic prostitution or facilitating same-sex acts),[26] the context does not suggest this; however, the text is significant in constructing gender difference. This is amplified by the imbalance in what is prohibited: the man is prohibited from wearing the garment (שמלה) of a woman, whereas the woman is to not have on her an object of a man (כלי גבר), an act which is abominable (תועבה), offending the moral order.[27] Bodies become the site of sexual and gender difference, and according to Boyarin, this law is symbolically linked with the prohibition on male–male penetrative sex in Lev. 18:22—it acts to enforce a boundary to prevent a blurring of male and female bodies.[28]

The Woman Accused of Not Being a Virgin by a Man Who Is Displeased with Her after Sleeping with Her, Where the Parents Have Evidence of Virginity (22:13-19)

The text demonstrates the importance of virginity and the male's right to protest a lack of virginity. It also constructs virginity as more important than sexual gratification—thus the punishment of a fine for the man who

---

26. For a review of scholarship on the verse, see Steffan Mathias, "Queering the Body: Un-Desiring Sex in Leviticus," in *The Body in Biblical, Christian and Jewish Texts*, ed. Joan E. Taylor, LSTS 85 (London: Bloomsbury T&T Clark, 2015), 30–1.

27. Ibid., 27.

28. Daniel Boyarin, "Are There Any Jews in 'The History of Sexuality'?" *Journal of the History of Sexuality* 5 (1995): 342–3.

slanders the woman. It suggests the parents would have evidence of her virginity: they are to display a cloth, presumably stained with the hymenal blood, implying that sexual intercourse occurred within the woman's father's house, or, if in the husband's house, with family close by. This again constructs sexual activity in a particularly patriarchal and controlled setting, rather than, say, defining it as an act of pleasure or consummation.

The Woman Proved Not to Be a Virgin (22:20-21)

If no evidence of her virginity is found, she is to be brought to her father's house and stoned to death. Her previous sexual activity (and presumably all "premarital" sex of women)[29] is constructed as זנה, something akin to "playing the harlot";[30] it is also said to bring evil, רע, which is to be driven away. Women's sexual autonomy outside of particular relations is constructed as offensive. The punishment is still organized in terms of her father. The death is to take place at the entrance of his house, and Jeffery Tigay suggests this law corresponds to the law of the rebellious son; together they assert fatherly control over his progeny.[31] The action is, moreover, communal—the men of the town are to stone her to death. If the evidence provided is hymenal blood, the text does not appear to consider the possibility of hymenal breakage other than through intercourse or the possibility that bleeding will not occur. Thus, women's sexual organs are inscribed with a particular kind of virginity and an overall sexual meaning.

The Man and the Woman Found in Adultery (22:22)

If a man is found lying (שכב) with the wife of another man, then they are both to die. Here the term for adultery (נאף) is not used as in 5:18, but that it is an act of intercourse is suggested by the verb that does occur (שכב).

---

29. By "premarital," we should understand, more accurately, before she is taken by or given over to a man, rather than something related to a contemporary notion of marriage.

30. For more on the use of זנה in the Pentateuch, see Hilary Lipka, "The Offense, Its Consequences, and the Meaning of זנה in Leviticus 19:29," Chapter 6 in this volume.

31. Jeffrey H. Tigay, *Deuteronomy: The Traditional Hebrew Text with the New JPS Translation* (Philadelphia: Jewish Publication Society, 1996), 204. See also Adele Berlin, "Sex and the Single Girl in Deuteronomy 22," in *Mishneh Todah: Studies in Deuteronomy and Its Cultural Environment in Honor of Jeffrey H. Tigay*, ed. Nili Sacher Fox, David A. Glatt-Gilad, and Michael J. Williams (Winona Lake: Eisenbrauns, 2008), 131–48.

The Engaged Virgin Who Has Sex with another Man in the Town (22:23-24)

Both the man and woman are to be put to death, the woman "because she did not cry for help in the town"[32] and the man "because he violated (ענה) his neighbour's wife." Again, the woman's sexuality is constructed in relation to the man, and the man's transgression is constructed in relation to violating another man's sexual rights. This "evil" is to be purged.

The Engaged Virgin Seized in the Country (22:25-27)

The text states that the man in the open country "seizes her and lies with" the engaged virgin. The word for seize (a *hiphil* form of חזק) suggests brute strength. It prescribes death for the man but nothing for the woman: "the young woman has not committed an offense punishable by death, because this case is like that of someone who attacks and murders a neighbor." It suggests she may have cried for help. The use of חזק, together with the woman's crying out, appears to construct rape as an exclusively violent act.[33] Interestingly, the text constructs guilt based on intent: it is not the woman's body being penetrated that leads to her exoneration but rather her intent. Because she cried out, the law goes to the extent of explicitly explaining why she is not to be punished.

The Virgin Who Is Not Engaged and Seized by a Man (22:28-29)[34]

This law is particularly significant for contextualizing the former two. If she is not engaged, the man is to pay the father 50 shekels of silver, and she will "become his wife." Because he has violated her, he is not permitted to divorce her. The penalty the man takes is based not on the offense towards the woman—her virginity is not constructed as somehow sacrosanct—but rather on the violation done to the man understood as having sexual authority over her. The text understands the

---

32. Although not directly relevant to our discussion, the text's construction of sexual consent as being based on the ability to cry out should be something which is deeply troubling to a contemporary audience.

33. This is not to say that all rape is not an act of violence, but this notion is reminiscent of a kind of contemporary discourse that tends to characterize rapists as violent strangers.

34. Cf. Exod. 22:15-16. If the law in Deuteronomy is based on the law in Exodus, the redactor has done away with the father's right to refuse the daughter to the man. See Tikva Frymer-Kensky, *Studies in Bible and Feminist Criticism* (Philadelphia: Jewish Publication Society, 2006), 244.

violation done to her as mediated through her relation to another man, as in the above laws. Here she is presumably perceived as "damaged," since the man's purchase from the father is constructed as an act of punishment. The fact that he is unable to divorce her suggests that she may struggle to remarry.

Marriage to the Father's Former Wife (23:1)

A man is prohibited from marrying his father's wife. This is understood as violating the father's rights, but no context is given. Anderson suggests it delineates between generations of a household.[35]

Prohibition on Being a Cult Prostitute or Bringing Wages of Prostitutes into the Temple (23:18-19)

Cultic prostitution is not permitted for any of the "daughters of Israel" or "sons of Israel," and the fee of a prostitute is not allowed to be brought into the temple. There appears to be a boundary between the temple and its cult and the practice of prostitution, such that not even the money of a prostitute can be brought into the temple. However, the text seems to acknowledge the existence of both male and female prostitution.

Remarriage to a Former Wife, Who Has Been Married to another Man in the Intervening Period (24:1-4)

The law is obscure in parts. Still, it does indirectly legislate for divorce of some kind: "but [if] she does not please him (לא תמצא חן בעיניו) because he finds something objectionable about her (מצא בה ערות דבר), and so he writes her a certificate of divorce, puts it in her hand, and sends her out of his house." ערוה is somewhat unclear. The previous legislation in Deut. 22:22 would imply that it could not be an issue of infidelity, since the woman would be put to death in that situation. On the other hand, the law here may be a discreet way of actually allowing divorce instead of death for infidelity.[36] These laws, prescribing permitted sexual relationships,

---

35. Anderson, *Women, Ideology and Violence*, 45.
36. Unlike Prov. 6:34-35, Deut. 22:22 does not offer the husband the possibility of pardoning the wife. The text of Deut. 24:1, in contrast, may subtly be allowing the husband to forego the full punishment mandated for adultery. Kenneth Bergland's treatment of this law suggests that no scholarly explanation has yet found a consensus. For an overview of the scholarship on this passage, see Bergland's discussion in "Divorce Instruction and Covenantal Unfaithfulness: A New Examination of the Reuse of Deuteronomy 24:1-4 as Metaphor in Jeremiah 3:1-10," Chapter 11 in this

appear to define sexual possibility in terms of pre-existing social relationships—who someone is engaged or married to, who someone has been sexually intimate with. Still, as George notes, Deuteronomy constructs a world of male sexual possibility: "Several laws prohibit a man having sex with a woman, be she married or promised in marriage...which means that Israelite men are having sex with women, whether those women are single, virgin, or married."[37] He observes that the potential sexual partners imagined for Israelite men are varied: married and engaged women, virgins, former wives, father's wives, mothers-in-law, sisters, temple prostitutes, and women captured in war. While some of these may be prohibited, Deuteronomy creates, by virtue of its prohibitions, a specific kind of knowledge of a man as highly sexualized. These regulations construct sex in terms of proscriptions (these are the women you cannot have sex with) rather than by restriction (you are only to have sex with a wife). Male sexual power manifests itself in a particular form of knowledge about the male body and libido. It is one that is active, penetrating, and authorized. Women's sexuality is, conversely, only known in terms of its relation to men: father, husband, etc. It is understood in terms of virginity, which may be related to a notion of sexual ownership. It could also be framed as an issue of paternity: based either on the need to be sure that one's wife is carrying one's child, or the need to know that there is no notion of split loyalties. This is especially the case when this perspective is brought into comparison with Deut. 25:5-10 and levirate marriage, which emphasizes the crucial role of progeny in perpetuating the male name and family unit. Fundamentally, sexuality is only partially constructed in terms of desire (male desire, say, in the case of the woman captured in war), whereas female desire is not inscribed into the law. Instead, it is constructed predominantly relationally, and these relations are not just between sexual partners but also between family and community.

This discussion highlights an additional crucial construction of sexuality. It is not simply a matter of personal relationships, but of social organization. Cynthia Edenburg notes that the formula "expunge the evil" appears repeatedly in Deut. 22:13-29. By stamping the laws with this injunction, maintains Edenburg, "the author implies that their

---

volume. Particularly interesting for our purposes is his reference to the possibility of the grounds for divorce being infertility; cf. Anthony Phillips, *Deuteronomy*, CBC (Cambridge: Cambridge University Press, 1973), 160.

37. George, "Masculinity," 70–1.

purpose is to ensure the integrity of the social fabric." She goes on to argue that "the concentration of the formula in the women's sex laws implies that maintaining the proper relations between the sexes—particularly with regard to the uncompromising fidelity incumbent upon women to maintain toward their patron, be he father, present husband, or future spouse—is as critical to preserving the proper social order as maintaining exclusive fidelity to YHWH."[38] Here sexuality operates within a particular discourse. It is not constructed as bodily acts or emotional acts or even erotic acts but as the ability to "know" sex is tied up with a deep relation to societal order. It furthermore connects to fidelity to YHWH, which forms the core component of social stability, as will be seen below. Whereas Foucault traces the internalization of sexual life through the early modern period, we can witness here a kind of externalized sexual life, not simply confined to individuals or the family unit, but to society as well. This again explains the heightened public attention towards, and ownership of, virginity (such as the communal murder of the non-virgin by the men of her town at her father's door). If social stability is incumbent on adherence to the law, even in relation to sex, it follows that sexuality is in some way everyone's business.

Reproductive Dynamics in Legal Material

The following laws also construct sexual knowledge; however, there is a special emphasis on discourses of reproduction, and so they will be considered here separately.

No Admittance into the Congregation (קהל) for One with Crushed Testicles or Whose Penis is Cut Off (23:1) (פצוע דכא וכרות שפכה)

The text seems to construct the identity of the קהל as, firstly, based on the integrity of the male sexual organs. Here it seems to be that one admitted into the Torah community, the community adopted by YHWH, has to be able to reproduce. Masculinity is defined here, but so is proper social functioning—Israelite men are to be sexually intact and reproductive. If this is a reworking of Lev. 21:18-20, it significantly reduces the reasons for exclusion, from general bodily disfigurement to disfigurement of reproductive organs.

---

38. Edenburg, "Ideology and Social Context," 57.

No Admittance into the Congregation for Misbegotten Children (ממזר), Followed by No Admittance for Ammonites or Moabites (23:3-7), although an Edomite or Egyptian May Be Admitted in the Third Generation (23:8-9)

A ממזר cannot be admitted into the congregation, suggesting family membership is contingent on family integrity. Moreover, inclusion is restricted to those who bear some relation to the community.[39] Thus, YHWH here prescribes not only how sexual relations are to function within the community, but he also delineates the sexual boundary between the people he has made a covenant with and those who may disrupt it.

First Year of Marriage (24:5)

This verse states: "When a man is newly married, he shall not go out with the army or be charged with any related duty. He shall be free at home (לביתו) for one year, to be happy (שמח) with the wife whom he has married." Jacob Wright suggests that this text specifically refers to a period of allowing reproduction, with לביתו suggesting that the husband and wife are allowed an opportunity to reproduce for the sake of their household, and שמח being euphemistic for pregnancy. He relates this to Deut. 20:7, which suggests that any man engaged to a woman should have military service delayed so no other man can use her first sexually should he die.[40] This constructs marriage/sexual union as both a kind of right, but also as fundamentally procreative—the right of procreation being under- stood as integral to family life. It also relates to Deut. 25:5-10, discussed below.

Woman Who Intervenes in a Fight and Seizes her Husband's Enemy's Genitals (25:11)

It has been suggested that the issue here is women taking charge of the male reproductive body[41] and having power over something that is a seat of the patriarchal promise.[42]

---

39. Hannah Harrington explores this both in terms of admittance into the temple community and with respect to intermarriage, the offspring of which was believed to cause a sacrilege. See her "Sexual Relations and the Transition from Holy People to Human Sanctuary in Second Temple Times," Chapter 12 in this volume.

40. Jacob L. Wright, "Making a Name for Oneself: Martial Valor, Heroic Death, and Procreation in the Hebrew Bible," *JSOT* 36 (2011): 150–1.

41. Tikva Frymer-Kensky, "Deuteronomy," in *The Women's Bible Commentary*, ed. Carol Ann Newsom and Sharon H. Ringe (Louisville: Westminster John Knox, 1998), 67.

42. Both in terms of circumcision and the use of male genitals as a place of oath-making in relation to dynastic issues (Gen. 24:2-9; 47:28-31).

Levirate Marriage (25:5-10)

While some have argued this text is about inheritance or the widow's rights,[43] the text does not present this as its primary cause:[44]

> When brothers reside together, and one of them dies and has no son, the wife of the deceased shall not be married outside the family to a stranger. Her husband's brother shall go in to her, taking her in marriage, and performing the duty of a husband's brother to her, and the firstborn whom she bears shall succeed to the name of the deceased brother, so that his name may not be blotted out of Israel. But if the man has no desire to marry his brother's widow, then his brother's widow shall go up to the elders at the gate and say, "My husband's brother refuses to perpetuate his brother's name in Israel; he will not perform the duty of a husband's brother to me." Then the elders of his town shall summon him and speak to him. If he persists, saying, "I have no desire to marry her," then his brother's wife shall go up to him in the presence of the elders, pull his sandal off his foot, spit in his face, and declare, "This is what is done to the man who does not build up his brother's house." Throughout Israel his family shall be known as "the house of him whose sandal was pulled off."

Instead of focusing on inheritance, the text indicates that the woman's sexuality is used fundamentally for the procreation of a child to preserve the name of her deceased husband. While the brother is offered the opportunity to refuse, the wife is not—she is constructed, sexually, entirely in service to her husband's social reproduction, so that his name may not be blotted out of Israel. Here knowledge of women's sexuality is understood entirely in terms of her husband's use of her body, even after his death.

These laws, rather than simply constructing sexual difference and ownership, reveal a discourse where sexuality is tied up with reproduction and paternity and where procreation is intimately and symbolically connected with men's and women's bodies and with the operations of power over these bodies. Pressler states:

---

43. See Raymond Westbrook, *Property and the Family in Biblical Law* (Sheffield: Sheffield Academic, 1991); Eryl W. Davies, "Inheritance Rights and the Hebrew Levirate Marriage: Part 1," *VT* 31 (1981): 138–44; Davies, "Inheritance Rights and the Hebrew Levirate Marriage: Part 2," *VT* 31 (1981): 257–68. I discuss Davies' wider work on levirate marriage, particularly his understanding that the law relates to a form of marriage for the widow, in Mathias, *Paternity, Progeny, and Perpetuation*. Davies gives an overview of his argument in "Judah, Tamar, and the Law of Levirate Marriage," Chapter 4 in this volume.

44. Mathias, *Paternity, Progeny, and Perpetuation*.

> The deuteronomic family laws examined have as their primary focus neither women, per se, nor men, per se, but the family. They support the family, however, by affirming parental and especially paternal authority, by asserting the husband's unilateral and exclusive claims over his wife's sexuality, and by addressing a man's need for a male heir. In these laws, the interests of the family are largely identified with the interests of the man.[45]

Here male sexuality and social integrity coalesce around a particular discourse at work in these laws. Female sexuality appears highly constrained, whereas male sexuality is constrained only in terms of other men but made highly fruitful in terms of procreation. Crucially, as in Deut. 25:5-10, female sexuality (or female sexual bodies) are configured as social tools. As will now be seen, the discourse of the legal material relates to the blessings and promises of YHWH, but non-compliance distorts the social order and gives YHWH sexual control.

Deuteronomy and YHWH's Children

Deuteronomy begins with an abundance of references to ancestors (Deut. 1:18), descendants (1:11), children, and Torah. The relationship between hearer/reader and their progeny is repeated throughout (4:25, 40; 5:26; 6:2, 7, 20-21; 11:19, 21; 12:12, 18; 16:11, 14), focusing especially on the teaching of Torah precepts to children:

> Teach them to your children, talking about them when you are at home and when you are away, when you lie down and when you rise. Write them on the doorposts of your house and on your gates, so that your days and the days of your children may be multiplied in the land that the Lord swore to your ancestors to give them, as long as the heavens are above the earth. (11:19-21)

There is something almost exaggerated about the relationship between parent, child, and Torah. Torah becomes total—within and outside of the home, throughout the time periods of the day, physically inscribed on the home—and is carefully connected with the promise of multiplication of descendants and security in the land. This multiplication is directly contingent on the observation of the law (7:12-13). God will bless them and multiply them; God will bless the fruit of their womb and the ground, as well as their grain, wine, oil, cattle, and flocks. It is taken to hyperbolic levels with declarations such as 7:14: "You shall be the most

---

45. Pressler, *The View of Women*, 101.

blessed of peoples, with neither sterility nor barrenness among you or your livestock." Those faithful to the Torah are constructed as fertile and reproducing, to the extent that even livestock will not suffer infertility. Torah is to be repeatedly reinternalized by the people:

> But take care and watch yourselves closely, so as neither to forget the things that your eyes have seen nor to let them slip from your mind all the days of your life; make them known to your children and your children's children— how you once stood before the Lord your God at Horeb, when the Lord said to me, "Assemble the people for me, and I will let them hear my words, so that they may learn to fear me as long as they live on the earth, and may teach their children to do so." (Deut. 4:9-10)

Deuteronomy constructs the community through this recalling of the past: "the idea of the assembly symbolizes the idea that each man stood before Yhwh at Mt. Horeb."[46] This recollection of the past, the placing of the community in relation to the giving of the Torah, is intensified in ch. 16. In the month of Abib, the people are to keep the Passover, offering the sacrifice "at the place that the Lord will choose as a dwelling for his name" (v. 2), and to re-enact the circumstances of the original Passover (vv. 3-4), offering the sacrifice in the evening, "the time of day when you departed from Egypt" (v. 6). This re-enactment of the Passover, carried out by the whole (male?) community, acts as a re-adoption of the community by YHWH. If, as Levinson argues, the people become the sons (or children) of YHWH, then the re-enactment allows the community to become, year after year, not only that first community, liberated from slavery by YHWH, but also the community that heard the Torah being spoken and that gave assurances for its transmission to their children.

Moreover, there is sexualized imagery in some of the admonitions to observe the law:

> Keep the commands of the Lord your God.... The Lord set his heart in love on your ancestors alone and chose you, their descendants after them, out of all the peoples, as it is today. Circumcise, then, the foreskin of your heart. (Deut. 10:13-16)

If, for the Priestly writer, fruitfulness and reproduction is contingent on the circumcision of the penis, the symbolism is borrowed and transferred here to the heart and the keeping of Torah.[47] It becomes the location of

---

46. George, "Masculinity," 77.
47. For the relationship between circumcision, sexual reproduction, and fruitfulness, see Howard Eilberg-Schwartz, *The Savage in Judaism: An Anthropology*

circumcision and is connected to both the observance of the law *and* the promise to descendants. This is later intensified in Deut. 30:6-9:

> Moreover, the Lord your God will circumcise your heart and the heart of your descendants (ומל יהוה אלהיך את לבבך ואת לבב זרעך), so that you will love the Lord your God with all your heart and with all your soul.... You shall again obey the Lord, observing all his commandments that I am commanding you today, and the Lord your God will make you abundantly prosperous in all your undertakings, in the fruit of your body (בפרי בטנך), in the fruit of your livestock....

YHWH becomes the one doing the circumcision, across the generations, and the circumcision is specifically linked with observation of the commandments and fruitfulness of the body. If paternal circumcision is a male rite symbolically connected to fertility, then YHWH is claiming a particular role in procreation by virtue of having a paternal relationship with the people and establishing a place of preeminence for the law among the people.

Procreative language abounds in the blessings and warnings that have to do with the importance of obedience (concentrated in Deuteronomy 28–31). The initial items in each section appear to intentionally parallel each other:

> Blessed shall be the fruit of your womb, the fruit of your ground, and the fruit of your livestock, both the increase of your cattle and the issue of your flock. (28:4)

> Cursed shall be the fruit of your womb, the fruit of your ground, the increase of your cattle, and the issue of your flock. (28:18)

But, whereas Deut. 28:4 and 28:18 complement each other, the short blessing of 28:11 (that if the people follow the commandments, they will "abound in prosperity" in the "fruit of your womb," the "fruit of your livestock," and the "fruit of your ground") is far outdone by a later passage in ch. 28, which sets forth an extended set of reproductive curses. Male sexual control is undone: "you shall become engaged to a woman, but another man shall lie with her" (28:30); your sons and daughters (בניך ובנתיך) will be "given to another people" (28:32); oxen and sheep will be lost or slaughtered (28:31); seed will not bear fruit (28:38), vineyards will not produce anything (28:29); and olives will fail to grow

of Israelite Religion and Ancient Judaism (Bloomington: Indiana University Press, 1990), 141–76.

(28:40). The text then descends into a terrifying warning of what will happen to offspring. The people will eat the fruit of their womb, their sons and daughters (28:53). A man will not share the flesh of his children, which he eats, with his wife or remaining offspring (28:55), and a woman will not share the afterbirth of her labor or the children she bears, because she will eat them in secret (28:57). If they do not obey the words of the book, the Lord, who made them as numerous as the stars in heaven and delighted in making them numerous, will delight in their destruction (28:58-63). YHWH's dominion over the people does not just extend to the matter of multiplication, however. The text constructs non-observation of the law as directly related to the destruction of children. YHWH's role is constructed such that fertility is presented as his possession, dependent on the faithful keeping of the law, and so he takes on a role as a destroyer of reproduction and progeny. As the mother and father take on this role in the death of the rebellious child (21:12-21), or as the father's house acts as the place of death for a woman found not to be a virgin (22:20-21), so YHWH, here, takes on the rights of parents against children in destroying his disobedient people. If Deuteronomy elsewhere constructs a kind of reproductive utopia, where there is no infertility (7:14), it here offers a picture not just of a people who cannot procreate, but of a sexual and reproductive dystopia, where women's bodies are no longer the preserve of the men they are engaged or married to, and the fruit of these bodies suffers grotesque consequences.[48] Following Foucault, one can say that YHWH's power is exercised in the production of a type of knowledge that places him firmly in control of sexuality and reproduction, even when this infringes on normal male sexual control. The text asserts him as the dominant sexual male, even if he is one who does not procreate himself.

YHWH's body, or lack of body, is, as Howard Eilberg-Schwartz argued,[49] negotiated at different points in the Hebrew Bible. But where the legal material controls human procreation, YHWH in Deuteronomy stakes his claim to the process. George states:

> An Israelite male needs to, indeed must, live on after his death by having his name carried on by his sons. If this is true for Israelite males, how much more must this be true for Israel's deity, Yhwh? The deity, however, has no female deity partner, either wife, consort, or virgin, with whom he may

---

48. It is interesting that, while the text promises in 7:14 that there will be no barrenness in the land, sterility is not mentioned as a curse—only the destruction of children after birth.

49. I am thinking here, of course, of Howard Eilberg-Schwartz, *God's Phallus and Other Problems for Men and Monotheism* (Boston: Beacon, 1995).

procreate, at least according to Deuteronomy. How does he perpetuate his name? Through his chosen people and their observance of his Torah. Should they fail to observe it, then Yhwh will blot out their names from upon the earth.[50]

The text is indeed saturated with references to the name: human names are to be blotted out (7:14; 9:14; 12:3; 25:6-7), whereas YHWH's is treated very differently. His name is protected from blasphemy (5:11), is to be sworn by (6:13; 10:20), is used to bless (10:8; 21:5), and is to be proclaimed (32:3) and feared (29:20). People speak and minister in YHWH's name (18:7, 19-20, 22), and the nation is called by it (28:10). But the greatest concentration of references are to its dwelling in the place he has chosen (12:5, 11, 21; 14:23-24; 16:2, 6, 11; 26:2). His name is also to be magnified, as is the name of the deceased in the law of levirate marriage, but human names and descendants, if they do not comply with YHWH's law, will be erased.

In the end, the mechanism that YHWH chooses to use for reproduction in Deuteronomy is Torah, and Torah, therefore, assumes a procreative role. While for the Priestly writer circumcision is the preeminent mode of the transmission of fertility, for Deuteronomy it is the repeated teaching and passing down of Torah, culminating in YHWH's adoption and circumcision of the hearts of the people that they may follow Torah. If divine–human sexuality and fertility rites and practices were commonplace in the mythology of ancient West Asia,[51] and the Hebrew Bible renegotiates these norms throughout its pages, Deuteronomy places itself in the place of the reproductive God.[52] It is through *Torah* that sexual

---

50. George, "Masculinity," 76.

51. These do not have to be as explicit a reference as Inanna's exploits with a gardener's boy; see Gwendolyn Leick, *A Dictionary of Ancient Near Eastern Mythology* (London: Routledge, 1998), 90–1. For example, in the Sumerian hymn *Enki and the World Order*, Enki ejaculates, filling the Euphrates with flowing water, and brings forth living things. Elsewhere in *Atrahasis* and *Enki and Ninmah*, Nintu, the womb goddess, infuses Enki's "water" with her clay, which she forms into human beings; see Stephanie Lynn Budin, "Fertility and Gender in the Ancient Near East," in *Sex in Antiquity: Exploring Gender and Sexuality in the Ancient World*, ed. Mark Masterson, Nancy Sorkin Rabinowitz, and James Robson (Routledge Handbooks Online, 2014), 32, 34.

52. The closest explicit reference to a reproductive deity in the Hebrew Bible may well come in the mention of the infamous נפילים of Gen. 6:1-4 or in references to the opening of wombs in Genesis (e.g., ויפתח את רחמה in Gen. 30:22). Indeed, we get strong hints of this notion particularly in prophetic literature, such as in Isaiah 5 and Hosea 2.

reproduction is regulated, for the purpose of having fruitful men who will maintain their name, and it is by the transmission of Torah that the people will remain fruitful, that proper social continuity will be ensured, and that YHWH will reassert his role as head of the household. It is in the very Torah itself that the mechanisms of fertility are ensured and their destruction foretold. Thus, male sexuality within Deuteronomy can be read as autonomous, but it is always subservient to the procreative rights of YHWH.

Bibliography

Anderson, Cheryl. *Women, Ideology and Violence: Critical Theory and the Construction of Gender in the Book of the Covenant and the Deuteronomic Law*. JSOTSup 394. London: T&T Clark, 2004.

Baden, Joel S. *The Composition of the Pentateuch: Renewing the Documentary Hypothesis*. AYBRL. New Haven: Yale University Press, 2012.

Berlin, Adele. "Sex and the Single Girl in Deuteronomy 22." In *Mishneh Todah: Studies in Deuteronomy and Its Cultural Environment in Honor of Jeffrey H. Tigay*, edited by Nili Sacher Fox, David A. Glatt-Gilad, and Michael J. Williams, 131–48. Winona Lake: Eisenbrauns, 2008.

The Bible and Culture Collective. *The Postmodern Bible*, edited by George Aichele et al. New Haven: Yale University Press, 1995.

Boyarin, Daniel. "Are There Any Jews in 'The History of Sexuality'?" *Journal of the History of Sexuality* 5 (1995): 333–55.

Brenner, Athalya. *The Intercourse of Knowledge: On Gendering Desire and "Sexuality" in the Hebrew Bible*. BibInt 26. Leiden: Brill, 1997.

Budin, Stephanie Lynn. "Fertility and Gender in the Ancient Near East." In *Sex in Antiquity: Exploring Gender and Sexuality in the Ancient World*, edited by Mark Masterson, Nancy Sorkin Rabinowitz, and James Robson, 30–49. Routledge Handbooks Online, 2014, https://www.routledgehandbooks.com/doi/10.4324/9781315747910.ch2.

Carroll, Robert P. "Poststructuralist Approaches: New Historicism and Postmodernism." In *The Cambridge Companion to Biblical Interpretation*, edited by John Barton, 50–66. Cambridge: Cambridge University Press, 1998.

Davies, Eryl W. "Inheritance Rights and the Hebrew Levirate Marriage: Part 1." *VT* 31 (1981): 138–44.

Davies, Eryl W. "Inheritance Rights and the Hebrew Levirate Marriage: Part 2." *VT* 31 (1981): 257–68.

Edenburg, Cynthia. "Ideology and Social Context of the Deuteronomic Women's Sex Laws (Deuteronomy 22:13–29)." *JBL* 128 (2009): 43–60.

Eilberg-Schwartz, Howard. *God's Phallus and Other Problems for Men and Monotheism*. Boston: Beacon, 1995.

Eilberg-Schwartz, Howard. *The Savage in Judaism: An Anthropology of Israelite Religion and Ancient Judaism*. Bloomington: Indiana University Press, 1990.

Ellens, Deborah L. *Women in the Sex Texts of Leviticus and Deuteronomy: A Comparative Conceptual Analysis*. LHBOTS 458. New York: T&T Clark, 2008.

Foucault, Michel. *The Archaeology of Knowledge*. Translated by Alan Sheridan. London: Tavistock, 1972.

Foucault, Michel. *Discipline and Punish: The Birth of the Prison*. Translated by Alan Sheridan. New York: Vintage, 1977.
Foucault, Michel. *The History of Sexuality, Volume 1: An Introduction*. Translated by Robert Hurley. 5th ed. New York: Vintage, 1990.
Frymer-Kensky, Tikva. "Deuteronomy." In *The Women's Bible Commentary*, edited by Carol Ann Newsom and Sharon H. Ringe, 57–68. 2nd ed. Louisville: Westminster John Knox, 1998.
Frymer-Kensky, Tikva. *Studies in Bible and Feminist Criticism*. Philadelphia: Jewish Publication Society, 2006.
George, Mark. "Masculinity and Its Regimentation in Deuteronomy." In *Men and Masculinity in the Hebrew Bible and Beyond*, edited by Ovidiu Creangă, 68–82. Sheffield: Sheffield Phoenix, 2010.
Hens-Piazza, Gina. *The New Historicism*. Minneapolis: Fortress, 2002.
Hodge, Robert. *Literature as Discourse: Textual Strategies in English and History*. Cambridge: Polity, 1990.
Leick, Gwendolyn. *A Dictionary of Ancient Near Eastern Mythology*. London: Routledge, 1998.
Levinson, Bernard M. *Deuteronomy and the Hermeneutics of Legal Innovation*. New York: Oxford University Press, 1997.
Levinson, Bernard M. "The Reconceptualization of Kingship in Deuteronomy and the Deuteronomistic History's Transformation of Torah." *VT* 51 (2001): 511–34.
Mathias, Steffan. *Paternity, Progeny, and Perpetuation: Creating Lives after Death in the Hebrew Bible*. London: Bloomsbury T&T Clark, forthcoming.
Mathias, Steffan. "Queering the Body: Un-Desiring Sex in Leviticus." In *The Body in Biblical, Christian and Jewish Texts*, edited by Joan E. Taylor, 17–41. LSTS 85. London: Bloomsbury T&T Clark, 2015.
Phillips, Anthony. *Deuteronomy*. CBC. Cambridge: Cambridge University Press, 1973.
Pressler, Carolyn. *The View of Women Found in the Deuteronomic Family Laws*. BZAW 216. Berlin: de Gruyter, 1993.
Tigay, Jeffrey H. *Deuteronomy: The Traditional Hebrew Text with the New JPS Translation*. Philadelphia: Jewish Publication Society, 1996.
Westbrook, Raymond. *Property and the Family in Biblical Law*. Sheffield: Sheffield Academic, 1991.
Wright, Jacob L. "Making a Name for Oneself: Martial Valor, Heroic Death, and Procreation in the Hebrew Bible." *JSOT* 36 (2011): 131–62.

10

DIVORCE IN ARCHAIC CRETE:
COMPARATIVE PERSPECTIVES
ON DEUTERONOMY 24:1-4

Anselm C. Hagedorn

This essay investigates how the procedure of divorce stipulated in the laws of Gortyn negotiates status and property.[1] Ancient Crete provides us with a remarkable set of laws, of which the oldest written statutes date back to late seventh century BCE.[2] In contrast to ancient Athens, writing down the law in Crete did not lead to the development of a democratic society; Crete thus represents an alternative to the legal culture of Athens. It is further noteworthy that we have almost no other epigraphical evidence from Crete apart from laws, and this points to the importance of written law for its society.[3] The most well-known collection is the one

1. For a general overview on divorce in ancient Greece, see the old but still useful study by Walter Erdmann, *Die Ehe im alten Griechenland*, MBPF 20 (Munich: C. H. Beck, 1934), 384–409; and on Greek marriage law, see Hans Julius Wolff, "Die Grundlagen des griechischen Eherechts," *The Legal History Review* 20 (1952): 1–29, 157–81.

2. An inscription from the polis of Dreros (*Nomima* I.81) that can be dated to ca. 650 BCE is generally regarded as the oldest Cretan, if not the oldest Greek, inscription.

3. On Cretan society, see Stefan Link, *Das griechische Kreta: Untersuchungen zu seiner staatlichen und gesellschaftlichen Entwicklung vom 6. bis zum 4. Jahrhundert v. Chr.* (Stuttgart: Steiner, 1994); Karen Rørby Kristensen, "Archaic Laws and the Development of Civic Identity in Crete, ca. 650–450 BCE," in *Cultural Practices and Material Culture in Archaic and Classical Crete: Proceedings of the International*

from the site of Gortyn and is known as the Gortyn Code, consisting of twelve columns written on one of the city's famous walls.[4] Scholars of the Hebrew Bible look mostly to Mesopotamia and other parts of the ancient Near East for background data as they seek to understand biblical texts in their sociocultural context. They often overlook ancient Greece and its environs. This study seeks mainly to glean insights from the laws in Crete governing marriage and divorce; toward the end of the discussion, it will explore how those insights might inform an interpretation of Deut. 24:1-4.

Marriage at Gortyn

The great Code of Gortyn (*IC* IV 72) contains a variety of laws dealing with marriage and divorce. Those specifically relating to the divorce of couples are addressed in the following sections:

II.45–III.16   Divorce between free citizens

III.40-44   Divorce between slaves

III.44–IV.8   Children of divorced women

The lengthy section *IC* IV 72 III.17-40 addresses the issue of disposition of property after the death of a spouse, showing the importance of property ownership within the culture at large. "As in a divorce, the death of a

---

Conference, Mainz 20–21, 2011, ed. Oliver Pilz and Gunnar Seelentag (Berlin: de Gruyter, 2014), 141–58; Gunnar Seelentag, *Das archaische Kreta: Institutionalisierung im frühen Griechenland*, Klio Beihefte 24 (Berlin: de Gruyter, 2015); and Saro Wallace, *Ancient Crete: From Successful Collapse to Democracy's Alternatives, Twelfth to Fifth Centuries BC* (Cambridge: Cambridge University Press, 2010), 353–75. On the importance of written law and of writing down legal stipulations, see Michael Gagarin, *Writing Greek Law* (Cambridge: Cambridge University Press, 2008); Michael Gagarin, "Inscribing Laws in Greece and the Near East," in *Symposion 2003: Vorträge zur griechischen und hellenistischen Rechtsgeschichte*, ed. H. A. Rupprecht, Akten der Gesellschaft für griechische und hellenistische Rechtsgeschichte 17 (Vienna: Österreichische Akademie der Wissenschaften, 2003), 9–20; and Rosalind Thomas, "Writing, Law, and Written Law," in *The Cambridge Companion to Ancient Greek Law*, ed. Michael Gagarin and David Cohen (Cambridge: Cambridge University Press, 2005), 41–60.

4. See Homer, *Il.* 2.645-49. On the architectural context of Cretan monumental inscriptions, see Paula J. Perlman, "Writing on the Walls: The Architectural Context of Archaic Cretan Laws," in *Crete Beyond the Palaces: Proceedings of the Crete 2000 Conference*, ed. Leslie P. Day, Margaret S. Mook, and James D. Muhly, Prehistory Monographs 10 (Philadelphia: INSTAP Academic, 2004), 181–97.

spouse requires a separation of the husband's property from the wife's."[5] Although marriage is the prerequisite for any divorce, Cretan laws do not provide information about the procedure for the act of marriage.[6] It is, however, likely that, as elsewhere in the Eastern Mediterranean, marriage was arranged between families.[7] This mirrors the evidence from other early laws; Solon, for example, only regulates marriage between brother and sister:

ὁ μὲν οὖν Ἀθηναῖος Σόλων ὁμοπατρίους ἐφεὶς ἄγεσθαι τὰς ὁμομητρίους ἐκώλυσεν.

"In fact, Solon the Athenian allowed marriage with a paternal half-sister, but forbade it with a maternal half-sister."[8]

The word to indicate the act of marrying at Gortyn is ὀπυίω for men and ὀπύεσθαι in the middle voice for women.[9] Whether the woman had any say in the decision to marry is difficult to ascertain, but the Gortyn

---

5. Michael Gagarin and Paula Perlman, *The Laws of Ancient Crete, c. 650–400 BCE* (Oxford: Oxford University Press, 2016), 354. Unless otherwise stated, all English translations of laws from ancient Crete are taken from this volume.

6. It is debated whether *IC* IV 72 VIII.20-22 (*vac.* αἰ δέ κα πατρὸ- | ς δόντος ἒ ἀδελπιō πατροιō- | κος γένεται) can be applied to any marriage procedure; in fact it has been argued that γένεται here refers only to betrothal (Alberto Maffi, "Le mariage de la patrôoque 'donnée' dans le Code de Gortyne [col. VIII, 20–30]," *Revue historique de droit français et étranger* 65 [1987]: 507–25; cf. Maffi,"Studi recenti sul Codice di Gortina," *Dike* 6 [2003]: 204–12).

7. See already Josef Kohler and Erich Ziebarth, *Das Stadtrecht von Gortyn und seine Beziehungen zum gemeingriechischen Rechte* (Göttingen: Vandenhoeck & Ruprecht, 1912), 67: "Die Eheschließung erfolgt nach dem alten Recht; das Gesetz gibt keine korrektorische Bestimmung." Demosthenes 46.18 (*Against Stephanos II*) quotes a law stating who is allowed to give a woman in marriage: ἣν ἂν ἐγγυήσῃ ἐπὶ δικαίοις δάμαρτα εἶναι ἢ πατὴρ ἢ ἀδελφὸς ὁμοπάτωρ ἢ πάππος ὁ πρὸς πατρός, ἐκ ταύτης εἶναι παῖδας γνησίους. ἐὰν δὲ μηδεὶς ᾖ τούτων, ἐὰν μὲν ἐπίκληρός τις ᾖ, τὸν κύριον ἔχειν, ἐὰν δὲ μὴ ᾖ, ὅτῳ ἂν ἐπιτρέψῃ, τοῦτον κύριον εἶναι.

8. Solon, fr. 47b (see Eberhard Ruschenbusch, *Solon: Das Gesetzeswerk—Fragmente*, Übersetzung und Kommentar, Historia Einzelschriften 215 [Stuttgart: Steiner, 2010], 86–8); English translation according to Delfim F. Leão and P. J. Rhodes, *The Laws of Solon: A New Edition with Introduction, Translation and Commentary*, Library of Classical Studies 7 (London: I. B. Tauris, 2015), 75.

9. See *IC* IV 44.4-6 (...) ὀπυιέθ[ο ...) and *IC* IV 72 III.19-20; III.54-55; IV.4; IV.19; IV.50; VI.44; VII.1, 16, 20-21, 23, 27, 30, 35, 36-38, 40, 42-43, 46, 47, 52, 54; VIII.5-6, 12, 14, 16-17, 19, 22-24, 26, 28-29, 32, 35, 37, 39-40, 53; XII.17-18. The word is already attested in Homer, *Il*. 13.429 for a man (πρεσβυτάτην δ' ὤπυιε

Code allowed for the possibility that an heiress could refuse to marry a possible suitor:

>   vac. αἰ δέ κα τō-
>   ι ἐπιβάλλοντι ἐβίονσα μὲ λε͂-
>   ι ὀπυίεθαι ἒ ἄνορος ε͂ι ὀ ἐπιβ-
> 55 άλ[λ]ον [κα]ὶ μ[ὲ λε͂ι μέν]εν
> col. VIII
>   ἀ πατροιο͂κος, στέγαμ μέν,
>   αἴ κ' ε͂ι ἐν πόλι, τὰμ πατροιο͂κο-
>   ν ἔκεν κάτι κ' ἐνε͂ι ἐν τᾶι στέγ-
>   αι, τōν δ' ἄλλον τὰν ἐμί<ν>αν δ-
> 5   ιαλακόνσαν ἄλλοι ὀπυίεθ-
>   αι τᾶς πυλᾶς τōν αἰτιόντον
>   ὄτιμί κα λεῖ. vac.

vac. And if the heiress | is past puberty[10] but does not | wish to marry the claimant, or the | claimant has not reached puberty and | she does not wish to wait, | (col. VIII) the | heiress is to have the house, if there is | one in the city, and whatever is in the | house, and she is to receive half of the | remaining (estate) and is to marry | | another from the tribe, whomever she | wishes of those who ask. *vac.*[11]

Additionally, the peculiar laws regulating the matrimonial union between a free woman and a slave seem to imply that the woman was able to have a say in the matter.

> 55   τō ἐλευθέρο τὸν
>   δε [— — — — αἴ κ' ὀ δο͂λος]
> col. VII
>   ἐπὶ τὰν ἐλευθέραν ἐλθὸν ὀπυίει,
>   ἐλεύθερ' ἔμεν τὰ τέκνα. vac. αἰ δέ κ'
>   ἀ ἐλευθέρα ἐπὶ τὸν δο͂λον, δο͂λ' ἔμ-
>   εν τὰ τέκνα. vac. αἰ δέ κ' ἐς τᾶς αὐτ-

θυγατρῶν Ἱπποδάμειαν) and in Homer, *Il.* 8.304 for a woman (τόν ῥ' ἐξ Αἰσύμηθεν ὀπυιομένη τέκε μήτηρ).

10. *IC* IV 72 XII.17-19 states that "women acquired matrimonial capacity" (Eva Cantarella, "Greek Law and the Family," in *A Companion to Families in the Greek and Roman Worlds*, ed. Beryl Rawson, Blackwell Companions to the Ancient World [Malden: Wiley-Blackwell, 2011], 342) at the age of twelve (ὀπυί- | εθαι δὲ δυοδεκαϝετία ἒ πρεί- | γονα. *vac.*), but we do not know whether this stipulation reflects common practice or draws attention to a change in procedure.

11. *IC* IV 72 VII.52–VIII.7.

5   ἆς ματρὸς ἐλεύθερα καὶ δõλα
    τέκνα γένεται, ἒ κ' ἀποθάνει ἀ
    μάτερ, αἴ κ' ἔι κρέματα, τὸνς ἐλε-
    υθέρονς ἔκεν. αἰ δ' ἐλεύθεροι
    μὲ ἐκσεῖεν, τὸνσς ἐπιβάλλον-
10 τανς ἀναιλε͂θαι. vac.

...of the free man [c. 7 If the | slave] (col. VII) goes to a free | woman and marries her, their | children are to be free; vac. but if | the free woman (goes to) the | slave, their, children are to be | slaves. vac. And if free and slave | children are born from the same | mother, when the mother dies, if | there is property, the free chil- | dren are to have it; but if there | should be no free children, her | relatives are to inherit it. vac.[12]

First of all, the law stipulates that the status of the children born out of wedlock between a free woman and a slave depends on where they reside. Similar stipulations are known from the Laws of Hammurabi where the status of the children is determined by the status of the free woman, without reference to the place of habitation.[13] The Gortynian law only regulates the marriage of a free woman with a slave and not vice versa.[14] That it is envisaged that a slave goes to the free woman (ἐπὶ τὰν ἐλευθέραν ἐλθὸν ὀπυίει) probably suggests that the free woman was in possession of a house and possibly some wealth and that the place of residence was perhaps determined by the economic status of the woman.[15] In any

---

12. *IC* IV 72 VI.55–VIII.10.

13. See LH §§175-176. The text of §175 seems to suggest that the slave resides with the woman: "If a slave of the palace or a slave of a commoner marries a woman of the *awīlu*-class and she then bears children, the owner of the slave will have no claims of slavery against the children of the woman of the *awīlu*-class" (translation according to Martha T. Roth, *Law Collections from Mesopotamia and Asia Minor*, ed. Piotr Michalowski, SBLWAW 6 [Atlanta: Scholars Press, 1997], 115). In contrast, §176 explicitly mentions that the free woman enters the house of the slave. This, however, does not seem to affect the status of the children since, with respect to the division of property after the death of the slave husband, the text states: *mišlam mārat awīlim ana mārīša ileqqe* ("the woman of the *awīlu*-class shall take half for her children" [ibid., 116]).

14. Henri van Effenterre and Françoise Ruzé, eds, *Nomima: Recueil d'inscriptions politiques et juridiques de l'archaïsme grec I–II*, Collection de l'École Française de Rome 188 (Paris: de Boccard, 1995), 132, speculate: "Il faut croire qu'avec les guerres et les naufrages, il pouvait y avoir un déséquilibre numérique entre les sexes."

15. Monique Bile, "Prolégomènes aux lois Gortyne I: Statut de la femme et ordre social," in *Folia Graeca in honorem Edouard Will: Linguistica*, ed. Claude Brixhe and Guy Vottéro, Études anciennes 50 (Nancy: de Boccard, 2012), 59–60.

case, "it seems unlikely that the girl's father or other relatives would be involved in arranging such a marriage, let alone arrange it without consulting the girl."[16]

Furthermore, a passage in *IC* IV 72 VII.27-29 that is difficult to interpret seems to limit the number of heiresses a man could marry:

μίαν δ'
ἔκεν πατροι[ō]κον τὸν ἐπιβάλ-
λοντα, πλίαδ δὲ [μ]έ. vac.

And the claimant is to have one heiress and not more.

This clause has been linked to the prohibition of polygamy at Gortyn,[17] but we have to note that polygamy is not mentioned in any of the Cretan laws. The context suggests that this stipulation is probably connected to divorce, prohibiting a claimant from successively marrying heiresses.[18]

Divorce at Gortyn

At Gortyn the issue of divorce is treated after matters of sexual offenses. As is common elsewhere in the Great Code, the law distinguishes between free persons (*IC* IV 72 II.45–III.16) and serf couples (*IC* IV 72 III.40-44). The stipulations are supplemented by rules for children born after the divorce (*IC* IV 72 III.44–IV.23) and additional stipulations in regard to women's oaths in the addenda to the laws (*IC* IV 72 XI.46-55).[19]

col. II
45   vac. αἴ κ' ἀνὲρ [κ]αὶ γυνὰ διακρ[ί]νον[τ]αι, τὰ ϝὰ α-
ὐτᾶς ἔκεν, ἄτι ἔκονσ' ἔιε π-
ὰρ τὸν ἄνδρα, καὶ τō καρπō τ-
ὰνν ἐμίναν, αἴ κ' ἔι ἐς τον ϝō-

---

16. Michael Gagarin, "Women and the Law in Gortyn," *Index* 40 (2012): 59.

17. Kohler and Ziebarth, *Das Stadtrecht von Gortyn*, 67; Ronald F. Willetts, *The Law Code of Gortyn*, Kadmos Supplement 1 (Berlin: de Gruyter, 1967), 24–5.

18. Gagarin and Perlman, *The Laws of Ancient Crete*, 393.

19. These addenda are recognizable by large gaps at the end of a line in col. XI.23, 25, 45, and most of the laws preserved in col. XI.24–XII.19 modify or supplement earlier legislation. See also John K. Davies, "Deconstructing Gortyn: When Is a Code a Code?" in *Greek Law in its Political Setting: Justification Not Justice*, ed. L. Foxhall and A. D. E. Lewis (Oxford: Clarendon, 1996), 33–56, who has argued that these provisions were carved by a different hand.

50 ν αὐτᾶς κρεμάτον, κὄτι
κ' ἐνυπάνει τὰν [ἐμίνα]ν ἄτι
κ' ἔι, καὶ πέντε στατἒρανς, αἴ κ' ὁ ἀ-
νὲρ αἴτιος ἔι τᾶς κε[ρ]εύσι-
ος· α[ἰ] δὲ πονίοι ὁ ἀνὲρ [αἴτι]-
55 [ος μὲ ἔ]μεν, τὸν δικαστὰν
col. III
ὀμνύντα κρίνεν. αἰ δέ τι ἄλλ-
ο πέροι τὸ ἀνδρός, πέντε στατἒρανς καταστασεῖ κὄτι
κα πέρει αὐτόν, κὄτι κα παρ-
5 έλει ἀποδότο αὐτόν. ὂν δέ κ'
ἐκσαννέσεται δικάκσαι τ-
ὰν γυναῖκ' ἀπομόσαι τὰν Ἄρ-
τεμιν πὰρ Ἀμυκλαῖον πὰρ τὰν
Τοκσίαν. ὄτι δέ τίς κ' ἀπομο-
10 σάνσαι παρέλει, πέντε στατἒρανς καταστασεῖ καὶ τὸ κρ-
έος αὐτόν. vac. αἰ δέ κ' ἀλλόττρι-
ος συνεσάδδει, δέκα στ[ατ]ἒ-
ρανς καταστασεῖ, τὸ δὲ κρέ-
15 ιος διπλεῖ ὄτι κ' ὁ δικαστὰς
ὀμόσει συνεσσάκσαι. vac.

If a husband and wife are divorced | she is to have her own things, what- | ever she had when she came to her | husband, and half of the produce, if | there is any from her own property, | and half of what she has woven, | whatever it is, and five staters if the | husband is responsible for the separ- | ation; but if the husband affirms that | he is not responsible, the judge (col. III) is to swear an oath and decide. But | if she should take away something else | of her husband's, she will pay five | staters and (return) the object that she | carries away, and let her give back | whatever she has stolen. But with | regard to things she denies, (the judge) | is to rule that the woman is to take an | oath of denial by Artemis, before (the | statue of) | the Archeress at Amyklaion. | And whatever anyone may steal from | her after she has sworn an oath of | denial, he will pay five staters and the | thing itself. vac. And if some other | person helps her remove (something), | he will pay ten staters and twice the | value of whatever the judge swears he | helped remove. vac.[20]

---

20. *IC* IV 72 II.45–III.16, modified according to Gagarin and Perlman, *The Laws of Ancient Crete*, 350–1.

The legal stipulation is not concerned with the actual procedure for divorce, but instead addresses the division of property after the separation of the spouses has occurred. The verb used for the separation is διακρίνονται, not otherwise attested in archaic and classical Crete.[21] It is equivalent to κρίνεται, which is used to indicate divorce in III.41 and XI.46.

The grounds for divorce are not given, but II.52-53 describes the husband as ὁ ἀνὲρ αἴτιος implying that he is responsible for the divorce, without, however, distinguishing whether he has left his wife or whether his behavior was the reason for his wife leaving him.[22] "It appears that divorce could be initiated by either spouse."[23] This concurs with the evidence from Athens, though it seems that it was considerably easier for a husband to initiate a divorce than for a wife.[24] In Athens the husband simply had to expel the wife from his house,[25] while "a divorce proceeding from a woman was only valid if it had been reported in writing to the archon."[26]

Whether divorce was usually amicable cannot be determined and is, admittedly, not of concern to the lawgiver. Evidence from Athens suggests that Greeks knew both hostile and amicable separations of spouses. Isaeus recounts the proceedings of a certain Menacles, who divorced his young wife:

[6] ἐκδόντες τοίνυν τὰς ἀδελφάς, ὦ ἄνδρες, καὶ ὄντες αὐτοὶ ἐν ἡλικίᾳ ἐπὶ τὸ στρατεύεσθαι ἐτραπόμεθα, καὶ ἀπεδημήσαμεν μετὰ Ἰφικράτους εἰς Θρᾴκην· ἐκεῖ δὲ δόξαντές του εἶναι ἄξιοι περιποιησάμενοί τι κατεπλεύσαμεν δεῦρο, καὶ καταλαμβάνομεν τῇ πρεσβυτέρᾳ ἀδελφῇ ὄντα δύο παιδία, τὴν δὲ νεωτέραν, ἣν

---

21. In Attic Greek, words like ἀποπέμπειν, ἐκπέμπειν, and ἐκβάλλειν are used when the husband initiates the divorce and ἀπολείπειν when the wife does so (cf. A. R. W. Harrison, *The Law of Athens, vol. 1: The Family and Property* [Oxford: Oxford University Press, 1968], 40).

22. Reinhard Koerner, *Inschriftliche Gesetzestexte der frühen griechischen Polis*, Akten der Gesellschaft für griechische und hellenistische Rechtsgeschichte 9 (Cologne: Böhlau, 1993), 474.

23. Gagarin and Perlman, *The Laws of Ancient Crete*, 352.

24. For divorce in classical Athens, see Louis Cohn-Haft, "Divorce in Classical Athens," *Journal of Hellenic Studies* 65 (1995): 1–14; and the documents assembled in David D. Phillips, *The Law of Ancient Athens*, Law and Society in the Ancient World (Ann Arbor: University of Michigan Press, 2013), 153–7.

25. Lysias 14.28 (*Against Alcibiades I*) mentions that a certain Hipponikos summoned witnesses to attest to his actions (Ἱππόνικος δὲ πολλοὺς παρακαλέσας ἐξέπεμψε τὴν αὑτοῦ γυναῖκα, φάσκων τοῦτον οὐχ ὡς ἀδελφὸν αὐτῆς ἀλλ' ὡς ἄνδρα ἐκείνης εἰς τὴν οἰκίαν εἰσιέναι τὴν αὑτοῦ), but this seems to have been an exception.

26. Harrison, *The Family and Property*, 42.

εἶχε Μενεκλῆς, ἄπαιδα. [7] καὶ ἐκεῖνος δευτέρῳ μηνὶ ἢ τρίτῳ, πολλὰ ἐπαινέσας τὴν ἀδελφήν, λόγους ἐποιεῖτο πρὸς ἡμᾶς, καὶ ἔφη τήν τε ἡλικίαν ὑφορᾶσθαι τὴν ἑαυτοῦ καὶ τὴν ἀπαιδίαν· οὔκουν ἔφη δεῖν ἐκείνην τῆς χρηστότητος τῆς ἑαυτῆς τοῦτο ἀπολαῦσαι, ἄπαιδα καταστῆναι συγκαταγηράσασαν αὐτῷ· ἱκανὸς γὰρ ἔφη αὐτὸς ἀτυχῶν εἶναι. [8] <...> ἐδεῖτο οὖν ἡμῶν δοῦναι χάριν ταύτην αὐτῷ, ἐκδοῦναι ἄλλῳ αὐτὴν μετὰ τῆς γνώμης τῆς ἑαυτοῦ. καὶ ἡμεῖς ἐκελεύομεν αὐτὸν πείθειν αὐτὴν περὶ τούτων· ὅ τι γὰρ <ἂν> ἐκείνη πεισθῇ, τοῦτ' ἔφαμεν ποιήσειν. [9] κἀκείνη τὸ μὲν πρῶτον οὐδ' ἠνέσχετ' αὐτοῦ λέγοντος, προϊόντος δὲ τοῦ χρόνου μόλις ἐπείσθη· καὶ οὕτως ἐκδίδομεν αὐτὴν Ἠλείῳ Σφηττίῳ, καὶ ὁ Μενεκλῆς τήν τε προῖκα ἐπιδίδωσιν αὐτῷ, μετασχὼν τοῦ οἴκου τῆς μισθώσεως τῶν παίδων τῶν Νικίου, καὶ τὰ ἱμάτια, ἃ ἦλθεν ἔχουσα παρ' ἐκεῖνον, καὶ τὰ χρυσίδια, ἃ ἦν, δίδωσιν αὐτῇ.

[6] So we gave our sister in marriage, gentlemen, and then ourselves joined the army, as we were of military age. We served abroad with Iphicrates of Thrace, where we proved our worth and saved some money before sailing back to Athens. Here we found our elder sister with two children but the younger one, Menacles' wife, childless. [7] Two or three months later, while lavishing praise on our sister, he spoke to us and said that he was worried about his age and childlessness. He said she ought not to be rewarded for her virtue by growing old with him and remaining childless; it was enough, he said, that he was himself unfortunate. [8] He therefore begged us to do him the favor of marrying her to someone else with his blessing. We told him to persuade her of this and said that we would do whatever she agreed. [9] At first she would not even listen to his proposal, but after a while she reluctantly agreed. So we married her to Elius of Sphettus, and Menacles, who had obtained part of the estate of Nicias' children by lease, handed over her dowry to him, and gave her the clothes she'd brought with her to his house and the jewelry she had.[27]

Here the husband initiates the proceedings, but it is stressed quite clearly that no blame for the divorce should fall upon the woman. Menacles only proceeds with the divorce after first gaining the acquiescence of the woman and her brothers.[28] He also begs the brothers to ensure that she is married to somebody younger.[29] As part of the divorce proceedings, Menacles returns the dowry as well as the personal possession of his wife to the brothers (καὶ τὰ ἱμάτια, ἃ ἦλθεν ἔχουσα παρ' ἐκεῖνον, καὶ τὰ χρυσίδια, ἃ ἦν, δίδωσιν αὐτῇ); this seems to have been common practice.

27. Isaeus, II.6-12; English translation according to Michael Edwards, *Isaeus*, The Oratory of Classical Greece 11 (Austin: University of Texas Press, 2007), 33–4.
28. Cohn-Haft, "Divorce in Classical Athens," 3.
29. A similar procedure is attested in Plutarch, *Pericles* 24.5, when Pericles ensures that his (foreign) wife Aspasia is immediately remarried.

Things are different in Lysias's first speech against Alcibiades. Here it is reported that Hipponicos divorces Alcibiades's daughter because he has discovered that she had an incestuous affair with her brother:

> ὅσα μὲν οὖν, ὦ ἄνδρες δικασταί, ἢ εἰς τοὺς πολίτας ἢ εἰς τοὺς ξένους ἢ περὶ τοὺς αὑτοῦ οἰκείους ἢ περὶ τοὺς ἄλλους ἡμάρτηκε, μακρὸν ἂν εἴη λέγειν· Ἱππόνικος δὲ πολλοὺς παρακαλέσας ἐξέπεμψε τὴν αὑτοῦ γυναῖκα, φάσκων τοῦτον οὐχ ὡς ἀδελφὸν αὐτῆς ἀλλ' ὡς ἄνδρα ἐκείνης εἰς τὴν οἰκίαν εἰσιέναι τὴν αὑτοῦ.

Well, to relate all the offenses that he has committed, gentlemen, either against the citizens, or against foreigners, or in his dealings with his own relations or with ordinary people, would be a lengthy affair; but Hipponicus assembled a number of witnesses and put away his wife, stating that this man had been entering his house, not as her brother, but as her husband.[30]

The incest may add to the overall scandal, but the issue is really adultery, which may require an immediate divorce from the wife.[31] Demosthenes in his speech against Neaera reports that a husband named Phrastor simply threw out (ἐκβάλλει) his wife Phano after he had learned that she was not an Athenian, and refused to pay back the dowry (καὶ τὴν προῖκα οὐκ ἀποδίδωσιν).[32] Since a law in the same speech stipulates that marriage of an Athenian with a non-Athenian was a criminal offense, the union between Phano and Phrastor may not have been considered a valid marriage.[33]

---

30. Lysias, 14.28 (Lamb, LCL).
31. Such a law is stated as Νόμος Μοιχείας in Demosthenes 59.87. The authenticity of the law is disputed; cf. the discussion in Mirko Canevaro, *The Documents in the Attic Orators: Laws and Decrees in the Public Speeches of the Demosthenic Corpus* (Oxford: Oxford University Press, 2013), 190–6. The issue of adultery in Athens is complex; see the detailed debate in David Cohen, *Law, Sexuality, and Society. The Enforcement of Morals in Classical Athens* (Cambridge: Cambridge University Press, 1991), 98–132; Rosanna Omitowoju, *Rape and the Politics of Consent in Classical Athens*, Cambridge Classical Studies (Cambridge: Cambridge University Press, 2002), 72–115; and Winfried Schmitz, "Der nomos moicheias: Das athenische Gesetz über den Ehebruch," *Zeitschrift der Savigny-Stiftung für Rechtsgeschichte: Romanistische Abteilung* 114 (1997): 45–110.
32. Demosthenes 59.51.
33. See Demosthenes 59.16; see also the discussion of the law's authenticity in Canevaro, *The Documents in the Attic Orators*, 183–7.

Probably the most powerful statement regarding a woman's feelings relating to separation and divorce can be found in Euripides's *Medea*.[34] In the opening monologue, the heroine's nurse recounts the situation in Corinth:[35]

> νῦν δ' ἐχθρὰ πάντα, καὶ νοσεῖ τὰ φίλτατα.
> προδοὺς γὰρ αὑτοῦ τέκνα δεσπότιν τ' ἐμὴν
> γάμοις Ἰάσων βασιλικοῖς εὐνάζεται,
> γήμας Κρέοντος παῖδ', ὃς αἰσυμνᾷ χθονός.
> 20 Μήδεια δ' ἡ δύστηνος ἠτιμασμένη
> βοᾷ μὲν ὅρκους, ἀνακαλεῖ δὲ δεξιᾶς
> πίστιν μεγίστην, καὶ θεοὺς μαρτύρεται
> οἵας ἀμοιβῆς ἐξ Ἰάσονος κυρεῖ.

But now all is enmity, and closest ties are diseased. For Jason, abandoning his own children and my mistress, is bedding down in a royal match, having married the daughter of Creon, ruler of this land. Poor Medea, finding herself thus dishonored, calls loudly on his oaths, invokes the mighty assurance of his sworn right hand, and calls the gods to witness the unjust return she is getting from Jason.[36]

Greek tragedy is generally silent about the issue of divorce, though the motif of the "other woman" bringing distress to a household occurs quite frequently, and a common cause of marital strife in this literature is the husband's infidelity.[37] In *Medea* the separation is the result of Jason's decision to enter into a more economically advantageous union. It should

---

34. On the play, see Donald J. Mastronarde, ed., *Euripides: Medea*, Cambridge Greek and Latin Classics (Cambridge: Cambridge University Press, 2002); and Edith Hall, *Greek Tragedy: Suffering under the Sun* (Oxford: Oxford University Press, 2010), 242–5.

35. Medea is the only tragedy that is set in Corinth and is probably playing with the reputation of the city in antiquity; cf. Kate Gilhuly, *Erotic Geographies in Ancient Greek Literature and Culture* (New York: Routledge, 2018), 11–42.

36. Euripides, *Medea* 16–23 (Kovacs, LCL).

37. Mastronarde, *Euripides*, 278. On sexual jealousy in the play, see Ed Sanders, "Sexual Jealousy and *Erôs* in Euripides' Medea," in *Erôs in Ancient Greece*, ed. Ed Sanders et al. (Oxford: Oxford University Press, 2013), 41–57; see also Homer, *Od.* 1.429-433, when Laertes avoids the wrath of his wife by not sleeping with Eurycleia; and Euripides, *Andromache* 465–470, when the chorus states that the "doubleness" of marriage is not recommended (οὐδέποτε δίδυμα λέκτρ' ἐπαινέσω) and that a husband should be content with a single companion and an unshared bed.

be noted that there would have been a problem with classifying the union of Jason and Medea as a proper marriage and that Athenian audiences would have immediately recognized this: "Since she was not given in marriage by a father or brother, and indeed was not even a Hellene, in Athenian eyes the marriage to Jason was not a legal union; moreover, she had no family to whom she could be sent back, and whose reaction to the dismissal of their relative had to be taken into consideration, as would normally have been the case in Athenian marriage."[38] Nevertheless, throughout the play, issues known from regular marriage and divorce proceedings are alluded to. In lines 230-251, Medea describes women as being most unfortunate (γυναῖκές ἐσμεν ἀθλιώτατον φυτόν) since they are in fact forced to buy a husband—an allusion to the dowry—making him master over their bodies (ἃς πρῶτα μὲν δεῖ χρημάτων ὑπερβολῇ | πόσιν πρίασθαι, δεσπότην τε σώματος). She continues to label separation as disreputable for women and states that a woman is unable to refuse wedlock (οὐ γὰρ εὐκλεεῖς ἀπαλλαγαὶ | γυναιξὶν οὐδ' οἷόν τ' ἀνήνασθαι πόσιν).[39] "The vengeful, competitive and sexually honest Medea, in escaping without punishment, was any Athenian husband's worst nightmare realized."[40]

Such passionate outbursts are, of course, not part of the Gortynian law, but the mentioning of the unlawful removal of property not belonging to the wife (αἰ δέ τι ἄλλ- | ο πέροι τῶ ἀνδρός, πέντε στ- | ατερανς καταστασεῖ), as well as the possibility that she might enlist someone to help her remove more than she has the right to (αἰ δέ κ' ἀλλόττρι- | ος συνεσάδδει), may indicate that proceedings were not always as amicable as one may have hoped.

Property and Divorce

As already noted above, the main concern of the stipulations regulating the separation of spouses in the Gortyn Code is the correct allocation of property. In a divorce, the woman was only allowed to take what belonged to her at the time of her marriage (ἄτι ἔκονσ' ἔιε πὰρ τὸν ἄνδρα), and the language of the code makes it quite clear that this is her own property (τὰ ϝὰ αὐτᾶς).[41] The reference to "her own things" is often

---

38. Cohn-Haft, "Divorce in Classical Athens," 1.
39. In lines 638–644, the Chorus urges Aphrodite to bless marriages that are peaceful.
40. Hall, *Greek Tragedy*, 243.
41. *IC* IV 72 V.1-4 refers to a woman who does not own property: γυνὰ ὀ[τ]εία κ- | ρέματα μὲ ἔκει ἒ [πα]τρὸδ δό- | ντος ἒ ἀ[δ]ελπιὸ ἒ ἐπισπέν- | σαντος ἒ ἀπολα[κ]όνσα.

understood as identifying the dowry,[42] but as we will see below, Gortyn does not seem to know this institution. In addition to her own property, she is to have half of the produce (καρπός) from her property (κρέματα),[43] the other half presumably remaining with the husband. The term καρπός here probably refers to the actual agricultural product rather than general profit, implying that a Gortynian woman could own land.[44] Lastly, she is to have half of the profit she generated during the marriage (κὅτι κ' ἐνυπάνει τὰν [ἐμίνα]ν ἄτι κ' ἔι). The use of the Aorist in (ἐν)υφαίνω seems to refer to activities in the house, as the use of ἐναιλεθέντος in line 30 of the same column suggests. The term ὑφαίνω refers to the stereotypical occupation of females, most famously Penelope, in a Greek household.[45] The wording, however, does not only refer to woven cloth(ing), which the following ἄτι κ' ἔι seems to emphasize.[46] The male property remains unaffected by the separation, and he retains half of what his wife has woven. If the husband is responsible for the separation, there is a fine to be paid by him of five staters. Should the woman remove additional property, she, too, is to pay five staters, and so is the person who steals from her.[47]

Also, the law allows for the possibility that the woman might deny that she has taken more than she was allowed to. In this case, it is her word

---

42. Franz Bücheler and Ernst Zitelmann, *Das Recht von Gortyn*, RhM 40 (Frankfurt: Sauerländer, 1885), 115; Koerner, *Inschriftliche Gesetzestexte*, 475.

43. On the basis of ἐπιπολαία κρεμάτα in V.41, κρεμάτα seems to refer to immovable property here.

44. Gagarin and Perlman, *The Laws of Ancient Crete*, 352–3; against Claude Brixhe and Monique Bile, "La circulation des biens dans les Lois de Gortyne," in *Des dialectes grecs aux Lois de Gortyne*, ed. Catherine Dobias-Lalou, Études Anciennes 21 (Nancy: de Boccard, 1999), 101–2, who, on the basis of *IC* IV 162 (second half of the third century BCE), have argued that the phrase καρπῶ ὠνίοι is a clear indication that καρπός in the Great Code has to be understood as profit. In *IC* IV 72 V.39-41, καρπός clearly refers to produce.

45. Cf. Homer, *Od.* 2.104-105, for Penelope, and *Il.* 3.125; 6.456.

46. Koerner, *Inschriftliche Gesetzestexte*, 475.

47. The value of such payment is difficult to assess; Koerner (ibid., 476) thinks the financial setback for the husband is minimal ("eine wahrlich nicht sehr hohe Summe"). The highest fine attested in the legal material from Gortyn is 100 staters for the rape of a free man or woman (double if the offender was a slave) in *IC* IV 72 II.11-16 and possibly for plunder (see *IC* IV 78 = *Nomima* I.16). The law in *IC* IV 63 (= *Nomima* I.59) mentions a payment of five staters per day: κατ' ἀμέραν πέντε στατέραν[ς].

against her husband's, and the matter can only be decided by an oath of denial (ἀπόμνυμι).⁴⁸ This oath is to be sworn by Artemis and seems to be a specific female form of the oath, given that men at Gortyn swear by other deities.⁴⁹ The place of the oath is specified in detail: πὰρ Ἀμυκλαῖον πὰρ τὰν Τοκσίαν. Artemis Toxia is unknown in Greece,⁵⁰ though the reference to archery fits the general portrait of the deity quite well.⁵¹ The temple of Artemis is located at Amyclaion,⁵² which was probably an extra-urban sanctuary.⁵³ This would require the woman to travel and thus add to the significance of the oath.

The procedure of the oath is specified in more detail in the amendment to the law about the separation of spouses in *IC* IV 72 XI.46-55:

---

48. Outside the Gortyn Code, this oath is also attested in *IC* IV 72 22 (= *Nomima* II.84) and maybe in *IC* II xii 17 (from the site of Eleutherna on Crete).

49. See *IC* IV 51 (= *Nomima* II.13), where men swear by Apollo, Athene, and Hermes; van Effenterre and Ruzé, *Nomima: Recueil d'inscriptions*, 64, following an old proposal by Johannes Brause ("ΓΟΡΤΥΝΙΩΝ ΟΡΚΟΣ ΝΟΜΙΜΟΣ," *Hermes* 49 [1914]: 107), suggest—in light of the prominence of Zeus in Crete—that Zeus should be added too.

50. A sacred law from Cos, however, mentions τὸ ἱερὸν τᾶς Ἀρτάμ[ιδος τᾶς Τοξίτιδος (*LSCG*, no. 154).

51. On the character of Artemis, see Walter Burkert, *Griechische Religion der archaischen und klassischen Epoche*, 2nd ed., Die Religionen der Menschheit 15 (Stuttgart: Kohlhammer, 2011), 231–5; and in more detail, Stephanie Lynn Budin, *Artemis*, Gods and Heroes of the Ancient World (London: Routledge, 2016).

52. The term is also attested as the name of a month at Gortyn (*IC* IV 182), and it has been interpreted in light of information provided by Conon (FrGrH 26 fr. 1) "that Laconians from Amyklai emigrated to Crete and settled at Gortyn" (Paula J. Perlman, "Reading and Writing Archaic Cretan Society," in *Cultural Practices and Material Culture in Archaic and Classical Crete: Proceedings of the International Conference, Mainz 20–21, 2011*, ed. Oliver Pilz and Gunnar Seelentag [Berlin: de Gruyter, 2014], 198; cf. Paula J. Perlman, "Gortyn: The First Seven Hundred Years [Part I]," in *Polis and Politics: Studies in Ancient Greek History Presented to Mogens Hansen on His Sixtieth Birthday*, ed. Pernille Flensted-Jensen, Thomas Heine Nielsen, and Lene Rubinstein [Copenhagen: Museum Tusculanum, 2000], 67–71).

53. The identification is difficult, and scholars normally locate it in Western Mesara, near Kommos (Paula J. Perlman, "Crete," in *An Inventory of Archaic and Classical Poleis: An Investigation Conducted by The Copenhagen Polis Centre for the Danish National Research Foundation*, ed. Mogens Herman Hansen and Thomas Heine Nielsen [Oxford: Oxford University Press, 2004], 1145; and Joseph W. Shaw, *Kommos: A Minoan Harbor Town and Greek Sanctuary in Southern Crete* [Princeton: Princeton University Press, 2006], 134–5).

γυνὰ ἀνδρὸς ἄ κα κρίνεται,
ὀ δικαστὰς ὅρκον αἴ κα δικάκ-
σει, ἐν ταῖς ϝίκατι ἀμέραις ἀ-
πομοσάτο παριόντος τō δικα-
50 στᾶ ὅτι κ' ἐπικαλῆι. προϝειπάτ-
ο δὲ ὀ ἄρκον τᾶ<δ> δίκας τᾶι γυνα-
ικὶ καὶ τōῖ δικα<σ>τᾶι καὶ [τ]ōῖ
μνάμονι προτέταρτον ἀντὶ μ-
αίτυρος πεντεκαιδεκαδρόμο⁵⁴
55 ἒ πρείγονος. vac.

If the judge rules that a woman being | divorced from her husband (swear) an | oath, let her swear the oath of denial | regarding what he charged within twenty | days with the judge present. And let the | initiator of the suit declare to the woman | and the judge and the rememberer on | the fourth day before (the oath) in front | of a witness who has been adult for fifteen years or more. vac.

The amendment presupposes the existing legislation (γυνὰ ἀνδρὸς ἄ κα κρίνεται) and specifies that this oath has to be sworn within twenty days. Additionally, the husband has to declare beforehand (προϝειπάτο) what he is accusing her of. This must refer to the property she allegedly took, and it has been suggested that "the declaration here may be a formal act, but its purpose must be to remind everyone of the charge in preparation for the oath swearing."⁵⁵ The official act is further emphasized by the presence of the "rememberer."⁵⁶ As such the oath introduces a sacred dimension that is universally accepted, never questioned, and simply employed as a protective measure for the accused woman.⁵⁷

54. The word is a *hapax legomenon* in Greek (Monique Bile, *Le Dialecte Crétois Ancien: Étude de la langue des inscriptions. Recueil des inscriptions postérieures aux IC*, École Française d'Athènes Études Crétoises 27 [Paris: Geuthner, 1988], 344). In *IC* IV 72 VII.35-41, the term ἀποδρόμος is used to denote a minor and δρόμος to describe an adult (male) person.
55. Gagarin and Perlman, *The Laws of Ancient Crete*, 425.
56. On this office, see Seelentag, *Das archaische Kreta*, 194–203.
57. On the various problems surrounding the process of oath-taking, see Robert Parker, "Law and Religion," in *The Cambridge Companion to Ancient Greek Law*, ed. David Cohen and Michael Gagarin (Cambridge: Cambridge University Press, 2006), 69–74; Gerhard Thür, "Oath and Dispute Settlement in Ancient Greek Law," in *Greek Law in its Political Setting: Justification Not Justice*, ed. L. Foxhall and A. D. E. Lewis (Oxford: Clarendon, 1996), 57–72; and, especially for Gortyn, Alan H. Sommerstein and Andrew J. Bayliss, *Oath and State in Ancient Greece*, Beiträgezur Altertumskunde 306 (Berlin: de Gruyter, 2013), 63–7.

The various differences from, for example, Athenian law have mainly to do with the fact that women at Gortyn "had considerably more freedom than their counterparts in classical Athens."[58] Women at Gortyn were able to own property and could possibly manage it independently from a male *kyrios*.[59] That women's property is treated in the same way as its male equivalent can be seen from the terminology employed. Only in Crete do we find the distinction between ματρōια and πατρōια, i.e., the maternal and paternal estate.[60] The Gortyn Code states clearly that the maternal estate is to be treated in the same way as the paternal one:[61]

δ-
ατε̄θ[θ]αι δὲ καὶ τὰ ματρōια, ε̃
45 κ' ἀποθά[νε]ι, ἄιπερ τὰ [πατρō]ι'
γ[ρατ]ται.[62]

58. Gagarin, "Women and the Law in Gortyn," 57.

59. On the issue of women's property at Gortyn, see Michael Gagarin, "Women and Property at Gortyn," *Dike* 11 (2008): 5–25; Michael Gagarin, "Women and the Law in Gortyn," 57–67; Gagarin, "Women's Property at Gortyn," *Dike* 15 (2012): 73–92; and the contrasting view of Alberto Maffi, "Ancora sulla condizione giuridica della donna nel Codice di Gortina," *Dike* 15 (2012): 93–123. See also Raphael Sealey, *Women and Law in Classical Greece* (Chapel Hill: University of North Carolina Press, 1990), 74–80; Karen Rørby Kristensen, "Inheritance, Property, and Management: Gortynian Family Law Revisited," in *Symposium 2005: Vorträge zur griechischen und hellenistischen Rechtsgeschichte (Salerno, 14.–18. September 2005)*, ed. Eva Cantarella, Akten der Gesellschaft für griechische und hellenistische Rechtsgeschichte 19 (Vienna: Österreichische Akademie der Wissenschaften, 2007), 89–100.

60. ματρōια in *Nomima* II.39 (from Phaistos), *IC* IV 72 IV.44, VI.34, VI.45, XI.44-45, and *IC* IV 20 line 4 (= *Nomima* II.37). πατρōια in *IC* IV 21 line 5 (= *Nomima* II.38) and *IC* IV 72 IV.45, IV.54, XI.43-44.

61. An inscription (διαγράμμα) from Hellenistic Teos, dating to 324/3 BCE (*IPArk* 5 = P. J. Rhodes and Robin Osborne, *Greek Historical Inscriptions, 404–323 BCE* [Oxford: Oxford University Press, 2003], no. 101), regulates the restoration of exiles and mentions τὰ πατρῶια and τὰ ματρῶια together (lines 4-5 and 52-56). It has been suggested that this relates to the Gortynian practice (Alberto Maffi, "Lo statuto dei 'beni materni' nella Grecia classica," *Index 40* [2012]: 91–111). The text, however, defines τὰ ματρῶια in lines 5–6 as ὅσαι ἀ- | νέσδοτοι τὰ πάματα κατῆχον καὶ οὐκ ἐτύνχανον ἀδ- | ελφεὸς πεπαμέναι, "i.e., in cases when women were not married and held their property and did not possess brothers" (Rhodes and Osborne, *Greek Historical Inscriptions*, 527). This would suggest that we have a different concept here (cf. Gagarin, "Women's Property at Gortyn," 87).

62. *IC* IV 72 IV.43-46.

Women could acquire property, including land, by inheritance or gift, but the amount a man was allowed to give a woman was limited by the law. The rules of inheritance clearly favored the male members of a household, since the women only received half the amount of each son's share (*IC* IV 72 IV.31-43).[63] The ability to own property may also be the reason why the laws from Gortyn do not seem to know the concept of a dowry.[64]

                vac. αἰ δέ κα λε̃-
        ι ὀ πατὲρ δοὸς ἰὸν δόμεν τᾶ-
50   ι ὀπυιομέναι, δότο κατὰ τ-
        ὰ ἐγραμμένα, πλίονα δὲ μέ. vac.

vac. If her father while he is alive wishes to | give to (his daughter) who is getting | married, let him give according to what is written, but not more. *vac.*

Though the gift of a father to his daughter who is getting married in *IC* IV 72 IV.48-51 may resemble a dowry "in that it conveys family property to a daughter," there are significant differences.[65] The arrangement is made between the father and his daughter and—in contrast to the dowry—not with the future husband.[66] The stipulation regarding divorce above makes it clear that the gift remains in the sole possession of the woman.[67] As far as the nature of the gift is concerned, it should probably be regarded as an advance on her inheritance.[68]

---

63. The heiress, i.e., a woman who does not have a father or a brother from the same father (see *IC* IV 72 VIII.40-42), presents a special and important matter, which falls beyond the scope of this essay. For further discussion, see Seelentag, *Das archaische Kreta*, 360–8; Gagarin and Perlman, *The Laws of Ancient Crete*, 389–403.

64. Thus already Bücheler and Zitelmann, *Das Recht von Gortyn*, 115–17; followed by Gagarin, "Women and the Law in Gortyn," 58–9.

65. Gagarin and Perlman, *The Laws of Ancient Crete*, 368.

66. *IC* IV 17 mentions bridal gifts, which are also known from Homer (e.g., *Il.* 16.190l; *Od.* 8.38), making it "la première mention en prose—et la seule en Crète" (van Effenterre and Ruzé, *Nomima: Recueil d'inscriptions*, 198); due to the fragmentary state of the inscriptions, it cannot be determined what the function of this gift was.

67. See the recurring phrase τὰ ϝὰ αὐτᾶς in *IC* IV 72 II.46, 49; III.25, 32, 36, 42; IV.26 (cf. the wording in VI.16-18). Athenian rhetoric is different when it speaks of the woman bringing the dowry into her husband's house; cf. Demosthenes 27.4, and the accusation of stinginess despite a dowry in Theophrastus, *Characters* 22.10.

68. Bile, "Prolégomènes aux lois Gortyne I," 16 ("une avance d'héritage"); followed by Gagarin and Perlman, *The Laws of Ancient Crete*, 368.

The law regarding the divorce of a serf couple in *IC* IV 72 III.40-44 reads like an abbreviated version of the preceding one for free persons:[69]

40   *vac.* αἴ κ-
α ϝοικέος ϝοικέα κριθῆι δοō
ἒ ἀποθανόντος, τὰ ϝὰ αὐτᾶ-
ς ἔκεν· ἄλλο δ' αἴ τι πέροι, ἔνδ-
ικον ἔμεν. *vac.*

If a serf woman is separated from her | serf husband either while she is living | or by his death, she is to have her | own things, but if she should carry | away anything else, it is a matter for | trial. *vac.*

The "similarity in language…indicates that the legislator saw both unions as essentially the same."[70] Instead of διακρίνω, which is used in the case of free persons, κρίνω occurs here, but there is no difference in meaning, given that *IC* IV 72 XI.46 can say of a free woman γυνὰ ἀνδρὸς ἄ κα κρίνεται.[71] A serf woman is also able to own property (τὰ ϝὰ αὐτᾶς), though probably not including land.[72] The social status of the serf is not clearly defined in the Gortyn Code, as slave and serf occasionally seem to be assimilated into one and the same group. It seems, however, that the ϝοικεύς was engaged in agricultural work and could reside in houses as well as own livestock.[73] As in the case of free women, it is a matter for trial when she removes more than belongs to her.[74]

69. An earlier inscription from Gortyn (*IC* IV 23 = *Nomima* II.25) may have referred to serf marriages as well (in lines 7–8), but the inscription is too fragmentary to glean any information apart from it being the first attestation of the term ϝοικεύς at Gortyn and the first attestation of the collective term "Gortynians" (τὸν Γ[ο]ρτύνιον in line 8b).
70. Gagarin and Perlman, *The Laws of Ancient Crete*, 356.
71. Bile, *Le Dialecte Crétois Ancien*, 275, remarks in regard to the prefix δια-: "Dans ses occurrences crétoises, le préverbe indique la dissociation."
72. On the status of serf and slave, see Michael Gagarin, "Serf and Slaves at Gortyn," *Zeitschrift der Savigny-Stiftung für Rechtsgeschichte: Romanistische Abteilung* 127 (2010): 14–31. For a different view, see David Lewis, "Slave Marriage in the Laws of Gortyn: A Matter of Rights?" *Historia* 62 (2013): 390–416; and Stephan Link, "Dolos und Woikeus im Recht von Gortyn," *Dike* 4 (2001): 87–112.
73. See *IC* IV 72 III.31–37.
74. How this is done is not stated. Willetts (*The Law Code of Gortyn*, 63) assumes that "[n]o doubt her master would be involved in the legal proceedings," but since the master of the serfs is not mentioned, this seems unlikely. Gagarin and Perlman (*The Laws of Ancient Crete*, 357) are probably right when they claim that "it is more likely that the two serfs would resolve their differences through litigation on their own."

Children and Divorce

The last issue related to the separation of a husband and wife concerns children who are born after the divorce (*IC* IV 72 III.44–IV.23):

```
              vac. αἰ τέκοι γυνὰ κ-
45   ε[ρ]ε[ύο]νσα, ἐπελεῦσαι τõι ἀ-
     νδρὶ ἐπὶ στέγαν ἀντὶ μαιτ-
     ύρον τριõν. αἰ δὲ μὲ δέκσαι-
     το, ἐπὶ τᾶι ματρὶ ἔμεν τὸ τέκ-
     νον ἒ τράπεν ἒ ἀποθέμεν· ὀρκ-
50   ιοτέροδ δ' ἔμεν τὸς καδεστ-
     ὰνς καὶ τὸς μαίτυρανς, αἰ
     ἐπέλευσαν. vac. αἰ δὲ ϝοικέα τέ-
     κοι κερεύονσα, ἐπελεῦσαι
     τõι πάσται τõ ἀνδρός, ὃς ὄ-
55   πυιε, ἀντὶ μαιτύρον δ[υ]õν.
col. IV
     αἰ δέ κα μὲ δέκσεται, ἐπὶ τõι
     πάσται ἔμεν τὸ τέκνον τõι τ-
     ᾶς ϝοικέας. αἰ δὲ τõι αὐτõι αὐ-
     τιν ὀπυίοιτο πρὸ τõ ἐνιαυτ-
 5   õ, τὸ παιδίον ἐπὶ τõι πάσται
     ἔμεν τõι τõ ϝοικέος. κὀρκιό-
     τερον ἔμεν τὸν ἐπελεύσαν-
     τα καὶ τὸς μαίτυρανς. vac. γ-
     υνὰ κερεύονσ' αἰ ἀποβάλοι
10   παιδίον πρὶν ἐπελεῦσαι κατ-
     ὰ τὰ ἐγραμμένα, ἐλευθέρο μ-
     ὲν καταστασεῖ πεντέκοντα
     στατε̃ρανς, δόλο πέντε καὶ ϝ-
     ίκατι, αἴ κα νικαθε̃ι. ο̃ι δέ κα μ-
15   ὲ 'ἴ[ε] τις 'τέγα ὀπυῖ ἐπελευσε
     ῖ, ἒ αὐτὸν μὲ ὀρε̃ι, αἰ {αι} ἀποθ-
     είε τὸ παιδίον, ἄπατον ἔμεν.
     vac. αἰ κύσαιτο καὶ τέκοι ϝοικ-
     έα μὲ ὀπυιομένα, ἐπὶ τõι τõ
20   πατρὸς πάσται ἔμεν τὸ τ-
     έκνον· αἰ δ' ὁ πατὲρ μὲ δόοι, ἐ-
     πὶ τοῖς τõν ἀδελπιõν πάσ-
     ταις ἔμεν. vac.
```

If a divorced woman should bear a | child, (she) is to bring it to her (former) | husband at his house before three wit- | nesses; and if he should not accept it, it | is to be in the hands of the mother | either to rear or to expose the child;

and | the relatives and witnesses are to be the | ones who swear, whether they brought | it. *vac*. If a divorced serf woman should | bear a child, (she) is to bring it to the | master of her husband, who married | (her), in the presence of two witnesses. | (col. IV) And if he does not accept it, | the child is to be in the hands of the | master of the serf woman. And if she | should marry the same man again | within a year, the child is to be in the | hands of the male serf's master. The | person who brought (the child) and the | witnesses are the ones who swear. *vac*. | If a woman separated (by divorce) | should dispose of her child before | bringing it in accordance with what is | written, (she) will pay fifty staters for a | free (child), twenty-five for a slave, if | she is convicted. And if there should not | be a house to which (she) will bring it or | (she) does not see him (there), if (she) | should expose the child, there is to be | immunity. *vac*. If an unmarried serf | woman should be pregnant and give | birth, the child is to be in the hands of | the master of her father; but if the father | is not alive, it is to be in the hands of the masters of her brothers. *vac*.

What the lawgiver envisages here is that the woman was pregnant when she separated from her husband and gave birth to a child after the divorce became final and she had left his house. The stipulations regarding free and unfree persons are closely connected here,[75] adding further weight to the view that unions of unfree persons are considered proper marriages at Gortyn. As long as the (former) husband is alive, this rule applies. But in the case of a deceased husband, the rules of *IC* IV 72 III.17-40 would probably apply.

As in Athens, lineage at Gortyn is thought to be patrilineal, and so children were under the control of the father.[76] This would imply that after a divorce, the children would remain with the father, and that right seems to extend to unborn children as well. Therefore, the woman is to bring the newborn child to her former husband, who has the right to accept the child as his own or to reject it. The wording of the stipulation is interesting. The verb "to bring" (ἐπελεύο) lacks a subject, and this leaves open the possibility that someone else apart from the mother can present the child to the father.[77] Also, that the husband is never called "father" may allude to doubts regarding his paternity; on the other hand, it could simply be due to the fact that the law regulates issues between the husband and his (former) wife. The presentation has to be done in the house (στέγα) of

---

75. Koerner, *Inschriftliche Gesetzestexte*, 490.
76. *IC* IV 72 IV.23-25 states this clearly: τὸν πατέρα τὸν | τέκνον καὶ τὸν κρεμάτον κ- | αρτερὸν ἔμεν τᾶδ δαίσιος.
77. Willetts, *The Law Code of Gortyn*, 63, assumes that the subject is τὸς καδεστὰνς in lines 50-51, but see Gagarin and Perlman, *The Laws of Ancient Crete*, 359.

the husband,⁷⁸ a requirement that stresses the rightful place of residence for a lawful child.⁷⁹ The process is validated by three formal witnesses,⁸⁰ indicating proper legal procedure and allowing for the possibility that the father could have denied the proper presentation. If he does not accept the child into his house (αἰ δὲ μὲ δέκσαιτο), the child is to remain in the hands of the mother, and she can decide whether to rear or expose it (ἐπὶ τᾶι ματρὶ ἔμεν τὸ τέκνον ἒ τράπεν ἒ ἀποθέμεν). The mention of the relatives of the woman (τὸς καδεστὰνς) indicates that she is probably living with them,⁸¹ and this might be why they are part of the process.⁸² Nothing is said about the future status of the child living with his or her mother.⁸³

78. στέγα is the normal term for house in Gortyn; see *IC* IV 72 III.46; IV.15; IV.32-33; IV.47; VIII.1; VIII.2-4. See also *IC* IV 73 (= *Nomima* II.91); *IC* IV 80 (= *Nomima* I.7); *IC* IV 97; *IC* IV 106.

79. The importance of the house is further stressed later in the stipulation (col. IV.14-16), when the law states that the woman is exempt from punishment (ἄπατον ἔμεν) for abandoning the child before presenting it to the father, when the father has no house.

80. Apart from a fragmentary inscription from Lyktos (Gagarin and Perlman, *The Laws of Ancient Crete*, 482–4 = Koerner, *Inschriftliche Gesetzestexte*, no. 98), witnesses in Crete are only known from Gortyn. Here "formal witnesses" have to be distinguished from "accidental witnesses"; see Michael Gagarin, "The Function of Witnesses at Gortyn," in *Symposion 1985: Vorträge zur griechischen und hellenistischen Rechtsgeschichte (Ringberg, 24.–26. Juli 1985)*, ed. Gerhard Thür, Akten der Gesellschaft für griechische und hellenistische Rechtsgeschichte 6 (Cologne: Böhlau, 1990), 24–54.

81. For such an arrangement, see *IC* IV 72 II.16-29, where a woman lives with her relatives.

82. Bile ("Prolégomènes aux lois Gortyne I," 51–2), assumes that the male relatives make the decision for the mother, but this is speculation, since the lawgiver could have said so (see Gagarin and Perlman, *The Laws of Ancient Crete*, 359).

83. Adoption by a male member from the maternal side is certainly a possibility (see *IC* IV 72 X.33-34). An adoption by the mother is excluded since *IC* IV 72 XI.18–19 forbids adoption by women. The reason for such a prohibition seems to be that a woman could not participate in the assembly where adoptions took place (*IC* IV 72 X.34-36). If an adoption did not take place, it has been suggested (Bile, "Prolégomènes aux lois Gortyne I," 52) that the child would become a member of the ἀπέταιροι, i.e., a free person of lower status, only known from Gortyn (cf. Seelentag, *Das archaische Kreta*, 286–9). Nowhere is it said that the child was classified as a "bastard"; the law code may speak of "legitimate children" (τοῖς γνεσίοις [*IC* IV 72 X.44-45]), but the term νόθος is never mentioned. This suggests that the concept is unknown, but see Angelos Chaniotis, "Some Cretan Bastards," *Cretan Studies* 7 (2002): 51–2, who has argued on the basis of τοῖς γνεσίοις that bastardy must have been recognized in Gortyn.

In regard to the divorced serf couple, things are a bit more complicated, because the owner of the serfs is involved. Here, the master of the male serf takes over the position of the husband of a free woman and is granted the power to decide whether the child is accepted or not. If he chooses not to accept the child, it seems likely that the same procedure would be repeated in the presence of the master of the female serf. Again, the master is granted the same rights as a free woman here.[84] The acceptance by the master would imply that the child would join the body of serfs of the household.[85] As in the case of a free couple, the procedure is seen as a proper legal act and witnesses are therefore required. Only the case of the female serf's remarriage with the same man within a year is regulated. As in the previous stipulation, it is envisaged that the serfs had different masters, and thus the ownership of the child becomes an issue. Since the child becomes the property of the master of the male serf in the case of remarriage, it is presupposed that he had previously declined to accept the child; this suggests "that in a significant number of cases the father's master would refuse the baby when the couple was separated."[86] Maybe the stipulation protects against any conflict of ownership between the two masters.[87] Remarriage of free persons is not regulated, and we do not know whether it happened or, if it did occur, how it was conducted.[88]

The Gortyn Code and Deuteronomy 24:1-4

Marriage is seen as a contractual relationship at Gortyn, and its dissolution is thus mainly concerned with the restitution of the goods involved in the contract. Since Gortyn does not seem to know the concept of dowry, the issue of its return is not in need of regulation.[89] The lawgiver's language of

---

84. Koerner, *Inschriftliche Gesetzestexte*, 491.

85. Willetts, *The Law Code of Gortyn*, 63, rightly emphasizes that "the rearing of the child was obviously the mother's responsibility."

86. Gagarin and Perlman, *The Laws of Ancient Crete*, 360.

87. Koerner, *Inschriftliche Gesetzestexte*, 491; and van Effenterre and Ruzé, *Nomima: Recueil d'inscriptions*, 130, who stress that the Gortyn Code "s'intéresse au statut de 'inférieurs.'"

88. IC IV 72 VI.44–46 stipulates that a widower who remarries loses control of the maternal estate of his deceased wife.

89. For such restitutions, see, e.g., LH §§138-140; and Günther Häge, *Ehegüterrechtliche Verhältnisse in den griechischen Papyri Ägyptens bis Diokletian*, Graezistische Abhandlungen 3 (Cologne: Böhlau, 1968), 238–44 (for Hellenistic and Roman Egypt). On the issue of divorce in the ancient Near East, see Marten Stol, *Women in the Ancient Near East* (Berlin: de Gruyter, 2016), 209–33; see also

divorce is quite simple (διακρίνονται / κρίνεται) and does not reflect any of the emotions behind it as, for example, the papyri from Elephantine tend to do.[90] At Gortyn both partners could initiate a divorce—something that the biblical law of divorce in Deut. 24:1-4 does not envisage.[91]

In contrast to the stipulations regarding divorce at Gortyn, the Torah does not offer a detailed treatment of the issue.[92] This ties in with the observation that there "are no formal laws in the Bible that deal with the customary solemnities involved on the formation of marriage."[93] Only

---

Betina Faist, "Der abgewiesene Bewerber: Zur Eheschließung in der altbabylonischen Zeit," in *Grenzüberschreitungen: Studien zur Kulturgeschichte des Alten Orients— Festschrift für Hans Neumann zum 65. Geburtstag am 9. Mai 2018*, ed. Kristin Kleber, Georg Neumann, and Susanne Paulus, Dubsar 5 (Münster: Zaphon, 2018), 187–93, on the use of the dowry as part of slander.

90. On the use of שנא at Elephantine, see Alejandro F. Botta, "Hated by the Gods and Your Spouse: The Legal Use of שנא in Elephantine and its Ancient Near Eastern Context," in *Law and Religion in the Eastern Mediterranean: From Antiquity to Early Islam*, ed. Anselm C. Hagedorn and Reinhard G. Kratz (Oxford: Oxford University Press, 2013), 105–28; and, in general, Annalisa Azzoni, *The Private Lives of Women in Persian Egypt* (Winona Lake: Eisenbrauns, 2013), 64–80. For the biblical context, see Bruce Wells, "First Wives Club: Divorce, Demotion, and the Fate of Leah in Genesis 29," *Maarav* 18 (2013): 101–29.

91. However, this does not necessarily warrant the conclusion that women in ancient Israel could not initiate divorce. See the discussion in Pamela Barmash, "The Daughter Sold into Slavery and Marriage," Chapter 2 in this volume, 59–62. While the complex issues surrounding the biblical law of divorce and its Rabbinic transformation will not be addressed in detail here, see the extensive discussions in Samuel Greengus, *Laws in the Bible and in Early Rabbinic Collections* (Eugene: Cascade, 2011), 35–40; Shalom E. Holtz, "'To go and marry any man that you please': A Study of the Formulaic Antecedents of the Rabbinic Writ of Divorce," *JNES* 60 (2001): 241–58; Étan Levine, *Marital Relations in Ancient Judaism*, BZABR 10 (Wiesbaden: Harrassowitz, 2009), 126–36; Eckart Otto, *Gottes Recht als Menschenrecht: Rechts- und literaturhistorische Studien zum Deuteronomium*, BZABR 2 (Wiesbaden: Harrassowitz, 2002), 253–68; Otto, *Deuteronomium 12–34, Zweiter Teilband: 23,16–43,12*, HThKAT (Freiburg: Herder, 2017), 1801–6; and Moshe A. Zipor, "Divorce and Restoration of Marriage (Deut 24:1-4)," *ZABR* 20 (2014): 127–40.

92. Zipor, "Divorce and Restoration of Marriage," 127.

93. Greengus, *Laws in the Bible*, 35. While this is the case, there is the possibility that some of the narrative texts might be able to shed light on what was customary for betrothal and marriage procedure. See, for example, the analysis of Gen. 29:14-30 in F. Rachel Magdalene, "Rachel's Betrothal Contract and the Origins of Contract Law," Chapter 3 in this volume. Magdalene contends that this narrative is an account of the

Deut. 24:1-4 addresses the issue, and the passing note in Deut. 22:19 (לא־יוכל לשלחה כל־ימיו) seems to suggest that the concept is known but probably belonged to the realm of (family) custom.

1) כי־יקח איש אשה ובעלה והיה אם־לא תמצא־חן בעיניו כי־מצא בה ערות דבר וכתב לה ספר כריתת ונתן בידה ושלחה מביתו:
2) ויצאה מביתו והלכה והיתה לאיש־אחר:
3) ושנאה האיש האחרון וכתב לה ספר כריתת ונתן בידה ושלחה מביתו או כי ימות האיש האחרון אשר־לקחה לו לאשה:
4) לא־יוכל בעלה הראשון אשר־שלחה לשוב לקחתה להיות לו לאשה אחרי אשר הטמאה כי־תועבה הוא לפני יהוה ולא תחטיא את־הארץ אשר יהוה אלהיך נתן לך נחלה:

> If a man takes a woman and possesses her and she fails to please him because he finds something objectionable about her and he writes her a bill of divorce, hands it to her, and sends her away from his house, (2) and she leaves his household and becomes the wife of another man (3) and then this later man hates [i.e., rejects] her, writes her a bill of divorce, hands it to her, and sends her away from his house, or the man who married her last dies, (4) then the first husband who divorced her shall not take her as wife again, since she has been defiled—for that would be an abhorrence to YHWH. You must not bring sin upon the land that YHWH your God is giving you as an inheritance.

The Deuteronomic law of divorce is part of an early collection of family laws that has been integrated into the book of Deuteronomy.[94] Deuteronomy 24:1-4 and Deut. 24:5 are connected to 22:13-21 via the identical introduction כי יקח איש אשה. A later postexilic redaction in 24:4b introduces the themes of the purity and giving of the land, thus joining the law to similar stipulations in 22:22-24 and 23:18-19.[95] The law of divorce, together with 25:5-10, concludes the various laws addressing the issue of marriage. While the text of Deut. 22:13-19 addresses a case

---

creation of a legally enforceable oral contract for services in exchange for a bride, its breach by one of the parties (Laban), a renegotiation leading to a settlement, and the ultimate fulfillment of the contract.

94. See Alexander Rofé, "Family and Sex Laws in Deuteronomy and the Book of the Covenant," in *Deuteronomy: Issues and Interpretation*, OTS (London: T&T Clark, 2002), 169–92; Anselm C. Hagedorn, *Between Moses and Plato: Individual and Society in Deuteronomy and Ancient Greek Law*, FRLANT 204 (Göttingen: Vandenhoeck & Ruprecht, 2004), 200–201; and Eckart Otto, *Deuteronomium 12–34, Erster Teilband: 12,1–23,15*, HThKAT (Freiburg: Herder, 2016), 1689–92.

95. Otto, *Deuteronomium 12–34, Zweiter Teilband*, 1786.

where a husband tries to rid himself of his newly wedded wife without any financial loss, the law in 24:1-4 regulates divorce proceedings that ensue after a marriage has been well established. Although the Covenant Code knows of the marriage of (Hebrew) slaves in Exod. 21:1-11,[96] the law in Deuteronomy probably only applied to free persons. In contrast to the laws from the Gortyn Code, Deut. 24:1-4 provides a reason for the divorce (ערות דבר).[97] The interpretation of the term is difficult, and "the phrase seems to be intended to cover the whole range of customary reasons for divorce."[98] This range also included adultery, as the reference to defilement seems to indicate,[99] since it prevents the husband from circumventing the divorce by remarriage.[100] In contrast to the Gortynian Laws,[101] Deut. 24:1-4 displays a certain gender asymmetry—or in the

96. For a detailed discussion of the Covenant Collection's treatment of the marriage of slaves, especially with respect to daughters sold into slavery for the purpose of marriage and the provisions for the dissolution of such arrangements, see Barmash, "The Daughter Sold into Slavery and Marriage."

97. On the different terminology used for the first and second divorce, see Raymond Westbrook, "The Prohibition on Restoration of Marriage in Deuteronomy 24:1-4," in *Law from the Tigris to the Tiber: The Writings of Raymond Westbrook, vol. 2: Cuneiform and Biblical Sources*, ed. Bruce Wells and F. Rachel Magdalene (Winona Lake: Eisenbrauns, 2009), 387–404.

98. Richard D. Nelson, *Deuteronomy: A Commentary*, OTL (Louisville: Westminster John Knox, 2002), 287.

99. For an alternative explanation of the cause and nature of the woman's defilement, see the discussion at n. 8 and nn. 17–18 in Kenneth Bergland, "Divorce Instruction and Covenantal Unfaithfulness: A New Examination of the Reuse of Deuteronomy 24:1-4 as Metaphor in Jeremiah 3:1-10," Chapter 11 in this volume. Bergland suggests that in this passage the woman is defiled by her second marriage and only in relation to her first husband. If he were to remarry her, that would be an abomination that brings sin upon the land. Bergland also notes that the range of מצא בה ערות דבר in this context may include the possibility that the wife did nothing wrong and is blameless and that the husband wants a divorce simply because he found something about her that he disliked. See also Sarah Shectman, "Priestly Marriage Restrictions," Chapter 7 in this volume, who argues, contrary to this essay's position, that the notion of ערות דבר cannot include adultery.

100. See Otto, *Gottes Recht als Menschenrecht*, 261–2; and Otto, *Deuteronomium 12–34, Zweiter Teilband*, 1803–6. Since Deut. 22:22a only regulates adultery *in flagrante delicto*, it seems difficult to conclude that the "indecency could be something sexual, although not adultery" (Jack R. Lundbom, *Deuteronomy: A Commentary* [Grand Rapids: Eerdmans, 2013], 671).

101. For comparable evidence from Elephantine, where women were able to initiate divorce proceedings without cause, see Azzoni, *The Private Lives of Women in Persian Egypt*, 64–80.

words of the Mishnah: "The man who divorces is not like the woman who is divorced, for the woman is divorced with her consent or without her consent whereas the man divorces only with his consent."[102] Legal security for the divorced woman is ensured by the issuing of a bill of divorce (ספר כריתת). In light of Jer. 3:8 and Isa. 50:1, the "writing of a formal record of divorce may thus have been a means of creating a clear and public break in a marital relationship."[103] At the same time, such written documents may have also recorded any financial issues related to the divorce proceedings.[104]

Returning to the Gortyn Code, we have observed that it distinguishes between marriages of free and serf couples, but leaves no doubt that serf unions are considered as valid marriages. Only when children were involved is the status of the marriage partners of concern, because the owner of the serf woman is granted the rights normally reserved for the free person. Remarriage of the same wife, so important to the biblical authors,[105] is only regulated when property and ownership are involved, i.e., when serf couples (with children) divorce and remarry. The laws of Gortyn do not mention the remarriage of the same partner for free persons (all stipulations regarding remarriage concern widowers); perhaps it was not practiced or simply regarded as a regular—i.e., new—marriage. Though the law code extensively regulates sexual offenses (*IC* IV 72 II.2-45), sexuality is absent from the stipulations regarding the separation of spouses. We may be able to see some allusions to possible (sexual) neglect in the formulation ἀνὴρ αἴτιος, but this is never recounted in detail. Rather, the laws of Gortyn focus on the maintenance of the status of the person and the correct allocation or division of property. Even though the social position of the free woman is significantly better than, for example, in Athens,[106] in divorce proceedings the husband (guilty or not) profits from his wife's estate, and he keeps the children born in wedlock.

---

102. *m. Yebam.* 14:1, quoted in Levine, *Marital Relations in Ancient Judaism*, 134.

103. Greengus, *Laws in the Bible and in Early Rabbinic Collections*, 37.

104. This can be gleaned from *m. Ketub.* 4:7, quoted in Levine, *Marital Relations in Ancient Judaism*, 132: "Even if one didn't write out a document for her, or did not write, 'All the goods that I possess are surety for your marriage settlement,' he is still liable, for that is a condition established by the Court."

105. Reuven Yaron, "The Restoration of Marriage," *JJS* 17 (1966): 1–13.

106. Wolff, "Die Grundlagen des griechischen Eherechts," 160–1.

Bibliography

Azzoni, Annalisa. *The Private Lives of Women in Persian Egypt*. Winona Lake: Eisenbrauns, 2013.
Bile, Monique. *Le Dialecte Crétois Ancien: Étude de la langue des inscriptions. Recueil des inscriptions postérieures aux IC*. École Française d'Athènes Études Crétoises 27. Paris: Geuthner, 1988.
Bile, Monique. "Prolégomènes aux lois Gortyne I: Statut de la femme et ordre social." In *Folia Graeca in honorem Edouard Will: Linguistica*, edited by Claude Brixhe and Guy Vottéro, 7–63. Études anciennes 50. Nancy: de Boccard, 2012.
Botta, Alejandro F. "Hated by the Gods and Your Spouse: The Legal Use of שנא in Elephantine and its Ancient Near Eastern Context." In *Law and Religion in the Eastern Mediterranean: From Antiquity to Early Islam*, edited by Anselm C. Hagedorn and Reinhard G. Kratz, 105–28. Oxford: Oxford University Press, 2013.
Brause, Johannes. "ΓΟΡΤΥΝΙΩΝ ΟΡΚΟΣ ΝΟΜΙΜΟΣ." *Hermes* 49 (1914): 102–9.
Brixhe, Claude, and Monique Bile. "La circulation des biens dans les Lois de Gortyne." In *Des dialectes grecs aux Lois de Gortyne*, edited by Catherine Dobias-Lalou, 75–116. Études Anciennes 21. Nancy: de Boccard, 1999.
Bücheler, Franz, and Ernst Zitelmann. *Das Recht von Gortyn*. RhM 40. Frankfurt: Sauerländer, 1885.
Budin, Stephanie Lynn. *Artemis*. Gods and Heroes of the Ancient World. London: Routledge, 2016.
Burkert, Walter. *Griechische Religion der archaischen und klassischen Epoche*. 2nd ed. Die Religionen der Menschheit 15. Stuttgart: Kohlhammer, 2011.
Canevaro, Mirko. *The Documents in the Attic Orators: Laws and Decrees in the Public Speeches of the Demosthenic Corpus*. Oxford: Oxford University Press, 2013.
Cantarella, Eva. "Greek Law and the Family." In *A Companion to Families in the Greek and Roman Worlds*, edited by Beryl Rawson, 333–45. Blackwell Companions to the Ancient World. Malden: Wiley-Blackwell, 2011.
Chaniotis, Angelos. "Some Cretan Bastards." *Cretan Studies* 7 (2002): 51–7.
Cohen, David. *Law, Sexuality, and Society: The Enforcement of Morals in Classical Athens*. Cambridge: Cambridge University Press, 1991.
Cohn-Haft, Louis. "Divorce in Classical Athens." *Journal of Hellenic Studies* 65 (1995): 1–14.
Davies, John K. "Deconstructing Gortyn: When Is a Code a Code?" In *Greek Law in its Political Setting: Justification Not Justice*, edited by L. Foxhall and A. D. E. Lewis, 33–56. Oxford: Clarendon, 1996.
Edwards, Michael. *Isaeus*. The Oratory of Classical Greece 11. Austin: University of Texas Press, 2007.
Effenterre, Henri van, and Françoise Ruzé, eds. *Nomima: Recueil d'inscriptions politiques et juridiques de l'archaïsme grec I–II*. Collection de l'École Française de Rome 188. Paris: de Boccard, 1995.
Erdmann, Walter. *Die Ehe im alten Griechenland*. MBPF 20. Munich: C. H. Beck, 1934.
Faist, Betina. "Der abgewiesene Bewerber: Zur Eheschließung in der altbabylonischen Zeit." In *Grenzüberschreitungen: Studien zur Kulturgeschichte des Alten Orients—Festschrift für Hans Neumann zum 65. Geburtstag am 9. Mai 2018*, edited by Kristin Kleber, Georg Neumann, and Susanne Paulus, 187–93. Dubsar 5. Münster: Zaphon, 2018.

Gagarin, Michael. "The Function of Witnesses at Gortyn." In *Symposion 1985: Vorträge zur griechischen und hellenistischen Rechtsgeschichte (Ringberg, 24.–26. Juli 1985)*, edited by Gerhard Thür, 29–54. Akten der Gesellschaft für griechische und hellenistische Rechtsgeschichte 6. Cologne: Böhlau, 1990.

Gagarin, Michael. "Inscribing Laws in Greece and the Near East." In *Symposion 2003: Vorträge zur griechischen und hellenistischen Rechtsgeschichte*, edited by H. A. Rupprecht, 9–20. Akten der Gesellschaft für griechische und hellenistische Rechtsgeschichte 17. Vienna: Österreichische Akademie der Wissenschaften, 2003.

Gagarin, Michael. "Serf and Slaves at Gortyn." *Zeitschrift der Savigny-Stiftung für Rechtsgeschichte: Romanistische Abteilung* 127 (2010): 14–31.

Gagarin, Michael. "Women and Property at Gortyn." *Dike* 11 (2008): 5–25.

Gagarin, Michael. "Women and the Law in Gortyn." *Index* 40 (2012): 57–67.

Gagarin, Michael. "Women's Property at Gortyn." *Dike* 15 (2012): 73–92.

Gagarin, Michael. *Writing Greek Law*. Cambridge: Cambridge University Press, 2008.

Gagarin, Michael, and Paula Perlman. *The Laws of Ancient Crete, c. 650–400 BCE*. Oxford: Oxford University Press, 2016.

Gilhuly, Kate. *Erotic Geographies in Ancient Greek Literature and Culture*. New York: Routledge, 2018.

Greengus, Samuel. *Laws in the Bible and in Early Rabbinic Collections*. Eugene: Cascade, 2011.

Guarducci, Margherita, ed. *Inscriptiones Creticae*. 4 vols. Rome: La Libreria dello stato, 1935–50.

Häge, Günther. *Ehegüterrechtliche Verhältnisse in den griechischen Papyri Ägyptens bis Diokletian*. Graezistische Abhandlungen 3. Cologne: Böhlau, 1968.

Hagedorn, Anselm C. *Between Moses and Plato: Individual and Society in Deuteronomy and Ancient Greek Law*. FRLANT 204. Göttingen: Vandenhoeck & Ruprecht, 2004.

Hall, Edith. *Greek Tragedy: Suffering under the Sun*. Oxford: Oxford University Press, 2010.

Harrison, A. R. W. *The Law of Athens, Volume 1, The Family and Property*. Oxford: Oxford University Press, 1968.

Holtz, Shalom E. "'To go and marry any man that you please': A Study of the Formulaic Antecedents of the Rabbinic Writ of Divorce." *JNES* 60 (2001): 241–58.

Koerner, Reinhard. *Inschriftliche Gesetzestexte der frühen griechischen Polis*. Akten der Gesellschaft für griechische und hellenistische Rechtsgeschichte 9. Cologne: Böhlau, 1993.

Kohler, Josef, and Erich Ziebarth. *Das Stadtrecht von Gortyn und seine Beziehungen zum gemeingriechischen Rechte*. Göttingen: Vandenhoeck & Ruprecht, 1912.

Kovacs, David. *Euripides I: Cyclops—Alcestis—Medea*. LCL 12. Cambridge: Harvard University Press, 2001.

Kristensen, Karen Rørby. "Archaic Laws and the Development of Civic Identity in Crete, ca. 650–450 BCE." In *Cultural Practices and Material Culture in Archaic and Classical Crete: Proceedings of the International Conference, Mainz 20–21, 2011*, edited by Oliver Pilz and Gunnar Seelentag, 141–58. Berlin: de Gruyter, 2014.

Kristensen, Karen Rørby. "Inheritance, Property, and Management: Gortynian Family Law Revisited." In *Symposium 2005: Vorträge zur griechischen und hellenistischen Rechtsgeschichte (Salerno, 14.–18. September 2005)*, edited by Eva Cantarella, 89–100. Akten der Gesellschaft für griechische und hellenistische Rechtsgeschichte 19. Vienna: Österreichische Akademie der Wissenschaften, 2007.

Lamb, W. R. M. *Lysias*. LCL 244. Cambridge: Harvard University Press, 1988.

Leão, Delfim F., and P. J. Rhodes. *The Laws of Solon: A New Edition with Introduction, Translation and Commentary*. Library of Classical Studies 7. London: I. B. Tauris, 2015.
Levine, Étan. *Marital Relations in Ancient Judaism*. BZABR 10. Wiesbaden: Harrassowitz, 2009.
Lewis, David. "Slave Marriage in the Laws of Gortyn: A Matter of Rights?" *Historia* 62 (2013): 390–416.
Link, Stefan. *Das griechische Kreta: Untersuchungen zu seiner staatlichen und gesellschaftlichen Entwicklung vom 6. bis zum 4. Jahrhundert v. Chr.* Stuttgart: Steiner, 1994.
Link, Stefan. "Dolos und Woikeus im Recht von Gortyn." *Dike* 4 (2001): 87–112.
Lundbom, Jack R. *Deuteronomy: A Commentary*. Grand Rapids: Eerdmans, 2013.
Maffi, Alberto. "Ancora sulla condizione giuridica della donna nel Codice di Gortina." *Dike* 15 (2012): 93–123.
Maffi, Alberto. "Le mariage de la patrôoque 'donnée' dans le Code de Gortyne (col. VIII, 20–30)." *Revue historique de droit français et étranger* 65 (1987): 507–25.
Maffi, Alberto. "Lo statuto dei 'beni materni' nella Grecia classica." *Index* 40 (2012): 91–111.
Maffi, Alberto. "Studi Recenti sul Codice di Gortina." *Dike* 6 (2003): 161–226.
Mastronarde, Donald J., ed. *Euripides: Medea*. Cambridge Greek and Latin Classics. Cambridge: Cambridge University Press, 2002.
Nelson, Richard D. *Deuteronomy: A Commentary*. OTL. Louisville: Westminster John Knox, 2002.
Omitowoju, Rosanna. *Rape and the Politics of Consent in Classical Athens*. Cambridge Classical Studies. Cambridge: Cambridge University Press, 2002.
Otto, Eckart. *Deuteronomium 12–34. Erster Teilband: 12,1–23,15*. HThKAT. Freiburg: Herder, 2016.
Otto, Eckart. *Deuteronomium 12–34. Zweiter Teilband: 23,16–43,12*. HThKAT. Freiburg: Herder, 2017.
Otto, Eckart. *Gottes Recht als Menschenrecht: Rechts- und literaturhistorische Studien zum Deuteronomium*. BZABR 2. Wiesbaden: Harrassowitz, 2002.
Parker, Robert. "Law and Religion." In *The Cambridge Companion to Ancient Greek Law*, edited by David Cohen and Michael Gagarin, 61–82. Cambridge: Cambridge University Press, 2006.
Perlman, Paula J. "Crete." In *An Inventory of Archaic and Classical Poleis: An Investigation Conducted by The Copenhagen Polis Centre for the Danish National Research Foundation*, edited by Mogens Herman Hansen and Thomas Heine Nielsen, 1143–95. Oxford: Oxford University Press, 2004.
Perlman, Paula J. "Gortyn: The First Seven Hundred Years (Part I)." In *Polis and Politics: Studies in Ancient Greek History Presented to Mogens Hansen on His Sixtieth Birthday*, edited by Pernille Flensted-Jensen, Thomas Heine Nielsen, and Lene Rubinstein, 59–89. Copenhagen: Museum Tusculanum, 2000.
Perlman, Paula J. "Reading and Writing Archaic Cretan Society." In *Cultural Practices and Material Culture in Archaic and Classical Crete: Proceedings of the International Conference, Mainz 20–21, 2011*, edited by Oliver Pilz and Gunnar Seelentag, 177–206. Berlin: de Gruyter, 2014.
Perlman, Paula J. "Writing on the Walls: The Architectural Context of Archaic Cretan Laws." In *Crete Beyond the Palaces: Proceedings of the Crete 2000 Conference*, edited by Leslie P. Day, Margaret S. Mook, and James D. Muhly, 181–91. Prehistory Monographs 10. Philadelphia: INSTAP Academic, 2004.

Phillips, David D. *The Law of Ancient Athens*. Law and Society in the Ancient World. Ann Arbor: University of Michigan Press, 2013.

Rhodes, P. J., and Robin Osborne. *Greek Historical Inscriptions, 404–323 BCE*. Oxford: Oxford University Press. 2003.

Rofé, Alexander. "Family and Sex Laws in Deuteronomy and the Book of the Covenant." In *Deuteronomy: Issues and Interpretation*, 169–92. OTS. London: T&T Clark, 2002.

Roth, Martha T. *Law Collections from Mesopotamia and Asia Minor*. Edited by Piotr Michalowski. SBLWAW 6. Atlanta: Scholars Press, 1997.

Ruschenbusch, Eberhard. *Solon: Das Gesetzeswerk—Fragmente*. Übersetzung *und Kommentar*. Historia Einzelschriften 215. Stuttgart: Steiner, 2010.

Sanders, Ed. "Sexual Jealousy and *Erôs* in Euripides' *Medea*." In *Erôs in Ancient Greece*. Edited by Ed Sanders, Chiara Thumiger, Chris Carey, and Nick J. Lowe, 41–57. Oxford: Oxford University Press, 2013.

Schmitz, Winfried. "Der nomos moicheias: Das athenische Gesetz über den Ehebruch." *Zeitschrift der Savigny-Stiftung für Rechtsgeschichte: Romanistische Abteilung* 114 (1997): 45–110.

Sealey, Raphael. *Women and Law in Classical Greece*. Chapel Hill: University of North Carolina Press, 1990.

Seelentag, Gunnar. *Das archaische Kreta: Institutionalisierung im frühen Griechenland*. Klio Beihefte 24. Berlin: de Gruyter, 2015.

Shaw, Joseph W. *Kommos: A Minoan Harbor Town and Greek Sanctuary in Southern Crete*. Princeton: Princeton University Press, 2006.

Sokolowski, Franciszek. *Lois sacrées des cités greques*. 2nd ed. Paris: de Boccard, 1969.

Sommerstein, Alan H., and Andrew J. Bayliss. *Oath and State in Ancient Greece*. Beiträge zur Altertumskunde 306. Berlin: de Gruyter, 2013.

Stol, Marten. *Women in the Ancient Near East*. Berlin: de Gruyter, 2016.

Thomas, Rosalind. "Writing, Law, and Written Law." In *The Cambridge Companion to Ancient Greek Law*. Edited by Michael Gagarin and David Cohen, 41–60. Cambridge: Cambridge University Press, 2005.

Thür, Gerhard. "Oath and Dispute Settlement in Ancient Greek Law." In *Greek Law in its Political Setting: Justification Not Justice*, edited by L. Foxhall and A. D. E. Lewis, 57–71. Oxford: Clarendon, 1996.

Wallace, Saro. *Ancient Crete: From Successful Collapse to Democracy's Alternatives, Twelfth to Fifth Centuries BC*. Cambridge: Cambridge University Press, 2010.

Wells, Bruce. "First Wives Club: Divorce, Demotion, and the Fate of Leah in Genesis 29." *Maarav* 18 (2013): 101–29.

Westbrook, Raymond. "The Prohibition on Restoration of Marriage in Deuteronomy 24:1-4." In *Law from the Tigris to the Tiber: The Writings of Raymond Westbrook, Volume 2: Cuneiform and Biblical Sources*, edited by Bruce Wells and F. Rachel Magdalene, 387–404. Winona Lake: Eisenbrauns, 2009.

Willetts, Ronald F. *The Law Code of Gortyn*. Kadmos Supplement 1. Berlin: de Gruyter, 1967.

Wolff, Hans Julius. "Die Grundlagen des griechischen Eherechts." *The Legal History Review* 20 (1952): 1–29, 157–81.

Yaron, Reuven. "The Restoration of Marriage." *JJS* 17 (1966): 1–11.

Zipor, Moshe A. "Divorce and Restoration of Marriage (Deut 24:1-4)." *ZABR* 20 (2014): 127–40.

11

Divorce Instruction and Covenantal Unfaithfulness: A New Examination of the Reuse of Deuteronomy 24:1-4 as Metaphor in Jeremiah 3:1-10*

Kenneth Bergland

Introduction

The purpose of this study is to evaluate the textual basis for claiming that Jer. 3:1-10 reuses and depends upon the prohibition against a husband remarrying his formerly divorced wife in Deut. 24:1-4 and to demonstrate how the latter is incorporated into the line of thought of the former. Since Winfried Thiel's two-volume work, *Die deuteronomistische Redaktion von Jeremia*, the majority of scholars see Jer. 3:1-10 as dependent upon Deut. 24:1-4. Yet, the textual support provided for this claim is often weak.[1] First,

---

* This essay is an abbreviated version of the chapter, "Instructions on Divorce and Remarriage," in Kenneth Bergland, *Reading as a Disclosure of the Thoughts of the Heart: Proto-Halakhic Reuse and Appropriation between Torah and the Prophets*, BZAR 23 (Wiesbaden: Harrassowitz, 2019), 109–28.

1. Winfried Thiel, *Die deuteronomistische Redaktion von Jeremia 1–25*, WMANT 41 (Neukirchen-Vluyn: Neukirchener Verlag, 1973), especially 280–2; Thiel, *Die deuteronomistische Redaktion von Jeremia 26–45: Mit einer Gesamtbeurteilung der deuteronomistischen Redaktion des Buches Jeremia*, WMANT 52 (Neukirchen-Vluyn: Neukirchener Verlag, 1981). See also Georg Fischer, *Jeremia: Der Stand der theologischen Diskussion* (Darmstadt: Wissenschaftliche Buchgesellschaft, 2007), 134–6; Jack R. Lundbom, *Jeremiah 1–20: A New Translation with Introduction and Commentary*, AB 21A (New Haven: Yale University Press, 2008), 300–301, 303, 307; Michael Fishbane, *Biblical Interpretation in Ancient Israel* (Oxford: Clarendon, 1985), 307–12; William L. Holladay, *Jeremiah 1: A Commentary on the Book of the Prophet Jeremiah, Chapters 1–25*, Hermeneia (Philadelphia: Fortress, 1986), 112–16; and

I want to argue that a case for reuse between Jer. 3:1-10 and Deut. 24:1-4 can be made. Second, I will point out textual indicators for why Jer. 3:1-10 seems to be dependent upon Deut. 24:1-4, and not vice versa.² Third, I will explore the role that Deut. 24:1-4 appears to play in Jer. 3:1-10.

A Case for Reuse

Deut. 24:1-4	Jer. 3:1-10
¹ כי־יקח איש אשה ובעלה והיה אם־לא תמצא־חן בעיניו כי־מצא בה ערות דבר וכתב לה ספר כריתת ונתן בידה ושלחה מביתו: ² ויצאה מביתו והלכה והיתה לאיש־אחר: ³ ושנאה האיש האחרון וכתב לה ספר כריתת ונתן בידה ושלחה מביתו או כי ימות האיש האחרון אשר־לקחה לו לאשה: ⁴ לא־יוכל בעלה הראשון אשר־שלחה לשוב לקחתה להיות לו לאשה אחרי אשר הטמאה כי־תועבה הוא לפני יהוה ולא תחטיא את־הארץ אשר יהוה אלהיך נתן לך נחלה: ס	¹ לאמר הן ישלח איש את־אשתו והלכה מאתו והיתה לאיש־אחר הישוב אליה עוד הלוא חנוף תחנף הארץ ההיא ואת זנית רעים רבים ושוב אלי נאם־יהוה: ² שאי־עיניך על־שפים וראי איפה לא שגלת על־דרכים ישבת להם כערבי במדבר ותחניפי ארץ בזנותיך וברעתך: ³ וימנעו רבבים ומלקוש לוא היה ומצח אשה זונה היה לך מאנת הכלם: ⁴ הלוא מעתה קראתי לי אבי אלוף נערי אתה: ⁵ הינטר לעולם אם־ישמר לנצח הנה דברתי ותעשי הרעות ותוכל: פ ⁶ ויאמר יהוה אלי בימי יאשיהו המלך הראית אשר עשתה משבה ישראל הלכה היא על־כל־הר גבה ואל־תחת כל־עץ רענן ותזני־שם: ⁷ ואמר אחרי עשותה את־כל־אלה אלי תשוב ולא־שבה ותראה בגודה אחותה יהודה: ⁸ וארא כי על־כל־אדות אשר נאפה משבה ישראל שלחתיה ואתן את־ספר כריתתיה אליה ולא יראה בגדה יהודה אחותה ותלך ותזן גם־היא: ⁹ והיה מקל זנותה ותחנף את־הארץ ותנאף את־האבן ואת־העץ: ¹⁰ וגם־בכל־זאת לא־שבה אלי בגודה אחותה יהודה בכל־לבה כי אם־בשקר נאם־יהוה: פ

Nathan Mastnjak, *Deuteronomy and the Emergence of Textual Authority in Jeremiah* (Tübingen: Mohr Siebeck, 2016), 165–72. For representatives of those who do not see reuse and dependence between Jer. 3:1-5 and Deut. 24:1-4, but rather a common legal inheritance, see T. R. Hobbs, "Jeremiah 3:1-6 and Deuteronomy 24:1-4," *ZAW* 86 (1974): 23–9; James D. Martin, "The Forensic Background to Jeremiah 3:1," *VT* 19 (1969): 82–92.

2. In my approach to the discussion of reuse and direction of dependence, I have found the lists of what I prefer to call indicators of reuse and direction of dependence proposed by Michael A. Lyons and William A. Tooman helpful (Michael A. Lyons, *From Law to Prophecy: Ezekiel's Use of the Holiness Code*, LHBOTS 507 [London: T&T Clark, 2009], 59–75; William A. Tooman, *Gog of Magog: Reuse of Scripture and Compositional Technique in Ezekiel 38–39*, FAT 2/52 [Tübingen: Mohr Siebeck, 2011], 26–34).

¹ When a man takes a wife and marries her, but it happens that she does not find favor in his eyes because he found *something unseemly* with her, and he writes a letter of divorce to her and gives [it] in her hand, and he sends her from his house, ² and she leaves his house and she goes and becomes [the wife] of another man, ³ then this latter man hates her and writes her a letter of divorce and gives [it] in her hand, and he sends her from his house, or if the latter man who took her as wife dies, ⁴ the first husband, who sent her away, cannot return to take her to be his wife, after she *was defiled*. For this is an abomination to YHWH, and you must not *bring sin upon the land* which YHWH your God gives you as an inheritance.	¹ …saying: "If a man divorces his wife, and she leaves him and becomes [wife] to another man, can he return to her again? *Would this not certainly pollute the land?* But you have whored with many lovers. So [can you] return to me?" says YHWH. ² "Lift your eyes to the bare heights and see: where have you not been ravished? You were sitting along roads [waiting] for them, as *an Arab in the desert*. And *you polluted the land* with your whoring and your wickedness. ³ When showers were withheld and there was no late rain, you had the forehead of a whore. You refused to be ashamed. ⁴ Have you not now called to me 'My father, you are the companion of my youth! ⁵ Does one hate forever? Does one guard forever?' That is what you said. But you did evils, and you still can." ⁶ Now YHWH said to me during the days of King Josiah, "Have you seen what *faithless* Israel has done, going to every high mountain and under every green tree and whored there? ⁷ And I said, 'After she has done all this, she will return to me.' But she did not return. Rather, her treacherous sister, Judah, saw [her/it]. ⁸ And I viewed [it such] that because of all by which *faithless* Israel had committed adultery, I sent her away, and I gave her her letter of divorce. But treacherous Judah did not fear and went away and she whored also. ⁹ And from all her whorings *she defiled the land*, and she committed adultery with the stone and with the tree. ¹⁰ And even in all this her treacherous sister, Judah, did not return unto me with all her heart, except with a lie," says YHWH.

Distinctiveness

First, the phrase ספר כריתת ("bill of divorce") is only found in Deut. 24:1, 3; Isa. 50:1; and Jer. 3:8.[3] In the same contexts (Deut. 24:1, 3-4; Isa. 50:1; Jer. 3:1, 8), we also find the *piel* of שלח used in a technical sense to refer to the dismissal of a wife.[4] Although Isa. 50:1 is similar to Deuteronomy 24 and Jeremiah 3 in that it uses ספר כריתת + the *piel* of שלח, the closer similarity between the clauses והלכה מאתו והיתה לאיש־אחר in Jer. 3:1 and והלכה והיתה לאיש־אחר in Deut. 24:2 provides a stronger basis for identifying possible reuse. These two sets of clauses are identical, with the exception of Jer. 3:1 adding מאתו. It is possible that this might relate to the presence of ויצאה מביתו in the preceding clause of Deut. 24:2, with both texts identifying the location from where the woman is expelled. The two clauses והלכה מאתו והיתה לאיש־אחר in Jer. 3:1 could be a conflation of the three clauses ויצאה מביתו והלכה והיתה לאיש־אחר in Deut. 24:2, or the latter could be an elaboration of the former.

Second, we also find an indication in the LXX that the translators saw a reuse between Jer. 3:1-10 and Deut. 24:1-4. Jeremiah 3:8 LXX reads εἰς τὰς χεῖρας αὐτῆς where MT has אליה. If LXX rendered proto-MT here, similar to MT, this would not be a precise translation. Alternatively, perhaps the LXX had a different *Vorlage*. Since the Greek can be retroverted into Hebrew with the phrase בידה, it is difficult to ignore that this is the exact phrase we find in Deut. 24:1 MT,[5] where LXX also has εἰς τὰς χεῖρας αὐτῆς. In this instance, the LXX translator seems to have recognized the reuse and to have taken the liberty to make the link even clearer. The fact that the prepositional phrase בידה is not frequent in the Hebrew Bible makes it even more likely that the translator of Jer. 3:8 LXX took a glance at Deut. 24:1.[6] It is still possible, of course, that LXX had a

---

3. David Instone-Brewer points out that "there is no equivalent to the divorce certificate in any ancient Near Eastern culture outside Judaism" (*Divorce and Remarriage in the Bible: The Social and Literary Context* [Grand Rapids: Eerdmans, 2002], 32). For a discussion of the possible purpose of the bill of divorce in ancient Israel, see Anselm C. Hagedorn, "Divorce in Archaic Crete: Comparative Perspectives on Deuteronomy 24:1-4," Chapter 10 in this volume, 264.

4. Cf. Richard M. Davidson, *Flame of Yahweh: Sexuality in the Old Testament* (Peabody: Hendrickson, 2007), 394; Lundbom, *Jeremiah 1–20*, 301.

5. Even though בידה is also used in Deut. 24:3, it seems to me that Deut. 24:1 was in the mind of the LXX translator. The close proximity between βιβλίον ἀποστασίου and εἰς τὰς χεῖρας αὐτῆς in Jer. 3:8 LXX, just as with ספר כריתת and בידה in Deut. 24:1 MT, indicates this connection.

6. Cf. Gen. 39:12-13; Exod. 15:20; 35:25; Judg. 4:21; Isa. 51:18; Prov. 14:1; Lam. 1:17. A similar point has been made by William McKane, *A Critical and Exegetical Commentary on Jeremiah*, ICC (Edinburgh: T&T Clark, 1986), 65.

Vorlage different from Jer. 3:8 MT. Nevertheless, this does not undermine the observation in regard to reuse. Thus, the inclusion of the phrase εἰς τὰς χεῖρας αὐτῆς in Jer. 3:8 LXX seems to indicate that either the LXX translator or its Hebrew *Vorlage* included this additional link between Deut. 24:1 and Jer. 3:8 as compared to the MT.[7]

Third, the phrase איש + אחר is found in Gen. 29:19; Lev. 27:20; Deut. 20:5-7; 24:2; 28:30; 1 Sam. 10:6; 2 Sam. 18:26; 1 Kgs 20:37; and Jer. 3:1; but only in Deut. 24:2 and Jer. 3:1 is it used in relation to the issue of marriage to "another man." There might be a link between the curse אשה תארש ואיש אחר ישגלנה ("You shall betroth a woman, but another man ravish her") in Deut. 28:30 and והלכה מאתו והיתה לאיש־אחר...שאי־עיניך על־שפים וראי איפה לא שגלת ("and she leaves him and becomes [wife] to another man...; lift your eyes to the bare heights and see: where have you not been ravished?") in Jer. 3:1-2, given the parallels between the phrase איש + אחר and שגל. The link would, however, need to be stronger to lend confidence to such a claim.

Thematic Correspondence

Jeremiah 3:1-10 MT seems to contain more parallels to Deut. 24:1-4 than Jer. 3:1-10 LXX does. Christl Maier points out that Jer. 3:1-10 MT reflects Deut. 24:1-4 in showing the husband returning to the wife. This contrasts with Jer. 3:1-10 LXX, where the woman returns to the husband.[8] I will come back to this difference below. For now the important point is that the return of the husband to the former wife in Jer. 3:1-10 MT again establishes a parallel with Deut. 24:1-4.[9] Further, Lundbom points out that the MT's idea of the defilement of the land in Jer. 3:1-2, 9 MT also reflects

---

7. Another difference here is that the phrase וכתב לה is dropped and not reused in Jeremiah 3. Thus, ספר כריתת does not become the indirect object of וכתב לה as in Deuteronomy 24, but of ואתן + אליה in Jeremiah 3. This again means that the verb נתן (ונתן / ואתן) is not followed by the prepositional phrase בידה as in Deuteronomy 24, but by אליה in Jeremiah 3. Further, in Jer. 3:8 the phrase ספר כריתתיה receives the 3fs suffix, and this is different from what occurs in Deuteronomy 24.

8. Commenting on the woman's defilement in Jer. 3:1, Craigie, Kelley, and Drinkard argue that it reflects more the legal tradition in Deut. 24:1-4, while the LXX "reflects an attempt to continue the surface logic of the preceding lines" (Peter C. Craigie et al., *Jeremiah 1–25*, WBC 26 [Dallas: Word, 1991], 49). Deuteronomy 24:4 uses the strange *pual* form הטמאה. The expression אחרי אשר הטמאה (lit. "after which she was defiled") implies that she was defiled by the second marriage, and if she then returns to the first husband, it is תועבה ("an abomination"), ולא תחטיא את־הארץ ("and you must not bring sin upon the land").

9. Christl M. Maier, *Daughter Zion, Mother Zion: Gender, Space and the Sacred in Ancient Israel* (Minneapolis: Fortress, 2008), 105.

the idea of the defilement of the land in Deut. 24:2, in contrast to the LXX, which only views the woman as defiled.[10]

Holladay's comment on the use of שוב in Jer. 3:1 is also worth noting:

> Jrm [Jeremiah] presses the verb "return" (שוב) in the fourth colon beyond the usage in Deuteronomy. In Deut. 24:4* we read, "Her first husband... cannot turn (שוב) to take her [i.e., cannot again take her] to be a wife to him": the verb שוב carries here the idiomatic meaning "do something again." But Jrm says, "Would he (re)turn to her again?" Here is the adverb "again" (עוד), implied by שוב in Deuteronomy, while שוב carries its full value "(re)turn." The result in Jrm's metaphor is that Yahweh is the active agent, as the husband is in the Deuteronomic law, but the meaning of the verb here suggests a kind of humbling action on Yahweh's part, as if Israel is the stable one and Yahweh contemplates moving back to her.[11]

Beyond such a possible reworking of שוב in Jer. 3:1 and dependence upon Deuteronomy 24, there may also be a further wordplay on שוב in the rest of the passage. Could משבה ישראל in Jer. 3:6, 8 also be a play on the verb שוב from Deuteronomy 24? Note how the same consonantal form שבה is used in Jer. 3:7, 10. The instruction in Deuteronomy 24 dealt with the possibility of a return (שוב). In Jer. 3:7 YHWH expressed his desire for Israel to return (שוב / שבה), yet they did not return. Likewise, in Jer. 3:10 Judah is said not to have returned (שוב / שבה), with the result that the people in Jeremiah's days have become faithless (משבה).

---

10. Lundbom, *Jeremiah 1–20*, 301. Jonathan Klawans has shown that defilement of the land is particularly associated with moral impurity, in contrast to ritual impurity (Jonathan Klawans, *Impurity and Sin in Ancient Judaism* [Oxford: Oxford University Press, 2000], 26–7). Dalit Rom-Shiloni argues that the author of Jer. 3:1-5 is familiar with the so-called Priestly terminology and conceptions of Leviticus 18, 20, and Numbers 35 but does not reuse either one intentionally in his composition of Jer. 3:1-5 (Dalit Rom-Shiloni, "Compositional Harmonization: Priestly and Deuteronomic References in the Book of Jeremiah—An Earlier Stage of a Recognized Interpretive Technique," in *The Formation of the Pentateuch*, ed. Jan C. Gertz et al., FAT 111 [Tübingen: Mohr Siebeck, 2016], 928–32).

11. Holladay, *Jeremiah 1–25*, 112–13. He goes on to claim that this also becomes an argument for the priority of MT over LXX (ibid., 113). Fishbane writes that the phrase לשוב in Deut. 24:4, where it means "return," "undergoes a semantic transformation [in Jer. 3:1-5], and refers to *religious return*—or repentance—not palingamy" (Fishbane, *Biblical Interpretation in Ancient Israel*, 309).

Direction of Dependence

Lack of Integration

Having argued for a reuse between Deut. 24:1-4 and Jer. 3:1-10, I now turn to arguing for why I believe it was Jeremiah that borrowed from Deuteronomy, and not vice versa.[12] First, there is something awkward about the sequence of actions in Jer. 3:8. In Deut. 24:1 we find the formulation וכתב לה ספר כריתת ונתן בידה ושלחה מביתו ("and he shall write a letter of divorce to her and give it into her hand and send her from his house"). These same clauses, in identical form, are repeated in 24:3 in relation to the second husband's divorce of the woman. This repetition highlights these clauses as describing the technical procedure of divorce. The sequence of events here follows the natural and expected order. First the husband would write the bill of divorce, then give it to the wife, and finally send her off. But when we come to Jer. 3:8, we read שלחתיה ואתן את־ספר כריתתיה אליה ("I sent her and I gave her letter of divorce to her"). Here the metaphorical wife, apostate Israel, is first sent off and then given a bill of divorce. This could be an example of Seidel's law of inversion,[13] in which case it would indicate Jeremiah's reuse of Deut. 24:1-4 due to the awkward sequence of events introduced in Jer. 3:1-10 MT. I cannot see another reason for why the author should alter an otherwise natural flow of events.[14] If this is a case of intentional

---

12. Fishbane takes the disputed לאמר in Jer. 3:1 as a "citation formula" introducing the reinterpretation of Deut. 24:1-4 (ibid., 284, 307).

13. See M. Seidel, "Parallels between Isaiah and Psalms," *Sinai* 38 (1955–56): 149–72, 229–40, 272–80, 333–55 (Hebrew).

14. Jan Joosten writes that a *wayyiqtol* following a *qatal* in discourse will usually take over the temporal perspective of the *qatal* and thus indicate "an event time preceding the reference time" (*The Verbal System of Biblical Hebrew: A New Synthesis Elaborated on the Basis of Classical Prose*, JBS 10 [Jerusalem: Simor, 2012], 182). In that case we could expect that the combination *qatal+wayyiqtol* represents a sequence. Still, it is also possible to understand the ואתן of ואתן את־ספר כריתתיה אליה as having an epexegetical function ("in the sense that I gave her a bill of divorce") or a pluperfect connotation ("having given her a bill of divorce"). In both cases this clause would explicate what was seen as implicit in שלחתיה (Bruce K. Waltke and Michael O'Connor, *An Introduction to Biblical Hebrew Syntax* [Winona Lake: Eisenbrauns, 1990], 551–3). This could be taken to weaken the use of these clauses to argue for the direction of dependence. Still, there is a clear reversal in verbal sequence between נתן and שלח in the two passages that invites an explanation. In light of the evidence for reuse between Jer. 3:1-10 and Deut. 24:1-4 in other parts

inversion, I list it here as an indication of the direction of dependence rather than reuse, since the lack of integration in the context of Jer. 3:8 creates an awkward sequence.

Wordplay

There seems to be a word-play in Jer. 3:2 that has, as far as I have seen, not been noted in previous scholarship. In Deut. 24:1, ערות דבר constitutes the legitimate basis for divorce. The debate regarding the meaning of this phrase by later commentaries is well known and needs no repetition here.[15] In Jer. 3:2 the promiscuous people are seen as כערבי במדבר ("like an Arab in the desert"). Why does the author make this comparison? It is used as a simile for the idea expressed in the preceding clause, which describes the people and reads על־דרכים ישבת להם ("you were sitting by roads [waiting] for them"). Prostitutes would typically sit by the side of a road, waiting for passersby (e.g., Gen. 38:14; Prov. 7:10-12).[16] The phrase כערבי במדבר would therefore seem to have a sexual connotation. The consonantal and phonetic similarity to ערות דבר is striking. In both cases the phrases are used for something objectionable, possibly including a sexual offense. The phrase ערות דבר in Deut. 24:1 does not necessarily imply a fault with the wife, but rather simply that the husband came to find something he disliked about the wife.[17] Through the wordplay in Jer. 3:1, the situation is intensified on several levels. While the Deuteronomic

---

of the passages, the more complex syntax of Jer. 3:8 compared to Deut 24:1 needs an explanation. Further, reading ואתן in an epexegetical or a pluperfect sense can be taken as compatible with the idea that the author of Jer. 3:8 wanted to mark dependence on Deuteronomy 24 by inverting the sequence, while still retaining a logical sequence of events. Another possibility is to understand שלח as a literal expression in Deut. 24:1 for sending away, but as a technical expression in Jer. 3:8 for divorce. If so, the altered order could make better sense. In Jer. 3:8 the husband would first divorce his wife by, for example, a public statement such as "You shall not be my wife," and then afterward he would write her a divorce certificate and send her off. However we explain the altered verbal sequence in Jer. 3:8, it is at least likely that it was meant as an intentional inversion of Deut. 24:1.

15. See Jacob Neusner, *The Rabbinic Traditions about the Pharisees before 70*, part 2: *The Houses* (Eugene: Wipf & Stock, 1971), 37–9; Fishbane, *Biblical Interpretation in Ancient Israel*, 309; Instone-Brewer, *Divorce and Remarriage*, 110–14.

16. Georg Fischer, *Jeremia 1–25*, HThKAT (Freiburg: Herder, 2005), 186; and Lundbom, *Jeremiah 1–20*, 302.

17. Cf. Eve Levavi Feinstein, *Sexual Pollution in the Hebrew Bible* (Oxford: Oxford University Press, 2014), 53–65.

instruction prohibits the husband from returning to a divorced wife that has meanwhile been married a second time, in Jer. 3:1 the Judah-wife has been sexually promiscuous through sexual contact with "many lovers" (רעים רבים). Further, while ערות דבר in Deut. 24:1 may be understood as implying no real fault on the wife's part, in Jer. 3:1 כערבי במדבר seems not only to imply sexual promiscuity and adultery, but also prostitution.[18] The adultery described in Jeremiah 3 would be liable to capital punishment, in contrast to Deuteronomy 24 where the remarried wife has only become defiled. In other words, while both the first husband in Deuteronomy 24 and the YHWH-husband in Jeremiah 3 have formally divorced their wives, Jeremiah 3 reverses culpability compared to Deuteronomy 24. Deuteronomy 24 can be read as the first husband having the sole responsibility for the dissolution of the relationship and pollution, with the wife as morally innocent, while in Jeremiah 3 it is the Judah-wife that has the sole responsibility for the dissolution of the relationship and pollution, and the YHWH-husband is morally innocent. The LXX apparently misunderstood the root and took it as ערב ("a raven") rather than ערבי ("an Arab/Bedouin"), showing that the translator missed the point of the wordplay in Hebrew.[19]

---

18. For a further discussion of prostitution, see Hilary Lipka, "The Offense, Its Consequences, and the Meaning of זנה in Leviticus 19:29," Chapter 6 in this volume, 163–4; and Sarah Shectman, "Priestly Marriage Instructions," Chapter 7 in this volume, 190–1.

19. For a discussion on whether MT or LXX represents the earlier version, see Emanuel Tov, *The Septuagint Translation of Jeremiah and Baruch: A Discussion of an Early Revision of the LXX of Jeremiah 29–52 and Baruch 1:1–3:8*, Harvard Semitic Monographs 8 (Missoula, MT: Scholars Press, 1976); Tov, "The Literary History of the Book of Jeremiah in the Light of Its Textual History," in *Empirical Models for Biblical Criticism*, ed. Jeffrey H. Tigay (Philadelphia: University of Pennsylvania Press, 1985), 211–41; Alexander Rofé, "The Arrangement of the Book of Jeremiah," *ZAW* 101 (1989): 390–8; Emanuel Tov, *The Text-Critical Use of the Septuagint in Biblical Research*, JBS 8 (Jerusalem: Simor, 1997), 243–4; Christl Maier, *Jeremia als Lehrer der Tora: Soziale Gebote des Deuteronomiums in Fortschreibungen des Jeremiabuches* (Göttingen: Vandenhoeck & Ruprecht, 2002), 26–30, 252–4, 257–60; Maier, *Daugther Zion, Mother Zion*, 105; Alexander Rofé, "The Arrangement of the Book of Jeremiah (MT and LXX)," *Beit Mikra* 56 (2011): 126–37 (Hebrew); Aaron D. Hornkohl, "The Language of the Book of Jeremiah and the History of the Hebrew Language" (PhD diss., Hebrew University, 2011), vi–vii (Hebrew); and Hornkohl, *Ancient Hebrew Periodization and the Language of the Book of Jeremiah: The Case for a Sixth-Century Date of Composition* (Leiden: Brill, 2014), 356–73.

In his study of paronomasia, or allusive wordplay, in the Hebrew Bible, Jonathan Kline writes:

> What constitutes similarity of sound? Paronomasia can be (1) homonymic (referring to words that sound identical and are spelled identically but differ in meaning; e.g., "bear" as noun or verb), or (2) homophonic (referring to words that sound identical but differ in spelling and meaning; e.g., "bear" and "bare"), or (3) can involve words that sound similar but are not identical and that differ in spelling and meaning (e.g., "bear" and "pear"). These three categories are differentiated by increasing degrees of markedness: the first is unique in that examples can be identified only on the basis of semantics (but not visually or orally/aurally); examples of the second category can be identified on the basis of semantics as well as visually (though not orally/aurally); and examples of the third category can be identified on the basis of semantics, visually, and orally/aurally. Given these differences in markedness, a useful distinction can be made between homonymic paronomasia (the first category) and nonhomonymic paronomasia (the second and third categories).[20]

The phrase כערבי במדבר in Jer. 3:2 sounds similar to but differs in spelling and meaning from ערות דבר in Deut. 24:1. Thus, Jer. 3:2 would belong to Kline's third category. Both Edward Greenstein and L. J. de Regt have emphasized that, for words to be identified as paronomasia, they need to appear "in proximity" and "in the same context."[21] Kline argues that several recent studies have demonstrated the phenomenon of allusive paronomasia as well.[22] Understanding כערבי במדבר in Jer. 3:2 as a wordplay on ערות דבר in Deut. 24:1 would be to see an example of allusive wordplay crossing book boundaries within the Hebrew Bible. Greenstein elaborates further: "because Hebrew words comprise a consonantal root interspersed with changing vocalic schemes, we generally demand of wordplay that at least half the consonants, usually two of the common root's three, are identical or phonologically similar."[23] This is fulfilled with two consecutive consonants ער followed by a possibly similar sound created by the consonants ו and ב between ערות and כערבי, and the three

---

20. Jonathan G. Kline, *Allusive Soundplay in the Hebrew Bible*, SBLAIIL 28 (Atlanta: SBL Press, 2016), 9.

21. Edward L. Greenstein, "Wordplay, Hebrew," *ABD* 6:968; L. J. de Regt, "Wordplay in the OT," *NIDB* 5:898.

22. Kline, *Allusive Soundplay*, 11, cf. 17, 24–9. He finds Benjamin D. Sommer, *A Prophet Reads Scripture: Allusion in Isaiah 40–66* (Stanford: Stanford University Press, 1998) especially noteworthy in this regard.

23. Greenstein, "Wordplay, Hebrew," 969.

consecutively following consonants דבר in דבר and במדבר. That we have two lexemes that, in addition, follow in the same order in the two passages further strengthens the case. A case like this without definite supporting evidence may be perceived as weak. But the similarity in consonants and order between the phrases, together with the additional evidence for reuse and direction of dependence discussed above and a distinct function for this proposed case of paronomasia in Jer. 3:2,[24] makes this a strong case for allusive sound-play. We can therefore formulate this in more general terms: if a passage shows additional evidence of reuse from a specific source, then similarity in sound and/or spelling with a different meaning is a more likely case of allusive paronomasia.

There might be another dimension as well to the possible wordplay of כערבי במדבר in Jer. 3:2 on the key and much contested phrase ערות דבר in Deut. 24:1. It is significant to note, especially given the Deuteronomic flavor of Jeremiah as a whole, that Deut. 1:1 opens the book by describing Moses as addressing the people בערבה במדבר ("in the desert, in the Arabah"). There are other verses using מדבר and ערבה together, referring to a similar location, but not in as tight a combination as in Deut. 1:1.[25] A significant parallel is found in Jer. 2:6, המוליך אתנו במדבר בארץ ערבה ושוחה ("who led us in the wilderness, in a land of desert and pit"). This seems to evoke Deut. 1:1 and the experience in the desert. Jeremiah 17:6 also compares the people to someone living in the desert and wilderness, but again not in as tightly constructed a phrase as in Deut. 1:1 and Jer. 3:2. While כערבי במדבר in Jer. 3:2 is the only place in the Hebrew Bible to use ערבי + מדבר, likely playing on ערות דבר in Deut. 24:1 as argued here, it simultaneously may be drawing from motifs of the people in the desert, בערבה במדבר, from the opening passage of Deuteronomy (1:1). The question here is why Jer. 3:2 and 17:6 describe the people in terms of being in the desert. While Jer. 17:6 simply states that the people were in the desert, Jer. 3:2 goes a step further and personalizes the term, suddenly giving it sexual connotations by alluding to an Arab prostitute sitting and

---

24. Kline writes: "The best way to demonstrate that a possible example of allusive paronomasia performs a clear function is to show that the word in the source text and its proposed patronym in the alluding texts are in *close proximity* with respect to the words or text-segment(s) that the alluding text reproduces from the source text and, even more importantly, that the *similarity in sound* and *difference in meaning* between the word in the source text and its proposed patronym in the alluding text combine to produce a striking effect in the message of the alluding text" (Kline, *Allusive Soundplay*, 29, cf. 28).

25. Cf. Deut. 1:1; 2:8; Josh. 12:8; 1 Sam. 23:24; 2 Sam. 17:16; Isa. 35:1, 6; 40:3; 41:19; 51:3; Jer. 2:6; 17:6; 50:12; Job 24:5.

waiting for lovers in the desert. The phrase כערבי במדבר in Jer. 3:2 does seem to simultaneously draw upon במדבר בערבה in Deut. 1:1 and ערות דבר in Deut. 24:1. If this is the case, it also means that Jeremiah 3 had a version of Deuteronomy likely similar to the received text we have, including the superscription of Deut. 1:1-5.

Conceptual Dependence

Jeremiah uses literal divorce between a man and his wife as a metaphor for the relationship between God and his people.[26] By definition, metaphorical language is secondary. This in itself cannot establish that Jer. 3:1-10 reused Deut. 24:1-4. But the metaphorical use of divorce here presupposes that a certain norm in regard to divorce was well-known both by Jeremiah and his readers. Without such a norm as a benchmark for comparison, Jeremiah's line of logic falls flat.[27] Given that there is reuse between these two passages, the metaphorical use of technical terms in Jer. 3:1-10 could therefore be taken as support for saying that Jeremiah is the one borrowing from the norm expressed in Deuteronomy, and not vice versa.

Appropriation

My line of argumentation began with evidence of reuse between Jer. 3:1-10 and Deut. 24:1-4. The close parallels between the clauses והלכה מאתו והיתה לאיש־אחר in Jer. 3:1 and והלכה והיתה לאיש־אחר in Deut. 24:2, where both passages use the phrase ספר כריתת ("bill of divorce") and the *piel* of שלח as a technical term for divorce, draw the two passages together and strongly indicate a literary relation between the two. There is also a possible adaptation of ויצאה מביתו והלכה והיתה לאיש־אחר from Deut. 24:2 into והלכה מאתו והיתה לאיש־אחר in Jer. 3:1.

Once reuse between the two passages was established, the next question was the direction of dependence. I have mentioned three main reasons for seeing Jeremiah as dependent upon Deuteronomy: (1) the awkward sequence of שלחתיה ואתן את־ספר כריתתיה אליה in Jer. 3:8;

---

26. Lundbom calls Jer. 3:6-11 "a 'pesher' on the surrounding oracles"; in his opinion, "much of the vocabulary is quarried from 3:1-5" (Lundbom, *Jeremiah 1–20*, 306). In his terms we could thus speak of reuse and direction of dependence within the two sections in 3:1-11 itself. I am not convinced, though, by his division between vv. 5 and 6. The parallels within Jer. 3:1-11 that he mentions could also be taken as signifying the unity of this passage.

27. Craigie, Kelley, and Drinkard call Jer. 3:1 a "paraphrase of the substance of the law also known in Deut 24:1-4" (Craigie et al., *Jeremiah 1–25*, 50).

(2) the wordplay of כערבי במדבר in Jer. 3:2 on ערות דבר in Deut. 24:1; and (3) the metaphoric use in Jer. 3:1-10 of language for divorce, which is used literally in Deut. 24:1-4. Even if we should use wordplay and metaphor with care to argue for the direction of dependence, the use of wordplay and metaphor in Jer. 3:1-10 with key concepts found in Deut. 24:1-4 does seem to point to the former's dependence on the latter. This would point in the direction that the author of Jer. 3:1-10 was aware of a text like Deut. 24:1-4, or something very similar to it, and not simply that the two passages shared a common legal inheritance.

Reuse of Deut. 24:1-4 can be seen both in Jer. 3:1-10 MT and LXX. Still, a certain difference between the two manuscripts can also be observed. On the one hand, Jer. 3:1-10 MT follows Deut. 24:1-4 in having the first husband return to the wife, in contrast to the wife returning to the husband in LXX. The defilement of the land in Jer. 3:1-2, 9 MT also reflects the idea of the defilement of the land in Deut. 24:2, in contrast to LXX, which only regards the woman as defiled. On the other hand, the MT אליה is rendered in Jer. 3:8 LXX as εἰς τὰς χεῖρας αὐτῆς, which is also used in Deut. 24:1 LXX. At this point the translator of Jer. 3:1-10 LXX appears to have incorporated a phrase taken from Deut. 24:1-4 LXX itself, instead of simply providing a literal translation of a text like Jer. 3:1-10 MT.

According to Jer. 3:1, it was God who divorced his people due to their adulterous behavior. It was not the fornication itself that constituted the divorce. The ערות דבר in Deut. 24:1 did not necessarily imply a fault with the wife but might simply denote that the husband had come to dislike the wife for some reason. Through the wordplay in Jer. 3:1 the situation is intensified. While the Deuteronomic instruction prohibits the husband from taking back a divorced wife who meanwhile has been married a second time, in Jer. 3:1 the Judah-wife has had sexual contact with "many lovers" (רעים רבים). Further, while ערות דבר in Deut. 24:1 may be understood as implying no real fault on the wife's side, in Jer. 3:1 כערבי במדבר denotes not only adultery but also prostitution—with adultery deserving capital punishment (e.g., Deut. 22:22). Based on the analogy of Deut. 24:1-4, the people in Jeremiah's day would have deserved to be wiped out. However, the analogy does not legally bind YHWH to the dictates of Deut. 24:1-4 in terms of how to treat Judah; it simply throws the situation into relief.

In Deut. 24:4 the prohibition against bringing sin upon the land, ולא תחטיא את־הארץ, is directed against the male. With the reuse of Deut. 24:1-4, the implication in Jeremiah 3 could be that the YHWH-husband himself would bring sin upon the land by taking back his people. Jeremiah, however, seems to studiously avoid this connotation. First of all, in 3:1, 7, and 10, it is the unfaithful people who are expected to return to God.[28] Further, while Jer. 3:1 MT does follow the legal lead of Deut. 24:4 in speaking about the impossibility of the husband returning to his divorced wife, since this would pollute the land (הלוא חנוף תחנף הארץ ההיא), in the rest of the passage the danger of polluting the land is defined otherwise. In 3:2 (ותחניפי ארץ בזנותיך וברעתך) and 3:9 (ותחנף את־הארץ) it is the adultery of the people that has defiled the land. Jeremiah therefore places the sole blame for defiling the land upon the people.[29]

In Jer. 3:4-5a the people are described as invoking God's first love toward them, in their initial walk in the wilderness together (cf. 2:2), and as asking a rhetorical question to affirm that God will not rage against the people forever: "Do you not now call to me: 'My father, you are the companion of my youth! Does one hate forever? Does one rage forever?' That is what you said." But in 3:5b, God exposes this as vain talk: "But you did evil and had your way." As Georg Fischer points out, not only have they acted promiscuously with multiple lovers and therefore deserve the capital punishment of Deut. 22:22, but by appealing to God to take them back, they also become guilty of setting Deut. 24:1-4 aside.[30] Still, as pointed out above, this is exactly what God says he needs to do—and is willing to do—to receive the people back again.

When we compare the dating in v. 6 ("Now YHWH said to me during the days of King Josiah") with the introductory statement in Jer. 1:2-3 ("The word of YHWH came to him in the days of King Josiah son of Amon of Judah, in the thirteenth year of his reign, and throughout the days of King Jehoiakim son of Josiah of Judah, and until the end of the eleventh year of King Zedekiah son of Josiah of Judah, when Jerusalem

---

28. It would have been easier if Jer. 3:1-10 MT had rendered it like the LXX, only speaking of the woman being defiled and the woman returning to the husband. But as Jer. 3:1-10 MT appears to be bound by Deut. 24:1-4 MT, it needed circumspectly to avoid placing the blame on YHWH for the defilement of the land. For a further discussion on defilement of the land, see Lipka, "The Offense, Its Consequences, and the Meaning of זנה in Leviticus 19:29," Chapter 6 in this volume.

29. It is possible that the LXX translator imported the scenario from Jer. 3:6-11 MT, with the wife returning to the husband, into his rendering of 3:1 (μὴ ἀνακάμπτουσα ἀνακάμψει πρὸς αὐτὸν ἔτι). A difference, however, is that LXX only has the wife being defiled (οὐ μιαινομένη μιανθήσεται ἡ γυνὴ ἐκείνη) and not also the land as in Deut. 24:4. The text of Jer. 3:1-10 MT focuses more upon the land being defiled. Hobbs argues that probably the "LXX reflects the original reading," while the MT is a later edition (Hobbs, "Jeremiah 3:1-6 and Deuteronomy 24:1-4," 23).

30. Fischer, *Jeremia 1–25*, 185.

went into exile in the fifth month" [NJPS; see also Jer. 25:3]), we find that the time of reference in 3:6 would be from the thirteenth year of Josiah to his death. Edwin Thiele has dated Josiah's reign to 641/640–609 BCE and the beginning of Jeremiah's ministry to 627 BCE.[31] If we accept all of this, then to say that Jeremiah was dependent on Deuteronomy would place the composition of Deuteronomy, at least this part of Deuteronomy, prior to this time.

Even if Jer. 3:1-10 assumes knowledge of Deut. 24:1-4, it should not be understood as a legal exegesis of the latter. Pushing the legal connection too much creates a legal issue with the incest laws (Lev. 18:6-7) and the prohibition against marrying two sisters (Lev. 18:18), in addition to the question of God possibly violating his own restriction on return after a divorce, as Jeremiah 3 describes both Israel and Judah as wives and daughters in this passage. If the connection is pushed this far, then YHWH is presented as married to his daughters, who also happen to be sisters. Instead, Jeremiah 3 uses the law of divorce and remarriage from Deut. 24:1-4 metaphorically for the relationship between God and his people. We should therefore not use Jer. 3:1-10 to expound upon the legal meaning of the law in Deut. 24:1-4. The reuse functions rather as a warning to Judah that it may suffer exile as Israel did in 722 BCE, when God "divorced" the northern kingdom. Even more importantly, the entire thrust of Jer. 2:1–4:4 is a call to Judah to repent and return to God. It is an open invitation, describing how God is willing to defy any expectations based on the legal boundaries in Deut. 24:1-4 to welcome his people back again.

---

31. Edwin R. Thiele, *The Mysterious Numbers of the Hebrew Kings* (Grand Rapids, MI: Kregel, 1983), 180–1, 217. Even if Lundbom finds it difficult to precisely date the passage, he sees no problems in dating it to the time of Josiah, even though he sees vv. 6–11 as a later interpolation (Lundbom, *Jeremiah 1–20*, 308–9). The dating of Jer. 3:1-10 on the basis of the historical information in v. 6 and the content of the context is also supported to some extent by linguistic studies. Aaron Hornkohl concludes, after having studied the linguistic phenomena in Jeremiah: "On the basis of a detailed examination of over forty linguistic features—representing the full spectrum of linguistic categories: orthography, phonology, morphology, syntax, and lexicon—the conclusion of the present study is that, though likely composite, the extant book of Jeremiah was written in a form of TBH, the literary medium employed in works composed in the span of time linking the First and Second Temple Period, probably approximately conterminous with the 6th century BCE" (Hornkohl, *Language of the Book of Jeremiah*, 371). Cf. Hornkohl, "The Language of the Book of Jeremiah," v.

Bibliography

Bergland, Kenneth. "Instructions on Divorce and Remarriage." In *Reading as a Disclosure of the Thoughts of the Heart: Proto-Halakhic Reuse and Appropriation between Torah and the Prophets*, 109–28. BZAR 23. Wiesbaden: Harrassowitz, 2019.

Craigie, Peter C., Joel F. Drinkard, and Page H. Kelley. *Jeremiah 1–25*. WBC 26. Dallas: Word, 1991.

Davidson, Richard M. *Flame of Yahweh: Sexuality in the Old Testament*. Peabody: Hendrickson, 2007.

Feinstein, Eve Levavi. *Sexual Pollution in the Hebrew Bible*. Oxford: Oxford University Press, 2014.

Fischer, Georg. *Jeremia 1–25*. HThKAT. Freiburg: Herder, 2005.

Fischer, Georg. *Jeremia: Der Stand der theologischen Diskussion*. Darmstadt: Wissenschaftliche Buchgesellschaft, 2007.

Fishbane, Michael. *Biblical Interpretation in Ancient Israel*. Oxford: Oxford University Press, 1988.

Greenstein, Edward L. "Wordplay, Hebrew." *ABD* 6:968–71.

Hobbs, T. R. "Jeremiah 3:1-6 and Deuteronomy 24:1-4." *ZAW* 86 (1974): 23–9.

Holladay, William L. *Jeremiah 1: A Commentary on the Book of the Prophet Jeremiah, Chapters 1–25*. Hermeneia. Philadelphia: Fortress, 1986.

Hornkohl, Aaron D. *Ancient Hebrew Periodization and the Language of the Book of Jeremiah: The Case for a Sixth-Century Date of Composition*. Leiden: Brill, 2014.

Hornkohl, Aaron D. "The Language of the Book of Jeremiah and the History of the Hebrew Language." PhD diss., Hebrew University, 2011 (Hebrew).

Instone-Brewer, David. *Divorce and Remarriage in the Bible: The Social and Literary Context*. Grand Rapids: Eerdmans, 2002.

Joosten, Jan. *The Verbal System of Biblical Hebrew: A New Synthesis Elaborated on the Basis of Classical Prose*. JBS 10. Jerusalem: Simor, 2012.

Kitchen, Kenneth A. *On the Reliability of the Old Testament*. Grand Rapids: Eerdmans, 2003.

Klawans, Jonathan. *Impurity and Sin in Ancient Judaism*. Oxford: Oxford University Press, 2000.

Kline, Jonathan G. *Allusive Soundplay in the Hebrew Bible*. Atlanta: SBL, 2016.

Lundbom, Jack R. *Jeremiah 1–20: A New Translation with Introduction and Commentary*. AB 21A. New Haven: Yale University Press, 2008.

Lyons, Michael A. *From Law to Prophecy: Ezekiel's Use of the Holiness Code*. LHBOTS 507. London: T&T Clark, 2009.

Maier, Christl M. *Daughter Zion, Mother Zion: Gender, Space and the Sacred in Ancient Israel*. Minneapolis: Fortress, 2008.

Maier, Christl M. *Jeremia als Lehrer der Tora: Soziale Gebote des Deuteronomiums in Fortschreibungen des Jeremiabuches*. Göttingen: Vandenhoeck & Ruprecht, 2002.

Martin, James D. "The Forensic Background to Jeremiah 3:1." *VT* 19 (1969): 82–92.

Mastnjak, Nathan. *Deuteronomy and the Emergence of Textual Authority in Jeremiah*. Tübingen: Mohr Siebeck, 2016.

McKane, William. *A Critical and Exegetical Commentary on Jeremiah*. ICC. Edinburgh: T&T Clark, 1986.

Neusner, Jacob. *The Rabbinic Traditions about the Pharisees before 70*. Part 2: *The Houses*. Eugene: Wipf & Stock, 1971.

Phillips, Anthony. *Deuteronomy*. CBC. Cambridge: Cambridge University Press, 1973.

Regt, L. J. de. "Wordplay in the OT." *NIDB* 5:898–900.
Rofé, Alexander. "The Arrangement of the Book of Jeremiah." *ZAW* 101 (1989): 390–8.
Rofé, Alexander. "The Arrangement of the Book of Jeremiah (MT and LXX)." *Beit Mikra* 56 (2011): 126–37 (Hebrew).
Rom-Shiloni, Dalit. "Compositional Harmonization: Priestly and Deuteronomic References in the Book of Jeremiah – An Earlier Stage of a Recognized Interpretive Technique." In *The Formation of the Pentateuch*, edited by Jan C. Gertz, Bernard M. Levinson, Dalit Rom-Shiloni, and Konrad Schmid, 913–42. FAT 111. Tübingen: Mohr Siebeck, 2016.
Seidel, M. "Parallels between Isaiah and Psalms." *Sinai* 38 (1955–56): 149–72, 229–40, 272–80, 333–55 (Hebrew).
Sommer, Benjamin D. *A Prophet Reads Scripture: Allusion in Isaiah 40–66*. Stanford: Stanford University Press, 1998.
Thiel, Winfried. *Die deuteronomistische Redaktion von Jeremia 1–25*. WMANT 41. Neukirchen-Vluyn: Neukirchener Verlag, 1973.
Thiel, Winfried. *Die deuteronomistische Redaktion von Jeremia 26–45: Mit einer Gesamtbeurteilung der deuteronomistischen Redaktion des Buches Jeremia*. WMANT 52. Neukirchen-Vluyn: Neukirchener Verlag, 1981.
Thiele, Edwin R. *The Mysterious Numbers of the Hebrew Kings*. Grand Rapids: Kregel, 1983.
Tooman, William A. *Gog of Magog: Reuse of Scripture and Compositional Technique in Ezekiel 38–39*. FAT 2/52. Tübingen: Mohr Siebeck, 2011.
Tov, Emanuel. "The Literary History of the Book of Jeremiah in the Light of Its Textual History." In *Empirical Models for Biblical Criticism*, edited by Jeffrey H. Tigay, 211–41. Philadelphia: University of Pennsylvania Press, 1985.
Tov, Emanuel. *The Septuagint Translation of Jeremiah and Baruch: A Discussion of an Early Revision of the LXX of Jeremiah 29–52 and Baruch 1:1–3:8*. HSM 8. Missoula, MT: Scholars Press, 1976.
Tov, Emanuel. *The Text-Critical Use of the Septuagint in Biblical Research*. JBS 8. Jerusalem: Simor, 1997.
Waltke, Bruce K., and Michael O'Connor. *An Introduction to Biblical Hebrew Syntax*. Winona Lake: Eisenbrauns, 1990.

12

Sexual Relations and the Transition from Holy People to Human Sanctuary in Second Temple Times

Hannah K. Harrington

Several Second Temple authors interpret Israel's holiness to mean that the bodies of Israel form a sacred residence, or sanctuary. Authors as disparate as Philo, Paul, and the author of 4QFlorilegium refer to Israel as a temple. Furthermore, desecration of this "sanctuary" is possible by sexual relations with non-Jews. How did such a concept develop?

There are various factors that may have contributed to the view that the people form a temple. Some scholars suggest that Jews compensated for the temple's loss during the exile by focusing on the identity of the people.[1] Persian thought emphasized the spirit world. Hellenistic philosophy replaced the corrupt with the ethereal and perfect.[2] While these views have validity, they are external to the core of Jewish tradition. This chapter looks inside the Torah itself to discover the effect, if any, of

---

1. Mary Douglas, *Jacob's Tears: The Priestly Work of Reconciliation* (Oxford: Oxford University Press, 2004), 154, 174; cf. also Jacob Neusner, *The Idea of Purity in Ancient Judaism*, SJLA 1 (Leiden: Brill, 1973), 28.

2. The emphasis on the spirit world in post-biblical Judaism can be attributed to foreign influence. For one, the Persians envision a world of dueling spirits of good and evil. Another possibility is Middle Platonism (Eibert Tigchelaar, private communication). Philo regards the holy spirit as a daemonic being that makes voiceless contact through the mind, an idea that may come from Plato and his interpreters. According to Philo, insight into the Torah and the mind of God "comes from a voice in my own soul" (*Cher.* 27) when "the invisible spirit, the familiar secret tenant" speaks (*Somn.* 2.252).

biblical legal traditions on the notion of people-as-temple in various forms of Second Temple Judaism. What aspects of the received tradition led to, or at least supported, the idea of the sanctuary of the body in Judaism? Below I will examine interpretations of four traditions from biblical law that reveal a shift in emphasis from the sanctuary as the temple and its cult to the notion that the people of Israel form a sanctuary which houses the presence of God and can be desecrated by illicit sexuality.

First a note on language. An analogy can be made between temple and people already during the biblical period through the term קדש, "holy," or "holiness." The term קדש occurs 470 times in the Hebrew Bible, usually indicating the sacred character of an item dedicated to YHWH (e.g., holy ark, 2 Chron. 25:33; holy garments, Exod. 28:2; holy ground, Exod. 3:5; holy food, Lev. 22:10; holy day, Lev. 23:4). In 70 of these instances, קדש, like מקדש, "sanctuary," refers to a holy place, building, or room within it (e.g., Exod. 28:29, 35; Lev. 10:17; Ezek. 42:14). However, some instances of קדש refer to the holiness of Israel (e.g., "people of holiness," אנשי קדש in Exod. 22:30 and עם הקדש in Isa. 62:12) and even קדש יהוה, "the holiness of the Lord" (Mal. 2:11). Thus, קדש in biblical literature already associates the holiness of YHWH with both the sanctuary and the people of Israel.

Purpose of the Tabernacle

According to the laws of the tabernacle, the sanctuary was not just a separate location for God; it also functioned to facilitate his presence among Israel. According to Exodus, YHWH wishes to reside among the people of Israel and not only in the sanctuary: ועשו לי מקדש ושכנתי בתוכם, "Let them construct a sanctuary for me, that I may dwell among them" (Exod. 25:8; see also Exod. 29:45-46, "I will dwell among the sons of Israel and will be their God"). The purpose of building the sanctuary was so that YHWH could live בתוכם, "among them (the people)," not בתוכו, "within it (the sanctuary)." The term for sanctuary, משכן, derives from the root שכן, "to dwell, reside." In priestly literature משכן refers to the holy enclosure of the tent or building where God's presence resides, not the whole compound.[3] But Leviticus emphasizes God's presence as

---

3. Jacob Milgrom, *Studies in Levitical Terminology, vol. 1: The Encroacher and the Levite: The Term 'Aboda*, Near Eastern Studies 14 (Berkeley: University of California Press, 1970), 23 n. 78: "Indeed, מקדש in P never means the sanctuary building. It either refers to 'the sacred area,' the holy place (Lev. 12:4, 16:33, 20:3, 21:12, 12, 26:2 = 19:30; Num. 19:20) or to 'the sacred objects,' the sancta (Lev. 21:23, 26:31; Num. 3:38, 10:21, 18:1).... It should also be noted that Ezekiel, just like P,

active among Israel (Lev. 26:11), not just the sanctuary: "Moreover, I will establish my presence (משכני) among you and I will not expel you. I will walk about (והתהלכתי) in your midst: I will be your God, and you shall be my people" (Lev. 26:11-12). Because of this spillover of God's holiness from inside the sanctuary to the whole people, Jacob Milgrom interprets משכן as a metaphor for God's "ethereal, spatially unbounded presence."[4] Much later, Paul quotes this verse to make his claim that believers in Christ are a temple of God: "For we are the temple of the living God; just as God said, 'I will dwell in them and walk among them; and I will be their God, and they shall be my people'" (2 Cor. 6:16b NASB).

The verb התהלך, "to walk about," indicates that God's presence was not considered static within the tabernacle but moved everywhere among the Israelites.[5] The term is first used in the Bible in Gen. 3:8 where YHWH walks about (התהלך) in the garden with Adam and Eve, indicating God's personal relationship to his people. The participle (מתהלך) is also used in Deut. 23:15 to indicate YHWH's movement throughout Israel's war camp:

כי יהוה אלהיך מתהלך בקרב מחנך להצילך ולתת איביך לפניך והיה מחניך קדוש
ולא־יראה בך ערות דבר ושב מאחריך:

Since YHWH your god walks in the midst of your camp to deliver you and to defeat your enemies before you, therefore your camp must be holy; and he must not see anything indecent among you or he will turn away from you.

---

never uses מקדש for the sanctuary building." Cf. Philip Jenson, *Graded Holiness: Key to the Priestly Conception of the World*, JSOTSup 106 (Sheffield: JSOT Press, 1992), 90; and Israel Knohl, *The Sanctuary of Silence: The Priestly Torah and the Holiness School* (Minneapolis: Fortress, 1995), 63.

4. Milgrom, *Leviticus 23–27: A New Translation with Introduction and Commentary*, AB 3B (New York: Doubleday, 2000), 2300; see also Milgrom, *Leviticus 1–16: A New Translation with Introduction and Commentary*, AB 3 (New York: Doubleday, 2000), 516, on the cognate Aramaic term משכנא, "which stands for the innermost, forbidden portion of the Temple" (citing the work of D. R. Hillers, "*MŠKN*' 'Temple' in Inscriptions from Hatra," *BASOR* 207 [1972]: 54–6). Note also rabbinic development of the term into the concept of the Shekinah—God's glorious presence. In addition to Shekinah, "the divine presence," the Rabbis frequently use the terms, "Glory," "The Name," and "the Holy Spirit," to describe God's nearness and goodness to his people (*b. Shab.* 22b; *b. Ber.* 6a). It is his nearness rather than his transcendence that they emphasize most. Cf. Hannah K. Harrington, *Holiness: Rabbinic Judaism in the Graeco-Roman World* (London: Routledge, 2001), 32–3.

5. Milgrom, *Leviticus 23–27*, 2300. The term appears only seven times in the Hebrew Bible.

YHWH's holy presence among the troops ensures their victory in battle but also requires a high state of purity from them, including abstinence from sexual relations and even covering excrement.

Another Torah term for an Israelite sanctuary, "tent of meeting" (אהל מועד), indicates its purpose as a meeting place between God and his people, through the mediation of Moses or the high priest. "...There I will meet you (Moses) and speak to you; I, [*YHWH,*] *will also meet the Israelites there* and it will be sanctified by my glory" (ונעדתי שמה לבני ישראל ונקדש בכבדי, Exod. 29:43-44).[6] Indeed, non-Torah traditions of all stripes emphasize this desire of YHWH to live among Israel, sustained by their praises and humble hearts (Isa. 57:15; 66:1-2; Ps. 22:3). Thus, the sanctuary was not just a safe house for YHWH, protecting him from the impurities of Israel and protecting Israel from the high voltage of his holiness. Rather, it is clear that YHWH wishes to "move about" among Israel. The real sanctuary of YHWH could be understood to be the nation itself.

The Nation as a Royal Priesthood

The meeting of Israel and YHWH at Sinai required a high level of purity of all Israel on account of the holiness of the divine revelation. The entire nation was required to abstain from sexual relations for three days and perform ritual ablutions (Exod. 19:10-15). For their obedience to

---

6. "The Tent is Israel's oracular center.... This is why the sanctuary is indispensable" (Milgrom, *Leviticus 23–27*, 2300–301). Milgrom distinguishes between P's view that YHWH is confined to a sanctuary and H's view that he is present everywhere in the land. The sanctuary enables communication and a relationship between God and Israel. Even though the Israelite laity may not enter the sanctuary, the rituals of the cult mediate the relationship between God and Israel, atoning for impurities and reinforcing bonds of fellowship. Purgation rituals atone for the sins of Israel. Purification rituals keep the sanctuary free of impurity and effective. Other rituals, e.g., lighting the continuous menorah fires or setting out the sacred bread, symbolize the presence of and provision for YHWH among Israel. These rituals form the framework through which the penitent, supplicant, and jubilant can express themselves to YHWH. The cult thus maintains and strengthens the relationship between God and his people. The firecloud (Exod. 40:38) which rested on it, and the altar fire (Exod. 40:29; Lev. 6:6), were visible manifestations to the entire assembly that YHWH was "home" and happy. Non-priestly traditions describe the Israelites communicating through prayer and praise to YHWH when they came to worship him at the sacred courts (2 Kgs 8:12-54; 2 Chron. 20:28).

the covenant, they are offered the status of "a royal priesthood" (Exod. 19:6a). In this context, even laity gained direct access to the deity. Some Jews in Second Temple times understood the "royal priesthood" promise somewhat literally and applied priestly restrictions (cf. Leviticus 21–22) to the nation in terms of marriage.

In terms of law, the priesthood is distinguished in Israel by additional requirements to protect their purity and holiness. The sexuality of the priests is especially restricted. All priests are forbidden to marry certain women (e.g. prostitute, rape victim, and divorcee), and the high priest must marry a virgin from within the clan (Lev 21:7, 14). The priesthood depends on holy seed to produce the next generation of priests and if that seed is compromised by illicit sex, there is no way to remedy the outcome (see the desecration of "holy seed" in Ezra 9:1-2). When the nation is regarded as priestly, the matter becomes critical for all the people. It is not just the priest's wife who must be selected with such care, but it is the spouses of all the men. For Second Temple Judaism, the illicit sex at issue is frequently intermarriage.

Aramaic Levi Document

Using the Exodus tradition that Israel is a royal priesthood (Exod. 19:6), the author of the Aramaic Levi Document (ALD) applies a priestly dynamic to Israel's sexuality.[7] The longer version of the Testament of Levi correlates intermarriage and desecrating the sanctuary: "Be on

---

7. The longer Greek version of this document from Mt. Athos, the Testament of Levi, dates back only to medieval times, but the antiquity of its core is supported by fragments from Qumran, which suggest an original date during the third century BCE. Other attestations include two sets of vellum in Aramaic from the Cairo Geniza, two possible citations in Greek from the fourth-century monk Ammonas, and a small Syriac fragment. See Jonas C. Greenfield, Michael E. Stone, and Esther Eshel, *The Aramaic Levi Document: Edition, Translation, Commentary*, SVTP 19 (Leiden: Brill, 2004). For more on the date of ALD, see the discussion in Armin Lange, "Your Daughters Do Not Give to Their Sons and Their Daughters Do Not Take for Your Sons (Ezra 9,12): Intermarriage in Ezra 9–10 and in the Pre-Maccabean Dead Sea Scrolls," *Biblische Notizen* 139 (2008): 79, who argues for a third- or late fourth-century BCE date; so also Henryk Drawnel, *An Aramaic Wisdom Text from Qumran: A New Interpretation of the Levi Document*, JSJSup 86 (Leiden: Brill, 2004), 71. Lange claims that *Jubilees* incorporates ALD (cf. *Jub.* 30:1-32), pointing to a non-polemic use of the solar calendar, an ethical dualism that does not reflect the Hellenistic religious reforms, and an appreciation of the absolute authority of the high priest; but see J. L. Kugel, "How Old is the Aramaic Levi Document?" *DSD* 14 (2007): 292–300, who prefers a Hasmonean date.

guard against the spirit of promiscuity, for it is constantly active and through your descendants it is about to defile the sanctuary. Therefore, take for yourself a wife while you are still young, a wife who is free of blemish or pollution, who is not from the race of alien nations" (*T. Levi* 9:9-10). Promiscuity here refers to intermarriage resulting in irremediably profaned children.[8]

The third-century BCE fragments of ALD make an explicit connection between Jews, the priesthood, and the sanctuary. The patriarch Isaac exhorts his grandson Levi, "Marry a woman from my family and do not defile your seed with illicit sexual partners (Aram. זניאן = Heb. זנות), since you are holy seed, but sanctify your seed *like the holy place* since you are called a holy priest for all the seed of Abraham" (ALD 6:4, col. a 17-18).[9] The writer makes an explicit association between Levi and the temple itself, one which illicit sexual relations threaten to destroy. While the priests are most at issue in the matter of marriage, Joseph Baumgarten claims, "For the time of the patriarchs, ancient Judaism perceived the family (משפחה) of Levi and the peoples (עמי) of Israel as identical."[10] Indeed the author regards intermarriage as a desecration for anyone in

---

8. Ultimately, sexual immorality brings destruction to the temple and people (*T. Levi* 14:1-8; 15:1-4).

9. The term זנות can refer to any illicit sexuality, especially intermarriage. For references throughout Second Temple literature to the understanding of זנות as "sexual wrongdoing," cf. William Loader, *The Dead Sea Scrolls on Sexuality: Attitudes towards Sexuality in Sectarian and Related Literature at Qumran* (Grand Rapids: Eerdmans, 2009), 362.

10. See the citation of Baumgarten in Lange, "Your Daughters Do Not Give to Their Sons," 80–1 n. 10; see also William Loader, *Enoch, Levi, and Jubilees on Sexuality: Attitudes towards Sexuality in the Early Enoch Literature, the Aramaic Levi Document, and the Book of* Jubilees (Grand Rapids: Eerdmans, 2007), 94. For the view that ALD is concerned only with the priestly line, see Robert A. Kugler, "Halakhic Interpretive Strategies at Qumran: A Case Study," in *Legal Texts and Legal Issues: Proceedings of the Second Meeting of the International Organization for Qumran Studies, Published in Honour of Joseph M. Baumgarten*, ed. M. Bernstein, F. Garcia Martinez, and J. Kampen (Leiden: Brill, 1999), 134 n. 15; Christine E. Hayes, *Gentile Impurities and Jewish Identities: Intermarriage and Conversion from the Bible to the Talmud* (Oxford: Oxford University Press, 2002), 72; and Martha Himmelfarb, "Levi, Phinehas, and the Problem of Intermarriage at the Time of the Maccabean Revolt," *JSQ* 6 (1999): 5, who (following J. Kampen, "4QMMT and New Testament Studies," in *Reading 4QMMT: New Perspectives on Qumran Law and History*, ed. J. Kampen and M. J. Bernstein [Atlanta: Scholars Press, 1996], 135–8) takes זנות in this context to include women of non-priestly families as unsuitable marriage partners for priests; but see the rebuttal by Loader, *Enoch, Levi, and Jubilees*

Israel, not just the priests. He presents the example of Dinah, whose intercourse with Shechem he sees as a desecration (4Q213a, 3-4). The writer holds Dinah responsible for Shechem taking advantage of her (Gen. 34:2), stating that she "profaned her name (i.e., herself) and the name of her ancestors, and shamed all her brothers" (4Q213a 3 + 4).[11] To guard against further sacrilege, the author warns his readers to sanctify their children as they would the temple.[12]

Jubilees

When making much the same case against intermarriage as ALD, the book of *Jubilees*, usually dated to the mid-second century BCE, explicitly connects all Israel with the priesthood:

> No sin is greater than the sexual impurity which they commit on the earth because Israel is a holy people for the Lord its God. It is the nation which he possesses; it is a priestly nation; it is a priestly kingdom: it is what he owns. No such impurity will be seen among the holy people. (*Jub.* 33:20, trans. Loader)

Leviticus teaches that a priest's intercourse with a prohibited woman profanes him (Lev. 21:7). *Jubilees* forbids intermarriage between any Jew and gentile on the basis of the nation's "royal priesthood" status.

---

on Sexuality, 102, on the basis of the parallel biblical marriage instructions from Isaac to Jacob (Genesis 28), which endorses any woman of the clan, as well as Levi's subsequent actions according to ALD 11:1.

11. Drawnel's translation prefaces this line with "every virgin," indicating that Dinah's shame applies to any Jewish woman who has sexual relations with a gentile (Drawnel, *An Aramaic Wisdom Text from Qumran*, 235–6); see further discussion in Loader, *Enoch, Levi, and Jubilees on Sexuality*, 92–4.

12. Lange, "Your Daughters Do Not Give to Their Sons," 80–1, claims that ALD's point here is to require gentiles to convert to Judaism before they marry Jewish women. However, that misses the point of the Dinah story reported by the author. Shechem was willing to convert; however, Simeon and Levi not only rebuffed his offer but murdered him along with all the men of his town (Gen. 34:15-27). I would argue that, like Ezra–Nehemiah, the author of ALD does not support any type of conversion. The same type of interpretation of the Dinah story is evident in *Jubilees* (see below) where the author commends Jacob's sons for destroying Shechem, even though a covenant had been made and circumcision of the townsmen performed, so that the marriage of Dinah with even a converted gentile would not take place. See Hayes, *Gentile Impurities*, 72, who argues that ALD rejects even gentile converts as marriage partners for priests.

Dead Sea Scrolls

Several of the scrolls found at Qumran designate the community of the elect as a "holy house" or "human sanctuary."[13] Devorah Dimant suggests this self-designation reflects an attempt to fulfill Israel's mission of a "royal priesthood" (Exod. 19:6): "In this context, each action within the sectarian framework acquires the character of a sacrifice, and thus becomes 'a work of thanksgiving.'"[14] In fact the primary goal of the group is to invite a spirit of holiness within the community which will effect atonement for the land. The Community Rule affirms that the community is a "holy house for Aaron," even a "holy of holies," and its mission is "to establish a/the spirit of holiness [רוח קודש] in eternal truth, to make atonement for the guilt of transgression and the unfaithfulness of sin, and that the land may be accepted without the flesh of burnt-offerings and without the fat of sacrifices" (1QS IX, 3-4).[15]

This priestly identity also accounts for the exclusion of the physically disabled from the assembly, as if they were priests in the temple and for the name of the Yaḥad as "The Sons of Zadok," a priestly title (e.g., CD IV, 13; V, 4; 1QS V, 2, 9; cf. Ezek. 44:15), and "faithful [priestly] house" (CD III, 19–IV, 6; cf. 1 Sam. 2:35). To be sure, not all of the community were priests, but this "priestly" character represented an aspiration to an intense level of holiness.

---

13. See, e.g., "holy house for Aaron" (1QS IX, 6); "holy among all the peoples" (1Q34 3 II, 6); "assembly of holiness" or "holy community" (1QS V, 20; IX, 2; 1Q28a I, 9, 13; 4Q181 1 II, 4); "holy council" (1QH XV, 10 [VII, 10]; 1QM III, 4; CD XX, 25; 1QS II, 25; 1Q28a II, 9); "human sanctuary" (4Q174 I, 6); "the holy ones" (1Q33 VI, 6); God's holy people (1Q33 XIV, 12); "men of holiness" (1QS VIII, 17); "congregation of the men of perfect holiness" (CD XX, 2-7; 1QS IX, 20); "precious cornerstone" (1QS VIII, 5-7); and "most holy dwelling for Aaron" (1QS VIII, 8). The community refers to itself as a group sanctified for Torah study in the desert (1QS VIII, 13–15). Each member is considered "a holy man" (1QS V, 13, 18; VIII, 17, 23; IX, 8).

14. Devorah Dimant, "4QFlorilegium and the Idea of the Community as a Temple," in *History, Ideology and Bible Interpretation in the Dead Sea Scrolls: Collected Studies*, FAT 90 (Tübingen: Mohr Siebeck, 2014), 287.

15. New Testament writers often refer to the elect as sacrifices or priests and even a temple for the spirit of God. The priestly role of Israel is taken over by the church's mission. Later, the author of Hebrews would refer to both of these activities as sacrifices to God: "Through him [Jesus] then let us continually offer up a sacrifice of praise to God, that is, the fruit of lips that acknowledge his name. Do not neglect to do good and to share what you have, for such sacrifices are pleasing to God" (Heb. 13:15-16; cf. also Rom. 12:1). Paul is explicit that the spirit of God lives within believers as it does in the temple.

For the sect, the elect were the temple, not in terms of dormant housing like wood and stone but as holy personnel who embodied the cult's activities. Just like workers in a business can be referred to as "the office," so priests can be referred to as "the temple," and for these writers the righteous form a type of temple (see also 2 Cor. 6:16-17). Like the priests, but not at the same level of sanctity, the nation is co-extensive with the sanctuary. Indeed, the people-as-sanctuary notion appears stronger among the sect, which had rejected the authority of the current priesthood of the Jerusalem temple and looked for communal ways to continue the cult's major functions.

The "Assembly of YHWH"

A legal tradition that contributes to the notion of the body of Israelites as sanctuary comes from Deuteronomy's restrictions on who may enter the "assembly of YHWH."

לא־יבא עמוני ומואבי בקהל יהוה גם דור עשירי לא־יבא להם בקהל יהוה עד־עולם:

> No Ammonite or Moabite may enter the assembly of YHWH. Even to the tenth generation, none of them may enter the assembly of YHWH forever. (Deut. 23:4)

The phrase "enter the assembly of YHWH" is ambiguous: does it refer to entering the temple courts or to joining Israel by marriage?[16] Ancient

---

16. Commentators, both ancient and modern, have interpreted the law variously as forbidding (1) entry into the sanctuary, (2) service in a national governing assembly, (3) participation in worship assemblies, and (4) membership among the people of Israel. Shaye J. D. Cohen, *The Beginnings of Jewishness: Boundaries, Varieties, Uncertainties* (Berkeley: University of California Press, 1999), 243 n. 5, claims that the clearest interpretation is simply that these ethnic groups were not allowed into the Israelite temple. But the context of Deuteronomy 23, with its list of forbidden marriage partners, points to intermarriage as the key concern; cf. Milgrom, *Leviticus 1–16*, 360, who presumes that Deuteronomy 23 was originally intended to ban intermarriage. Both interpretations appear in later texts; cf. a certain Simeon who claimed that Agrippa I was not allowed in the temple because of his foreign descent (*Ant.* 19.332). See Daniel R. Schwartz, "On Two Aspects of a Priestly View of Descent at Qumran," in *Archaeology and History in the Dead Sea Scrolls*, ed. L. H. Schiffman (Sheffield: JSOT Press), 166. Some rabbinic texts apply this verse to the entire city of Jerusalem, although the Mishnah and Talmud assume that intermarriage was the issue (*m. Qidd.* 4:3); Cohen, *The Beginnings of Jewishness*, 249–51. So also Philo, *Spec. Laws* 3.29; Josephus, *Ant.* 8.190-96; cf. 11.139-53. But cf. Bernard Levinson,

sources attest to both interpretations. After the Babylonian destruction of the temple, the writer of Lamentations protests, "She [Jerusalem] has seen her sanctuary invaded by nations concerning which you have commanded that they may not 'enter your congregation'" (1:10). However, the author of 1 Kings and Ezra–Nehemiah after him both regard this passage as a prohibition of intermarriage. Both add the Moabites and Ammonites (Deut. 23:4) to the list of forbidden gentile marriage partners in Deuteronomy 7 (Deut. 7:1), making the issue about marriage rather than entry to the temple. 1 Kings 11 reads:

> But King Solomon loved many foreign women, together with the daughter of Pharaoh, women of the Moabites, Ammonites, Edomites, Zidonians, and Hittites; of the nations concerning which the Lord said unto the children of Israel, You shall not go in to them, neither shall they come in unto you; for surely they will turn away your heart after their gods; Solomon clung unto these in love.... For it happened when Solomon was old, that his wives turned away his heart after other gods. (1 Kgs 11:1-2)

According to Nehemiah 13, after the Jews heard the Deuteronomic law "that the Ammonite and the Moabite should not enter the assembly of God forever," they "separated all the alien admixture from Israel" (Neh. 13:3; cf. Ezra 9:1-2).[17] The author of Ezra–Nehemiah interprets "enter the congregation" in a sexual manner as a prohibition against intermarriage because he regards not only the temple but the bodies of Israel as a cultic sanctum (Ezra 9:1-2, "holy seed"). Nehemiah 13:25-26 reads: "Then I [Nehemiah] made them [the offenders] swear by God, saying 'You will not give your daughters in marriage to their sons, nor take any of their daughters in marriage for your sons, or yourselves. Was it not on account of such women that Solomon, king of Israel, sinned?'" For both Ezra–Nehemiah and 1 Kings, the primary issue is not who can enter the temple but whom an Israelite may marry. Their main concern is to maintain holiness within the *human* sanctuary of Israel.

"Deuteronomy," in *The Jewish Study Bible*, ed. Adele Berlin and Marc Zvi Brettler (Oxford: Oxford University Press, 1999), 418, who contends that the assembly "served as the national governing body, akin to a popular legislature, that was charged with a broad range of judicial, political and policy matters (Judg 20.2)." Levinson adds that these prohibited ethnicities were probably also banned from marriage within the community and entry into the temple.

17. Ezra–Nehemiah utilizes Deuteronomy's prohibition against certain ethnicities, who "...may not enter the congregation of YHWH" (Deut. 23:4) and represents it as, "...may not enter the congregation of God" (Neh. 13:1).

The Dead Sea Scrolls connect Deuteronomy 23 with intermarriage and desecration of the sanctuary of human beings. Miqtsat Ma'ase ha-Torah (4QMMT), the most vocal of the Qumran texts against intermarriage, associates it explicitly with the defilement of the sanctuary. 4QMMT B 39-49 protests marriage with ineligible persons and supports this with Deuteronomy's prohibition on foreigners entering the "assembly" (קהל, Deut. 23:1):

> [And concerning the Ammonite] and the Moabite...who (nevertheless) enter the assembly [and...and] take [wives to be]come one bone [and enter the sanctuary...]. We are of the opinion [that one must not...and one must not coha]bit with them, [...and] one must not let them be united (with an Israelite) and make them [one bone...and one must not] let them en[ter] [the sanctuary].[18]

The rationale given for prohibiting intermarriage is a twofold cord: "[Beware] of any impure sexual unions (עְרוֹבֶת[ת] [ה]גבר), and be afraid of (polluting) the sanctuary (יראים מהמקדש)" (MMT B 48-49).[19] It is curious that intermarriage immediately raises the concern to protect the holiness of the sanctuary. However, the underlying text in Deuteronomy 23 prohibiting entry into the assembly provides the clue. The קהל יהוה, "assembly of YHWH," even if it is understood as the temple, has to do with the people who worship at the temple. Wandering into the sacred precincts is not the main issue for 4QMMT, but rather joining the sacred assembly. Intermarriage will bring unholy partners and their children into Israel and cause a sacrilege. Appearing in the middle of this passage against inter- marriage, the reference to the sanctuary probably refers both to protecting the sanctity of the temple as well as the sanctity of Jewish bodies.[20] Like many other Jews in this period, the author's concern to protect cultic sanctity in Israel is not limited to the temple but is focused on the sanctity and solidarity of the people.[21]

---

18. See Cohen, *The Beginnings of Jewishness*, 248–52, for evidence that many ancient interpreters of Deut. 23:2-9 understood the prohibition on entering the assembly of the Lord as a ban against intermarriage.

19. The translation, "Be full of reverence for the sanctuary," by Elisha Qimron and John Strugnell, *Qumran Cave 4, V: Miqsat Ma'ase Ha-Torah*, DJD 10 (Oxford: Clarendon, 1994), 51, does not convey the sense of dread for defilement of the sanctuary that is implied.

20. Cf. Hayes, *Gentile Impurities*, 89, 250.

21. See also Steffan Mathias, "Reproducing Torah: Human and Divine Sexuality in the Book of Deuteronomy," Chapter 9 in this volume, who points out that according to Deut. 23:1-9 solidarity is directly connected to sexuality, since the author

4QFlorilegium also interprets Deuteronomy 23 as a ban on marriage with outsiders. The author refers to a future temple which will be free of all illegitimate worshippers:

> ...It is the house which [he will establish] for h[im] in the latter days, as it is written in the book of [Moses: "The sanctuary] of the Lord which thy hands have established; The Lord will reign forever and ever"; This is the house to which shall not come [the uncircumcised in heart and the uncircumcised in fl]esh [for]ever, nor Ammonite nor Moabite nor bastard nor foreigner nor *resident alien* [Dimant: proselyte] forever because he will reveal his holy ones there, [and] eternal [glory] will continually appear upon it. And foreigners shall not make it desolate again, as they have desolated formerly the sanctuar[y of Is]rael because of their sin.... (1Q174 I, 2-6)

The translation above follows that of Devorah Dimant except where indicated. The author is clearly discussing an eschatological, renewed temple and cult that will take the place of the corrupt past (and present) temple. Like Ezra–Nehemiah, the writer presents certain types of people who will be prohibited from entering this sanctuary following the list of outcasts in Deuteronomy 23, but he also excludes the "foreigner" (בן נכר) as in Ezek. 44:6-9 and the "resident alien/proselyte" (גר). The rationale for these exclusions is "because his holy ones (angels) are there." The singular form קדושו here seems odd, leading to the emendation, קדושיו, "his holy ones." In other words, foreigners cannot join the assembly, because of the intense holiness which resides there, including even the holy angels.

The author of 4QFlorilegium goes on to discuss a less concrete temple as well: "And he commanded to build for him a human sanctuary (מקדש אדם) for there to be in it offered for him (as incense), before him works of thanksgiving..." (4Q174 I, 6-7). The sentence begins with "And he commanded." The syntax dictates that because of the dysfunctional situation mentioned in the previous sentences, it was necessary to introduce a new reality. That is, due to the devastated and corrupt condition of the past and current temples (CD III, 20–IV, 2; VI, 11-20; XI, 17-21; XVI, 13; 4Q390 2 I, 9), respectively, God has ordered a human sanctuary to fulfill the function of atonement (1QS VIII, 10; IX, 3-5).[22] The phrase, מקדש אדם, "human sanctuary," or "temple of man," does

---

constructs "the identity of the קהל as, firstly, based on the integrity of the male sexual organs" (229), and excludes ממזרים and those who are not descendants of Israel from the assembly.

22. Dimant, "4QFlorilegium and the Idea of the Community as a Temple," 281.

not refer to the temple building, which has just been discussed, but to the sectarian community itself which contains the holiness of God (4Q174 I, 6). According to the sect, angels are already present in this current reality as well (CD XV, 15-18; 1Q33 VII, 6; 1Q28a II, 3-9). So also the exclusions mentioned in line 4 undoubtedly apply to both the eschatological temple and the current temple-community.[23]

In addition to Deuteronomy 23, the writer utilizes the temple's birth narrative. In 2 Samuel 7 David desires to build God a house. YHWH is pleased but redirects the temple notion from a physical building to a human royal house, suspending the fulfillment of the building of the temple to a later time. The sect found fruitful soil: "[And] the Lord [de]clares to you that he will build you a house. 'And I will raise up your seed after you, and I shall establish the throne of his kingdom [for ev]er. I will be to him as a father, and he will be to me as a son" (1Q174 I, 10-11; cf. also 2 Cor. 6:16-18). God's promise of a royal house and sonship to David comes as a result of his desire to build the temple. It appears that the sect utilized this passage for their own aspirations.[24] The building of stone with a renovated cult would have to wait until a future time, but the human house, like the lineage of David, could begin now to fulfill the eschatological promise.

In fact, both ideas, a ban on temple entry and a ban on intermarriage, are linked. For example, if these groups are banned from the temple, that is, they then cannot enter holy precincts and worship with Israel, they will not be good marriage partners for Israel's children. If the meaning of the ban is that intermarriage is forbidden, it is likely that they will be rejected also as full partners in worship at the Israelite temple (Deut. 23:2-9).[25]

23. According to 4Q174, the "rise of the sect constitutes the onset of the end of days" (Lawrence H. Schiffman, "Messianic Figures and Ideas in the Qumran Scrolls," in *Qumran and Jerusalem: Studies in the Dead Sea Scrolls and the History of Judaism* [Grand Rapids: Eerdmans, 2010], 280–1).

24. Paul also makes use of the Davidic model for his concept of believers as a sanctuary. After his statement that believers are the "temple of the living God" who promises to "dwell in them and walk among them," he continues with an exhortation to purity and then gives the Father's welcome, quoting and adding to the Davidic covenant promise, "I will be your father, and you will be my *sons and daughters*" (2 Cor. 6:18). Like the author of 4QFlorilegium, Paul combines the two metaphors: people as temple and people as children of God. For Paul, both benefits are made possible by Christ, who is both David's son and the son of God.

25. Hayes, *Gentile Impurities*, 45–6, 62, notes that Second Temple sources that forbid intermarriage also forbid gentiles within the sanctuary. She traces this notion back to Neh. 13:1-9, which employs the Deuteronomic prohibition on various peoples entering the assembly to mean exclusion from the temple as well as from marriage

Defilement of the Sanctuary by Giving Seed to Molek

The final biblical passage on law we will trace concerns profaning the sanctuary by illicit sexual relations. The Levitical tradition reads:

ואני אתן את־פני באיש ההוא והכרתי אתו מקרב עמו כי מזרעו נתן למלך למען טמא את־מקדשי ולחלל את־שם קדשי

> I also will set my face against that man, and will cut him off from among his people; because he has given of his seed unto Molek, to defile my sanctuary, and to profane my holy name. (Lev. 20:3)

This law is directed against those who would offer a child as a sacrifice to the god Molek. The parallel text in Lev. 18:21 makes it clearer that child sacrifice is intended with the words: ומזרעך לא־תתן להעביר למלך, "giving any of your offspring to pass through [fire] for Molek."

A look at the Targumic tradition, although difficult to date, reveals that Jews read the child sacrifice prohibitions in terms of intermarriage. *Targum Pseudo-Jonathan* omits the phrase "to pass through (fire) for Molek" (Lev. 18:21) and understands the whole verse as prohibiting the desecration of marrying one's child to a foreigner:

ומן זרעך לא תיתן בתשמישתה לציד בת עממין למעברא לפולחנא נוכראה ולא תפיס ית שמא דאלקך אנא יי

> And you shall not give of your offspring to lie sexually with the daughters of the gentiles, to pass (them) over to strange worship; nor shall you profane the name of your God: I am YHWH. (*Targ. Ps-Jon.* on Lev. 18:21)

Furthermore, the author omits the גר from the prohibition against child sacrifice in Lev. 20:2-3 and reinterprets the law as a ban on intermarriage.[26] This gives the impression that the גר is not a member of the community; he is part of the problem.

Malachi, usually dated from the time of Ezra and Nehemiah, shares their concerns about intermarriage. He echoes the text of Lev. 20:3 which states that giving a child to Molek pollutes the sanctuary and profanes

---

within Israel. For a full discussion of Second Temple interpretations of Deuteronomy 23, see Cohen, *The Beginnings of Jewishness*, 248–52.

26. The oldest copies of Lev. 20:1-3 are two fragments of the Dead Sea Scrolls, Frags 4 and 8 of 4Q26a. Among the few words that remain, [מבני ישראל ומן הגר] הגר בישרא[ל אשר יתן מזרעו למ]לך, "[strangers that] sojourn in Israel" are quite clear in the original text, line 8. 11QPaleo Leviticus includes the whole phrase ומן הגר הגר בישראל, "or of the strangers who live as foreigners in Israel."

God's name. Malachi does not mention Molek, but he is concerned about the profanation of "the sanctuary of YHWH (קדש יהוה)," by intermarriage:

בגדה יהודה ותועבה נעשתה בישראל ובירושלם כי חלל יהודה קדש יהוה אשר אהב ובעל בת־אל נכר:

> Judah has dealt treacherously, and an abomination has been committed in Israel and in Jerusalem; for Judah has profaned the sanctuary of YHWH which he loves by engaging in sexual intercourse with the daughter of a foreign god. (Mal. 2:11)

The concern for profaning God's sanctuary echoes Lev. 20:3, but the medium is intermarriage, not child sacrifice. Malachi's concern that Judah has profaned "the sanctuary of YHWH" rests in the same vein as the warning in Lev. 20:3 against טמא את־מקדשי ולחלל את־שם קדשי, "defiling my sanctuary, and profaning my holy name."

Many modern scholars understand the terms קדש יהוה to refer to the sanctuary edifice, such as, מקדשי in Lev. 20:3. Indeed, קדש can refer to the temple, but it is also possible to interpret it as the "holiness" or the people of Israel.[27] The focus here is clearly on the holiness of Israel because illicit sexuality (marital infidelity and intermarriage) is the means by which the violation occurs, and it is the only offense developed in this passage. The previous verse (Mal. 2:10) uses חלל for desecrating the ancestral covenant with the nation:

הלוא אב אחד לכלנו הלוא אל אחד בראנו מדוע נבגד איש באחיו לחלל ברית אבתינו:

> Do we not all have one father? Has not one God created us? Why do we betray each man his brother so as to profane the covenant of our fathers?

In other words, the solidarity of the nation that derives from one father and one God is threatened by the desecration of intermarriage, which is considered an act of betrayal, each man against his relatives, and a profanation of the covenant made with the ancestors. The sacrilege here is not directed primarily against the temple building or its cult but against the people itself.[28] The two actions are placed in symmetry: "For

---

27. Versions are split between translating קדש יהוה as the "sanctuary" (ESV, NASB, NAS) or "holiness" (KJV, JPS, ASV) of YHWH. The translation "holiness" lends itself better to the notion of the holy people as the issue, but the connection to the sanctuary profanation concern of Lev. 20:3 should be retained.

28. Some suggest that it is idolatry introduced by the pagan women that makes the temple ineffective, or the physical entrance of these women into the temple precincts

Judah has profaned the sanctuary of the Lord which he loves." How? He has "engaged in sexual intercourse with the daughter of a strange god" (Mal. 2:11). It is tempting to translate the "sanctuary of the Lord which he (the man) loves" as the husband's abandoned Jewish wife. However, more plausible is that Judah (i.e., Jews, not just priests) has profaned the "sanctuary" of the community which is coextensive with the temple, by introducing an idolatrous, gentile element. It appears that Malachi is reading Leviticus' desecration of the sanctuary in a new way which includes the profanation of Jewish people.[29]

Jubilees

The book of *Jubilees*, like ALD, intensely opposes any sexual relations with foreign women on account of Israel's intrinsic holiness (*Jub*. 30:8).[30] The author combines the law to burn a priest's daughter who has had illicit sexual relations (Lev. 21:9) with Lev. 20:3 and rules that a father pollutes his daughter by marrying her to a non-Jew and in the process becomes defiled as well (*Jub*. 30:9-11).[31] *Jubilees* 30:10-11 states:

that defiles it; others point to the general effect of sin of any kind on the sanctuary. See Milgrom, *Leviticus 1–16*, 258–61. Qimron and Strugnell (*Miqṣat Ma'ase ha-Torah*, 131) point out that "in early Judaism, contaminating the Temple was considered the most severe sin"; cf. Jonathan Klawans, *Impurity and Sin in Ancient* Judaism (Oxford: Oxford University Press, 2000), 58, who suggests that profaning or polluting the sanctuary may simply be an abstract way of saying that God will destroy the sanctuary.

29. Alternatively, the holiness profaned here could be of the man and his wife. Whereas Ezra–Nehemiah emphasize the seed of the mixed couple as profaned (Ezra 9:1-2), the emphasis here is on the adults (cf. Gen. 34:2; 49:4; Lev. 21:14).

30. Holiness for *Jubilees* is a status that can be applied only to ethnic Israel, not other nations; see Cana Werman, "The Concept of Holiness and the Requirements of Purity in Second Temple and Tannaic Literature," in *Purity and Holiness: The Heritage of Leviticus*, ed. M. J. H. M. Poorthuis and J. Schwartz (Leiden: Brill, 2000), 173, who argues that holiness is only for Israel, not as a goal but a status. Werman cites J. Kugel, "The Holiness of Israel and the Land in Second Temple Times," in *Text, Temple and Tradition. A Tribute to Menahem Haran*, ed. M. V. Fox et al. (Winona Lake: Eisenbrauns, 1996), 25–9. Accordingly, *Jubilees* rejects the notion of conversion "though the idea developed at the time of the book's composition"; see Milgrom, "The Concept of Impurity," 282. Since for *Jubilees*, like Ezra, Israel's holiness is biological, even converts cannot share that status and hence they must not be allowed to intermarry among Israel.

31. Whereas Leviticus probably intends a stigma on the father, rather than pollution, *Jubilees* insists that the father or brother responsible be stoned for causing this impurity. For the original intention of Lev. 21:9 as banning premarital sex in

This law has no temporal limit. There is no remission or any forgiveness; but rather the man who has defiled his daughter within all of Israel is to be eradicated *because he has given one of his descendants to Molech and has sinned by defiling them*. Now you, Moses, order the Israelites and testify to them that they are not to give any of their daughters to foreigners and that they are not to marry any foreign women because it is despicable before the Lord. (trans. VanderKam)

The author directly quotes Lev. 20:3, following the Targum's interpretation, and, like Malachi, links the people with the sanctuary:

If one does this or shuts his eyes to those who do impure things, *pollute the Lord's sanctuary and profane his holy name, then the entire nation will be condemned* together because of all this impurity and this contamination, so is any man or woman in Israel to be who defiles his sanctuary. (*Jub*. 30:8-16; see also 7:33; 16:5; 21:19; 23:18-23; cf. Jdt 9:2-4)

The writer is concerned about the desecration and pollution of the people of Israel just as one would be about the pollution/profanation of the sanctuary and God's name. The relationship is symbiotic. That is, the same cultic holiness that is on the sanctuary rests on all Israel, and the pollution caused by illicit sex among Israel pollutes the sanctuary. The pollution is far beyond the couple involved. Following the lead of Lev. 20:3, intermarriage profanes God's name and sanctuary and defiles both the offender and the land of Israel (cf. also Lev. 18:21, 24-25). The illicit sexuality of an individual negatively impacts the whole community, people, sanctuary, and land, and it profanes God's name, which is on all of them. The close association of the impurity of intermarriage and the impurity of the sanctuary brings irremediable consequences to both (cf. *Jub*. 41:26; Lev. 18:24-28). Israel cannot get rid of this impurity, and neither can the cult.

Dead Sea Scrolls

Although a direct quotation of Lev. 20:3 is not present in other Second Temple texts, the notion of the people forming a human sanctuary that can be defiled by illicit sexuality is evident. Several of the Dead Sea Scrolls refer to the people as a human sanctuary or holy house, and some make reference to the divine spirit acting within them.[32] The author of

priestly families, see Milgrom, *Leviticus 17–22*, 1810. Sarah Shectman, "Priestly Marriage Restrictions," Chapter 7 in this volume, agrees in part with this view but probes further for a rationale for excluding the divorcee as a priestly wife.

32. See n. 13 above for references to the elect as some type of sanctuary.

the Hodayot, for example, declares, "I know that no one can be righteous apart from you, and so I entreat you with *the spirit that you have placed in me* that you make your kindness to your servant complete forever, purifying me by *your holy spirit* and drawing me nearer through your goodwill, according to your great kindness which you have showed to me and causing my feet to stand in the whole station of your good favor, which you have chosen for those who love you and for those who keep your commandments that they may take their stand before you forever" (1QHa VIII, 29-32).[33]

Each person, according to the hymnist, receives an allotment of the divine spirit. The understanding the spirit provides acquaints the individual with the mind of God himself: "By your holy spirit you have opened up knowledge within me through the mystery of your wisdom" (1QHa XX, 15-16). The hymnist praises God for letting him in on these mysteries: "I, the instructor, have known you, my God, through the spirit which you put in (נתן ב) me...wonderful secrets through your holy spirit..." (1QHa XII, 11-13). The use of נתן ב echoes Ezek. 11:19-20 and 36:26-27 where God promises to put a new spirit within his people to make them obey him. Indeed, by his holy spirit, YHWH reveals himself to Israel, thus extending himself toward them and allowing them access to him (1QS VIII, 16; 2 Tim. 3:16).

Even as water can fill a container or breath fills the body, so the divine spirit dwells within the receptacle of a human being (cf. 1QHa XVI, 14, "water of holiness" in the garden of Eden). Indeed, the creation of life, and, ultimately, the resurrection of the dead, is accomplished by divine breath/ spirit within human bodies (Gen. 2:7; Ezek. 37:6, 14).[34] Furthermore,

---

33. The purifying work of the spirit of holiness works internally on individuals to rid them of guilt. It is significant that while the biblical texts usually place the spirit's activity after a person has been purified, the Scroll authors often (but not always) refer to the spirit of holiness as the purifying agent. Eibert Tigchelaar, "Historical Origins of the Early Christian Concept of the Holy Spirit: Perspectives from the Dead Sea Scrolls," in *The Holy Spirit, Inspiration, and the Culture of Antiquity: Multidisciplinary Perspectives*, ed. Jörg Frey and John R. Levison, Ekstasis 5 (Berlin: de Gruyter, 2014), 167–240, points out the difference in biblical texts where purification is required before the agency of the spirit (cf. Ezek. 36:25-26). However, see Zech. 12:10 where God pours out his spirit on Jerusalem, causing them to mourn their transgressions, after which he immediately provides them with a fountain of purification from sin (Zech. 13:1).

34. Another quotation from Genesis (namely, Gen. 6:3) emphasizes the residence of the spirit within humanity: "My spirit shall not dwell (ידור) in man forever" (4Q252 I, 2). The scroll replaces ידון, "strive," with ידור, "dwell."

throughout the Scrolls, the spirit within humanity is not just a matter of giving life but establishing an ongoing conduit of divine blessing to God's people. The author of the Hodayot uses the phrase "placing a spirit within me" not just to acknowledge the God-given breath of life but also to accompany blessings of the divine spirit. The writer explains that it is via the holy spirit that knowledge has sprung up within him (1QHa XX, 11-13), thus creating an intellectual link between the writer and himself.[35] Related ideas can be found in other scrolls. According to the writer of the Incantation, "a spirit of knowledge and understanding, truth and righteousness, God put in my heart" (4Q444 1-4 + 5). Here there seems to be some connection between the granting of the spirit of knowledge and the writing of the laws of God in the heart, internalizing Isa. 11:2, which speaks of these attributes upon the messiah, and Jer. 31:31-34, which promises a new heart in the future.

The sanctuary of the human being is always in danger of profanation and pollution. Several scrolls are concerned with the possibility of polluting one's spirit of holiness. 4QBarkhi Nafshi, although fragmentary, appears to contrast the "evil inclination" (יצר רע) with the "spirit of holiness" (רוח קודש), which is threatened by "sexual immorality of the eyes (זנות עינים)" (cf. Treatise of the Two Spirits, רוח זנות, "a spirit of sexual wrongdoing," 1QS IV, 10).[36] Parts of Psalm 51 are quoted throughout

---

35. Carol Newsom claims, in her work on the Hodayot, that the text never states explicitly that the holy spirit has been placed within the righteous. See Carol A. Newsom, "Flesh, Spirit, and the Indigenous Psychology of the Hodayot," in *Prayer and Poetry in the Dead Sea Scrolls and Related Literature: Essays in Honor of Eileen Schuller on the Occasion of Her 65th Birthday*, ed. Jeremy Penner, Ken M. Penner, and Cecilia Wassen, STDJ 98 (Leiden: Brill, 2012), 339–54; and Carol A. Newsom, *Self as Symbolic Space: Constructing Identity and Community at Qumran*, STDJ 52 (Leiden: Brill, 2004), 106. Nevertheless, the context proves that the holy spirit was thought to be placed within the righteous. As Tigchelaar ("Historical Origins," 195) notes, "In this quotation [1QHa XX, 11–13], the juxtaposition of 'the spirit that you have placed in me' and 'your holy spirit,' and the connection of both with knowledge, suggests they are synonymous, though in other texts this need not be the case." In fact, Tigchelaar states that the Hodayot hymnist repeatedly thanks God for placing a spirit in him, "and virtually each time this is followed by a description of the enablement by the spirit" (ibid., 187). Clearly, there is a shift from earlier, biblical material where references to holiness as a spirit of any kind are few and far between. Nevertheless, it is the aspect of holiness, already established in the holiness traditions of Leviticus, that brings divine goodness and enablement unto Israel.

36. Following Ezekiel, the damaged text of 4QBarkhi Nafshi refers to the removal of a stony heart and probably the insertion of a spirit of holiness: "A heart of stone] you [re]buked away from me / and in its place you set a pure heart; an evil inclination

the Scrolls, often mixed with ideas from Ezek. 36:26-27, which refers to replacing the evil within Israel with the holy spirit (cf. 11Q5 XIX, 14). In this vein, 4QCommunal Confession clearly associates the "new spirit" with getting rid of sin: "Our God, hide our sins from your face, and wipe out all our iniquities; create *a new spirit* in us, and establish in us a faithful inclination" (4Q393 1ii 2, 4-8).

The Damascus Document warns the elect against impurity and urges them on to greater holiness: "let no man defile [ישקץ] his holy spirit... perfect holiness" (CD VII, 3-4; cf. VI, 14–VII, 5; cf. also, defiling the holy spirit by blasphemy in V, 11-12; 4Q270 2 II, 11-14).[37] Illicit sexuality ranks at the top of the author's vice list, the first of the three "nets of Belial," and the profanation of the sanctuary is the third net (CD IV, 17-18). In fact, sidestepping the whole issue of sexuality, some members opt to live in "perfect holiness" as celibates, without having families at all (CD VII).[38] Leviticus 11:43, which orders Israel to avoid defilement (אל תשקצו את נפשתיכם), stands behind this passage in the Damascus

[you] rebuked away [from my kidneys / and a *hol*[*y* [*spirit*] you set in my heart" (4Q436 1 I, 10–II, 4 // 4Q435 2 I, 1-3a). If the editor's reconstruction is correct, the author refers to the transformation of the inner person by means of the holy spirit to align with the divine will. The Scrolls emphasize the holy character of these attributes and the availability to all of the community. The contrast between the evil inclination and holiness as well as the parallel line regarding the removal of sexual immorality make a striking antithetical association between wrongful sexual relations and holiness similar to the association of *yetzer* and sexual urge often found in rabbinic literature. But cf. Loader, *The Dead Sea Scrolls on Sexuality*, 256.

37. According to Loader (ibid., 128), the defilement here "almost certainly includes reference to sexual wrongdoing." Indeed, the Molek prohibition of Lev. 20:3, taken by Second Temple exegetes to refer to intermarriage, is followed by a warning against impure spirits and an exhortation to be holy.

38. Loader (ibid., 374–5) suggests that the best evidence for celibacy is in CD 7 with the distinction between two camps, one which is celibate and the other which is not, and also in the motif of living for a thousand generations taken up in Pliny where it is linked with celibacy. Loader (ibid., 375) explains the assumed celibacy as "probably best understood in relation to a choice for a life of more stringent purity." See also Annette Steudel, "Ehelosigkeit bei den Essenern," in *Qumran kontrovers: Beiträge zu den Textfunden vom Toten Meer*, ed. Jörg Frey and Hartmut Stegemann, Einblicke 6 (Paderborn: Bonifatius, 2003), 124. The archaeological evidence reveals a predominantly male settlement at Qumran with no evidence of families; in over 150 years only one spindle whorl, five beads, and 3–4 women have been positively identified (not including the southern cemetery which represents Bedouin burials in the modern period). Cf. Jodi Magness, *The Archaeology of Qumran* (Grand Rapids: Eerdmans, 2002).

Document.³⁹ Instead of נפשתיכם, "yourselves," however, the Damascus Document warns a person not to defile רוח קודשיו, "his holy spirit." The emphasis on spirit marks a conscious development of thought vis-à-vis Scripture, making violations and impurities a more personal, invasive matter. Indeed, activities of the cult are often internalized by the sect, including spiritual sacrifices.

New Testament writers inherit the notion of the elect as a sanctuary from their Jewish heritage (1 Cor. 3:16-17; 6:12-20; 2 Cor. 6:14-18; Eph. 2:20-22; 1 Pet. 2:5; Rev. 3:12). In particular, Paul is clear that the body of the elect is a temple for the spirit and illicit sexuality can desecrate it. In a challenge not to submit to the power of sexual immorality, Paul admonishes, "Do you not know that your body is a temple of the holy spirit within you, which you have from God, and that you are not your own?" (1 Cor. 6:19). Paul teaches that when individuals engage in sexual immorality, they sin against their own bodies as well as against the spirit of holiness that lives within them (6:17-18). Paul exhorts believers to keep their "temple" chaste so that holiness can join them fully with Christ.⁴⁰

Conclusion

In Second Temple times, the notion took hold that Israel's corporate and/or individual body was a sanctuary that could be polluted by wrongful sexual relations. The notion has a long history of development, some of which can be traced through specific interpretations of biblical law: (1) the purpose of the tabernacle/temple was for God to be resident among Israel, not just present in his house (Exod. 25:8); (2) Israel was given the status of a "royal priesthood" (Exod. 19:6), which some interpreted as having direct access to holiness; (3) intermarriage could prohibit entry into the assembly of Israel (Deut. 23:4) which linked the concepts of temple and people and fueled the notion that the people themselves were a place of holiness (a related notion was the humanizing of the temple David desired to build for God by granting him a royal house); and (4) giving children to idolatry desecrated the sanctuary and name of God, which was easily understood as giving children to idolaters in marriage, hence profaning the "sanctuary" of the people (Lev. 20:3).

---

39. Milgrom, *Leviticus 1–16*, 684, who translates נפשתיכם here as "your throats," points out that this usage is frequent in Scripture in contexts that deal with impure foods.

40. Indeed, he characterizes believers as the pure bride of Christ (2 Cor. 11:2-3; cf. Eph. 5:23-32), following the Hebrew tradition of YHWH's marriage to Israel.

Bibliography

Cohen, Shaye J. D. *The Beginnings of Jewishness: Boundaries, Varieties, Uncertainties*. Berkeley: University of California Press, 1999.

Dimant, Devorah. "4QFlorilegium and the Idea of the Community as a Temple." In *History, Ideology and Bible Interpretation in the Dead Sea Scrolls: Collected Studies*, 269–88. FAT 90. Tübingen: Mohr Siebeck, 2014.

Douglas, Mary. *Jacob's Tears: The Priestly Work of Reconciliation*. Oxford: Oxford University Press, 2004.

Drawnel, Henryk. *An Aramaic Wisdom Text from Qumran: A New Interpretation of the Levi Document*. JSJSup 86. Leiden: Brill, 2004.

Greenfield, Jonas C., Michael E. Stone, and Esther Eshel. *The Aramaic Levi Document: Edition, Translation, Commentary*. SVTP 19. Leiden: Brill, 2004.

Harrington, Hannah K. *Holiness: Rabbinic Judaism in the Graeco-Roman World*. London: Routledge, 2001.

Hayes, Christine E. *Gentile Impurities and Jewish Identities, Intermarriage and Conversion from the Bible to the Talmud*. Oxford: Oxford University Press, 2002.

Himmelfarb, Martha. "Levi, Phinehas, and the Problem of Intermarriage at the Time of the Maccabean Revolt." *JSQ* 6 (1999): 1–24.

Jenson, Philip. *Graded Holiness: Key to the Priestly Conception of the World*. JSOTSup 106. Sheffield: JSOT Press, 1992.

Kampen, John I. "4QMMT and New Testament Studies." In *Reading 4QMMT: New Perspectives on Qumran Law and History*, edited by John Kampen and Moshe J. Bernstein, 129–44. Atlanta: Scholars Press, 1996.

Klawans, Jonathan. *Impurity and Sin in Ancient* Judaism. Oxford: Oxford University Press, 2000.

Knohl, Israel. *The Sanctuary of Silence: The Priestly Torah and the Holiness School*. Minneapolis: Fortress, 1995.

Kugel, James L. "The Holiness of Israel and the Land in Second Temple Times." In *Texts, Temples and Traditions: A Tribute to Menahem Haran*, edited by M. V. Fox et al., 21–32. Winona Lake: Eisenbrauns, 1996.

Kugel, James L. "How Old is the Aramaic Levi Document?" *DSD* 14 (2007): 292–300.

Kugler, Robert A. "Halakhic Interpretive Strategies at Qumran: A Case Study." In *Legal Texts and Legal Issues: Proceedings of the Second Meeting of the International Organization for Qumran Studies, Published in Honour of Joseph M. Baumgarten*, edited by M. Bernstein, F. Garcia Martinez, and J. Kampen, 131–49. Leiden: Brill, 1999.

Lange, Armin. "Your Daughters Do Not Give to Their Sons and Their Daughters Do Not Take for Your Sons (Ezra 9,12): Intermarriage in Ezra 9–10 and in the Pre-Maccabean Dead Sea Scrolls." *Biblische Notizen* 139 (2008): 79–98.

Levinson, Bernard. "Deuteronomy." In *The Jewish Study Bible*, edited by Adele Berlin and Marc Zvi Brettler, 356–450. Oxford: Oxford University Press, 1999.

Loader, William. *The Dead Sea Scrolls on Sexuality: Attitudes towards Sexuality in Sectarian and Related Literature at Qumran*. Grand Rapids: Eerdmans, 2009.

Loader, William. *Enoch, Levi, and Jubilees on Sexuality: Attitudes towards Sexuality in the Early Enoch Literature, the Aramaic Levi Document, and the Book of Jubilees*. Grand Rapids: Eerdmans, 2007.

Magness, Jodi. *The Archaeology of Qumran*. Grand Rapids: Eerdmans, 2002.

Milgrom, Jacob. "The Concept of Impurity in Jubilees and the Temple Scroll." *RevQ* 16 (1993): 277–84.

Milgrom, Jacob. *Leviticus 1–16: A New Translation with Introduction and Commentary*. AB 3. New York: Doubleday, 2000.

Milgrom, Jacob. *Leviticus 23–27: A New Translation with Introduction and Commentary*. AB 3B. New York: Doubleday, 2000.

Milgrom, Jacob. *Studies in Levitical Terminology, Vol. 1: The Encroacher and the Levite: The Term 'Aboda*. Berkeley: University of California Press, 1970.

Neusner, Jacob. *The Idea of Purity in Ancient Judaism*. SJLA 1. Leiden: Brill, 1973.

Newsom, Carol A. "Flesh, Spirit, and the Indigenous Psychology of the Hodayot." In *Prayer and Poetry in the Dead Sea Scrolls and Related Literature: Essays in Honor of Eileen Schuller on the Occasion of Her 65th Birthday*, edited by Jeremy Penner, Ken M. Penner, and Cecilia Wassen, 339–54. STDJ 98. Leiden: Brill, 2012.

Newsom, Carol A. *Self as Symbolic Space: Constructing Identity and Community at Qumran*. STDJ 52. Leiden: Brill, 2004.

Qimron, Elisha, and John Strugnell. *Qumran Cave 4, V: Miqsat Ma'ase Ha-Torah*. DJD 10. Oxford: Clarendon, 1994.

Schiffman, Lawrence H. "Messianic Figures and Ideas in the Qumran Scrolls." In *Qumran and Jerusalem: Studies in the Dead Sea Scrolls and the History of Judaism*, 270–85. Grand Rapids: Eerdmans, 2010.

Schwartz, Daniel R. "On Two Aspects of a Priestly View of Descent at Qumran." In *Archaeology and History in the Dead Sea Scrolls*, edited by L. Schiffman, 157–79. Sheffield: JSOT Press, 1990.

Steudel, Annette. "Ehelosigkeit bei den Essenern." In *Qumran kontrovers: Beiträge zu den Textfunden vom Toten Meer*, edited by Jörg Frey and Hartmut Stegemann, 115–24. Einblicke 6. Paderborn: Bonifatius, 2003.

Tigchelaar, Eibert. "Historical Origins of the Early Christian Concept of the Holy Spirit: Perspectives from the Dead Sea Scrolls." In *The Holy Spirit, Inspiration, and the Culture of Antiquity: Multidisciplinary Perspectives*, edited by Jörg Frey and John R. Levison. Ekstasis 5. Berlin: de Gruyter, 2014.

VanderKam, James C. *The Book of Jubilees*. 2 vols. CSCO 510–511; Scriptores Aethiopici 87–88. Leuven: Peeters, 1989.

Werman, Cana, "The Concept of Holiness and the Requirements of Purity in Second Temple and Tannaic Literature." In *Purity and Holiness: The Heritage of Leviticus*, edited by M. J. H. M. Poorthuis and J. Schwartz, 163–79. Leiden: Brill, 2000.

Index of References

Hebrew Bible/Old Testament

Genesis

Ref	Pages	Ref	Pages	Ref	Pages
1–3	221	23:16	89, 99	29:27-30	97
2:7	303	23:17-18	89	29:27	97, 102, 103
2:18-24	28	23:20	208	29:28-29	97
2:18-20	33	24	95	29:28	97, 104
2:20	28	24:31-61	105	29:29	65, 97, 101, 104
2:23	62	24:34-61	100		
2:24	62, 65	24:53-60	67	29:30	97, 104
3:1-7	28	25:5-6	68	30:3	67
3:8	288	26	33, 34	30:4	68
3:16	62	26:10	102	30:9	66, 68
6:1-4	26, 33, 236	28	292	30:13	208
6:3	303	29	67, 79	30:22	236
9	36, 145	29:13	97	30:25-34	105
9:20-24	33	29:14-30	13, 79, 95, 104–6, 261	30:25-28	100
9:22	36			30:28-34	100
12	33, 34			31	101
16	33	29:14	79, 96, 97	31:14	209
16:1-6	34	29:15-19	96	31:15	63
16:1-3	66	29:15	79, 96, 98, 100	31:33-35	33
16:3	68			31:35	37
17:8	208	29:16-18	96	31:37	103
17:18	66	29:16-17	96	32:23	68
19	123	29:16	96, 98	34	33
19:1-11	33	29:17	96, 98	34:2	292, 301
19:1-5	26	29:18	96, 98, 99	34:14	67
19:30-38	33	29:19-20	65	34:15-27	292
20	33, 34, 154	29:19	96, 99, 273	35	136
21:10-13	68	29:20-26	96	35:22	33
21:10	59	29:20	96, 99	37–50	111
21:12	66, 68	29:21	96, 101	37:5	130
23	89, 100	29:22-25	96	38–39	33
23:3-16	88	29:22	96, 101	38	13, 34, 111, 112, 113, 117–20, 165
23:4	208	29:23	97, 101		
23:9	208	29:24	65, 66, 97, 101	38:8	113, 114
23:15	89	29:25-26	97	38:9	118
		29:25	97, 102	38:10	113
		29:26	97, 103	38:11	113

Genesis (cont.)
38:14	114, 276	21:9	51, 52
38:15	163	21:10-11	60
38:24	40, 164, 165	21:12–22:16	69
38:26	114, 119	21:20-21	54, 55
39	34	21:22-25	206
39:12-13	272	21:26-27	54, 55
39:17	70	21:32	55
41:12	70	22	189
49	143	22:1	206
49:4	33, 36, 132, 136–9, 143, 156, 169, 301	22:2	52
		22:7-8	50
		22:15-16	170, 202, 206, 226
		22:16	202
49:30	208	22:17–23:19	69
49:57	33	22:18	28, 33
		22:21-23	172, 206
Exodus		22:26	9
2:11	70	22:30	287
2:13	70	23:12	55
2:15-22	67	25:8	16, 287, 306
3:5	287	28:2	287
11:5	59	28:29	287
12:9	126	28:35	287
15:20	272	29:43-44	289
19:6	16, 290, 293, 306	29:45-46	287
		30:33	126
19:10-15	289	31:14	169
19:15	204	34:15-16	162
20:1-17	204	34:16	166
20:12	204	35:25	272
20:13	33	40:29	289
20:14	34, 162		
20:17	204	*Leviticus*	
20:22–23:19	205	1–16	6
21–23	6	2:2	40
21	186	2:12	40
21:1-11	50, 263	2:13	40
21:2-33	69	2:15-16	40
21:2-11	48, 53, 67, 70, 206	2:27	40
		5:15	126
21:2-7	70	6:6	289
21:2	52, 69, 71	6:21	168
21:4	56	10:1-2	40
21:7-11	12, 185, 186	10:17	287
21:7-8	172	11:43	305
21:7	52, 53	11:44-45	159
21:8	51, 56	12	205

12:2-5	38
12:4	287
12:6-8	37
15:18	129, 131, 205
15:19-33	205
15:19-30	37
15:24	37, 205
15:27	37
15:28-30	37
16:23-24	168
16:33	287
17–26	6, 123, 182
17:4	182
17:7	162
17:9	182
17:10	182
18–20	31
18	32, 34, 43, 125–7, 130, 144, 145, 147–9, 151–6, 159, 205, 274
18:3	155, 205
18:6-18	34
18:6-16	32
18:6-7	283
18:6	32, 36, 205
18:7-18	137
18:7-16	32
18:7	36
18:8	36, 126, 205
18:9	126, 153
18:10	126, 152, 205
18:11	126, 205
18:12-13	149
18:12	126
18:13	126, 145
18:14	126
18:15	120, 126
18:16	37, 120, 126, 154
18:17-18	32, 35
18:17	41, 126, 145, 147, 175

18:18	126, 145, 154, 283	20	32–4, 125–7, 130, 144, 145, 147–51, 153–6, 159, 274	20:18	32–4, 36–8, 40, 145, 149
18:19-23	32			20:19-21	33, 34
18:19	34, 37, 41, 126			20:19	40, 145, 149
				20:20	41, 149
18:20	34, 126, 186	20:1-5	26, 28	20:21	35–8, 40, 41, 120, 149, 154
18:21	26, 28, 3–4, 126, 169, 174, 299, 302	20:1-3	299		
		20:2-6	34		
		20:2-5	33	20:22-24	155, 176
		20:2-3	299	20:26	159
18:22	13, 32, 34, 36, 41, 123–8, 130–3, 137, 139, 142, 144, 147, 150, 151, 154, 155, 224	20:3	16, 169, 174, 182, 287, 299–302, 305, 306	20:27	26, 28, 33, 34
				21–22	290
				21	155, 169, 171, 180–2, 190, 191
		20:5-6	162		
		20:5	162		
		20:6	26, 28, 33	21:1	182
		20:7	159	21:4	169, 171, 182
18:23	28, 29, 34, 41, 125, 126, 151	20:9	148		
		20:10-21	32, 170	21:6	169, 174
		20:10-14	148	21:7-8	14
18:24-30	42, 43, 175, 176	20:10-12	205	21:7	163, 171, 173, 180, 182, 183, 290, 292
		20:10	33–5, 40, 148, 162		
18:24-28	155, 302				
18:24-25	302	20:11-14	33, 34		
18:24	152	20:11-13	149	21:8	183
18:26	34	20:11	149, 150	21:9	35, 40, 164, 166, 169, 171, 181, 182, 301
18:28	37	20:12	36, 41, 149, 150		
18:29	35, 37, 170, 182, 186	20:13	13, 32, 33, 36, 41, 123–5, 127, 128, 130–3, 137, 139, 142, 144, 147, 149–51, 154, 155		
19	14, 33, 43, 159, 161, 170, 176			21:11	173
				21:12	287
				21:13-15	14, 169, 174
				21:13-14	173, 180
19:2	159			21:14	163, 173, 182, 290, 301
19:8	169, 182				
19:12	169, 174				
19:16	182				
19:18	182	20:14	33, 36, 40, 41, 145, 149, 175	21:15	173, 181, 182, 184
19:20-22	33, 35, 40, 151, 159, 160				
				21:17-23	173
		20:15-16	28, 29, 32–4	21:17	41
19:20	55, 129	20:15	149	21:18-20	229
19:29	14, 33, 143, 160, 164–6, 169–71, 176	20:16	149	21:23	169, 287
		20:17-21	148, 205	22:2	169, 174
		20:17	33, 34, 36, 40, 144, 149, 154	22:9	169
19:30	287			22:10	287
19:31	166			22:13	185
		20:18-20	149	22:15	169

Leviticus (cont.)		31:35	134	6:2	232
22:32	169, 174	32	208	6:7	232
23:4	287	32:4	208	6:13	236
25	55, 208	32:19	208	6:20-21	232
25:25-28	70	32:32	208, 209	7	295
26:2	287	34:1-15	196	7:1	295
26:11-12	176	35	196, 208, 274	7:6	170
26:11	288			7:12-13	232
26:31	176, 287	35:5	209	7:14	232, 235, 236
27:20	273	35:22	209		
		35:29	209	9:14	236
Numbers		35:30	9	10:8	236
3:27	211	35:32	209	10:13-16	233
3:30	211	36	14, 15, 117, 194–201, 210, 213	10:20	236
3:35	211			11:19-21	232
3:38	287			11:19	232
5:11-31	33, 35, 186, 206	36:1-12	210	11:21	232
		36:1	200, 211	12–26	6, 222
5:13	129	36:2-4	211	12:3	236
6:13-20	168	36:2	211	12:5	236
10:21	287	36:3-4	195, 211	12:11	236
15:39	162	36:3	211	12:12	71, 232
18:1	287	36:4	211	12:18	71, 232
19:20	287	36:6	207, 210	12:21	236
25:1	162	36:7	210, 211	13	166
25:14	211	36:8	210	14:1	222
25:15	211	36:9	210, 211	14:2	170
26	196, 209, 210	36:11	194	14:21	170
		36:12	210	14:23-24	236
26:33	194, 210			14:29	172
26:52-56	196	Deuteronomy		15:1	70
27	53, 117, 196–201, 209, 213	1:1-5	280	15:12-18	48, 50, 69, 70
		1:1	222, 279, 280		
				15:12-14	71
27:1-11	14, 194, 210	1:11	232	15:17	71
27:1	194	1:18	232	16	233
27:3-4	207	2:8	279	16:2	233, 236
27:3	195	4:1-40	222	16:3-4	233
27:4	195, 196, 207, 210, 212, 213	4:9-10	233	16:6	233, 236
		4:25	232	16:9-15	172
		4:40	232	16:11	71, 232, 236
27:7	208–10, 212	5:6-21	204	16:14	71, 232
27:8-11	116, 211, 212	5:11	236	16:18– 18:22	222
		5:17	33		
27:8	195, 212	5:18	34, 162, 223, 225	17:6	9
31	134, 140			17:14-20	222
31:17	134	5:21	223	18:7	236
31:18	134	5:26	232	18:19-20	236

18:22	236	23:16	71	28:30	168, 234, 273
19:15	9	23:18-19	227, 262	28:31	234
19:19	175	23:19	163	28:38	234
20:5-7	273	24	185, 187, 189–92, 272–4, 276, 277	28:40	235
20:6	168			28:53	235
20:7	230			28:55	235
20:14	223			28:57	235
21	186	24:1-4	15, 16, 60, 64, 173, 187, 227, 239, 240, 260–3, 269, 270, 272, 273, 275, 280–3	28:58-63	235
21:5	236			29:10	71, 142
21:10-14	172, 223			29:17	71
21:12-21	235			29:20	236
21:14	185			30:6-9	234
21:15-17	224			31:12	71
21:17	51			31:16	26, 28, 162
21:18-21	224	24:1	91, 172, 185, 227, 272, 273, 275–81	32:3	236
22	189			47:28-31	230
22:5	224				
22:13–23:1	33			*Joshua*	
22:13-29	60, 228	24:2-9	230	2:1	163
22:13-21	206, 262	24:2	272–4, 280, 281	6:17	163
22:13-19	224, 262			6:22	163
22:13-14	172	24:3-4	272	6:25	163
22:19	185, 262	24:3	91, 272, 275	9:22	102
22:20-21	166, 170, 225, 235	24:4	185, 262, 273, 274, 281, 282	12:8	279
				13–21	209
22:21	164, 166	24:5	230, 262	15:16-19	207
22:22-29	205	24:16	9	15:18-19	65
22:22-27	205	24:17-22	172	17:3-6	211
22:22-24	262	25	154	17:3	194
22:22	34, 225, 227, 263, 282	25:5-10	13, 112, 115, 118, 119, 121, 218, 228, 230–2, 262	24:22	88
22:23-27	191, 203			*Judges*	
22:23-25	165			1:12-15	207
22:23-24	35, 226	25:5	115	1:14-15	65
22:25-27	35, 186, 226	25:6-7	236	2:17	162
22:28-29	202, 205, 226	25:9	116	4:21	272
22:29	185	25:10	116	5	200
23	294, 296–8	25:11	230	6–7	200
23:1-9	296	26:2	236	8:1	102
23:1	227, 229	26:12-15	172	8:27	162
23:2-9	296, 298	28–31	234	11:1	163
23:3-7	230	28	217, 234	14:1-5	63
23:3	16	28:4	234	14:6	127
23:4	294, 295, 306	28:10	236	16:1	163
		28:11	234	19–21	200
23:8-9	230	28:18	234	19	41, 123
23:15	142, 288	28:29	234	19:2	60

Judges (cont.)		9:22	164	3:2	276, 278–82
20:2	295	14:5-6	9	3:4-5	282
20:6	175	21:13	127	3:5	280, 282
21	134, 140, 201	22–23	69	3:6-11	280, 282, 283
21:11	134	*Isaiah*		3:6	274, 280, 282, 283
21:12	134, 194	1:17	172	3:7	274, 282
21:20-23	31	5	236	3:8-9	163
		8:1-2	90	3:8	91, 172, 264, 272–6, 280, 281
1 Samuel		10:14	127		
2:35	293	11:2	304		
6:15	130	23:9	170		
9:18	142	32:7	175	3:9	273, 281, 282
10:6	273	32:18	142		
17:53	142	35:1	279	3:10-10	269, 270
18:17-30	67	35:6	279	3:10	274, 282
18:25	65	40:3	279	13:27	163, 175
19:17	102	41:19	279	16:1-2	27
22:2	71	50:1-2	52	17:6	279
23:24	279	50:1	64, 91, 172, 264, 272	17:21	127
28:12	102			19:11	127
30:22	126	51:3	279	20:7-18	27, 28
		51:18	272	22:3	172
2 Samuel		56:2	169	23:8-15	89
4:5	129, 131	56:6	169	23:10	163
6:20	127	57:2	132	25:3	283
7	298	57:3	163	31:5	168
7:14	222	57:8	136, 137	31:31-34	304
11:9	129	57:15	289	32:10	90, 92
12:16	129	62:12	287	34:9	70
13:31	129	66:1-2	289	34:10	70
17:16	279			34:11	70
18:26	273	*Jeremiah*		34:14	69, 70
19:21	102	1:2-3	282	34:16	70
		2:1–4:4	16, 283	42:5	103
1 Kings		2:2	282	50:12	279
2:39-40	71	2:6	279		
3:16	163	3	272, 273, 277, 280, 281, 283	*Ezekiel*	
9:16	65			6:9	162
11	295			11:19-20	303
11:1-2	295	3:1-11	280	16	186
20:37	273	3:1-10	272, 273, 275, 280–3	16:8	60, 115
21	9			16:15-34	163
22:38	163	3:1-5	163, 270, 274	16:20	164
				16:26	162
2 Kings		3:1-2	273, 281	16:27	175
4:1	52, 58	3:1	272–7, 280–2	16:28-34	162
8:12-54	289			16:37	145

16:48-52	123	4–5	166	*Proverbs*		
16:58	175	4:10	166	2:17	60	
20:13	169	4:11	164	6:26	163	
20:16	169	4:13-14	163	6:34-35	227	
20:21	169	4:18	166	7:10-12	276	
20:24	169	5:3	166	7:10	163	
20:30	162	6:10	164	7:17	138	
20:39	169	7:14	132	14:1	272	
22:1-8	177			23:34	127	
22:8	169	*Amos*		24:9	175	
22:9-16	177	2:6	52	29:3	163	
22:9-10	41	2:7	43, 169			
22:9	177	2:8	9	*Job*		
22:10	175	7:17	164	2:10	127	
22:11	41, 42, 175,	8:6	52	24:5	279	
	177	9:9	127	24:15	162	
23	186			31:11	175	
23:1-21	162, 163	*Jonah*		36:19	142	
23:8	164	1:9	70	42:10	209	
23:11	164			42:13	209	
23:14	162	*Micah*		42:14	209	
23:17	164	2:1	132	42:15	209	
23:21	175	7:5	128, 129			
23:27	164, 175			*Song of Songs*		
23:29	164, 175	*Zechariah*		1:6	67	
23:35	175	3:7	142	8:8-9	67	
23:38	169	12:10	303			
23:44	175	13:1	303	*Ruth*		
23:48	175	13:9	127	2:20	115	
23:49	175	14:10	127	3:8	128, 129	
36:25-26	303			3:9	115	
36:26-27	303, 305	*Malachi*		3:14	129	
37:6	303	2:10	300	4	88	
37:14	303	2:11	287, 300,	4:5	209	
42:14	287		301	4:8-9	120	
44:6-9	297	2:14	60	4:9	209	
44:7	169			4:10	209	
44:15	293	*Psalms*				
44:22	14, 181, 182	8	31, 38	*Lamentations*		
		8:5-9	27	1:8	145	
Hosea		22:3	289	1:10	295	
1–3	163, 164	26:10	175	1:17	272	
1:2	164	50:18	162			
2	236	51	304	*Daniel*		
2:1-9	186	88:6	128, 129	11:6	60	
2:4-7	172	149:5	132	11:17	60	
2:4	163, 164					

Ezra		*Yavneh Yam (Meṣad*		*KUB*	
2:61	212	*Ḥashavyahu)*	49	13.4 iii 68-83	38
9–10	199				
9	181	CUNEIFORM TEXTS		*Laws of Eshunna*	
9:1-2	290, 295, 301	*CTH*		§24	62
		446	38		
		456.5	30	*Laws of Hammurabi*	
Nehemiah				§117	62
5:1-5	49	*CTN*		§§138-140	260
5:5	52, 58	2 247	146	§§170-171	67, 68
7:63	212			§§175-176	243
13	295	*Epic of Gilgamesh*		§176	243
13:1-9	298	II ii 44	131		
13:1	295			*Laws of Lipit-Ishtar*	
13:3	295	*Hittite Laws*		§25	68
13:15-22	169	§37	31, 45	§27	52
13:15	127	§§187-188	29	§32	52
13:17	102	§187	41		
13:25-26	295	§188	41	*Middle Assyrian Laws*	
		§189	36	§§19–20	151
1 Chronicles		§190	46	§19	151
5:1	136, 169	§190α	28	§20	151, 154
5:25	162	§190β	36	§33	118
		§190γ	36	§43	117
2 Chronicles		§191	44		
20:28	289	§192	35, 37	*Neo-Babylonian Laws*	
21:11	166	§193	35, 37, 118	§§12–15	147
21:13	166	§194	37, 43		
25:33	287	§195	36	*PBS*	
31:2	142	§196	35, 43	7 90	82
		§197α	35		
WEST SEMITIC		§197β	35	APOCRYPHA	
INSCRIPTIONS		§197γ	35	*Tobit*	
Khirbet Qeiyafa	49	§198	35	7:9-12	91
		§199	41	7:11	91
KTU		§199α	29, 30	7:12	91
4.195	132	§199β	29, 30, 43	7:13	91
4.385	132	§199γ	30		
		§200	41	*Judith*	
P. Yadin		§200α	30	9:2-4	302
10	61	§200aα	29		
		§200aγ	29	*1 Maccabees*	
TAD				14:43	91
B28	61	*KBo*			
B36	61	5.2	38	PSEUDEPIGRAPHA	
B41	61	5.2 i 4-5	38	*Jubilees*	
		17.65 rev. 5-9	38	7:33	302
				16:5	302

21:19	302	*1QM*			*4Q174*		
23:18-23	302	III, 4	293		I, 2-6	297	
30:1-32	290				I, 6-7	297	
30:8-16	302	*1QS*			I, 6	293, 298	
30:8	301	II, 25	293		I, 10-11	298	
30:9-11	301	IV, 10	304				
30:10-11	301	V, 2	293		*4Q181*		
33:20	292	V, 9	293		1 II, 4	293	
41:26	302	V, 13	293				
		V, 18	293		*4Q213a*		
Aramaic Levi Document		V, 20	293		3–4	292	
6:4, col. a 17-18	291	VIII, 8	293		3 + 4	292	
11:1	292	VIII, 10	297				
		VIII, 13-15	293		*4Q252*		
Testament of Levi		VIII, 16	303		I, 2	303	
9:9-10	291	VIII, 17	293				
14:1-8	291	VIII, 23	293		*4Q270*		
15:1-4	291	IX, 2	293		2 II, 11-14	305	
		IX, 3-5	297				
DEAD SEA SCROLLS		IX, 3-4	293		*4Q390*		
CD		IX, 6	293		2 I, 9	297	
III, 19–IV, 6	293	IX, 8	293				
III, 20–IV, 2	297				*4Q393*		
IV, 13	293	*1Q28a*			1 ii 2, 4-8	305	
IV, 17-18	305	I, 6	138				
V, 11-12	305	I, 8-11	138		*4Q435*		
V, 4	293	I, 9	293		2 I, 1-3a	305	
VI, 11-20	297	I, 10	139, 156				
VI, 14–VII, 5	305	I, 13	293		*4Q436*		
VII	305	II, 3-9	298		1 I, 10–II, 4	305	
VII, 3-4	305	II, 9	293				
XI, 17-21	297				*4Q444*		
XV, 15-18	298	*1Q33*			1-4 + 5	304	
XVI, 13	297	VI, 6	293				
XX, 2-7	293	VII, 6	298		*11Q5*		
XX, 25	293	XIV, 12	293		XIX, 14	305	
1QH		*1Q34*			ANCIENT JEWISH WRITERS		
VII, 10	293	3 II, 6	293		Philo		
XV, 10	293				*De cherubim*		
		4QMMT			27	286	
1QHa		B 39-49	296				
VIII, 29-32	303	B 48-49	296		*De somniis*		
XII, 11-13	303				2.252	286	
XVI, 14	303	*4Q26a*					
XX, 11-13	304	Frag. 4	299		*De specialibus legibus*		
XX, 15-16	303	Frag. 8	299		3.29	294	

Josephus
Antiquities
8.190-96   294
11.139-53   294
19.332   294

NEW TESTAMENT
Matthew
22:25-27   113

Mark
12:20-22   113

Luke
20:27-32   113

Romans
12:1   293

1 Corinthians
3:16-17   306
6:12-20   306
6:17-18   306
6:19   306

2 Corinthians
6:14-18   306
6:16-18   298
6:16-17   294
6:16   288
6:18   298
11:2-3   306

Ephesians
2:20-22   306
5:23-32   306

2 Timothy
3:16   303

Hebrews
13:15-16   293

1 Peter
2:5   306

Revelation
3:12   306

RABBINIC WORKS
Mishnah
Qiddušin
4:3   294

Yebamot
14:1   264

Babylonian Talmud
Berakot
6a   288

Šabbat
22b   288

Sanhedrin
19b   217

Targums
Pseudo-Jonathan
Lev. 18:21 299

Midrash
Deuteronomy Rabbah
2:25   32

Genesis Rabbah
16:6   32

GRAECO-ROMAN
LITERATURE
Demosthenes
27.4   255
46.18   241
59.16   248
59.51   248
59.87   248

Euripides
Andromache
ll. 465-470 249

Medea
ll. 16–23   249
ll. 230-251 250
ll. 683-644 250

FrGrH 26
fr. 1   252

Homer
Iliad
2.645-49   240
3.125   251
6.456   251
8.304   242
13.429   241
16.1901   255

Odyssey
1.429-433   249
2.104-105   251
8.38   255

Inscriptiones Creticae
II xii 17   252
III.54–55   241
IV.4   241
IV 17   255
IV.19   241
IV 20   254
IV 21 1   254
IV 23   256
IV 44.4–6   241
IV.50   241
IV 51   252
IV 63   251
IV 72 (Gortyn Code)
  II.2–45   264
  II.11–16 251
  II.16–29 259
  II.45–
   III.16   240
  II.46   255
  II.49   255
  II.52–53 246
  III.17–40 258
  III.19–20 241
  III.25   255
  III.31-37 256
  III.32   255
  III.36   255
  III.40–44 240
  III.41   246

III.44–		XI.18–19	259	VIII.14	241
IV.23	257	XI.23	244	VIII.16–17	241
III.46	246	XI.24–		VIII.19	241
III.50-51	258	XII.19	244	VIII.22–24	241
IV.14–16	259	XI.25	244	VIII.26	241
IV.15	259	XI.43–44		VIII.28–29	241
IV.23–25	258	XII.44–45	254	VIII.32	241
IV.26	255	XI.45	244	VIII.35	241
IV.32–33	259	XI.46	246	VIII.37	241
IV.31–43	255	XI.46–55	252	VIII.39–40	241
IV.43–46	254	XII.17–19	242	VIII.53	241
IV.44	254	IV 72 22	252	XII.17–18	241
IV.45	254	IV 73	259		
IV.47	259	IV 78	251	*IPArk* 5	
IV.48–51	255	IV 80	259	101	254
IV.54	254	IV 97	259		
V.1–4	250	IV 106	259	Isaeus	
V.39–41	251	IV 162	251	II.6-12	247
V.41	251	IV 182	252		
VI.16–18	255	VI.44	241	Lysias	
VI.34	254	VII.1	241	14.28	246, 248
VI.44–46	260	VII.16	241		
VI.45	254	VII.20–21	241	*LSCG*	
VI.55–		VII.23	241	no. 154	252
VIII.10	243	VII.27	241		
VII.27–29	244	VII.30	241	Plutarch	
VII.35–41	253	VII.35	241	*Pericles*	
VII.52–		VII.36–38	241	24.5	247
VIII.7	242	VII.40	241		
VIII.1	259	VII.42–43	241	Solon	
VIII.2–4	259	VII.46	241	fr. 47b	241
VIII.20–22	241	VII.47	241		
VIII.40–42	255	VII.52	241	Theophrastus	
X.33–34	259	VII.54	241	*Characters*	
X.34–36	259	VIII.5–6	241	22.10	255
X.44–45	259	VIII.12	241		

Index of Authors

Aaron, D. H. 194, 198, 209, 213, 214
Abramson, P. R. 3, 17
Adler, R. 205, 214
Ahituv, S. 49, 73
Alter, R. 111, 121
Amit, Y. 111, 121
Amorim, N. D. 168, 169, 173, 174, 177
Andersen, F. I. 161, 177
Anderson, C. 223, 227, 237
Asher-Greve, J. M. 21, 25, 46
Ashley, T. R. 161, 177
Assante, J. 165, 177
Avigad, N. 68, 73
Azzoni, A. 261, 263, 265

Baden, J. S. 210, 214, 217, 237
Barmash, P. 62, 65, 66, 69, 73, 93, 94, 107, 172, 186, 199, 201, 205, 206, 261, 263
Bayliss, A. J. 253, 268
Beattie, D. R. G. 115, 121
Bechtel, L. M. 116, 121
Becking, B. 49, 74
Beckman, G. M. 38, 46
Bekins, P. 111, 121
Ben-Barak, Z. 196, 207, 212, 214
Bergland, K. 185, 227, 263, 269, 284
Berlin, A. 171, 177, 225, 237
Berlinerblau, J. 124, 156
Bile, M. 243, 251, 253, 255, 256, 259, 265
Bird, P. A. 49, 57, 61, 74, 148, 156, 161–4, 177, 188, 193
Blenkinsopp, J. 109
Boecker, H. J. 80, 88, 95, 100, 102, 103, 107
Boer, R. 50, 74
Botta, A. 91, 107, 261, 265
Boyarin, D. 4, 17, 46, 135, 136, 156, 224, 237
Brause, J. 252, 265

Brenner, A. 9, 17, 161, 177, 221, 237
Brixhe, C. 251, 265
Brooten, B. 5, 17
Bücheler, F. 251, 255, 265
Budin, S. L. 236, 237, 252, 265
Buffington, R. M. 3, 17
Burdick, W. 82, 85, 107
Burkert, W. 252, 265
Burrows, M. 62, 63, 74, 78, 107, 112, 121

Caballero, J. 207, 214
Calamari, J. D. 77, 78, 82, 83, 87, 94, 98, 103, 104, 107
Campbell, W. 3, 17
Canevaro, M. 248, 265
Cantarella, E. 242, 265
Carmichael, C. M. 116, 121, 204, 206, 214
Carr, D. M. 134, 156
Carroll, R. P. 221, 237
Case, M. L. 56, 106, 117, 143, 167
Chaniotis, A. 259, 265
Chapman, C. R. 58, 59, 67, 74
Chirichigno, G. C. 6, 17, 53, 74
Claassens, J. 197, 214
Coats, G. W. 95, 102, 107, 111, 114, 115, 121
Cocks, R. C. J. 84, 107
Cohen, D. 248, 265
Cohen, M. S. 153, 156
Cohen, S. J. D. 294, 296, 299, 307
Cohn-Haft, L. 246, 247, 250, 265
Collinet, P. 85, 107
Collins, J. J. 109
Collins, O. E. 167, 177
Coogan, M. 160, 163, 177
Cooter, R. D. 1, 17
Corbin, A. L. 77, 78, 82, 94, 98, 103–5, 107
Craigie, P. C. 273, 280, 284

Crosby, R. A. 18
Crumley, C. L. 201, 202, 214
Cruveilhier, P. 112, 121
Cushing (Stahlberg), L. 134, 157

Daube, D. 86, 95, 97, 98, 107, 117, 121
Davenport, W. H. 3, 17
Davidson, A. I. 4, 17
Davidson, R. 79, 100, 107, 272
Davies, C. 155, 157
Davies, E. W. 112, 115, 119, 121, 231, 237
Davies, J. K. 244, 265
DeLamater, J. 2, 17
Derby, J. 197, 200, 214
Dershowitz, I. 152, 154, 157
Diamond, A. S. 86
Dillmann, A. 100, 107
Dimant, D. 293, 297, 307
Dommershausen, W. 161, 168, 173, 174
Douglas, M. 196, 214, 286, 307
Drawnel, H. 290, 292, 307
Drinkard, J. F. 284
Driver, S. R. 66, 74, 100, 107

Ebeling, J. 188, 193
Edenburg, C. 74, 223, 229, 237
Edwards, M. 247, 265
Effenterre, H. van 243, 252, 255, 260, 265
Eilberg-Schwartz, H. 233–5, 237
Ellens, D. L. 145, 148, 155, 157, 160, 162, 177, 218, 223, 237
Ellens, J. H. 160, 177
Emerton, J. A. 112, 121
Erdmann, W. 239, 265
Erlandsson, S. 162
Eshel, E. 290, 307
Eskenazi, T. C. 184, 193, 201, 214
Esler, P. 62, 74

Faist, B. 261, 265
Falk, Z. 6, 17
Feinstein, E. L. 134, 151, 152, 157, 162, 172, 173, 177, 181–8, 191, 193, 276, 284
Finkelstein, J. J. 8, 10, 17, 100, 107
Fischer, G. 269, 276, 282, 284
Fishbane, M. 51, 74, 79, 107, 149, 157, 269, 274–6, 284

Fisher, E. 165, 177
Fitzpatrick-McKinley, A. 8, 10, 17
Fleishman, J. 207, 214
Fohrer, G. 95, 107
Fokkelman, J. P. 98, 100, 107
Foucault, M. 4, 17, 21–3, 31, 32, 46, 219–21, 237, 238
Frahm, E. 141, 157
Freedman, D. N. 161, 177
Freedman, M. A. 61, 74
Freidman, R. E. 214
Friedman, R. E. 209, 214
Frymer-Kensky, T. 58, 74, 171, 178, 226, 230, 238

Gagarin, M. 240, 241, 244–6, 251, 253–6, 258–60, 266
Gagnon, R. A. J. 133, 136, 153, 157
Gane, R. E. 125, 157
García Martínez, F. 138, 157
Gebhard, P. H. 47
George, M. 218, 228, 233, 236, 238
Gericke, J. 25, 46
Gerstenberger, E. 81, 108
Gilhuly, K. 249, 266
Goldin, J. 111, 121
Gordon, C. H. 78, 108
Gottwald, N. K. 82, 108, 199, 214
Gow, M. D. 115, 121
Graetz, N. 186, 193
Graham, C. A. 18
Greenberg, S. 31, 46
Greenfield, J. C. 62, 76, 290, 307
Greengus, S. 61, 74, 82, 87, 92, 108, 261, 264, 266
Greenspahn, F. E. 113, 121
Greenstein, E. L. 278, 284
Grotius, H. 83, 108
Guarducci, M. 266
Gunkel, H. 102, 108
Gurney, O. R. 112, 121

Hackett, J. A. 200, 201, 214
Häge, G. 260, 266
Hagedorn, A. C. 262, 266, 272
Hall, E. 249, 250, 266
Harrington, H. K. 201, 230, 288, 307
Harrison, A. R. W. 246, 266
Hartley, J. E. 150, 157, 160, 178
Hasselbach, R. 141, 157

Hayes, C. E. 291, 292, 296, 298, 307
Hendel, R. 153, 157
Hens-Piazza, G. 219, 220, 238
Hiebert, P. S. 202, 214
Hill, B. J. 18
Hillers, D. R. 89, 108, 288
Himmelfarb, M. 291, 307
Hobbs, T. R. 270, 282, 284
Hodge, R. 220, 238
Hoffner, H. A., Jr. 29, 30, 39, 46
Holladay, W. L. 269, 274, 284
Holtz, S. E. 261, 266
Hoop, R. de 136, 157
Hornkohl, A. D. 277, 283, 284
Hornsby, T. J. 20, 21, 24, 46
Houston, W. 169, 176, 178
Huebner, R. 85, 108
Hundley, M. B. 139, 157

Instone-Brewer, D. 272, 276, 284

Jackson, B. M. 54, 64, 74
Jackson, B. S. 185, 193
Jakob-Rost, L. 30, 47
Japhet, S. 70, 74
Jassen, A. P. 127, 157
Jeansonne, S. P. 79, 108
Jenson, P. P. 168, 173, 176, 178, 288, 307
Jones, E. A. 115, 121
Joosten, J. 9, 17, 161, 168, 169, 174, 176, 178, 275, 284

Kalluveettil, P. 60, 74
Kamionkowski, S. T. 160, 178
Kampen, J. I. 291, 307
Kant, I. 83, 108
Kawashima, R. S. 202, 203, 206, 214
Kearns, T. R. 1, 19
Kedar-Kopfstein, B. 163, 178
Keefe, A. A. 161–4, 178
Kelley, P. H. 284
Kessler, R. 68, 74
King, P. J. 199, 200, 214
Kinsey, A. C. 24, 28, 47
Kitchen, K. A. 89, 108, 284
Klawans, J. 183, 193, 274, 284, 301, 307
Kline, J. G. 278, 279, 284
Knohl, I. 174, 176, 178, 288, 307
Koch, C. 89, 108
Koerner, R. 246, 251, 258–60, 266

Kohler, J. 241, 244, 266
Koschaker, P. 62, 74, 112, 115, 121
Kovacs, D. 266
Kratz, R. G. 79, 108
Kristensen, K. R. 239, 240, 254, 266
Kronfeld, C. 153, 157
Kruschwitz, J. 111, 121
Kugel, J. L. 290, 301, 307
Kugler, R. A. 291, 307

Lacheman, E. R. 116, 121
Lamb, W. R. M. 266
Lambe, A. J. 112, 121
Lange, A. 290–2, 307
Langer, S. K. 44, 47
Laroche, E. 30, 47
Larue, G. 160, 178
Lawrence, P. J. N. 89
Leão, D. F. 241, 267
Leggett, D. A. 112, 115, 122
Lehmann, M. R. 88, 108
Leick, G. 5, 18, 236, 238
Lemche, N. P. 6, 18
Lemos, T. M. 78, 108
Levine, B. A. 76, 160, 162, 175, 178, 194, 196, 198, 207–11, 213, 214
Levine, E. 52, 74, 78, 108, 168, 261, 264, 267
Levinson, B. M. 7, 18, 70, 75, 222, 238, 295, 307
Lewis, D. 256, 267
Lings, K. R. 124, 127, 140, 157
Link, S. 239, 256, 267
Lipka, H. 2, 4, 18, 33, 114, 143, 171, 178, 181, 182, 184, 193, 203, 225, 277, 282
Loader, W. 143, 157, 291, 292, 305, 307
Long, B. O. 102, 108
Lundbom, J. R. 263, 267, 269, 272, 274, 276, 280, 283
Lyons, M. A. 270, 284

Mace, D. R. 117, 122
Maffi, A. 241, 254, 267
Magdalene, F. R. 1, 18, 66, 67, 202, 261
Magness, J. 305, 307
Maier, C. 165, 178, 273, 277
Maier, C. M. 284
Maine, H. S. 83, 84, 108
Malul, M. 85, 88, 108
Marini, M. M. 2, 18

Martin, C. E. 24, 28, 47
Martin, J. D. 270, 284
Mastnjak, N. 270, 284
Mastronarde, D. J. 249
Mathias, S. 112, 122, 218, 224, 231, 238, 296
Mbuwayesango, D. R. 197, 215
McCarthy, D. J. 89, 108
McClenney-Sadler, M. G. 145, 157
McKane, W. 115, 122, 272, 284
McKinney, K. 2, 18
Mendelsohn, I. 49, 75
Mendenhall, G. E. 89, 108
Meyers, C. 49, 57, 58, 60, 62, 65, 75, 101, 108, 109, 199, 202, 215
Milgrom, J. 37, 47, 123, 125, 133, 148, 149, 153, 154, 157, 160, 162, 168, 169, 172, 174–8, 181–4, 193, 198, 215, 287–9, 294, 301, 302, 306, 308
Milhausen, R. R. 18
Miller, G. P. 81, 82, 95, 100, 102, 103, 108
Moran, W. L. 32, 47
Morgenstern, J. 120, 122
Mouton, A. 29, 38, 47

Nelson, R. D. 263, 267
Neufeld, E. 78, 87, 108, 112, 122
Neumann, H. 11, 18
Neusner, J. 276, 284, 286, 308
Newsom, C. A. 304, 308
Nicholson, E. W. 89, 108
Nickelsburg, G. W. E. 91, 108
Niditch, S. 120, 122, 163, 178
Nihan, C. 123, 124, 157, 159, 178
Nissinen, M. 148, 151, 153, 157
Noth, M. 196, 207, 215
Nwaoru, E. O. 198, 215

O'Callaghan, M. 112, 122
O'Connor, M. 142, 158, 167, 179, 275, 285
Oelsner, J. 11, 18
Olson, D. T. 197, 215
Olyan, S. 133–5, 139, 148, 153, 154, 158, 189, 193
Omitowoju, R. 248, 267
Osborne, R. 254, 268
Otto, E. 7, 10, 18, 124, 158, 187, 193, 261–3, 267

Padgug, R. A. 3, 18
Paradise, J. 87, 88, 91, 109, 212, 215
Pardes, I. 68, 75, 153, 157
Parker, R. 253, 267
Parpola, S. 89, 109
Patil, V. 202, 215
Paul, S. M. 51, 52, 75
Perdue, L. G. 78, 109
Perillo, J. 77, 78, 82, 83, 87, 94, 98, 103, 104, 107
Perlman, P. J. 240, 241, 244–6, 251–3, 255, 256, 258–60, 267
Peterson, N. E. 3, 17
Petschow, H. P. H. 10, 18, 88, 98, 109
Philip, T. S. 37, 38, 47
Phillips, A. 53, 75, 118, 120, 122, 228, 238, 284
Phillips, D. D. 246, 268
Pingree, D. 141, 158
Pinkerton, S. D. 3, 17
Pomeroy, W. B. 24, 28, 47
Porten, B. 61, 68, 75
Postgate, J. N. 146, 158
Postgate, N. 61, 75
Pressler, C. 51, 54, 75, 161, 171, 178, 218, 223, 232
Puhvel, J. 38, 47

Qimron, E. 296, 301, 308

Rabinowitz, J. J. 32, 47, 88, 109
Rad, G. von 53, 75, 79, 95, 109, 111, 115, 122
Radner, K. 61, 75, 146, 158
Rashkow, I. 160, 161, 178
Regt, L. J. de 278, 285
Rehefeldt, B. 85, 109
Reiner, E. 141, 158
Reinisch, J. M. 3, 19
Renger, J. 10, 11, 18, 92, 109
Rhodes, P. J. 241, 254, 267, 268
Richlin, A. 5, 18
Riegner, I. E. 162, 178
Ries, G. 10, 18
Rofé, A. 171, 178, 262, 268, 277, 285
Rom-Shiloni, D. 274, 285
Ron, Z. 197, 215
Roth, M. T. 61, 75, 87, 88, 99, 109, 151, 158, 243, 268
Rowley, H. H. 113, 117, 119, 122

Ruschenbusch, E. 241, 268
Ruzé, F. 243, 252, 255, 260, 265

Sakenfeld, K. D. 197, 198, 213, 215
San Nicoló, M. 92, 109
Sanders, E. 249, 268
Sanders, P. 49, 74
Sanders, S. A. 3, 18, 19
Sarat, A. 1, 19
Sarna, N. M. 79, 95
Sassoon, I. S. D. 154, 158
Schenker, A. 153, 158
Schiffman, L. H. 298, 308
Schipper, J. 129, 158
Schmitz, W. 248, 268
Schwartz, B. J. 160, 168, 170, 176, 179
Schwartz, D. R. 294, 308
Schwerin, C. F. von 85, 109
Sealey, R. 254, 268
Seebass, H. 196, 213, 215
Seelentag, G. 240, 253, 255, 259, 268
Segal, W. 85, 86, 109
Seidel, M. 275, 285
Shaw, J. W. 252, 268
Shectman, S. 40, 59, 60, 146, 155, 158, 173, 182, 183, 185, 186, 193, 263, 277, 302
Sherwood, S. K. 79, 95, 98, 103, 109
Silbermann, A. M. 102, 109
Skinner, M. B. 3, 5, 19
Sklar, J. 160, 179
Snaith, N. H. 215
Soden, W. von 131, 158
Sokolowski, F. 268
Sommer, B. D. 285
Sommerstein, A. H. 253, 268, 278
Southwood, K. E. 201, 215
Speiser, E. 79, 95, 101, 109, 116, 122
Stager, L. E. 199, 200, 214
Stanton, E. C. 95, 109
Stark, C. 165, 179
Steingrimsson, S. 175
Steudel, A. 305, 308
Stewart, D. T. 24, 25, 28, 30–2, 42, 43, 47, 133, 135–7, 158
Stiebert, J. 120, 122
Stieglitz, R. R. 132, 158
Stol, M. 61, 68, 75, 260, 268

Stone, M. E. 290, 307
Strugnell, J. 296, 301, 308

Taggar-Cohen, A. 202, 215
Tawil, H. 173, 179
Thiel, W. 269, 285
Thiele, E. R. 283, 285
Thomas, R. 240, 268
Thompson, D. 112
Thompson, T. 112, 122
Thür, G. 253, 268
Thurnwald, R. 86, 109
Tigay, J. H. 118, 122, 225, 238
Tigchelaar, E. 303, 304, 308
Toeg, A. 60, 75
Tooman, W. A. 270, 285
Tov, E. 277, 285
Tropper, J. 132, 158
Tsevat, M. 112, 122
Tubul, M. 132, 142, 158
Tucker, G. M. 81, 87, 88, 90, 91, 95, 109
Tucker, W. D. 215
Turner, B. S. 203, 215

Ulrich, D. R. 198, 215

Van Seters, J. 70, 75, 78, 109
Van de Mieroop, M. 7, 19
Van der Toorn, K. 203, 216
VanderKam, J. C. 308
Vaux, R. de 118, 122
Vermes, G. 138, 158
Viberg, Å. 88, 109

Wacker, M.-T. 165, 179
Wagenaar, J. A. 68, 75
Walker, D. M. 86, 109
Wallace, S. 240, 268
Walls, N. 27, 29, 47
Walsh, G. T. 130, 131, 136, 158
Waltke, B. K. 142, 158, 167, 179, 275, 285
Watanabe, K. 89, 109
Watson, A. 86, 95, 110
Watson, W. G. E. 212, 216
Weeks, J. 3, 19, 21, 47
Weinfeld, M. 71, 72, 75, 89, 110, 170, 179

Weingreen, J. 216
Weisberg, D. E. 112, 116, 122
Weiss, A. L. 184, 193
Wells, B. 6, 9, 19, 33, 78, 90, 110, 120, 146, 158, 159, 204, 216, 261, 268
Wenham, G. J. 160, 168, 169, 173, 179
Werman, C. 301, 308
Westbrook, R. 8, 9, 19, 61, 68, 75, 78, 81, 83, 87–95, 98, 99, 101, 110, 144, 148, 158, 216, 231, 238, 263, 268
Westenholz, J. G. 165, 179
Westermann, C. 79, 95, 100–103, 110, 114, 122
Willetts, R. F. 244, 256, 258, 260, 268
Williams, M. J. 119, 122
Williston, S. 77, 78, 94, 104
Wilson, R. 199, 200, 216
Wittgenstein, L. 25, 47

Wold, D. J. 154, 169, 179
Wolff, H. J. 239, 264, 268
Wright, D. P. 8, 19, 161, 168, 169, 174, 176, 179
Wright, J. L. 230, 238
Wunsch, C. 61, 75, 91, 110

Yadin, Y. 62, 76
Yarber, W. L. 18
Yardeni, A. 62, 68, 75, 76
Yaron, R. 93, 97, 98, 101, 110, 264, 268
Yee, G. A. 161, 164, 179

Zakovitch, Y. 60, 76, 185, 193
Ziebarth, E. 241, 244, 266
Zimmerli, W. 162, 175, 179
Zipor, M. A. 261, 268
Zitelmann, E. 251, 255, 265

www.ingramcontent.com/pod-product-compliance
Lightning Source LLC
Chambersburg PA
CBHW072121290426
44111CB00012B/1731